Biographies *and* Genealogical Abstracts *from* Hardin County, Illinois Newspapers 1872–1938

Ed Ferrell

HERITAGE BOOKS
2010

HERITAGE BOOKS
AN IMPRINT OF HERITAGE BOOKS, INC.

Books, CDs, and more—Worldwide

For our listing of thousands of titles see our website at
www.HeritageBooks.com

Published 2010 by
HERITAGE BOOKS, INC.
Publishing Division
100 Railroad Ave. #104
Westminster, Maryland 21157

Copyright © 1999 Ed Ferrell

Other books by the author:

*Biographics and Genealogical Abstracts from
Hardin County, Illinois Newspapers, 1872-1938*

*Biographies of Alaska-Yukon Pioneers, 1850-1950
Volumes 1-5*

Frontier Justice: Alaska 1898—The Last American Frontier

The Dangerous North

All rights reserved. No part of this book may be reproduced or transmitted in any form or by any means, electronic or mechanical, including photocopying, recording or by any information storage and retrieval system without written permission from the author, except for the inclusion of brief quotations in a review.

International Standard Book Numbers
Paperbound: 978-0-7884-1290-5
Clothbound: 978-0-7884-8465-0

Dedicated to my sister, Shirley Little Adkison
who continues the research on our family

Acknowledgements

I would like to thank Micah Nutt for converting the Kay Pro files to the IBM compatible format.

I wish to thank Noel E. Hurford, Publisher and Julie Rash, Editor for permission to use biographies and obituaries from the *Hardin County Independent*, published in Elizabethtown, Illinois.

Ed Ferrell
Juneau, Alaska
May 1999

This book will help to reconstruct some of the records destroyed in courthouse fires in Hardin County Illinois. The early newspapers of Hardin are rich in genealogical information, but are often hard to read. Additionally, the writers did not always make the family relationships clear, at least not to modern readers. I have listed the married women under their maiden name when known. However, as in any genealogical work these abstracts and biographies should be checked against the original sources. Microfilm copies of newspapers may be ordered from the Illinois State Historical Library via inter-library loan.

Military records are available from the National Archives and should be searched for information on men who served during the Civil War. In some entries I have identified their unit numbers. Records are available from the National Archives in Washington, D.C.

ABBREVIATIONS

HCB *Hardin County Bulletin*
HCI *Hardin County Independent*
HD   *Hardin Democrat*
HG   *Hardin Gazette*
HR   *Hardin Republican*
IS   *Independent Star*
*   Age calculated from information in Obituary
dau daughter
sis sister
bro brother
b.   born
d.   died
m.   married
inf infant
g.   grand
sur survivors

JOSHUA WOMACK, d. Jul? (07 Aug 1872 HD)
JOHN MARTIN, son of Isaac Martin, d. this wk.
(21 Nov 1873 HG)
MAHALA LEDBETTER d. last wk.(12 May 1876 HG)
LAURA CLAYTON, dau of J.J. Clayton, d. 15 Apr,
22 yrs old. (20 Apr 1877 HG)
A. De LEZYNSKI, d. Wed. (27 Apr 1877 HG)
J. ED CLARK d. 19th. (27 Apr 1877 HG)
LAURA FIELD funeral to be held 06 May.(27 Apr
1877 HG)
ABRAHAM DAVIS, son of Asa Davis, d. 7th.(26
Apr 1878 HG)
JEFFERSON HOBBS, d. 21 Apr, age 51 yrs, 1 mo.,
22 days. (26 Apr 1878)
JAMES FERRELL, b. 19 May 1819, d. 21 Sept 1878.
(27 Sept 1878 HG)
JAMES MOSELY'S wife d. Tues. (25 April 1879 HG)
RUFUS ANDERSON, d. May. (09 May 1879 HG)
LUKE HAMBRINK, d.? (09 May 1879 HG)
HORACE DAVIS'S dau, d. May ?(09 May 1879 HG)
MARTHA GINGER, only dau of E.T. Ginger, b. abt
1864, d. 27 Jun. (04 Jul 1879 HG)
JOHN Q.A.LEDBETTER'S inf son, Percy, d. last
Fri. (04 July 1879 HG)
BURFORD? ROSE'S son d.? (04 Jul 1879 HG)
JOHN CHEEK'S baby d. Jul. (11 Jul 1879 HG)
WM.B.MOSLEY'S child d.last Mon.(11 Jul 1879 HG)
HENRY FERRELL'S inf d. Sun.(18 Jul 1879 HG)
GEORGE SCHROLL, d. last Mon. (18 Jul 1879 HG)
GEORGE THOMAS'S inf, Francis, d. Jul.(01 Aug
1879 HG)
SARA ROSE'S baby d. Aug. (08 Aug 1879 HG)
WES HUGHES'S wife d. Mon. (08 Aug 1879 HG)
NANCY HOLLEMAN'S inf d. Aug (12 Aug 1879 HG)
SAMUEL MCMURPHY, d. Aug (12 Aug 1879 HG)
MATTHEW THOMPSON'S baby d. Aug.(15 Aug 1879 HG)
ISAIAH GUSTIN, d. Jul 1879? (22 Aug 1879 HG)
BOOKER JENKIN'S son, Mick, d. last Fri. (22 Aug
1879 HG)
WILLIAM WALTON, d. Sept ? (26 Sept 1879 HG)
SULLIVAN'S child d. Mon.(26 Sept 1879 HG)
ED SHAW'S baby d. Sept.(03 Oct 1879 HG)
HENRY BARNETT'S child d. Tues.(03 Oct 1879 HG)
ASA LANIER'S wife, Martha, d. Sept?, age 60?
(03 Oct 1879 HG)
--- HEMPHILL, father of Mrs. Judge Taylor, d.

Oct 1879.(24 Oct 1879 HG)
MARTHA M. JOYCE, b. Hardin Co., ILL., 28 Jun 1842, d. 7 Jun; m. James P. Joyce, 31 Jul 1873. 24 Oct 1879 HG)
JOHN TANNER'S child d.last Sun.(31 Oct 1879 HG)
ELISHA C. BROWN, d. 22 Nov.(28 Nov 1879 HG)
ELIZABETH SIMMS, d. last Mon, age 90? (28 Nov 1879 HG)
F.M. SHIPP'S baby d.--(?) (05 Dec 1879 HG)
L.J. SIMPSON d. 28 Nov 1879. (05 Dec 1879 HG)
MRS. L.B. ANDERSON, d. last wk.(05 Dec 1879 HG)
H.C. PEARSON'S wife d Tues.(12 Dec 1879 HG)
LOUISA A. CLANAHAN, wife of C.L. Clanahan, b. abt 1846, d. Metropolis, ILL., 19 Dec. (26 Dec 1879 HG)
J. MCKEE PEEPLES, b. abt 1826, d. Dec 1879; m. Harriet---, issue: John M., William A., Henry M., dau,(d.) (02 Jan & 23 Jan 1880 HG)
SAM FRITT'S child d. Dec. (02 Jan 1880 HG)
WM. STUBBY'S child d. Dec-Jan? (07 Jan 1880 HG)
W.J. PARIS'S child d. Dec-Jan? (07 Jan 1880 HG)
DICK INGRAM, son of Ben Ingram, d. Dec-Jan? (07 Jan 1880 HG)
GEORGE LEDBETTERS'S inf son, Walter, d. last Fri. (09 Jan 1880 HG)
NANCY LYONS, wife of John Lyons, sister of H.J. Belt, d. last Fri. (09 Jan 1880 HG)
RHODA JOINER, wife of Willie Joiner, d. 31 Dec 1879. (09 Jan 1880 HG)
BETTY BOYD, dau of the widow Boyd, d. 08 Jan 1880. (09 Jan 1880 HG)
--- EATON, d. Jan? (23 Jan 1880 HG)
JAMES TRENT, d. 22 Jan ? (23 Jan 1880 HG)
JOHN MURPHY, d. 20 Jan 1880. (23 Jan 1880 HG)
LIZA LEDBETTER d.? (23 Jan 1880 HG)
EPHRIAM FRIEND, father of M.B. Friend, d. 24 Jan 1880 in Wayne County. (06 Feb 1880 HG)
FANNY DOSSETT, wife of John T. Dossett, d. 19th; 2 children survive. (06 Feb 1880 HG)
CHARITY STEVENS, wife of John Stevens, d 30 Jan 1880. (06 Feb 1880 HG)
JAMES ISHAM, son of James M.Isham, d. 1 Feb 1880. (06 Feb 1880 HG)
PRY MCDOWELL'S wife d. Jan-Feb?(06 Feb 1880 HG)
HOSKINSON'S child d.? (06 Feb 1880 HG)
ANDY GIPSON'S child d. Feb? (13 Feb 1880 HG)

MARY LEMAR OWEN, b. Hardin Co. ILL., 29 Nov 1849, d.27 Jan 1880; m. Wm. Owen 25 Dec 1866; leaves husband & 3 small chld. (13 Feb 1880 HG)
TINA HAMPTON, d.? (27 Feb 1880 HG)
EMMA WALTON'S inf d. Mar (05 Mar 1880 HG)
CHARLES PLEASANTS, d. 24 Feb in New Orleans, bro of E. & W. Pleasants. (06 Mar 1880 HG)
ELIZABETH FERRELL, mother of C.M. Ferrell, d. Mar.(12 Mar 1880 HG)
ALEXANDER JONES, son of B.O. Jones of Massac County, d. 28 Mar 1880,age 11 years (09 Apr 1880 HG)
PLEAS. ROSE'S wife d. Apr. (16 Apr 1880 HG)
MRS. WM. ROSS, d. 10 Apr 1880. (23 Apr 1880 HG)
CHARLOTTE HAMP, wife of Dr. Henry Hamp, d. Sun the 25th; b. Hanover, Germany 1819; immigrated to Illinois 1854; leaves four children. (30 Apr 1880 HG)
LUCINDA CONRAD of Harrisburg d. last Sun at son-in-law, ---Freeman. (07 May 1880 HG)
JOE SHAW d. last Mon, abt 6 years old.(07 May 1880 HG)
JOHN BAYNE, d. 16 May. (21 May 1880 HG)
WM. OWEN, d. 11th. (21 May 1880 HG)
LULA CAVANDER, sis of J.C. Cavander, d.12th. (21 May 1880 HG)
WILLIAM H.A. HIGDEN, youngest son of William & Rebecca Higden; b. Franklin County, Tenn. 20 Sept 1858; d. 13 May 1880. (28 May 1880 HG)
JAMES CULLOM'S wife & child d. the 22nd. (28 May 1880 HG)
JOHN B. EDRINGTON, d. Jun? (02 Jul 1880 HG)
SOL DAVIS'S child d. 08 Jul. (09 Jul 1880 HG)
ELIZA BANK'S child d. Jul. (09 Jul 1880 HG)
ELIZABETH LEDBETTER'S inf son, Henry, d. Jul. (23 July 1880 HG)
A.C. FERRELL'S son, Albert, d. 14 Jul. (30 Jul 1880 HG)
CAIN CORTER'S child d. 18 Jul.(30 Jul 1880 HG)
CHAMP SMITH, d. at Evansville last wk. (06 Aug 1880 HG)
JAMES GENTRY, d.last Sun (13 Aug 1880 HG)
--- ROBINETT, d. 17 Aug at Bluford Robinett's. (27 Aug 1880 HG)
JEPPI YORK, d. 21 Aug? (27 Aug 1880 HG)
GEO. W. MCALLISTER'S child d. 23 Aug. (27 Aug

1880 HG)
JAS. S. ARTUR'S dau d. Aug.(27 Aug 1880 HG)
MR. BRANN'S boy d. Aug. (3 Sept 1880 HG)
JAMES JOHN'S boy d? (10 Sept 1880 HG)
ROSS MANNON, d. Sept.(10 Sept 1880 HG)
STEWART'S child d. Sept.(10 Sept 1880 HG)
Mrs. JOEL COGHILL, d. Sept (10 Sept 1880 HG)
ROSA BELL STUBBS, d. Sept, age 7 mos. (17 Sept 1880 HG)
TOMMY LAVANDER, d. Sept. (24 Sept 1880 HG)
WM. KING'S inf d. Sept. (01 Oct 1880 HG)
JAMES B.MCFARLAN'S inf d. Mon.(01 Oct 1880 HG)
MARY BELT, wife of Jonathan Belt, d. Mon, 20 Sept 1880 at son-in-law's, H. C. Pearson. (15 Oct 1880 HG)
GEO. A. WEATHERBY, d.last June.(15 Oct 1880 HG)
G.W. KIMBALL'S son d. Oct. (29 Oct 1880 HG)
JERRY COFFIELD, d. Oct. (29 Oct 1880 HG)
JOHN MOORE, d. last Sat. (29 Oct 1880 HG)
NAN RALPH, wife of James Ralph, d. Nov. (05 Nov 1880 HG)
J.S. WALTON, d. last Tues. (10 Dec 1880 HG)
GEO. RICKET, wife d. Nov; dau of Thomas Smock. (19 Nov 1880 HG)
ISSAC H. MASON'S baby d. Dec. (24 Dec 1880 HG)
MRS. HATHORN, d Nov (05 Nov 1880 HG)
ABROSE HARVEY d. last Sat.(06 Jan 1881 HG)
ELIZABETH BASSETT, d. last Sat.(06 Jan 1881 HG)
MRS. JOHN W. MILLER, d Wed. (06 Jan 1881 HG)
ANTON SHELTER, d. Jan? (06 Jan 1881 HG)
MRS. ED WALL, d. Wed. (06 Jan 1881 HG)
ELIZABETH KNUCKY, wife of Richard Knucky, d.12 Jan 1881. (14 Jan 1881 HG)
W.J. PARIS'S boy d. Jan.(14 Jan 1881 HG)
TOM LANE'S child d. Jan.(14 Jan 1881 HG)
ALEX ABNER'S child d. Jan. (14 Jan 1881 HG)
ELIZABETH KNUCKY,wife of Richard Knucky,d.12 Jan 1881.(14 Jan 1881 HG)
JOSHUA O. GASKILL, b St. Clair Co., 1814, d. 22 Nov 1880.(04 Feb 1881 HG)
SAMUEL E. STEELE JR., b 12 Jan 1859, d 23 Jan 1881.(04 Feb 1881 HG)
SAMUEL BROWN'S wife,d.Jan?1881.(28 Jan 1881 HG)
DAVID LAMBERT, son of B.J. Lambert, d. Jan? (28 Jan 1881)
JAMES YEAKEY'S wife d. ? (04 Feb 1881 HG)

---BARKMAN, father of H.H. Barkman, d.--. (04 Feb 1881 HG)
CICERO PATTON'S son d.--. (04 Feb 1881 HG)
ISSAC HOBBS' inf d. last Fri. (04 Feb 1881 HG)
JAMES GRACE'S son d.--. (04 Feb 1881 HG)
NANCY MACRAW, d. Mar. (04 Feb 1881 HG)
MRS. JUDGE DIMMICK, d Jan (04 Feb 1881 HG)
JAMES OLDHAM, d.-- Jan.(04 Feb 1881 HG)
JOSHUA O. GASKILL, b St. Clair Co.,1814, d 22 Nov 1880.(04 Feb 1881 HG)
JOHN T. GREATHOUSE, age 59 d.? (11 Feb 1881 HG)
MARY ANN PATTON, dau of Hannah Patton, d. 08 Feb.; issue 6. (18 Feb 1881 HG)
SAMUEL RUSSELL'S girl d. Feb. (18 Feb 1881 HG)
MARY ANN DENTON, wife of Allen Denton & oldest dau of Hannah Denton, d. 8 Feb 1881.(18 Feb 1881 HG)
LAURA ASHFORD, d. last Sun. (18 Feb 1881 HG)
AMANDA JANE DIMICK, b. 30 Jan 1826, d. 28 Jan; m. Franklin Dimick; issue: 4 sons & 4 daus. (18 Feb 1881 HG)
CICERO MOORE'S wife d.---.(25 Feb 1881 HG)
W.R. EDWARDS, d.---.(25 Feb 1881 HG)
ELIZABETH REED, mother of Lewis Reed, d. 17 th instant. (25 Feb 1881 HG)
MARION MOTT d. few days ago.(25 Feb 1881 HG)
MATTIX LANE, d.---.(25 Feb 1881 HG)
J.M. MILLER, d. Sun. (25 Feb 1881 HG)
MARY DENTON, wife of Allen Denton, d 08 Feb, age 30 yrs, 1 mo, 2 days.(04 Mar 1881 HG)
JOHN RICKETTE, d. last Sun.(04 Mar 1881 HG)
MELINDA MOTT, d. Feb? (04 Mar 1881 HG)
TOBE EDWARDS, d. 03 Feb 1881.(? Mar 1881 HG)
MOLLIE VAUGHN, d. 03 Feb 1881.(? Mar 1881 HG)
JAMES OLDHAM, d. 03 Feb 1881.(? Mar 1881 HG)
EDWARD GRACE, d. 04 Feb 1881.(? Mar 1881 HG)
THOMAS STEVENS, d. 05 Feb 1881.(? Mar 1881 HG)
CHARLES HOBBS, d. 08 Feb 1881.(? Mar 1881 HG)
MOLLIE RUSSELL, d. 10 Feb 1881.(? Mar 1881 HG)
T.L. WILLIAM'S baby d. Mar. (11 Mar 1881 HG)
JAMES W. VINYARD, d.---.(18 Mar 1881 HG)
OSCAR WINKLES, d.---. (18 Mar 1881 HG)
D.A. TURNER, d. ---. (18 Mar 1881 HG)
CATHERINE YEAKLEY, d.---.(18 Mar 1881 HG)
JABEEZ MOORE, d.---. (18 Mar 1881 HG)
AMBROSE WHITTAKER, d.---. (18 Mar 1881 HG)

SAMUEL S. CONN, d. Feb ?. (18 Mar 1881 HG)
W.R. EDWARDS, d.---.(18 Mar 1881 HG)
MRS. ED SHAW, d. Mar (25 Mar 1881 HG)
WILLIAM RALPH'S child d. Mar (25 Mar 1881 HG)
BUCHANAN MOORE, d. 09 Mar 1881, son of Jabez
Moore. (25 Mar 1881 HG)
BUCK MOORE, d. 10 Mar. 1881.(03 Apr 1881 HG).
CORA HUNTER, d. 16 Mar 1881. (03 Apr 1881 HG)
SUSAN PHILLIPS, d. 03 Mar 1881.(03 Apr 1881 HG)
EMILY KEELING, d. Feb ? 1881.(03 Apr 1881 HG)
MARY HOLLEMON, d. 28 Jun 1880.(03 Apr 1881 HG)
A.M. SCOTT, d. 10 Dec 1880. (03 Apr 1881 HG)
ELIZABETH REED, d. 19 Feb 1881.(03 Apr 1881 HG)
ABASALOM WINN, d. 19 Mar 1881. (03 Apr 1881 HG)
RICHARD HUGHES, d.08 Mar 1881.(03 Apr 1881 HG)
GEO. WILLIAMS, d. 04 Mar 1881.(03 Apr 1881 HG)
CARY DAVIS, wife of Asa Davis, d. Apr.(08 Apr 1881 HG)
WESLEY CALDWELL, d. Wed. (08 Apr 1881 HG)
JOHN JACKSON'S son d.---. (08 Apr 1881 HG)
DICK HOBBS, d. Apr ? (15 Apr 1881 HG)
THOS. H. CLARK, d.---, Golconda, ILL.(22 Apr 1881 HG)
CHARLOTTE HAMP, wife of Dr. Henry Hamp Sr., b. Hanover, Germany 1819, d. 25 Apr; husband & 4 chld survive. (29 Apr 1881 HG)
JONATHAN G. WATERS, b. Marion Co., Ky., 28 Jan 1805, d. Ky. 21 Feb 1881 at son-in-law's, J.H. Bruner; issue: Garrell, Robert, J.G., Ben, Emily (Mrs. John Miller) & Mary Ann (Mrs. Jacob Bruner). (22 Apr 1881 HG)
ELIZABETH LAMAR, d. 23 Apr. (29 April 1881 HG)
Mrs W.T. LAMAR Jr.,d. 22 Apr? (29 Apr 1881 HG)
JOHN RAY MITCHELL d.30 Apr 1881.(6 May 1881 HG)
BRAXTON GINGER, son of Eli Ginger, d. May. (06 May 1881 HG)
JOHN BAYNE, d. 16 May. (20 May 1881 HG)
CHARLES & HARRIET CASAD'S inf dau d. 20 May, 1 yr, 9 mos, 3 days.(27 May 1881 HG)
SUSAN PHILLIPS, wife of Manassa Phillips, d. May? (03 Jun 1881 HG)
LUCINDA Y. MATHENY, mother of Susan Phillips, d. May? (03 Jun 1881 HG)
THOMAS HINSON, oldest son of Joseph Hinson, d. May. (03 Jun 1881 HG)
J.R. OXFORD, d. May. (03 Jun 1881 HG)

JONATHON BELFOR, d. this wk. (03 Jun 1881 HG)
CHESTER CLARK'S wife d.? (03 Jun 1881 HG)
JAMES M. WARREN d. Wed?(17 Jun 1881 HG)
J.J. PARIS'S children d.? (01 Jul 1881 HG)
CALVIN MILLIGAN,d. 27 Jun.(01 Jul 1881 HG)
GEORGE BROWN'S child d. Jul.(22 Jul 1881 HG)
JAMES HASTIE'S wife d. Jul.(29 Jul 1881 HG)
EVAN DOGGETT, d. Jul? (29 Jul 1881)
MRS. E.C. WINGATE, d. Jul? (29 Jul 1881 HG)
JOHN & JOSEPHINE GRACE'S inf son d. 20 Jul.(05 Aug 1881 HG)
DICK LEDBETTER'S child d.4th Aug.(12 Aug 1881)
JIM CRAIG'S baby d. Wed. (19 Aug 1881 HG)
WILEY HOBB'S inf d. Thur. (19 August 1881 HG)
THOMAS CASAD'S dau d Aug. (02 Sept 1881 HG)
ELIAS & MARY PATTON'S inf dau, Clarissa Dell, d 27 Aug. (02 Sept 1881 HG)
EARL SHERWOOD'S inf d. Sept. (09 Sept 1881 HG)
MARY J. THOMAS, wife of George F. Thomas, dau of Wm. Millikan, d. Aug? (09 Sept 1881 HG)
GEORGE SHROLL, d. Mon. (16 Sept 1881 HG)
JOHN CREMEENS, d Sept? (16 Sept 1881 HG)
MRS. BRUMETTE, d Sept? (16 Sept 1881 HG)
EMMA A.HOSICK, age 19 years,2 mos, sis of Dora M.Hosick, d.Sept 1881.(16 Sept &14 Oct 1881 HG)
ABRAM DAVIS, d. Oct?(07 Oct 1881 HG)
J.A. OXFORD'S child d. last Mon.(7 Oct 1881 HG)
SARAH GRIFFIN, d. Wed.(07 Oct 1881 HG)
JOB MATHENY'S child d.Oct. (21 Oct 1881 HG)
M. PHILLIP'S child d.Oct. (21 Oct 1881 HG)
WILLIAM MOORE, d. Oct.(21 Oct 1881 HG)
JAMES HUNTER'S child d. Mon.(21 Oct 1881 HG)
JOHN B. TUCKER'S wife d.?(28 Oct 1881 HG)
ADAM KARBER, d?(04 Nov 1881 HG)
HIRAM STACEY, d. Nov.(18 Nov 1881 HG)
A.C.FERRELL'S dau d?(18 Nov 1881 HG)
MARY SHEWMAKER, d. the 8th, age 67 yrs.7 mo.7 days. (18 Nov 1881 HG)
THEODORE CHANCY'S wife d. Nov. (25 Nov 1881 HG)
MRS. JONAH PILAND, d. Wed. (09 Dec 1881 HG)
MRS. J.B. TUCKER, d. Nov? (09 Dec 1881 HG)
ROSS GOBLE'S inf child d. Tues (09 Dec 1881 HG)
SOLOMON SHELL, d. last week. (09 Dec 1881 HG)
J.W. GRIMSLY, d. Dec. (09 Dec 1881 HG)
MARTHA MEDORA HOSICK, b. 24 Dec 1858, White Co.,ILL., d. Elizabethtown.(23 Dec 1881 HG)

MILLARD FILLMORE GOODWIN, b. Leavenworth, Ind., 23 Dec 1856, d. New Haven, ILL., 16 Dec 1881. (23 Dec 1881 HG)
EDWARD KENNEDY'S child d. Tues.(29 Dec 1881 HG)
MOSES WILLIS SHELL d. 16 Jan.(20 Jan 1882 HG)
WILLIAM O'NEAL d. last Sat.(20 Jan 1882 HG)
MRS. ELISHA MORRIS, d. Sat.(24 Feb 1882 HG)
ANNIE COX, d. 30 Jan. (24 Feb 1882 HG)
MALVINA MORRIS, d. Feb. (24 Feb 1882 HG)
R.L. COFFIELD, d.--. (24 Feb 1882 HG)
FRANK SHOEMAKER, d. last Wed.(24 Feb 1882 HG)
MRS. MARSH ANGLETON, d. Fri.(24 Feb 1882 HG)
HENRY HAMP SR., d. last Wed.(17 Mar 1882 HG)
JAMES DEMERRIS, d. Mon.(17 Mar 1882 HG)
HENRY HAMP, b. Hanover,Germany, 15 Dec 1818, d. 15 Mar 1882.(24 Mar 1882 HG)
HENRY KARBER, son of Louis & Matilda Karber d. 27 Mar.(31 Mar 1882 HG)
SOLOMON STONE'S youngest dau d. last wk.(07 Apr 1882 HG)
POLLY ANN TYNER, wid of Samuel Tyner & dau of Hiram Belt, d.---; m.1st, Asa Mott(d.1872); m. 2nd, Samuel Tyner(d.1882). (12 Apr 1882 HG)
THOMAS BELT, son of Logan & Mary Belt, b. 10 June 1865; leaves:3 bros & 5 sis.(14 Apr 1882 HG)
CATHERINE DOUGHERTY, wid of Gov. Dougherty, d. Jonesboro, 28 Mar, age 74 yrs.(14 Apr 1882 HG)
JAS. GUESS, d. 21 Apr 1882.(28 Apr 1882 HG)
JOHN MOTT d. Wed of last week.(11 May 1882 HI)
DANIEL PLEW d. last week.(11 May 1882 I)
OLLIE ORLIN KIRKHAM,inf son of James & Lavina Kirkham, d.04 May.(11 May 1882 HI)
JAMES RUTHERFORD, d Sat.(23 Nov 1882 HG)
I.C. GRACE, d. Nov 1882?(23 Nov 1882 HG)
WILEY HOBBS, son of Abram Hobbs, b. Hardin Co. Ill.,04 June 1833; m. Jennie McElroy; d.16 June. (21 June 1883 I)
JOHN MARTIN, son of Isaac Martin, d. Nov.(07 Nov 1883 HG)
MRS. J.M. ANDERSON, d. Apr. (17 Apr 1884 I)
JOHN VINYARD,d. Apr?; dau Joe Vinyard.(17 Apr 1884 I)
THOMAS CLANTON, d. Mon.(17 Apr 1884 I)
MONNA H---, dau of Jacob & Lizzie H--, d? (17 Apr 1884 I)

JOHN JEWELL'S child   d.? (15 Apr 1886 I)
J.H. BEAVER'S child   d.? (15 Apr 1886 I)
JNO. TURNER d. last Sun. (15 Apr 1886 I)
Mrs. WM. PATTON d.?(14 Apr 1887 HI)
HIGH HUNTER, d. last Sun.(14 Apr 1887 I)
WM. GOSSAGE'S girl d. Sept? (06 Oct 1887 E)
- HILDORBECK, d.Sept, at 80 yrs.(06 Oct 1887 E)
PERRY COWSERT'S boy d last Sat.(06 Oct 1887 I)
ROBERT WILLIAMS'baby d. 20th.(04 Apr 1889 I)
CHRIS DALE'S dau d. 27th. (04 Apr 1889 1)
HOBBS, MARION, d, last wk. (04 Apr 1889 I)
NERRISSA KEELING, dau of J.J. & I Keeling, d.
11 Jan. (6 Feb 1890 I)
MRS. CHARLIE CRABBS'S twin baby d. Fri, buried
next to father.(03 Apr 1890 I)
JANIE GINGER, dau of Elia Ginger, b.10 Oct
1873, d. 11 Mar. (18 Mar 1891I)
FREDDIE MICK, Son of Spencer Mick, b. 23 Oct
1890; d. 14 Aug 1891.(Aug 1891 I)
ELIZABETH COX, dau of Arch & Julie Hobbs,
b.1849; d. 17 Aug; m. 1st, Wm. Abner; issue;4
(3 died), Mrs. Samuel Joiner survives; m.2nd
Solomon Cox; issue:3 sons,5 daus; daus Belle &
Mollie survive.(02 Sept 1891 I)
CARRIE DIMMICK, dau of Alice & George Dimmick,
b.17 Aug 1872, d. 24 Apr;m. Chester Baldwin,
1891.(11 May 1992 I)
MAMIE HURFORD, dau of Noah Hurford, d. 02 May.
(11 May 1892 I)
HENRY MATHEWS, son of John H. Mathews, d. 10
May? (11 May 1892 I)
BETSY ANN GINGER, wife of Arch Ginger, d. Mon.
(18 Oct 1892 I)
HARDIN PRICE, d. 27 Mar. (05 Apr 1893 I)
BIGGER MCFARLAND, son of James & Elizabeth
McFarland, b. 20? Apr 1820, d. 02 Apr;
m.Pernissa Stewart. (05 Apr 1893 HCI)
WILLIAM JACKSON,b.29 Feb 1816, Sumner Co.
Tenn., d. 30 Mar 1893; m. Barsheba Lee,1840
Hardin Co., Ill. (she died 05 Sept 1875);
issue:John,George,Charles,Joseph,William (who
died a few weeks ago)& Annie.(05 Apr 1893 I)
WILLIS SOWARD, d. Oct? (05 Oct 1894 HR)
PHIL PARIS, d. May? (01 Jun 1894 HR)
JAS LEE, d. May? (01 Jun 1894 HR)
JEFF RIGGS' inf d. May (01 Jun 1894 HR)

MACK LAVANDER'S child d. Jul (27 Jul 1894 HR)
WASHINGTON LIEHTENBERGER, d.30 Mar 1899.(04 Apr 1899 I)
CLARENCE MADDEN, son of Charles and Jane Madden, b.27 August 1874; d. 07 Oct 1899; m. Jennie Hubbard, step-dau of Thomas Jenkins; issue: 2(died). (12 Oct 1899 HN)
JULIA HAMP KARBER, wife of F.C. Karber, b. 27 Jul 1857, d.30 Aug; m. F.C. Karber, 25 Dec 1874.(04 Sept 1901 IS)
ALMA MCCONNELL, wid of Richard McConnell, d. Sun. (04 Sept 1901 IS)
HARDIN PRICE, d. 27 Mar (05 Apr 1893 I)
MRS. JAMES WALLACE, d.___; leaves husband and 2 small chld. (20 Nov 1895 I)
NANCY JANE ELLIOT, dau of Joseph and Harriett Elliot, b. Hardin Co.,ILL., 12 May 1833, d. 21? Feb; m. Marshall White 25 Dec 1850,(d.05 Mar 1894); issue: James, Anna Renfro, & Albert,who d.14 Mar 1888. (05 Mar 1902 IS)
MARSHALL N. MILLER, son of Hew and Sarah Miller, b. 2 May 1858, Hardin Co. ILL., d. 21 May; m. Mary Ginger, dau of Arch &Polly Ginger. (08 Jun 1905 I)
MARGARET OZEE, b. 4 Mar 1842, d. 10 Jun; m. George Winters,26 Feb 1860. (15 Jun 1905 I)
W.N. WARFORD, b 05 Sep 1822, Woodford Co. Ky., d. 24 May Elizabethtown, ILL; m. Mary J. Shearer, 8 Feb 1846; she d. 11 Aug 1886; issue: Annie (mother of J.W., Henry & Willie White), Mrs. Gregory, Mary C., Martha J., Sarah L., William P., John D., & Charles E.; m. 2nd, Martha J. Douglas, 13 Feb 1887;(d.01 Apr 1903) (15 Jun 1905 I)
MARY CORLEW, dau of William Hobbs, d. Sun. (06 Feb 1906 I)
OMER KOCH, son of John Koch, d. Sun. (23 Nov 1904 IS)
THOMAS PRICE, b. Wales, England, 5 June 1852, d.8 Jun 1906; m.---;issue: Mrs. W.R. Martin, Mrs. W. P. Warford, Mrs. J.W. Shaw, M. T. Price & Arthur Price. (14 Jun 1906 I)
LYDIA SIMMONS, dau of George Simmons, d. 7 Jun 1906; age 15. (14 Jun 1906 I)
JANE WALL,b.Wilson Co.Tenn.,05 Sept 1827, d.09 Jun 1906 at bro's,E.F.Wall Sr.(14 Jun 1906 I)

EFFIE D. WALL, b. Hardin Co. ILL., 23 Apr 1860, d. 4 Jun 1906; m. George Wall --Oct 1905; she d. in Monrovia, Cal. (14 Jun 1906 I)
MRS.SUSAN COLLINS, d. Mon at abt 60 years old; sis of Dan'l Davis. (30 Mar 1907 I)
JULIE MCGOWN, wife of Ed McGown, d. Sat.(14 Jun 1906 I)
DANIEL WINTERS, "old soldier" d. 02 Aug; Leaves wife & chlldren. (8 Aug 1907 I)
E.B. ROSE, d. last Sat; leaves son,Charles & Daus,Phoebe Lawrence & Mrs Voncree ? & bro.(08 Aug 1907 I)
MARTHA COOPER, d. 13 May, m. C. Cooper 1885; issue: Golda, Roy Mollie, Beula, Carl, Charles, Norah, Willard & Noah. (23 May 1907 I)
LEWIS HICKS, b. 18 ? Dec 1832, Hicks, Hardin Co. ILL.; d. 01 May; m. Margaret Patton, 27 Mar 1850;issue: 4 sons & dau, Sarah Ferrell;& Margaret Hicks (d.15 Oct 1863); m. 2nd Mary Johnson; issue: Charles, Ben, Marion (d), Henry, Milo, Fannie, & Loy; bro, Milas Hicks; sis, Mrs. James Carlisle & Mrs. Richard Benum. (23 May 1907 I)
CHAS LEE, d. last Mon, 68 yrs, 2 mo, & 9 days; leaves: wife, sons, Chas. R., John; daus Vina Gerhardt, & Lula Thompson. (25 Apr 1907 I)
CHAS A. FERRELL, son of Pernett Ferrell Sr., b. abt 1877, d. 12 Apr, N.Y. City; leaves, father, sis & 2 issue. (25 Apr 1907 I)
T.L. WILLIAMS, b. 18 Aug 1828, d 6. Jun; m. Harriett Mathews, 4 Feb 1856; issue: Joe, Jeff, Granville, Mary Ginger, Belle Hale & Hattie Rainer? (27 Jun 1907 I)
PATSY OXFORD, wid of Samuel Oxford, d Jun; issue; John C. Oxford ?(27 Jun 1907 I)
TABITHA OXFORD, sis to Patsy, wid of John W. Oxford, d. Jun (note: John Oxford was "half brother to the father of the old set of Oxfords, all of whom are now dead except for Hannah Patton, who will be 74 Aug 6, 1907." (27 Jun 1907 I)
WILLIAM MASON, son of Joseph Mason, d. Tues; leaves: wife, children, parents, & bros & sis. (27 Jun 1907 I)
MARTHA HINES, dau of Fount Hines, d 31. Jul? (01 Aug 1907 I)

AMY TUCKER, dau of J.B. Tucker, b Sept 1892, d.
31 Jul 1907. (08 Aug 1907 I)
PLEASANT ROSE SR, b 21 Feb 1836, d 17 Feb; m.
Mary Stacey abt 1862;issue: Pleasant Jr.,
Sarah Rose Dimmick & Ida Rose Finney; dau-
in-law, Maggie. (19 Apr 1908 I)
CORA RALPH, dau of Samuel Patton, b. 01 Jun
1879, d 09 Mar; m. Mack Ralph, 13 Dec 1903;
issue: 2 plus 4 step chld; sur, mother, 2 bros
& 1 sis. (02 Apr 1908 I)
PEARL SHIPP, dau of W.E., g dau of J.H. & Eliza
Shipp, b. Cincinnati, 26 Mar 1905, d. 26 Mar
1908. (02 Mar 1908 I)
FRED COWSERT, son of W.H. Cowsert, d. last
Tues. (16 Apr 1908 I)
ETTA GROSS, b. 20 Oct 1871, d. 21 Apr 1908;
m.---; issue: Elsie.(d. 20 Apr 1908), Eschol,
Eva, Sorado, Rachel.(30 Apr 1908 I)
NANCY VIRGINIA JENNINGS, b. 18 Jun 1848, d 21
Apr; m. Geo. A. Scott, 06 Apr 1857; issue:
Walter, Freedman, Gertude,(m. Walter McDowell),
& 2(d.). (07 May 1908 I)
ALICE GRAHAM, dau of Joseph Graham, b. 24 Mar
1890, d. 15 Apr Paducah, Ky; sur, parents, 5
sis, 1 bro. (07 May 1908 I)
DORA ALICE WATERS, dau of Jonathan G. & Martha
J. Waters, b. 23 Mar 1878, d. 29 Apr; m.
Charles Ginger, 7 Dec 1898; Issue: Hattie Mae,
& Willie. (07 May 1908 I)
SARAH CAMERON, b. 16 Aug 1833, d 09 Apr; m.
Wesley Reed, 20 Oct 1845; issue: Russell &
Rufus. (07 May 1908 I)
WILLIAM HARVEY HILL, b. abt 1856, d. 24 Apr; m.
Alice McCue abt 1874 (07 May 1908 I)
A.W. DUTTON, b 29 Jan 1845, d 29 Apr; m. Nancy
Rutledge;issue: Mary J. Pritchard,(wid of
Carroll Pritchard), Anice Julian, Chas. H.,
Margaret Rowland, Willie E., & Andrew R.
Dutton; m. 2nd Mrs. Polly Birch. (14 May 1908
I) LUCY A. SPIVEY, b. 18 Aug 1844, d 19 Apr
1908; m. --- Spivey; issue; Wade, Goolsby(?),
James & John Spivey. (21 May 1908 I)
MRS. SAM RAINER, sis of Chas. Baker, d. Pope
Co., ILL., last Thur. (28 May 1908 I)
CLARA LOWERY, dau of Jesse Lowery, b. 2 Feb
1883, d May; m. John Hill, May 1903; issue: 3

(Gladys died). (04 Jun 1908 I)
MILFORD PATTON, son of Grant & Alice Patton, b. 9 Feb 1886, Hardin Co.ILL., d. 21 Sept; m. Hattie Fellows, 06 Feb 1908 (01 Oct 1908 I)
MRS. JAMES LIVERS, d. Sat; leaves husband and 5 chld. (19 Mar 1908 I)
OSCAR MILLER, son of Jane Miller, b. 30 Dec 1885, d. 27 May 1908; leaves bro and sis.(18 Jun 1908 I)
W.W. GULLETTS, b.---, d. last week; m. Emma Wood abt 50 years ago; leaves wife & children. (29 Apr 1901 I)
PHOEBE PYLES, d. ---. (9 Dec 1910 I)
CLAUDE ILIFF, b. 10 Aug 1883, Hardin Co. ILL., d.12 Sept. (16 Sept 1909 I)
WILLIAM R. LEDBETTER, son of the late John T. Ledbetter's 1st wife, b. 15 Feb 1880, Hardin Co.,ILL., d. 16 Nov Marion, ILL; leaves: bros, James, Herbert; sis, Kate White, plus others; wife & 3 chld, deceased. He was nephew to D.A. Ledbetter, John Thorton, & J.L. Lowery.(25 Nov 1909 I)
ELIZA T. MARTIN, b. Caldwell Co. Ky., 09 Dec 1829, d. 25 Nov; m.1st,James D. Parton; issue: 5 living; m. 2nd, James W. Martin; issue: 2 (02 Dec 1909 I)
JOSEPH GRAHAM, b. 14 Jul 1870, d. 26 Nov; m. 1891 Margaret Joyner; issue:10 ?; sur, 1 chld, wife, 2 sis, & bro (09 Dec 1909 I)
---- TYLER,d. last Fri; George Tyler, grandson (09 Dec 1909 I)
JAMES PATTON, d. last Fri; sur, wife, 5 chld, bro, & 2 sis & mother; related to Oxfords, Pattons,&Pages of Hardin Co.ILL.(30 Dec 1909 I)
FINCH HOLDER, Civil War vet, d. Shawneetown, ILL., 28 Nov 1909. (09 Dec 1909 I)
PHOEBE LYONS PYLE, b. 1817 Jackson Co., Ohio, d. 03 Dec 1909; m. John Pyle abt 1831(who d. 1863) issue; 10, 5 living, Lucian Vinyard, Phoebe Riener, Mary Vinyard, John and Austin Pyle.(16 Dec 1909 I)
THOMAS HURFORD JR., d. Sun.(16 Dec 1909 I)
JOHN ROSE, d.--- .(16 Dec 1910 I)
---- MORMAN, d. Sun (16 Dec 1910 I)
BEN GRAHAM, d. 25 Dec 1909. (30 Dec 1910 I)
RAY COCHRAN, son of Joseph Cochran, b.12 Oct

1890?, d. 25 Dec 1909?;leaves:father,stepmother, 3 bros, 2 sis (06 Jan 1910 I)
EZRA REINER, son of Elmer & Katie Reiner, d---; leaves:parents,g.parents,& bro. (06 Jan 1910 I)
ARZIE VINYARD, son of Jefferson & Lucy Vinyard, b. 14 Dec 1877 Hardin Co. ILL., d. 20 Dec 1909; leaves: 5 bro. (13 Jan 1910 I)
CALVIN M. BAKER, b. 27 Dec 1824, d 21 Jan, m. Francis Calbert, 10 Jan 1814 (1844?); issue: 9, 6 sur, including Sarah M. Rose. (27 Jan 1910 I)
RAUM IRBY, son of L.P. & Nancy Irby, b. 12 Feb 1888, d 5 Jan. (27 Jan 1910 I)
LUIA CARTER, dau Elijah Carter, b. abt 1872, d. 25 Jan 1910 m. 3 Sept 1905 David Ledbetter, son of Millington & Mary Ledbeter; leaves husband, dau, father, 3 sis, & bro. (03 Feb 1910 I)
NANCY J. ANGLETON, dau of Elias & Nancy J. Oxford, b. 5 Sept 1849, d. 23 Mar 1910; m. 1st, James Oxford (d.Oct 1883); issue; Mrs. Peter Hambrink, Wilmer Oxford, 3(d); m. 2nd,Thomas Angleton, Sept 1885; issue: Millard; bros, J.A., S.C. & George W. Oxford); sis, Hanna Brownfield.(31 Mar 1910 I)
NOAH CARR, b. 4 Mar 1871, Pope Co., d. 29 Apr, Heaston, Okla; m. Cora M. Lambert(sis to Mrs. Henry Ferrell); issue: Pearl, Margaret, Moody, Madaline; Noah was a half-brother to Spencer & Alex Mick of Hardin Co.,ILL.(12 May 1910 I)
DONALD CONN, son of W.F. Conn, b. abt. 1897 Toronto, Jefferson Co. Ohio, d. 28 Apr 1910. (12 May 1910 I)
GRACE OXFORD, dau of the late Isaac N. Oxford and India (now Mrs India Hardesty), b. 1 Mar 1889, d. 4 Mar 1910 ; issue:Robbie; leaves mother & bro, Aaron Oxford.(12 & 19 May 1900 I)
EMMA DUNN DEWEY, b. 26 Jan 1839 Elizabethtown, Hardin Co., ILL., d. 15 June 1910; m. Jacob Dewey 18 Jul 1863; issue: John (d), Clyde, Frank L,.(23 Jun 1910 I)
OPHELIA KENDRICK, b. 17 Oct 1830, Hamilton Co. ILL, d. 23 Jul 1906 (1910?); m. W.P. Williams 30 Nov 1850 (d.11 Aug 1906); leaves 3 dau, 2 sons, and 11 g. children. (12 Aug 1910 I)
F.E. MATBENY (Matheny?), b. 30 Oct 1855 New Albany, Ind., d. 16 Aug 1910; m.1st, Adaline Hosick, 19 Nov 1881; issue: 3 boys, 1 girl,

Rolla, & Frank living; m. 2nd, Annie Clanahan, 6 Sept 1893; issue; 2, none living; m. 3rd, Mrs. Addie Irwin; issue: 3 boys, 1 girl, 1 boy (d). (25 Aug 1910 I)
MRS. HARRIET WILLIAMS, b. 1 Apr 1840, d. 23 Aug 1910; m. Thomas C. Williams, 4 Feb 1856;issue; 7 Boys, 3 girls;leaves 3 sons & 3 dau. (15 Sept 1910 I)
MRS. ELIZABETH HERI, b. abt 1842, d. 02 Sept 1910; m. 1st, Bill Herman;issue;Emanuel(d. Jan 1896) & John Herman; m. 2nd, John Heri (d.1908); issue: Bass, Rollie, Mrs A.F. Herman, & Mrs. Hugh Jordon. (15 Sept 1910 I)
HOMER FERRELL, son of J.W. & Belle Ferrell (nee Vinyard), b. 17 Jan 1896, d.06 Sept 1910; leaves parents, bros Bert, Ralph, Randal, Nolen & sis Eunice and Gladys.(05 Sept 1910 I)
CHARLES SWAGGART, b. 18 Jun 1849 in Penn., d. 5 Feb 1910; m. Sarah E. Womack, 7 May 1870; issue: 6 boys, 1 girl.(17 Feb 1910 I)
WM. DEAL, d. Sat at 79 years.(24 Feb 1910 I)
HARRIET JACKSON, wife of Geo. Jackson, d. Fri; leaves husband & 2 chld. (24 Feb 1910 I)
JACOB DEWEY, b. Penn. 30 Aug 1835, d. 15 Feb 1910; m.Emma Dunn, 8 Jul 1863; issue: 4, living (Frank, James, & Clyde Dewey). (24 Feb 1910 I)
WILLIAM DEAL, b. Jackson Co., ILL. abt 1831, d. 1910; m. Fannie Conley; issue: 7, living (Mrs. Segt, Mrs Johnson,& Anson Deal; m. 2nd, --- Beard, abt 1878; issue: 4, 1 living.(03 Mar 1910 I)
MANDY LANIER, wife of Sam Lanier & dau of Capt. Gibson; leaves husband and several children.(03 Mar 1910 I)
HARRIET JACKSON, wife of G. W. Jackson, b. 31 Nov 1841, d. 18 Feb 1910; leaves husband, 2 sons, step son, half bro & half sis; and Mrs. Charles Lee, sis. (24 Mar 1910 I)
MRS. W.L. WOMACK, d. in Ark.; leaves husband and 2 boys. (24 Mar 1910 I)
MOLLIE F. REAK, dau of Mat Reak, b. 1 Apr 1866, d. 14 Mar 1910 in Danville, Ark; m. W.L.Womack, 13 Jan 1887; issue 4, 2 living,George & Walter; leaves husband, parents, 5 bros & 3 sis. (24 Mar 1910 I)
MRS. NOAH LIGHTNER, d. last Fri; leaves husband

& 5 children. (14 Apr 1910 I)
ALBERT JENNINGS, d. Sun. (14 Apr 1910 I)
JOEL D. HART, d. Valparaiso, Ind. at 22 years
of age; bro to Ezra Hart, nephew to Joel Hart.
(19 May 1910 I)
MRS.W.H. MARTIN, b. abt 1889, d. Wed; leaves
husband, mother (Mrs. India Hardesty) & bro,
Aaron Oxford.(19 May 1910 I)
MRS. JULIA MASON, d. last Sat. (19 May 1910 I)
KATE MILLER, wife of Samuel D. Miller, d. Wed;
issue: Douglas Miller.(26 May 1910 I)
MAXIE BERNARD, d. in explosion on navy ship,
Charleston; leaves mother, bro (Austin) g.
mothers, Moore & Austin.(23 Jul 1910 I)
JAMES WONTING, b. McLeansboro, Hamilton Co.,
ILL., b. Aug ? 1850, d. Jul ? 1910; bro of Sam
Wonting.(7 Jul 1910 I)
WILEY HOBBS, son of Issac Hobbs, d. May 3(?)
(21 Jul 1910 I)
BRITTON STACEY, b. near Gainsboro, Johnson Co.,
Tenn. 1 May 1844, d. 07 Sept 1910; m. Emma J.
Tinsley 22 Mar--; issue: none; leaves wife, bro
Hiram Morton Stacey, & niece, Nancy Stacey, dau
of Hiram Morton Stacey. (15 Sept 1910 I)
LILLIE VINYARD, wife of Silas Vinyard, d. 25
May 1911. (01 Jun 1910 I)
CHAS. T. MILLER, b. Canada, 10 Nov 1812 ?, d.
22 Feb 1911; m. Mary E. Mitchell 1862; issue:
Charles Jr., Owen, & Daisy Barnet; leaves wife.
(09 Mar 1911 I)
PHILLIP J. HOWARD, b. Elizabethtown, ILL., 11
Mar 1840, d. 27 Feb 1911; m. Sarah J. Howe 15
Nov 1865; issue: 5; leaves 2 bro, 1 sis; served
in Civil War, Co. A 29 Ill. (09 Mar 1911 I)
MARTHA ENGLISH, d. 27 Feb 1911; leaves 2 sons,
1 dau, g.children (09 Mar 1911 I)
OLIVE BALL, wife of Claude Ball, b. 21 Oct
1889, Hardin Co.,ILL., d. 27 Feb 1911; m.
Claude Ball, 26 Oct 1908; issue: 1 son.
(16 Mar 1911 I)
WILLIAM RILEY LAMB, b. abt 1833, d. 17 Mar
1911; wife (d), 6 sons & 5 daus, one son,
Thomas (d). (23 Mar 1911 I)
HENRY ROSE, b. near Elizabethtown, Hardin Co.,
ILL., Dec 1827, d.17 Mar 1911; leaves: 2 sis,
Mrs. B.L. Lavander,& Mrs.Ile Dorssett; bro,

unnamed;2 sons, unnamed; 2 daus,Mrs Minerva Belt & Mrs. Alice Morgan.(27 Apr 1911 HCI) ANDERSON LEDBETTER, "very feeble", will have reached his 84th Year in June. (4 May 1911 I) LEWIS LAVANDER, b. Virginia, 1814; still living in 1911; m. India Whitesides in Pope Co, Il.; she d. 08 Jan 1897; issue: James and George named in article. (01 Jun 1911 HCI)
JOHN THORTON, b. Morgan Co., Tenn, 11 Aug 1839, d. 07 Jun 1911 Elizabethtown, ILL; m. Mary Ann Ledbetter,02 Jun 1859;issue: Rebecca (Mrs Richard Birch), Dr E. (Abliene, Texas), Martha (Mrs W.D. Aaron), Sidney (Mrs G.W. Patrick, Redlands, Cal), John A, Willis (d), Ida (Mrs Clarence Shearer, St. Petersburg, Fla), Phoebe (d), Lou (d., wife of Byrant Mason), & Henry Thornton. (15 Jun 1911 HCI)
JACOB PENNEL HOWE, b. 03 Aug 1892, d. 21 Aug 1910; leaves mother, stepfather (Mr. Davis), & 3 sis. (22 Jun 1911 HCI)
EMILY JACKSON, youngest dau of George & Susan Jackson, b. near Rosiclare, ILL., 24 Jul 1826, d. 18 Jul 1911. (27 Jul 1911 HCI)
JAS. HAYDEN, b. abt 1863, d. Wed; leaves bros Will, & Charley Hayden of Metropolis & sis, Mary Ferrell. (17 Aug 1911 HCI)
WILLIE -----, b. Hardin Co. ILL., 11 Oct 1887, d. 25 Sept 1911; leaves parents, bro & sis. (19 Oct 1911 HCI)
GERTRUDE WILLINGHAM, dau of R.H. Willingham, b. 25 Oct 1905, d. 13 Oct 1911. (19 Oct 1911 HCI)
ELIZABETH OXFORD, dau of J.A. & Sidney Oxford, b. Hardin Co. ILL., 21 Nov. 1873, d. 31 Oct 1911; m. George E. Rickets, 03 May 1900; issue: 5, 4 living. (09 Mar 1911 HCI)
BESSIE HOBBS (nee Collins), b. 08 Dec 1891, d. 08 Sept 1911; m. ---- Hobbs, 09 Dec 1907; Hobbs died 01 Oct 1910; issue: 1 dau; ---.Hobbs was son of Ezekial Hobbs ? (28 Sept 1911 HCI)
SARAH MORGAN, b. Hardin Co.ILL., d. 21 Nov 1911, Mt. Vernon, Ind.; m. Arthur Kneeling (d. 1905);issue: Addie(d., wife of William Gaines), Ernest, & John Knelling. (30 Nov 1911 HCI)
MARY ANN ROBERTSON, b. 14 Jan 1843, d. 15 Nov 1911; m. Millington Ledbetter, 12 Nov 1866; issue: 10, 5 living; leaves husband, 5 chld, 2

bros, & 3 sis. (30 Nov 1911 HCI)
SAMUEL GRINDSTAFF, d. last week; Civil War vet.
(15 Jun 1911 I)
MRS. J.N. MILLIGAN,d. 09 Jun 1911.(15 Jun 1911
HCI)
OSCAR BRUCE, d. last Week. (15 Jun 1911 HCI)
RITTA JACKSON, d. Mon. (27 Jul 1911 HCI)
MRS. LEE OXFORD, d. Mt. Vernon Ind. last week;
m.1st, Chas. Bloomer; m. 2nd, John C. Oxford;
leaves bros, Lace & Ab Edwards.(07 Dec 1911
HCI)
GEORGE WHEELER SR., d. Sun. (29 Feb 1912 HCI)
MRS. ELIZABETH MOORE, d.26 Mar 1912, dau of Eli
P. Vinyard; bros,Anderson & Daniel Vinyard.(04
Apr 1912 HCI)
MATTHEW REAK, "hopeless condition," 82 years
old. (11 Apr 1912 HCI)
MISSOURI BARNES, wife of Henry Barnes, d. Sat.
(12 Jun 1913 HCI).
THOS. HOBBS, son of Jefferson Hobbs, b abt
1888. (12 Jun 1912 HCI)
WILLIE WATERS, b Hardin Co. ILL., 01 Nov 1879,
d. 3 Jan 1912; leaves wife, 6 children, mother
& bro. (22 Feb 1912 HCI)
JOHN FRANKLIN DIMICK, b. 26 May 1858, d. 20 Mar
1912; m. Letitia Alice Calhoun, 18 Jul 1886;
issue: 7, 3 living, Otis, Ralph,& Mable; leaves
3 bros, C.C. Dimick, G.F. Dimick &--- Dimick of
Evansville, Ind. (21 Mar 1912 HCI)
JAS. A. ROSE, d. Mon. bro to J.M. Rose (09 May
1912 HCI)
JOHN T. MCAMIS,(son of Thomas Akin McAmis who
d. 03 Aug 1905 Tolu, KY.) b. Hardin Co.,ILL.
abt 1857, d. 24 Apr 1912; leaves bro Ross
(Calif) & sis, Mrs. E.E. Hodge, Mrs. Laura
Newman, Mrs. J.C. Taylor & Mrs. W.T. Crider.(09
Mar 1912 HCI)
JAMES HIRAM ROSE, b. Hardin Co., ILL. 16 Jun
1850, d. 06 May 1912; m. Mahallah Moreland;
issue:9,5 living; leaves wife, 2 bros, & sis.
(16 May 1912 HCI)
MRS.GOTLEIP STUBY, d. last week at her son's,
Charley. (16 May 1912 HCI)
THOMAS A. LEDBETTER, funeral last Sun. (16 May
1912 HCI)
EZRA HODGE, d. 21 Feb 1912, son of Mrs. George

Williams, grandson of Jim Hodge; leaves wife, Jessie Nelson Hodge.(22 Feb 1912 HCI)
ELSIE J. GUSTIN, b. Switzerland Co., Ind. 04 Jul 1847, d. 04 Mar 1913; m.1st, S.C.Oxford abt 1864; issue: 4, 3 living,Sarah Ellen Oxford, John Allen Oxford, & Kate Oxford; m. 2nd, John Miles 1873; issue: Arthur A. Miles, William A. Miles, Hannah Miles & Berdie Miles. (15 Mar 1913 HCI)
LEWIS LAVANDER, b. abt 1814, d. last week; leaves: sons Jas., Geo., Chas.; daus Katie & Josephine S. Barger(d).(10 Apr 1913 HCI)
HETTIE FELLOWS, dau of Willie & Fannie Fellows, d.06 Feb 1913; m. 1st, Milford Patton; m.2nd, Owen Decker; leaves mother, sis, bro, children; father & sis d."a few year back" (10 Apr 1913 HCI)
WILLIAM T. JACKSON, Hardin Co., ILL. 15 Oct 1837, d. 24 Mar 1913; m. Mollie Clanton 16 Jul 1873; children: 6. (10 Apr 1913 HCI)
MARION LOLENE WILLIAMS, dau of Milas Williams, b.21 Aug 1908, d. 22 Mar 1913.(10 Apr 1913 HCI)
HARM (Hiram?) B. COOK, b. 2 Dec 1847, d. 16 Mar 1913; m. Amanda K. Millikan, 04 Dec 1879;issue: 5, living:James, Fred, Ida (Mrs. Dan Patton), John & Herbert. (10 Apr 1913 HCI)
ALFRED OXFORD, son of Samuel Oxford, d. 28 Mar 1913; m. Minnie Curry, dau of Sigel Curry; leaves father, bros,Millard & Walter & 6 children, half-sis & mother(d).(10 Apr 1913 HCI)
WILLIAM ODOM ZIGLER, b. Hardin Co., ILL. 14 Nov 1885, d. 13 Mar 1913; m. Julie Matheny, 17 May 1911; leaves parents, 2 bros, 3 sis, wife & son.(10 Apr 1913 HCI)
MISSOURI BARNES, wife of Henry Barnes, d. last Sat. (12 Jun 1913 HCI)
JAMES GORDON BEARD, son of Mathew & Mamie Beard, b. 11 Oct 1911, d. 10 Sept 1913. (09 Oct 1913 HCI)
ARTHUR SUTTON, b. Virginia ? abt 1828 ?, d. 28 Sept 1913; m. 1st, Mrs. Miles; 2nd, Mrs Richardson; issue: 5 living; Arthur served 48th Reg. during Civil War. (09 Oct 1913 HCI)
HAZEL CURE, d. last night; leaves mother & 2 bros. (13 Nov 1913 HCI)
MRS. WALTER DAVIS, dau of Adam Zeigler, b.

Hardin Co., ILL., 07 Aug 1877, d. 30 Nov 1913;
m. Walter Davis, 03 Jun 1906; issue: Daisy, &
Marie; leaves husband, parents, bros Walter,
John & sis Minnie & Emma. (18 Dec 1913 HCI)
FREDERICK SPEILER, b. Gross Cothen (Anthault)
Germany, 14 Oct 1832, d. 01 Dec 1913; m. John
Leonberger(who d.10 Sept 1889), 20 Dec 1854,
New   Castle,Penn.;issue:10,6 living.(18 Dec
1913 HCI)
OMA PAULINE OXFORD, dau of Prof. & Seba Oxford,
b.---, d. 21 Dec 1913; leaves parents & bro.
(08 Jan 1914 HCI)
HENRY VAUGHN, son of Samuel and Ellen Vaughn,
b. 13 Sept 1894,d. 26 Jan 1914.(5 Feb 1914 HCI)
NANCY E. ASHFORD,dau of Wesley & Susan Ashford,
b. 13 Aug 1848 Allen Co., Ky., d. 19 Dec 1913;
m. J.B. Tucker, 27 Dec 1882; issue:sons, Weaver
(d), Henry, Elmer, & Roy; dau, Susan & Emma
(d); leaves husband, stepson,Willie Tucker,3
grandchld, sis, Mrs. Allen Love, half bro,
(Brittion York), & half sis, Mrs Eli Morris.
(19 Feb 1914 HCI)
THELMA MILLIKAN, son of Sam & Ora Millikan, b.
abt 1913, d. 07 Feb 1914. (19 Feb 1914 HCI)
NANCY BEBOUT HOOVER, b. Decab Co., Tenn, 21 Dec
1829, d.15 Apr 1914; m. George Moore 1844;
issue: 1 (d); George Moore d. 1845; m. 2nd,
Hinton Belt 1861; issue: Thomas & Marion Belt;
Hinton Belt d. Mar 1867; m. 3rd, Enoch Bebout;
he d.14 Dec 1906. (30 Apr 1914 HCI)
MARY A.GERHARDT, dau of C.W.& Melvina Gerhardt,
b. 22 Sept 1894; d.9 Apr 1914.(07 May 1914 HCI)
DANIEL V. GINGER, b. 1 Oct 1826, d. 03 May
1914; m. Ann Hicks, issue: 4 boys, 8 girls;
Daniel served in Civil War (14 May 1914 HCI)
STELLA MAE SHELBY, dau of James & Barbara
Shelby, b. 06 May 1893, d. 15 Apr 1914; m.
James Leonard Paris, 29 Oct 1911; issue: James
Archibald Mack Chestney Paris, & James Leonard
Paris Jr.; leaves parents; husband,2 boys, 3
sis, & 2 bros. (14 May 1914 HCI)
IRENE WINIFRED HOSSLER, dau of Aldolphus & Ida
Hossler, b. abt 1911, d. 2 may 1914; leaves
g.parents, David T. Warford & wife. (14 & 21
May 1914 HCI)
SARAH OXFORD, wid of Elihu Oxford;leaves 2 daus

Mrs. Griffith & Mrs. Curley Oxford; 4 others (d.),unnamed. (28 May 1914 HCI)
J.M. GREGORY, b. 14 Apr 1838, d.2? May 1914; leaves wife, sons, and dau; served in Civil War, 48 Ky Regiment.(28 May 1914 HCI)
JOE PALMER, son of Calvin & Sophia Palmer,b.06 Nov 1875, d.16 May 1914; m. Phoebe Mason, dau of John & Julie Mason; leaves wife, 8 children, 3 bros, 1 sis & 2 half sisters. (04 Jun 1914 HCI)
SARAH E. BROWNFIELD, b. 04 Nov 1837, d. 15 May 1914; m. Hugh Miller, 08 May 1866; he d. 28 Mar 1863 ?; m. 2nd, Elihu Oxford, 24 May 1887; issue; (by Miller) 6 boys, 3 girls, 2 living Mrs. John Oxford, & Mrs. Doc Griffith. (28 May 1914 HCI)
NETTIE BRAMBLET, dau of J.M.(Mit)Bramblet, b.08 Oct 1889, d. 24 May 1914; m. J.E. Ewell Jr.,03 Mar 1909;issue:Amerso & Icelez Ewell.(11 Jun 1914 RS)
Mrs. CAPT JOHN FERRELL," Mortal remains of Mrs. John Ferrell, mother of Capt. James Ferrell of this town was brought here from Paducah.... She was accompanied by her son, Mr. John T. Ferrell of Metropolis and Miss Joe Ferrell of Paducah." (23 Jul 1914 HCI)
LORA DOSSETT, dau of H.F. & Ida Dossett, b. Cave-in-Rock, Hardin Co., ILL., 27 Feb 1895, d. 27 Jun 1914 Sikeston, Missouri; m.Lester L. Reed, 21 Dec 1913, Moberly, Missouri; leaves husband, parents, 2 sis, Ethna & Minerva Dossett; bros Ile?,Henry, John, Bill, & Miem Dossett. (30 Jul 1914 HCI)
----- MORRIS, dau of Chas.? & Charlotte Morris, b. 1862, d. 5 Jul 1914; m. William Smith abt 1882; children: 5 sons, 1 dau, 5 living. (30 Jul 1913 HCI)
ETHEL BELT, dau of W.J. Belt of Oran, Mo., b. 19 Sept 1895, Hardin Co., ILL., d. 23 Jul 1914; m. W.T. Pate Jr. abt 1912; issue: son, John Albert; leaves husband, parents, bro, & 2 sis. (13 Aug 1914 HCI)
FRED LEONBERGER, b. Werternburg, Germany,09 Mar 1847, d. St. Louis, 06 Aug 1914; m.Lizzie Denton, issue: Sarah (Mrs. William Denton), Wiley,Ollie (Mrs. Sylvester),George & Clarence;

uncle: John Leonberger. (20 Aug 1914 HCI)
ANN SHERIDAN, b. Crittenden, Ky., May 1858, d.
Dell, Ark. 12 Aug 1914; m. William Sheridan in
Hardin Co., ILL., 1878; issue: Mrs. Della
Moore, Mrs. May McDowell, Roy Sheridan, Alice
Sheridan, & Chas. Sheridan. (20 Aug 1914 HCI)
HOWARD GIINTERT, son of Frank Giintert, b. abt
1895, d. Thur. (22 Jan 1914 HCI)
STEVE WALKER, d. Murphysboro Sat; bro of M.L.
Walker. (08 Jan 1914 HCI)
"GRANDMA" GUSTIN, d. 38 Jan at home of dau,
Mrs. Mary Lackey.(05 Feb 1914 HCI)
LOUIS LAVANDER, son of Charles Lavander, d.--.
(19 Feb 1914 HCI)
MARY JANE MABAN GARLAND, b. O'Byon Co., Tenn.
11 Mar 1833, d.22 Jun 1914; m. Wm. Garland,Aug
1854; issue 9, 8 living, Mary E.Shearer, Nancy
Jane Miles, Lizzie Farysey ?,Harriet Hoskinson
& Henry Garland, others? (25 Jun 1914 RS)
EDWARD ROWAN, son of Clara Oxford (now Mrs.
J.A. Oxford); d. 26 Jun 1914; father; Charles
Rowan (d.); bros, Paul & Don Rowan ?; aunts Ida
Stewart, Emma Woods, May Davis; uncles Frank
Rowan & Milton Martin. (09 Jul 1914 RS)
GEORGE RICKETS, b. Rising Sun Ind. 26 Dec 1851,
d. 13 Dec 1914; m. Bell Lowery, 13 Apr 1873;
issue: John, Charlie, George, Josie(Mrs. Luster
?) & Nellie (Mrs. Hurford).(17 Dec 1914 S)
OLLIE BIRCH, dau of Richard Birch, b. 26 Oct.
1882, d. 25 Aug. 1914; m. John Mayfield, 22 May
1912; leaves husband, parents, 1 bro, & 3 sis.
(03 Sept 1914 HCI)
EMMA TINSLEY dau of Jack & Nancy Tinsley, b. 13
Jul 1847, d.06 Sept 1914; m.Brittian Stacey, 22
Mar 1866; no issue. (08 Oct 1914)
OSCAR VINYARD, son of Bill Vinyard, d. Paducah,
Ky. 04 Oct 1914. (08 Oct 1914)
MARY RICKETS d.23 Oct 1914;bro, George Rickets.
(29 Oct 1914)
OLIVE JOYCE, dau of John & Lilly Joyce, b. 29
Apr 1910, d. 29 Sep 1915. (12 Nov 1914)
HANNAH HAWKER, b. 02 June 1840, near Berlin,
Germany, d. 07 Nov 1914; m. Henry Bath 1908;
children : 2 d, 9 living; Mrs Fred Shelter,
dau. (26 Nov 1914)
GENEVA HUMM, dau of J.F. & Marzella Humm, d.

last Wed (18th ?) 2 years old. (26 Nov 1914)
MRS. FRANCIS MILLER, mother of E.L. Robinsin &
Asa Brumly, b. abt 1832, d. last Thur.
(03 Dec 1914)
WILLIAM C. CLARK, d. last week; leaves widow;
no issue. (31 Dec 1914)
ELIZABETH HUMM, dau of Fredreick & Anna B.
Humm, b Rhinebar, Germany 01 Sept 1834, d. 21
Nov 1914; m. Anton Shelter (he d.1881) 1866;
issue: Rosa (Mrs. John Volkert), Fred, John,
Andrew, & grandson, Chas F. Volkert; sis Saloma
Shelter, Kate Shelter & Barbara Reif. (31 Dec
1914)
REV. A.G. PROCTOR, d. 05 Jan 1915. (14 Jan
1914)
PLEASANT T.ROSE, d. Salmon City, Id.,08 Dec
1914; relatives: nephew, Wiley J. Rose; cousins
William and George Rose, sis, Minerva Dossett &
Cassie Lavander. (07 Jan 1915)
ALTA MARIE HOLBROOKS, dau of Bruce & Minnie
Holbrooks, b.13 May 1912, d. 01 Jan 1915.
(14 Jan 1915)
HENRY VINYARD, son of Philip & Lucinda Vinyard,
b. Hardin Co., ILL., 27 Aug. 1845, d. 10 Jan
1915; m. Pinkneyette McFarland, 03 March 1869;
issue: Phillip, William, Lloyd, Sidney (Mrs.
W.P. Ledbetter), Henryette (Mrs. J.J. Scheytt),
& Della (Mrs. Charles Christensen); served in
Co. D 48 Ky. (21 Jan 1915)
BOSTY ROTES, d. 1915?; bro John Rotes, d. 20
Jan 1915; sis-in- law to Margaret Ledbetter.
(21 Jan 1915)
MRS.SAMUEL HOLBROOKS, d. Sun; leaves husband,
sons, Henry & Bruce Holbrooks; dau, Mrs. Annie
Smith. (28 Jan 1915)
THOMAS E. BIRCH, son of Ben & Viola Birch, b.
11 May 1912, d. 12 Jan 1915.(28 Jan 1915)
JOHN A. SPIVEY son of Jonas and Lucinda Spivey,
b. Jackson Co., Tenn., 08 Oct. 1845, d. 07 Jan
1915; m. Lucyann Golsby; issue: Jonas, James,&
John william Spivey; bro. Jonas Spivey. (04
Feb. 1915 HCI)
SAMUEL BLACK SR., 27 Jan 1915. (04 Feb 1915)
JAMES COVET. d. Tues; leaves wife.(11 Feb 1915)
J.K.P. FERRELL, d. 04 Feb 1915. (18 Feb 1915)
JOHN TYER, d. 8 Feb 1915. (25 Feb 1915)

Chambers, d. 24 Jan 1915; m.1st David Blanchard; issue: Anna; m 2nd, Samuel Holbrook; issue: Henry & Bruce Holbrook. (18 Feb 1915)
MOLLIE L. LEDBETTER, dau of the late J. N. Ledbetter, b. Hardin Co.ILL, about 1865, d. 17 Feb. 1915; m. Richard F. Taylor, 8 Oct. 1884; children: Eunice, Richard F., & Bennie.(25 Feb 1915)
R.A. FRAYSER, d. 22 Feb 1915. (04 Mar 1915)
ARTHUR LEE IRBY, son of James N.& Fannie Irby, b. Hardin Co.,ILL., 23 Mar 1884, d. 14 Feb. 1915; m. Lucy Spivey, 10 May 1914;leaves wife, parents, sis Laura Stacey & Hester Ladwig, half-sis Effie Livers and Mary Irby.(11 Mar 1915)
WILLIAM SEINER, bro of John Seiner d. Mon. (18 Mar 1915)
HENRY M. WINDERS, b. Hardin Co.ILL., 14 Apr 1848, d. 28 Mar 1915; m.1st, Mary J. Coltrin, nee Dunn (divorced); m 2nd, Mrs Mary F. Irons, 12 May 1876; leaves stepdaus, Mrs. Mary Belle Price,& Mrs. Dora Weaver. Winders served in Co. D 48 Ky. Mounted Vols, Civil War.(08 Apr 1915 HCI)
RAYMOND BALL, son of W.M. Ball, d. 29 Mar 1915. (15 Apr 1915 HCI)
CLARA DUTTON, d. 08 Apr. 1915; leaves 5 children , husband, Will; bro, mother, & 5 half bros & sis. (15 Apr 1915 HCI)
SIDNEY ANN PANKEY, b. Hardin Co,ILL., 14 Jul 1843, d. Virgina, City, Mon. 28 Mar 1915 ; m John Pankey in Elizabethtown, 1859; issue: J.H., C.A., Philip S., Mark, James, & Lula S. Badger. (22 Apr 1915 HCI)
MAURICE DECKER, son of Asa Decker, b.---, d. 10 Apr 1915; leaves parents, 5 sis, and 3 bro. (29 Apr 1915)
ZENAS PALMER, b. 19 Mar 1885, d. 7 Apr 1915; leaves wife, 3 chld, parents, 1 bro & 2 sis.(06 May 1915 HCI)
JAMES WARDEN GINGER, son of James B. & Lizzie Ginger, b. 30 Jan 1893, d.03 May 1915; leaves father, 2 bro, and 14 sis. (20 May 1915 HCI)
BILL COOK, d last Fri, served in Civil War. (20 May 1915 HCI)
MAY DAVIS, dau of Dick Davis, d 30 Apr 1915; m.

Lawrence Clark.(20 May 1915 HCI)
FRANK SEINER, son of John Seiner Sr., b. Hardin Co.ILL., 01 Nov 1876, d.17 May 1915; m. Clara Paris, dau of Mack Paris, 31 Aug 1914; leaves wife, parents, bros, Will, John Jr., Jacob, & sis, Tena Rotes & Lizzie Herrmann.(10 Jun 1915 HCI)
ADA HELEN GIINTERT, dau of Frank J. & Clara Giintert, b. Hardin Co. ILL., 02 Aug. 1891, d. 28 May 1915; leaves parents, 2 sis, 1 bro. (10 Jun 1915 HCI)
WILLIAM F.COOK, b. 22 Mar. 1836*, d. 14 May 1915; m. Frances L. Booth, 1872; children: 8, 2 survive, Harriet & James Cook. William Cook served in Civil War.(10 Jun 1915 HCI)
REBECCA RADCLIFFE, b. 29 Dec. 1830, Birmingham, Alabama area,d.11 May 1915; 1st m.Jas Hammonds, issue; Sidney & Sarah McDonald; 2nd m. William Radcliffe (d. 1896); issue; Susan (wife of George Liner) (01 Jul 1915 HCI)
TOM DOUGLAS d. last sun. (01 Jul 1915 HCI)
GEORGE W. LINER, b. 21 Aug. 1852*, d. 2 Jun 1915; m. Susan Radcliffe; issue: daus, Melissa Anderson, Maggie Signore, Allie Higgins, Mrs. Ed Perrin; sons, Harvey Liner, C. Liner, G. W. Liner Jr; sis, Ann Parkham.(01 Jul 1915 HCI)
ELIZABETH MILLER, b. Jan 1829, 18 Jun 1915; issue: 10, 7 survive. (08 Jul 1915 HCI)
ELIAS OXFORD, father of Roxie Oxford, d.04 Jul 1862,42 yrs old. (08 Jul 1915 HCI)
THOMAS DOUGLAS, b. Rising Sun Ind., 17 Oct. 1830, d. 27 Jun 1915; children: 8, 5 survive, Ida Renfro, Nora Winn, Cora Beaver, Louise Threlkeld, & Thomas Douglas. (15 Jul 1915 HCI)
EDWARD HESS, b. 26 Apr 1869*, d. 01 Jul 1915; m. Lizzie Fraily 1897, dau of Richard Fraily, 1897; issue: 1 son & 1 dau.(15 Jul 1915 HCI)
ALICE DEAN REED, b. 9 Apr 1865, d. 03 Jul 1915; m. Russell J. Reed, 03 Sept 1881; issue:10,7 survive. (22 Jul 1915 HCI)
HENRY C. REAK, son of Matthew & Rebecca Reak, b. 16 Sept 1868, d. 25 Jul 1915; mother, 4 bro, & 3 sis survive. (29 Jul & 12 Aug 1915 HCI)
FRED PILAND, son of Jerry Piland, d. Tues. (12 Aug 1915 HCI)
SARAH WALKER, wife of M.L. Walker, d. wed;

leaves husband,4 dau,& 2 sons.(19 Aug 1915 HCI)
GERTIE BISHOP, b. 19 Apr 1899, d. 11 Aug 1915.
(26 Aug 1915 HCI)
E.S. TINSLEY, b. Allen Co., Ky. 28 Aug 1840, d.
26 Aug 1908; issue:Clara & Marie.(02 Sept 1915
HCI)
WILLIAM W. WOMACK, d. 27 Aug 1915, 79 yrs old;
sons: Senator (title) Womack, Joseph Womack;
dau, Marion Williams; sis, Mrs. James Milligan.
(02 Sept 1915 HCI)
MRS. C.F. VINYARD, d. 1 Sept 1915.(16 Sept 1915
HCI)
TOMMY HALE, son of Alvin Hale, d. 26 Sept 1915;
grandmother, Martha Drumm. (16 Sep 1915 HCI)
C. W. BARNERD, b.Hardin Co. ILL., 19 Jul 1831,
d.26 Aug 1915; m.1st Elizabeth Hess (sis of
David and Jacob Hess); issue: 8; 2nd m. Riller
Walace (sis of Levy & W.R. Walace).(09 Sept
1915 HCI)
--- Love, dau of Allen and Mary Love, b. 12 Jul
1875, d. 1 Sept 1915; m.Charles Vinyard;issue:
4, 3 living (son,Willie).(16 Sept 1915 HCI)
MARY A. HOBBS, b. Hardin Co.ILL., 22 Feb. 1853,
d. 11 Jan 1886. (16 Sept 1915 HCI)
ORA HALE, son of Tom Hale, b. 09 Dec 1910, d.
23 Aug 1915. (09 Sept 1915 HCI)
George Waters, dau of Carl Waters, b. 01 May
1865, d. Oct 1915; m. Joseph Ginger, 23 Dec
1883 (son of H.L. & Flora Ginger); issue:
Henry, Fred, Junie, Pharris, Cradie, & Grover &
1(d.), leaves husband & 2 sis.(04 Nov 1915 HCI)
THOMAS HALE, son of Alvin & Belle Hale, b. 20
Dec 1887, d. 26 Sept 1915; m. Malissa Isham,
Mar 1910; issue: Ora & Alvin; leaves wife,
parents, 2 bro,& 1 sis.(11 Nov 1915 HCI)
MAYME TURNER, dau of Edward Turner, b. Hardin
Co.ILL., 17 Apr 1903, d. 12 Sept 1915; leaves
parents, 3 bro, & g.father.(30 Sept 1915 HCI)
LAURA HICKS, dau of Miles & Rebecca Hicks, b.
Hardin Co, 16 Apr 1877, d. 24 Oct. 1894; m.
John Joiner, 24 Oct 1894; issue: 6, 4 survive,
leaves husband, father, 2 bro,& 1 sis. (11 Nov
1910 HCI)
AMRENE BRITTAIN, b. Hardin Co. ILL., 14 Aug
1859, d. 24 Oct. 1915; m. Thomas Brittain, 20
Apr. 1883; issue: 7, 5 survive;leaves husband,

mother, & sis. (11 Nov 1915 HCI)
MRS. L.F. TWITCHELL, wid of Capt. Twitchell, d. last week in Bellevile,ILL., sons: L.F., Ben, Robert,& James Twitchell.(11 & 18 Nov 1915 HCI)
RACHEL ANN GENTRY, dau of Alex & Lutitia Gentry, b. Hardin Co., 08 Oct 1859, d. 25 Oct 1915 in Blytheville, Ark.; m. Thomas Lewis 25 Aug. 1880; issue: James Thomas (d. 23 Nov 1906), Harry Garfield Lewis; 2nd m. Thomas Robinson, 09 April 1893; issue: Jake, Fred, Richard, Mary & Eva Robinson; leaves husband, mother; sis, Mary Locke, Deal Mcdowell, Sarrah Smith, Ida Clement; bros, Tom Gentry & John Gentry. (18 Nov 1915 HCI)
HARRIET ANGIE STEELE b. Hardin Co. ILL., 01 Jun 1836, d. 06 Nov 1915; m. Lafayette Twitchell, 1 April 1856;issue; Robert, Lafayette, B.E., & J.W. Twitchell.(25 Nov 1915 HCI)
JOHN LITTLE HETHERINGTON, b. New York, 10 Jun 1850, d.11 Nov 1915: m. Sidney Jackson, 21 Mar 1872: issue; Anna Miller, Mrs. Walker, & John L. Hetherington; sis, Mary Jackson, Anna Morris, Laura Renfro; bro, W.T. Hetherington. (18 & 25 Nov 1915 HCI)
JAMES A. GERHARDT, son of Joseph & Isabell Gerhardt, b. 18 Apr. 1893, d. 20 Nov 1915; leaves parents,3 sis,& 3 bros.(09 Dec 1915 HCI)
MAY GREGORY, only dau of Will Gregory, wife of Millard Ledbetter, d.04 Dec 1915.(09 Dec 1915 HCI)
HORACE FOSTER, d. 03 Dec. 1916, New Haven, ILL; issue: 8, living: Tom, I.A., Alice, Julia, Mrs. M.L. Tyer, & William Foster. (09 Dec 1915 HCI)
HORACE FOSTER (JR), b. Pope Co., Nov 18, 1829, d. Dec 1, 1915, son of Horace & Phoebe Davis Foster(who married Sept 29, 1829); Horace Sr, b. Jan 8, 1811, d. 1847; Phoebe Davis b. May 1, 1808, d. --- ?; Horace Jr, m. Mrs. Elizabeth Hobbs, 09 Dec 1849;issue:12, Susa Ann Stevens, d. 25 Apr 1902, Joseph Alexander Foster, d. 05 Sept 1912, Mrs. Judge Tyer; others unamed. (16 Dec 1915 HCI)
MARIE HANDCOCK, eldest dau of J.J. Handcock, d. Sat. J.J. Handcock's wife d. Fri. (16 Dec 1915 HCI)
MRS. E.C. MCKERNAN, d. 25 Dec 1915; son,

Arthur.(30 Dec 1915 HCI)
WILLIAM CAMBELL, d. Dec. 1915 ?; dau, Mrs. Dan
Frailey.(30 Dec 1915 HCI)
DORIS RENFRO EICHORN, dau of George Renfro, d.
last week in East Prairie, Mo.(30 Dec 1915 HCI)
REBECCA FERRELL, b. Rising Sun, Ind. 17 Jun
1834, d. 30 Dec 1916, Harrisburg, ILL; m. A. J.
(Andrew Jackson) Ferrell 1854; issue; 8, 5
survive: Mrs. Ollie Conn, Mrs Martha Smock,
Orval, William, and Rev. C.H. (Clement)
Ferrell. (06 Jan 1916 HCI)
MINERVA ROSE DOSSETT, b. 01 Apr 1840,* d. 08
Jan ? 1916; m. I.F. Dossett; issue: Henry, W.J.
Dossett, & Mrs Reed; who was sis to Mrs. B.L.
Lavander. (13 Jan 1916 HCI)
MRS. MARGARET IRBY, b. 7 Jan 1900, d.28 Dec
1915; m. Earl Irby, 12 Oct 1914; leaves
husband, mother, 2 sis, 3 bro & grandparents.
(13 Jan 1916 HCI)
FLORA VAUGHN, wife of Warren Vaughn, d. wed;
leaves husband, & daus.(13 Jan 1916 HCI)
MINERVA ROSE DOSSETT, b. 29 Feb 1847, wife of
Ile F. Dossett, d. 2 weeks ago, Sikeston, Mo.;
sis of Mrs B.L. Lavander, nee Rose. (13 Jan
1916 HCI)
HANNAH OXFORD PATTON b. North Carolina, 08 Aug
1830*, d. 09 Jan 1916; M. Samuel S. Patton;
issue: Mary Ann Denton, William, Elias, James
W., Rebecca Sutton, Sarah Carr, Samuel G., &
Lizzie Oxford; deaths: Mary Ann, abt 1880;
Lizzie, Sept 1882; William, d. 10 Nov 1882;
Elias, Sept or Oct. 1905; James W., d. 24 Dec
1900.(20 Jan 1916 HCI)
JOHN WILKERSON, b. abt. 1841, d.17 Jan. 1916;
leaves wife, children, and half-sis, Mrs. Lydia
Rutherford. (20 Jan 1916 HCI)
MAE LEDBETTER, only dau of William G. & Dora
Gregory, b. 7 Oct. 1895*, d. 4 Dec. 1916; m.
Millard Ledbetter, 20 Feb 1915.
(27 Jan & 9 Mar 1916 HCI)
GEORGE E. HOKE, b. abt. 1834, d. 04 Mar. 1916.
(9 Mar 1916 HCI)
GEORGE F.DOMICK, d. last Sat. (16 Mar 1916)
HANNAH OXFORD BROWNFIELD, dau of Elias & Nancy
J. Oxford, b. Hardin Co. 08 Sept 1853, d. 26
Jan 1916; m. Benjamin F. Brownfield, 12 April

1874; issue: Ota (wife of E.N. Hall), Ida (wife of J.E. Denton), James, Girtie (wife of Wiley Leonberger), Nora (wife of Ernest Oxford) & Clarence; leaves 3 bros: J.A., Sam, & George Oxford; sis, Eva, wife of James Waters. (03 Feb 1916 HCI)
J.F. SHEWMAKER, b. Marion Co., Ky. 01 May 1846, d. 04 Jan 1916; m. Elizabeth Weston; issue: 8; m. 2nd, Eliza Vinyard 1885; issue: 5. (10 Feb 1916 HCI)
MRS PEYTON BOYD, d. 04 Mar 1916; son, W.T. Blakley: dau, Lizzie Blakley. (16 Mar 1916 HCI)
MRS.CHARLES BURKHART, dau of Wes Hughes, d. Shawneetown, 09 Mar 1916. (16 Mar 1916 HCI)
W.L. SCOTT, bro of F.E. Scott, d. Chicago,09 Mar 1916.(16 Mar 1916 HCI)
SALLY SHELTER, b. Markhammer, Germany, 04 Jul 1839, d. 16 Mar 1916; m. Joseph Shelter;issue: Anton, Mrs. Anna Mason, B.J., Andrew, Mrs. C.B. Humm, Nicholas, John E., & Mrs. Tenia Herrin; sis, Mrs. Nick Reif & Mrs. Andrew Shelter. (23 Mar 1916 HCI)
WALTER SCOTT, b. Hardin Co. 17 Oct 1876, d. Chicago, 09 Mar 1916; m. Anna Lundberg of Manistee, Mich., 09 Oct 1909; leaves adopted son Robert L., bro, Freeman Scott; & sis, Gertrude McDowell. (23 Mar 1916 HCI)
MARIA J. BLISS, b. 16 Jul 1843, d. 26 Mar 1916; m. Charles Lee, 24 Mar 1864; issue: Mrs C.W. Gerhardt, Mrs. Lula Thompson, Charles & John Lee; leaves bro and sis. (30 Mar 1916 HCI)
ELIZABETH WILLIS, wid of James Willis, d. Feb. (06 Apr 1916 HCI)
WILLIAM LACY EDWARDS, b. 15 Dec 1864, d. 28 Mar 1916; m. Ida Walton, dau of W.J. Walton, 07 Jul 1889; issue: 6, 5 living,(India died as infant) (13 Apr 1916 HCI)
CLARA JOINER, dau of John & Elizabeth Joiner, b. 31 Oct 1886, d. 02 Apr 1916; m.Lee Winn, 17 Dec. 1905; issue: James Orval Winn. (13 Apr 1916 HCI)
HATTIE HUBBARD, dau of Charles and Margaret A. Hubbard, b. 27 May 1874, d. 5 Apr 1916; m. Charles Cuttrell; issue: dau, Phoebe; son, Zenith. (20 Apr 1916 HCI)
JANE WINTERS, widow of Daniel Winters, a Civil

War soldier, d. 29 Apr 1916;leaves 2 sons &
stepson. (04 May 1916 HCI)
Mrs.RICHARD BLACK, dau of David Martin; sis of
Mrs. Samuel Bently, d. Sat. (04 May 1916 HCI)
JULIA FRAILY, d. 05 May 1916; m. L. H. Wallace;
issue: 2; 2nd m. Horace Foster; issue: 8, 6
survive, 3 sons & 3 dau (Mrs. Charlie Smith
named as dau);John Thornton,half bro.11 May
1916 HCI)
MINNIE DAYMON, dau of Wiley & Loucretia Daymon,
b. 25 Mar 1875, d. 11 May 1916; m. John
Thornton; issue: Electa, Willis, Theopolis;
leaves father, 2 bros, 1 sis (Mrs Dola Frayser)
(18 May 1916 HCI)
CLIFFORD LEDBETTER,d.20 May 1916; son of "Bunk"
Ledbetter,g.son of D.A. Ledbetter;leaves mother
& stepfather. (25 May 1916 HCI)
GORDON DUTTON, son of W.E. Dutton, b. May 1905,
d. 08 Jun 1916; leaves father, 2 sis, 2 bros, &
grandmother.(22 Jun 1916 HCI)
CHARLES M. CASAD, son of T.L.A. Casad & Elisa
Sutton, b. Hardin Co., 1849; d. 11 May 1916
Kerby,Oregon; m.1st, Harriet Thompson; issue:
5; m. 2nd,Ida Rose, dau of Blueford Rose;issue:
Walter, Orley, Raleigh, 4 others unnamed; bro
Otto Casad; sis, Mrs Sebary Wastson, Mrs. Vina
Womack, & Blanche Dutton.(22 Jun 1916 HCI)
ROBERT L. JENNINGS, b. Pope Co.,ILL.,10 May
1872, d.06 Apr 1916; leaves wife, Agnes & 4
children. (25 May 1916 HCI)
MRS. LUNCE SIMONEN, dau of Hiram Riley, d. 06
Jun 1916; leaves husband & 4 children. (29 Jun
1916 HCI)
MARY LOUISE JANE HURT, dau of William & Jane
Hurt, b. Mecklanburg Co., Va. 17 Oct 1829, d.
18 Jun 1916; m. Thomas Campbell; issue: Elvira
(Mrs.Daniel Austin),Virginia(Mrs.Jack Walton),
Mary (d. 4 yrs old),& Thomas Campbell(d.14 Aug
1852), 2nd m. ---- Cochran, issue: 2 (d.);Jane
Hurt's bro (Shackelford) fought in Rev. War.
(13 Jul 1916)
LUCIAN VINYARD, dau of W.M.M. & Mary Vinyard,
b. 23 Nov 1849, d. 28 Jun 1916; leaves 4 sis
(Sarah Shipp named);3 bros.(13 Jul 1916 HCI)
FRED SCHULTZ, b.Germany, d. 18 Jul 1916; leaves
wife. (03 Aug 1916 HCI)

JOHN DAUGHERTY, only son of W.E. Daugherty, d. 22 July 1916;leaves sis, Mrs.Jerry Barnerd,Lon, Ruby & Pauline; aunts,Kate,Ella Vaughn & Lottie Brown; uncles,John & James Daughterty. (03 Aug 1916 HCI)
MRS. ARTHUR DEVAULT, d. Jul 1916; sis-in-law of Mrs. George Grounds. (17 Aug 1916 HCI)
DR.J.H. ROSE, d.Saline Co.Mon, b.Elizabethtown, ILL.; leaves 2 dau, Gertrude Crane & ? (24 Aug 1916 HCI)
NORA FOSTER, dau of Horace & Mary Thomas,wife of Robert Ginger,b.10 Dec 1879, d.10 Sept 1916; leaves husband, 6 bro,4 sis,& 2 grandmothers. (14 & 28 Sept 1916 HCI)
H.L. BELT, b. Hardin Co.,11 Aug 1879, d.31 Aug 1916; m. Zora Baine, 09 Jan 1901;issue: dau Mabel; leaves father, 6 bro, 1 sis. (21 Sept 1916 HCI HCI)
EFIE DAVIS, dau of Donald & Sarah Davis, b. abt 1880, d. 10 Sept 1916; m. Frank Shelter 1898; issue: Gladys, Alma, Mythel, & Corlin.(28 Sept 1916 HCI)
JAMES M. MARGLIN, b. Pope Co.,ILL. abt 1843, d. 01 Oct. 1916; Civil War, Co. K, 1 Reg. Vol. Artillery; m. Nancy Jane Minor of Gallatin Co., 1866;issue:Robert F. Marglin;(12 Oct 1916 HCI)
JOHN WARREN LEONBERGER, son of William H. Leonberger, d.15 Sept 1916.(12 Oct 1916 HCI)
JOHN MARION BELT, son of Jonathan Belt, b. 01 Mar 1848, d.02 Oct 1916; m.Lucy Palmer, 22 Oct 1869; issue: 5 sons, 1 dau. (19 Oct 1916 HCI)
MRS.SARAH CLARK, wife of J. A. Clark, d. Thur; leaves husband & 6 children. (30 Nov 1916 HCI)
THOMAS J. LASATER, b. Hamilton Co.,ILL., 06 Jun 1841, d. 07 Dec 1916; m. Malissa Decker, 1878; issue: Mrs. House, Mrs. Mary Page, James, Connie, Gladys, & Robert. (21 Dec 1916 HCI)
ALVIN BRINKLEY, son of Richard & Catherine Brinkley, b. 27 Oct 1891, d. 22 Dec 1916; m. Frankie May Ginger, 16 Feb 1911; issue:Lester & Lessie; leaves wife, mother, 2 sis, & bro. (04 Jan 1917 HCI)
PITT YANDELL MCCOY, b. Golconda, Pope Co., ILL. 29 Jun 1841, d. Sun.(18 Jan 1917 HCI)
BESSIE TWITCHELL, b.31 Jul 1876, d. 09 Jan 1917; m. J.B. Twitchell 28 Feb 1900; issue: 6,

(Earl & Charlotte named);leaves husband,
father, 2 sis, & 3 bros. (25 Jan 1917 HCI)
SARAH A. HAWTHORNE CLARK, b. Cincinnati, Ohio
17 Feb 1845, d. 30 Nov 1916; m. J. A. Clark, 28
Nov 1869; issue, Mabel, d. 07 Dec 1910,(wife of
Edward Ferrell), Cora C. Waggoner, Ruth Travis,
Esther Lane, Cecil C. Clark, Royal C. Clark;
sis, Mary E. Shroeder, 2 half sis, Inez
Worrell, & Nettie Craig; husband survives (01
Feb 1917 HCI)
GERALDINE STACEY, son of Silas Stacey, b. 04
Oct 1909, d. 25 Dec 1916. (01 Feb 1917 HCI)
MARY SEINER, wife of John Seiner, d. Wed. (01
Feb 1917 HCI)
AGUSTUS PAUL CLARK, son of J. A. Clark, b.16
Nov, d. 5 Jan 1917. (01 Feb 1917 HCI)
S.L. JACKSON, d. 30 Jan 1917; leaves wife & 2
daus. (01 Feb 1917 HCI)
CHARLES R. CARTER, d. 25 Jan 1917; leaves
father,bro, & 3 sis.(01 Feb 1917 HCI)
MARY BARBARA EICHORN, dau of Sebastian & Anna
Eichorn, b. Germany 9 Aug 1847, d. 31 Jan 1917;
m. Sebastian Seiner 1870; issue: Wendlin, John,
Frank(d.) Jack, Christena, & Mary Elizabeth
Clark; bro, Jack Eichorn Sr. (08 Feb 1917 HCI)
MRS. JUNNIE OLDHAM, nee Fincham, funeral last
Sun. (08 Feb 1917 HCI)
CASSA LAVANDER, wife of B.L. Lavander, d. Sat.
(22 Feb 1917 HCI)
NANCY J. WINTERS,dau of J. W.Hughes, b.Hardin
Co., ILL., 08 Sept 1857, d. 29 Apr 1916; issue:
11, Paul, James, survive?; relatives: half bro,
William Hughes, John Hughes,& George Hughes.
(22 Feb 1917 HCI)
ESSIE SCHROLL, dau of John Schroll, b. 16 Jul
1893, d. 06 Feb 1917, leaves parents, 2 bros,&
sis. (22 Feb 1917 HCI)
JAKE DRUMM, b. abt 1853, d. 20 Feb 1917, m.
Martha---; issue: William & Mrs. Anna Parker.
(01 Mar 1917 HCI)
ALBERT RIGGS, d.--- 1917; issue:Henry, & Jewell
Riggs. (01 Mar 1917)
MRS. R.H. WILLINGHAM, dau of George Ledbetter,
d. 27 Feb 1917. (01 Mar 1917 HC1)
CASSANDER ROSE, b. Hardin Co.ILL., 29 Feb 1848,
d. 17 Feb 1917; m. Benjamin L. Lavander, 17 May

1868;issue: Wiley, & Della,(Mrs. John H. Tyre).
(08 Mar 1917 HCI)
JAMES A. HILL, d.15 Mar 1917, 89 yrs, 6 mo.
old. (22 Mar 1917 HCI)
ARCH GINGER, son of Eli T. Ginger, b. 05 Apr
1868, d. 09 Mar 1917; m. Maggie Volkert, 13 Apr
1896; issue: Katie (d. 25 Mar 1912); bro, James
Ginger. (15 & 29 Mar 1917 HCI)
BILL ZIMMER, d. Wed; dau, Mrs William Volkert.
(29 Mar 1917 HCI)
GEORGE W. DEVERS, son of F. M. Devers, b.
Hardin Co. ILL., 22 Dec 1882, d. 25 Feb 1917;
m. Katie Black 19 Feb 1905; relatives: John
Devers, Ben Devers, Mr. & Mrs. Tom Perry, Mr.&
Mrs. Archie Cleveland,& Mr. and Mrs. Dee
Burris; leaves wife, parents,9 bro & sis.(29
Mar 1917 HCI)
NOAH MCMURPHY, killed in Explosion at West
Frankfort, was brought here for burial. He was
son of Matt McMurphy; leaves leaves wife and 2
children. (12 Apr 1917 HCI)
MRS. HOLLMAN, mother of Mrs. S.G. Ramsey, d.
--1917.(12 Apr 1917 HCI)
MRS. HOLLY, mother of Grant& Columbus Holly, d.
Sun. (19 Apr 1917 HCI)
VIOLA PAGE, dau of J.J. & Louisa Page, b. 26
Oct 1881, d. 29 Mar 1917; m. Lewis H.Lane 9 Nov
1912; issue: 6, Woodrow Wilson Lane,(d.). (12
Apr 1917 HCI)
MRS. C. M. MILLER, b. abt 1844, d. Tues;
children: Charles Miller, Oren Miller, and
Daisy Barnett. (26 Apr & 3 May 1917 HCI)
ROBERT OXFORD, son of Elihu Oxford, b. abt
1845, d. 11 May 1917. (17 May 1917 HCI)
GEORGE BLAIN, d. Sun; leaves wife &3 sons.(17
May 1917 HCI)
LUCINDA DAVIS, wife of W.D. Davis, d. 15 May
1917. (17 May 1917 HCI)
MARY L KENRICKS, dau of James & Mary Kenricks,
b. Gallatin Co.ILL., 26 Mar 1853, d.15 May
1917; m. W.D. Davis, 3 Nov 1887; leaves husband
& sis, Mrs. Martha Hill. (14 Jun 1917 HCI)
ANDY HAMP, son of Louis Hamp, d. 14 Oct 1917.
(18 Oct 1917 HCI)
MATTIE F. JACKSON, nee Rash, b. 8 Jul 1872*, d.
15 Oct 1917; wife of W.L. Jackson; bro-in-law,

Marion Jackson. (18 Oct 1917 HCI)
JAMES LAMBERT, d.16 Oct 1917.(18 Oct 1917 HCI)
WILLIAM EDWARD CREASON, b.11 Mar 1845, d.17 Oct 1917.(18 Oct 1917 HCI)
MRS. MATTIE JACKSON, wife of W.L. Jackson, d. Mon.(18 Oct 1917 HCI)
ROBERT LANE, son of Rebecca Curry, d.----; leaves mother, 5 bro, wife & 5 or 6 children. (01 Nov 1917 HCI)
MATTIE RASH, b. 13 Jul 1872*, d.15 Oct 1917; m. William L. Jackson 26 Apr 1891; issue: twins (d.) in infancy. (08 Nov 1917 HCI)
SPENCER E. VAUGHN, b. 17 Mar 1843 Pope Co.ILL. d. 7 Nov 1917; m. 1st, Mary L. Hazell(d. 1863); 2nd, Sarah Lee Lamar 1873, sis of W.T. Lamar; issue: Loren F.; 3rd, Minerva Lambert 1876; issue: Mildred (wife of Green Parkinson); Nora (wife of Irving Hammach); Melissa (wife of Willis Joyner); Anna(Wife of Howard Canady); Dosia (wife of John A.Mc Neil)(15 Nov 1917 HCI)
JAMES A. VINYARD, son of John & Eliza Vinyard, b. Hardin Co. ILL.,08 Dec 1844, d.Springfield, ILL., 29 Oct 1917; m. Elizabeth O'Melveny, dau of George & Harriet O'Melveny, 27 Sept 1866; issue: son, John Vinyard; dau, Laura Sprecher; g.son, James H. Sprecher; sis, Mary Jenkins, Mrs. F.M. Fowler, Mrs. John Hubbard, & Mrs. D. W.Gustin; bros, W.H. Vinyard & Charles Vinyard. (22 Nov 1917 HCI)
MRS. E.S. HOSICK, formerly Mrs. Hollingsworth, d. 2 Dec 1917, Smithfield, Ky.(06 Dec 1917 HCI)
MRS. CASAD, nee Jackson, d. 02 Dec 1917; m. --- Casad abt 1877; sis of Mrs. S.T. Hosick and Mrs. Ben Hurford. (06 Dec 1917 HCI)
ETNA TENNIE SHAW, dau of George Shaw, b.14 Feb 1907, d. 28 May 1917. (6 Dec 1917 HCI)
SALINA EADS, dau of Riley Eads, b. Tenn.,03 Aug 1842, d. Elizabethown, ILL., 02 Dec 1917; m. Lewis Hollingsworth; issue: C.M. Hollingsworth, J.L. Hollingsworth, & 2 (d); m. 2nd, E.S. Hosick, 27 Jan 1902. (20 Dec 1917 HCI)
KENNETH L.FRAILEY, son of Richard H. Frailey, b.09 Jun 1915, d.11 Dec 1917.(20 Dec 1917 HCI)
CHARLEY E. FRAILEY, b. 26 Jan 1874, d. 21 Dec 1917; m.Laura Belt, dau of Logan belt, 24 Jan 1897; issue; 7, 6 survive (24 Jan 1917 HCI)

GUSTA REED, dau of R.J. and Alice Denia Reed, b. 4 Nov 1904, d. 4 Jan 1918; leaves father, 2 sis, & 4 bros. (24 Jan 1918 HCI)
JOHN PALMER,Civil War vet, d.last week at 80 years old; wife, Mary Palmer? (24 Jan 1918 HCI)
FANNIE ADAMS, youngest dau of the late J.R. Oxford and his wife of last marriage, d.last week; m. J.W. Fellows; issue: 4, Roy Fellows & Bessie Gross survive; m. 2nd Allen Adams;issue: Mrs. Hettie Decker(d.) (24 & 31 Jan & 7 Feb 1918 HCI)
FRANK GUEDRY, d. last Tues. (31 Jan 1918 HCI)
ALBERT HILL, d. 28 Feb 1918. (07 Mar 1918 HCI)
SYLVESTER SEINER ROTES, son of John E. Rotes, b. 07 Jul 1917, d.14 Jan 1918; leaves parents & 3 sis. (31 Jan 1918 HCI)
RICHARD BIRCH, b. Hartsville, Ind., 29 Aug 1850, d. 01 Feb 1918; m. Rebecca Thornton, dau of John Thornton, 16 Apr 1875; issue: 5; leaves wife, 3 bros & 3 sis, & dau, Ollie Mayfield. (07 Feb 1918 HCI)
SARAH ANN RENFRO, dau of W.J.B.& Ida Renfro, b. Hardin Co. ILL., 12 Dec 1884, d. 31 Dec 1917 m. Thomas Broadway, 09 Jun 1915; issue: William Franklin Broadway & Ida Irene Broadway; leaves parents; bros, Thomas, Raymond, Roscoe,& Howard Renfro. (21 Feb 1918 HCI)
MRS. ELLA JOYCE, b.18 Oct 1876, d.11 Feb 1918 m. George W. Joyce, 28 Jan 1891; issue: 9; 5 sons & 4 daus; leaves parents, husband, 2 bros & 3 sis. (28 Feb 1918 HCI)
ELIHU OXFORD, b. Hardin Co.ILL., 14 Mar 1844, d. 1918; leaves wife & 3 chld.(14 Mar 1918 HCI)
BERTHA NEWMAN, dau of George & Emma Newman,b. Wayne Co., 18 Dec 1896, d. 25 Feb 1918; m. Willie Reed, 25 Dec 1918; leaves husband, father, grandfather& 9 bros.(21 Mar 1918 HCI)
CHARLES RASH, d. 07 Feb 1918; leaves wife, son mother, & 4 bros. (21 Mar 1918 HCI)
CHARLES BEAVER, b.11 Oct 1870, d.23 Mar 1918, leaves wife, bro & sis,Harriet Garland.(04 Apr 1918 HCI)
NETTIE MILLER, also known as Nettie Banks, wife of Orren Miller, Civil War vet, d. last Sat; issue: dau, Mrs. Carlos Sisco.(11 Apr 1918 HCI)
A. M. MCTYRE d. Sat; son: Alfred. (11 Apr 1918)

SEBASTINE SHELTER, d. yesterday in Ky.; wife, Katie; sons, Walter & Gordon. (25 Apr 1918 HCI)
JOSIE FERRELL, b. Elizabethtown, 17 Jan 1855, d. 30 Apr 1918; m. Ed Stevens in 1871; leaves 2 bros,4 nephews (Omar Ferrell named),& 2 nieces. (09 May 1918 HCI)
WILEY JACKSON, d. Wed; sis, Mrs. Ben Hurford. (02 May 1918 HCI)
MRS. E.C. CULLUM, b. Hardin Co.ILL., dau of the late Noah & Mary Lightner; m.E.C. Cullum;issue: 3 ; bro, Jesse Lightner; sis, Maggie Gibbs, Ella Williams, & Ethel Cullum; leaves husband. (18 Jul 1918 HCI)
T.M. VINYARD, son of J.T., b.Hardin Co. ILL., 17 Jan 1867, d.23 Jul 1918; m.Virginia Oglesby, 25 Dec 1887; issue: Cordella Moore,Gertrude Pyles,Thomas Walter Vinyard,John Lacey Vinyard, Alpha Margaret Vinyard & Golden Vinyard.(08 Aug 1918 HCI)
QUILLER FIELDS, d. 09 Jul 1918, leaves mother, & bro, Jim Fields.(08 Aug 1918 HCI)
E.E. FRAYER, d. 27 Aug 1918. (05 Sept 1918 HCI)
NANNIE JENKINS, b. 26 Nov 1882, d. 31 Aug 1918; m. Waldo Jenkins, 15 Mar 1903;issue: 5; leaves husband, mother,(Mrs. Okerson); sis, (Mrs. Martha Huffman). (12 Sep & 10 Oct 1918 HCI)
JENNIE VINYARD, b. Karber's Ridge, ILL., 08 Jun 1890, d. 21 Aug 1918; leaves parents,bro,& 3 sis. (19 Sept 1918 HCI)
FRANCIS M. JONES, b.7 Feb 1844*, d. 16 Sept 1918; m. Susan Smith in 1862; issue: 5 sons, 4 daus; m. 2nd Elizabeth Watkins 1907; served in Civil War. (26 Sept 1918 HCI)
D.W. WRISTEN, b. abt 1839, d. Abliene, Tex. 16 Sept 1918; m.1st--; m. 2nd Mrs. Nettie Thornton, sis of John L. Lowery; son. D.W. Wristen Jr. (10 Oct 1918 HCI)
LOUIS H. HOSSLER, d. 05 Aug 1918.(10 Oct 1918)
OVERTON P. MORRIS, son of George Morris, d. 29 Sept 1918. (07 Nov 1918 HCI)
THOMAS W. VINYARD, son of T.M. & Virginia Vinyard, b.Hardin Co.ILL.,02 Jan 1895, d.27 Nov 1918; m.Hattie J.Vinyard, 02 Feb 1918; leaves wife, mother, 5 sis,& 1 bro.(16 Jan 1919 HCI)
MARION W.THOMAS, d.16 Nov 1918.(02 Jan 1919 HCI)

HARVEY HERRIN, son of Harvey Herrin, b. 20 Oct 1909, d. 30 Oct 1918. (09 Jan 1919 HCI)
ROBERT BROWNFIELD, d.1919 ?; bro, B.F. Brownfield; m.Nancy Duncan, sis of Opha Duncan, d.?; leaves 2 sons. (23 Jan 1919 HCI)
DELLA LEDBETTER, dau of D.A. Ledbetter, b. 01 Jun 1882, d. 12 Jan 1919; m. Lee Holloway, Nov 1899; issue: 3 sons, 3 daus. (22 Jan 1919 RS)
HERBIE OXFORD, son of Dock Oxford, b.18 Sept 1900, d.08 Nov 1918; leaves parents, 2 bros & 5 sis. (22 Jan 1919 RS)
ALLEN HOBBS, son of George Hobbs, b. abt 1901, d. Jan 1919; served, C Co. 48 Inf, ILL, Civil War. (30 Jan 1919 HCI)
MRS. GRACE EDWARDS, eldest dau of George Hobbs, d. Jan 1919. (30 Jan 1919 HCI)
JAMES ENGLISH, son of Isaac & Lissa English, b. 12 Apr 1894, d.04 Jan 1919; leaves parents, 4 bros,&1 sis.(06 Feb 1919 HCI)
OMER MOORE, son of Harrison and Sarah Moore, b. 26 Oct 1892, d. 19 Jan 1919; leaves bro,& sis,(Mrs. Earl Banks); parents & 3 bros (d.) (20 Feb 1919 HCI)
JOHN GRIFFIN HAWTHORNE, b. Cannelton, Ind., 18 Jun 1858, d.17 Feb 1919; m.Louise Edwards,18 Jun 1858;issue: Maude Vinyard, Lena Patterson, Goldie Joiner, Ethel Newton, Myrtle Yates, Will & Charlie Hawthorne who died 1905 & Inez Hawthorne who died 1884. (20 Feb 1919 HCI)
JOHN SHERIDAN, b. Rising Sun, Ind., 1846, d.06 Nov 1918; m.Sylvester Winders(d.1888); issue;? 5 living; m 2nd, Anna Below, issue: 5,3 living; leaves bro & sis. (20 Feb 1919 HCI)
GRACIE HOBBS, eldest dau of George Hobbs, b.08 Mar 1894, d. 24 Jan 1919; m. Ernest Edwards, 15 Aug 1917; issue: 1 dau; leaves parents, 3 bros, & 4 sis. (27 Feb 1919 HCI)
SEBBA HOBBS,eldest son of George & Flora Hobbs, b. 26 Apr 1912; d.21 Jan 1919.(27 Feb 1919 HCI)
ETTIE YARBER, wife of John Yarber, b. 24 Nov 1878, d. 18 Oct 1918; issue: 5, Wiley,b.18 Oct 1918, d. 22 Oct 1918; James, b. 21 Sept 1902, d. 24 Sept 1918; leaves husband, father, 3 children, 1 sis, 1 half bro, Harry Smith.(20 Mar 1919 HCI)
HATTIE BLAKLEY, dau of W.T. Blakley, b. 25 Mar

1904, d. 08 Mar 1919. (20 Apr 1919 HCI)
G.W.RENFRO, d.last Thur; dau, Mrs. Myrtle Rose; sons, Frank,& Johnny Renfro.(03 Apr 1919 HCI)
MRS. LOLA JOINER, b.07 Feb 1880, d. 05 Apr 1919; leaves husband,8 children; mother,& bro. (10 Apr 1919 HCI)
JOHN REYNOLDS, only son of Asa Reynolds, d.06 Apr 1919; wife & 2 daus sur.(10 Apr 1919 HCI)
FRANCE SUITS, son of David & Josie, b.Apr 1898, d.13 Mar 1919; leaves parents, 6 bros & 3 sis. (12 Apr 1919 HCI)
JAMES VINYARD, son of W.H. Vinyard, b. Hardin Co. ILL.,09 Nov 1889,d.18 Apr 1919; m.Elizabeth Champion; leaves wife, 2 bros,& 2 sis. (24 Apr 1919 HCI)
MRS. JAMES OLDHAM, d.21 Apr 1919, age 85. (01 May 1919 HCI)
VIRGINIA MAY BELT, infant dau of Non & Lilly Belt, d. 13 Apr 1919. (01 May 1919 HCI)
MILDRED WALTON, dau of Edgar & Maggie Walton, b.8 Feb 1916, d.16 Apr 1919. (01 May 1919 HCI)
THOMAS HOWARD RUSSELL, son of Loren Russell, b.16 Jun 1918, d. 12 Mar 1919.(01 May 1919 HCI)
MARY BRANTLY, dau of James Doggett, b. abt 1881, d. 22 Mar 1919; issue:Paul,Syble, Bessie, & Jimmy. James Doggett age 62, d.24 Mar 1919. He leaves bro.(01 May 1919 HCI)
CARTER BYRANT,d, Anna,ILL.Sun.(01 May 1919 HCI)
ALVIN JOYCE, son of G.W. & Ell--- Joyce, b. 03 Apr 1898, d. 16 Mar 1919. (08 May 1919 HCI)
  ORPHIA LORENE, dau of Jesse & Stella Lightener, b. 26 Apr ---, d. 25 Nov 1918.(08 May 1919 HCI)
ADRON PATTON, child of Alonzo & Gracie Patton, b. 15 Sept 1914, d. 20 Mar 1919; leaves sis, Loretta Patton, b. 10 Jul, d. 24 Mar 1919. (15 May 1919 HCI)
SALLIE OLDHAM, wife of James Oldham, b. 17 Nov 1840*, d. 22 Apr 1919; leaves husband & 6 children. (05 Jun 1919 HCI)
JOHN W. REYNOLDS, son of Asa & Anna Reynolds, b. 2 Jul 1892, d. 6 Apr 1919; m. Ida Sullivan 23 Aug 1914; issue: Wilma & Ima; sis, Janie Love. (19 Jun 1919 HCI)
HANNAH BROWNFIELD, b. 30 Oct 1896, d.08 May 1919; m. Thomas Brownfield, 30 Jun 1914; issue:

3, 2 survive; leaves husband, 3 bros, & 3 sis. (26 Jun 1919 HCI)
WILLIAM H. PARIS FRAILEY, son of D.M. & Martha Frailey, b. 29 Mar 1889, d. 22 Mar 1919; leaves parents, 1 sis and 4 bros. (26 Jun 1919 HCI)
WILLIAM H. CARMAN, son of Will & Belle Carman, b. 06 Jan 1896, d. 10 Mar 1919.(26 Jun 1919 HCI)
ANDREW SHELTER, b. Bavaria, Germany, 18 Apr 1838, d. 15 Jun 1919; m. Catherine Humm, 19 Jan 1865;issue: Mitch (d.), Joe (d.), Mrs. Henry Eckman, Mrs. Henry Bath, George, Mrs. Jacob Eichorn, Frank, Josie, Mrs. Grace Floyd,& Henry Shelter;leaves wife. (26 Jun 1919 HCI)
JOSIE PARROTT, dau of Daniel & Lucinda Parrott, b. Hardin Co. ILL., 20 Oct 1871, d. 06 Jun 1919; m. --- Holley; leaves 4 sons & sis, Mrs. Lula Ann Hurford. (17 Jul 1919 HCI)
ANDERSON A. VINYARD, son of the late A. A. Vinyard, d. 02 Aug 1919.(07 Aug 1919 HCI)
W. J. FLYNN, d. 17 Aug 1919. (21 Aug 1919 HCI)
MRS. F. E. LAWS, buried Mon; leaves child.(21 Aug 1919 HCI)
JOHN PRITCHARD, d. Aug 1919; leaves wife, bros, M.M. Pritchard & Andy Pritchard; sis, Mrs. S.N. Page & father.(21 Aug 1919 HCI)
MARY J. LAVANDER, b. Montgomery Co., Ind. 25 Aug 1832, d. 09 Sept 1927; m. W.H. Hill, 07 Aug 1859; issue: Mrs. L.E. Joiner, Mrs. Minnie Garland, Mrs. Hester Garland, W.J. Hill, C.O. Hill, Walter S. Hill, R.E. Hill, T.M. Hill, (d), Mrs. Nona Rich(d), 2 died in infancy; leaves bro, Ben Lavander. (12 Sept 1929 HCI)
JOSEPH E. TERRELL, b Caldwell Co., Ky., 19 Mar 1837, d. 13 Aug 1929 ; leaves widow, 2 sons, 1 dau; served in Co E, 52 Ky. Reg, Civil War. (12 Sept 1929 HCI)
MRS. HARVE HILL, b. Aug 1839, d. Sept 1929. (12 Sept 1929 HCI)
HIRAM PATTON, bro to Hardin and Lewis Patton, buried last Sat (12 Sept 1929 HCI)
W. H. DAVIS, b.Carresville, Ky. 7 Aug 1845*, d. 7 Sept 1929.(12 Sept 1929 HCI)
JAKE GOINS, d. 11 Sept 1928; sis Mrs. Mary Cowgill. (12 Sept 1929 HCI)
SARAH ANNA GINGER, dau of James B. & Lizzie

Ginger, b. 20 Feb 1896, d. 04 Sept 1919; m.
Clifford Mick;issue: Walter; leaves father, 3
sis, & 2 bros. (25 Sept 1919 HCI)
FLORA BARNETT LAWS, b. 12 Sept 1873, d. Aug
1919; m. F.E. Laws 3 May 1899; issue: 4, 3
survive.(25 Sept 1919 HCI)
JAMES ADAMS, d. Evansville, Ind, Mon. (02 Oct
1919 HCI)
ALFRED LOWE, son of James Lowe, d. Mon. (02 Oct
1919 HCI)
A. J. SHELL, d. Mon.(30 Oct 1919 HCI)
LUCINDA SIMMS, d. 02 Nov 1919; m. Jim Simms 14
Sept 1877; issue; Mrs. Frankie Conkley; leaves
husband, sis Mrs. Hester Bell; Mrs. Mary J.
Hill ; bro, B.L. Lavander & James Lavander.
(13 Nov 1919 HCI)
GROVER C. OXFORD, eldest son of John C. Oxford,
b. Elizabethtown,ILl., 25 Jan 1888,d.Sat; m.
Eunice Marie Decker,08 Jun 1910.(13 Nov 1919
HCI)
WILEY J. ROSE, b. Hardin Co., ILL., abt 1858,
d. Thur; leaves 1st cousin, Walter Rose; 2nd
cousins, Will & George Rose; sis; Minnie Belt.
(20 Nov 1919 HCI)
DENIA HUMPHREY, wife of George Humphrey, b.
Crittenden Co., Ky. 1873, d.10 Nov 1919; leaves
spouse & children.(20 Nov 1919,18 Mar 1920 HCI)
DAVID ORR, d. Evansville, Ind. 19 Nov 1919.(27
Nov 1919 HCI)
R. L. YEAKEY, d. last Sat. (22 Jan 1920 HCI)
JOHN B. TUCKER, d. Caseville, Ky. last week,
abt 75 yrs old; served in Ky. regiment, Civil
War; leaves wife & children.(19 Feb 1920 HCI)
MRS. GRADIE AARON HOLBROOK, dau of W.D. Aaron,
d. 29 Feb 1920; m. Dee Holbrook; issue: 2; sis,
Mrs. Walter Mason & Mrs. Milas Spivey; bros,
Dick & James Aaron. (04 Mar 1920 HCI)
JOHN Q.A. LEDBETTER, of McLeansboro, ILL., d.
01 Mar 1920;leaves wife & sons, Dossett, Willie
Ledbetter; dau, Grace Ledbetter; bros, George &
James A. Ledbetter.(11 Mar 1920 HCI)
MRS.ISSAC ROGERS, d. last Sun.(11 Mar 1920 HCI)
MOLLIE HUNTER, d. last Fri; children: J.A.
Hunter & Clora Pruett. (25 Mar 1920 HCI)
THOMAS BENTON LEE, b. Rutherford Co., Tenn. 24
Aug 1858, d. 06 Feb 1920; leaves bros & sis,

Mrs. Elizabeth Paris, Mrs. Mary Underwood, Mrs. Luela Page, Robert E. Lee, Charles R. Lee,& Mrs Cora Leonberger.(25 Mar 1920 HCI)
CLYDE ILIFF d. 24 Mar 1920, Oakland, Cal.(01 Apr 1920 HCI)
MRS. PHILLIP JOINER, dau of Samuel Winters, d. last week; leaves husband and children. (01 Apr 1920 HCI)
LEONARD WOOD, b. Winchester, New Hamshire, 6 Oct 1860, d. ?; m. Louise A. Condit Smith. (01 Apr 1920 HCI)
W. J. BYRAN DAVIS, son of C. M. and Martha Davis, b. 21 Aug 1896, d. 16 Mar 1920.(08 Apr 1920 HCI)
REEVIE ST JOHN, dau of John St John. b. Hardin Co.ILL.,03 Jul 1903,d.23 Mar 1920; m. Mr.Glass. (15 Apr 1920 HCI)
CHARLES W.WESTON, d.11 Apr 1920.(15 Apr 1920 HCI)
GRADIE HOLBROOK, b. 21 Sept 1889, d.26 Feb 1920, wife of Dee Holbrook, dau of W.D. Aaron; leaves 2 children. (22 Apr 1920 HCI)
ALFRED LOWE, b. 1 Mar 1893, d. 29 Sept 1919; leaves wife, 2 dau, 3 bro, 4 sis, & grandmother. (22 Apr 1920 HCI)
MRS. MOLLY WILLIAMS, dau of the late George Vinyard, d. in Kedron. (22 Apr 1920 HCI)
T.A. BIRCH, d. wed, age 60 yrs; half sis, Mrs. Ollie Saunders. (29 Apr 1920 HCI)
AUGUSTA FERRELL, widow of Henry Ferrell, b. 29 Oct 1849*, d. 23 Apr 1920; issue:Pernett, Edward, Mrs. Gertrude Jackson, Mrs. Grace Lavander, & dau, unnamed.(29 Apr 1920 HCI)
MRS. JOSEPHINE SCROGGINS, b. Hardin Co. ILL., 18 Oct 1852, d. 24 Apr 1920; m. Theoderic Belt 1870;issue: Walter Belt& Mrs. Thomas Smith; 2nd m., Saunders Scroggins.(06 May 1920 HCI)
LUTITIA BLAIR, dau of Thomas D.& Sarah Blair. b. Glasgow, Ky., 27 Nov 1833; m. Alexander Gentry (d. 16 Nov 1893)04 Oct 1849; issue:John J., James W.(d 08 Aug 1880), Mary J. Locke, Elizabeth McDowell, Rachel A.A. Robinson (d.25 Oct 1915), Thomas C., Sarah M. Smith, Martha (d. 04 Oct 1870) & Ida Clement. (06 May 1920 HCI)
THOMAS BIRCH, b. 30 Apr 1860, d. 28 Apr 1920;

m. Anna Burilson of Mt. Vernon, Ind.; issue:
Arthur C., Oscar T., Roy,& Allie.(13 May 1920
HCI)
MARGARET LEDBETTER, d. last Thur; dau, Mrs.
Charles Lamar. (13 May 1920 HCI)
JAMES WILLIAM FLYNN, b.Jackson Co., Tenn.11 May
1840, d. m. Mrs. Jane Lane, 12 May 1863 (she d.
26 May 1869);issue: Isabell (d.); 2nd m.,Martha
Vinyard;issue: Charlotte (d),Charles(d),& Clyde
L. Flynn; leaves bro, Jackson Flynn. (03 Jun
1920 HCI)
MRS.SERENA PLEW, d.at home of dau in Evans-
ville,Ind.,abt 90 yrs old.(10 Jun 1920 HCI)
MRS. LAURA BERTZIN, dau of Horace Foster, d. 12
Jun 1920, West Frankfort, ILL.(17 Jun 1920 HCI)
MRS.GEORGE PILLOW, d.Sun in Chicago; m. abt 20
yrs ago; son killed in France.(24 Jun 1920 HCI)
MRS. LAURA BANKS, b. 02 Oct 1853, d. 08 Mar
1920; m. Elijah Banks, 17 Jan 1870;issue:
Eller, Gertrude Ledbetter, Ida Johnson, Olie
Ferrell, Laura Wooten, Hattie Hamp, Earl, Deb,
and Lloyd Banks. (01 Jul 1920 HCI)
HENRY BARNES, d.last Fri. (01 Jul 1920 HCI)
MARY R. PEARSON, b. 16 Feb 1852, d. 23 June
1920; m. John L. Jackson, 1868; (he d. 1879);
issue: Alonzo (d), Martha, William, m. 2nd,
H.C. Pearson (d 21 May 1905); issue: Minnie,
Della, Maud, Essie, Bessie (Mrs. Robert
Randolph), and Wiley.(08 Jul 1920 HCI)
EMMA SCHNEIDER, b. Gallatin Co., ILL., 28 Mar
1862, d. 26 Jun 1920; m.Edward Schneider,15 Jan
1882; issue: Victor, Ernest, Carl, Oscar, and
Edward Schneider, plus 3 unnamed.(15 Jul 1920
HCI)
HESTER ADAMS,dau of James Adams d.Evansville,
Ind.?: leaves mother; sis, Belva,(d) two years
ago. (15 Jul 1920 HCI)
R.H. WILLINGHAM, d. Tues; m. at Elizabethtown,
ILL., Georgia Ledbetter, dau of George W.
Ledbetter; issue: Elizabeth.(19 Aug 1920 HCI)
FRED BROOKMIRE SR., b. Germany abt 1830, d.
Mon. (19 Aug 1920 HCI)
T.S."SPENCE"BERNARD,d.last wk.(19 Aug 1920 HCI)
JACOB P. GAINES, b. Lyon Co., Ky. 16 Feb 1865,
d.19 Aug 1920; m.Addie Cain;issue:Earl,Neme,
Ura.(26 Aug 1920 HCI)

BILL BARNERD, son of the late C.W."Kit" Barnerd, d.last Sat. (02 Sept 1920 HCI)
MAE WEAST,d. New York, City.(09 Sept 1920 HCI)
DICK BELT, d. Fri; leaves wife, father, 4 bros. (02 Sept 1920 HCI)
ARNIE KARRACKER, d. 31 Jul 1920; m. Roxie Lamar 27 Aug 1917; issue: Howard Karraker; leaves, wife, mother,4 bros, & 1 sis.(09 Sept 1920 HCI)
W.H. FERRELL, d. last Mon; leaves wife, Carrie; 3 sons, & 3 daus.(16 Sept 1920 HCI)
THOMAS JARRELLS, d. Thur; leaves wife & 3 daus. (23 Sept 1920 HCI)
T. A. EWELL, b. Pope Co., ILL., 7 Apr 1836, d. 28 Aug 1920; m. Harriet Parkinson, 1856; issue: Samuel, Mary (d. Aug 1919), Thomas (d.1913), and J. Ewell. (14 Oct 1920 HCI)
LAURA F. KILGORE, dau of Jeff & Willie Kilgore, b.17 Jun 1919, d. 27 Sep 1920.(14 Oct 1920 HCI)
ULA BAYLOU, dau of J.E. Baylou, d. 29 Sept 1920. (21 OCT 1920 HCI)
ELIZABETH WHEELER, wife of George Wheeler Sr, d. Sun; leaves son. (21 Oct 1920 HCI)
HALLENE DUNCAN, b. 25 Dec 1905, d. 09 Oct 1920; leaves sis, bro(d.)(21 Oct 1920 HCI)
JAMES MANHART, b. Hardin Co., ILL, 26 Apr 1840, d.16 Oct 1930; served in Morgan's Raiders, CSA, Civil War. (23 Oct 1930 HCI)
MRS. JULIA DALE, wife of Clarence Dale, d. 29 Oct 1920; leaves husband, child, father, 4 bros,& 1 sis. (4 Nov 1920 HCI)
WILLIAM W. WOMACK, b. abt 1836, d.16 Nov 1920. (25 Nov 1920 HCI)
BENJAMIN"BUCK"PRUETT,d. Tues.(09 Dec 1920 HCI)
HORATIO TINSLEY, son of E.S. Tinsley, d. Bay City, ILL.; leaves wife & children, 4 sis, & 3 bros, including, James Tinsley. (09 Dec 1920 HCI)
JAMES H.LEDBETTER, Perry, Okla., son of James A.Ledbetter, d. Dec 1920.(16 Dec 1920 HCI)
SALLIE MORRIS, funeral Mon; leaves dau, Mrs. Ruby Morris. (16 Dec 1920 HCI)
W.S. LEDBETTER, son of James and Margaret Ledbetter, d.last Fri; sis, Vola Lamar,& half sis, Alice Robinett. (16 Dec 1920 HCI)
JAMES LYON, d. Tues, Shawneetown; leaves wife & dau. (23 Dec 1920 HCI)

W.S. LEDBETTER, b. 24 Oct 1890, d. 10 Dec 1920; m. Emmer Lee Ferrell, 1911; leaves wife, 5 chld, 1 bro, 1 sis, 2 half sis. (23 Dec 1920 HCI)
CLARENCE LITTLE, b. 08 Jul 1896, d. 03 Dec 1920; m. Flora Downing, 22 June 1920; leaves wife, 7 bros, 1 sis. (23 Dec 1920 HCI)
JAMES H. LEDBETTER, b. Elizabethtown, ILL., 28 Jul 1877, d. 09 Dec 1929; m. Belle Dickman 1900; issue: James Jr. & Isabell Ledbetter; bro, Millard Ledbetter. (06 Jan 1921 HCI)
JAMES H. SHIPP, Napoleon, Gallatin Co., Tenn., d. last Sat; m. dau of Henry & Lucinda Ginger; leaves 1 son, & 3 or 4 daus. (06 Jan 1921 HCI)
NORA MILES, dau of Robert Miles, d. Tues at 20 yrs of age. (13 Jan 1921 HCI)
WILLIAM SMITH, d. Jan ? 1921; leaves children. (20 Jan 1921 HCI)
CLIFFORD FERRELL, son of John & Sallie Ferrell, b. Elizabethtown, ILL., d. 21 Sep 1918; m. Bessie Watson, 28 Aug 1906 (she d. 03 Feb 1911). (27 Jan 1921 HCI)
MRS. KATE SHELBY, d. Fri; leaves bro, V.C. Frayser. (03 Feb 1921 HCI)
JEWELL SWAGGART, dau of Wiley Swaggart, b. 25 Nov 1906, d. 28 Jan 1921. (03 & 17 Feb 1921 HCI)
MINNIE PEARL MITCHELL, b. Livingstone Co., Ky., 18 Mar 1882, d. 22 Jan 1921; m James Jefford May 1900; issue: 4 including Raymond and Kelly. (03 Feb 1921 HCI)
MRS. JAMES MORRIS, d. Sun, dau of Mrs. Joe Ratcliffe. (03 Feb 1921 HCI)
REUBEN C. VINYARD, son of H. T. & Nettie Vinyard, b. 19 Dec 1901, d. 21 Dec 1920. (10 Feb 1921 HCI)
NORA EASTER MILES, dau of R.N. Miles, b. Hardin Co. ILL., 15 Apr 1900, d. 04 Jan 1921; leaves sis Jannie Patton, Arvie Rogers, Amie Karber, Lottie DeVelle, & bro, Frank Miles. (10 Feb 1921 HCI)
LOREN JOYNER, dau of D. N. Cox, d.--; leaves 3 children, husband, parents, bros & sis. (10 Feb 1921 HCI)
PAUL HERSHEL GINGER, son of John and Bessie Ginger, b. Detroit, Mich. 27 Feb 1920, d. 02 Jan 1921. (17 Feb 1921 HCI)

MARY HESS, nee Pankey, d. last week at abt 76 yrs old; leaves sons, D.E. Hess (his wife d. wed, she was a Edwards) & Issac Hess, also sons & daus unnamed,also g. dau, Mrs.Phoebe Manhart. (17 Feb 1921 HCI)
MINO JOYCE, d. ---; leaves wife & childern: Hilbert, Oakley, John, Arvetta; 4 bros & 1 sis. (24 Feb 1921 HCI)
JOHN REYNOLDS, d. 06 Apr 1921.(03 Mar 1921 HCI)
NOEL HURFORD, son of David & Suda Hurford, b. 22 Nov 1910, d. 14 Jan 1921.(03 Mar 1921 HCI)
GORDON EUGENE STACEY, son of Raliegh Stacey, b. Rosiclare, ILL., 06 Jan 1918, d. 25 Feb 1921. (10 Mar 1921 HCI)
IDA FRANCIS VINYARD, dau of Elmer and Dulcie Vinyard, b. 18 Oct 1918, d. 24 Nov 1920. (17 Mar 1921 HCI)
WILLIAM MILES of DeQueen, Ark., d. last week; bro, J.W. Miles. (17 Mar 1921 HCI)
BILL FRAILEY, d.12 Mar 1921; leaves wife & children. (17 Mar 1921 HCI)
MRS. JOSEPH VINYARD Mrs. Joseph Vinyard of Kedron d. ?.(17 Mar 1921 HCI)
JOE VAUGHN, d. 06 Apr 1921; leaves wife; served in Civil War. (14 Apr 1921 HCI)
WILLENA DALTON, dau of H. D. Dalton, b. 19 Feb 1920, d. 15 Apr 1921. (21 Apr 1921 HCI)
LENORA J. RIGGS, b. 09 Dec 1837, d.18 Apr 1921; m.1st Dink Wright; issue: Jackie Wright; m. 2nd Franklin Riggs; issue: Mary Elizabeth Riley, John T.Riggs, Franklin Riggs(d), Henry Riggs, plus 5 (d.). (28 Apr & 5 May 1921 HCI)
ANNA BALL, wife of William Ball, d. last week; leaves husband & children. (12 May 1921 HCI)
ORA COX, dau of D. N. Cox, wife of George Ferrell, d. Tues. (19 May 1921 HCI)
PEARL LEDBETTER, dau of Riley and Sidney Ledbetter, d. Mar 1921; m. Richard English. (16 Jun 1921 HCI)
MARY A. HESS, b. 05 Feb 1870s?, d. 05 Feb 1921; m. Drura Hess, 11 Feb 1883, Hardin Co. ILL., issue: 12, 7 survive. (23 Jun 1921 HCI)
JAMES H. CARR, b. abt 1861, d. 23 Jun 1921; m.1st, Lucy Taylor;issue: 3 sons, 1 dau; m. 2nd, Mrs William Stokes; m. 3rd. Mrs. James Oxford. (07 Jul 1921 HCI)

ORA FERRELL, wife of George Ferrell, dau of D. N. Cox. b. 15 Apr 1898, d. 17 May 1921; leaves husband, 2 children, parents, 1 bro. (30 Jun & 07 Jul 1921 HCI)
SUSIE ISABELLA COLLINS, dau of John Collins, b. 17 Jan 1898, d. 2 Apr 1921; leaves 4 sis; 2 bros. (14 Jul 1921 HCI)
WILLIAM DANIEL TAYLOR, b. Macon Co., Tenn., 25 Feb 1856, d. 30 Jun 1921; m. Clara Lainer 1876; issue; 8, 6 survive, including dau in Arizona. (21 Jul 1921 HCI)
LOUISA ANTELL ROSE, b. 16 Jan 1849, d. 5 Jul 1921; m. Joseph L. Rose 12 Jul 1866; issue: Mrs. Ida Hampton, Milton Rose & three (d.) (21 Jul 1921 HCI)
PETE HOLBROOK, d. Jul ? 1921; m. Lucy Rogers. (28 Jul 1921 HCI)
MRS. JAMES SPIVEY, dau of Alex Vinyard, d. 23 Jul 1921; leaves husband & 2 children. (28 Jul 1921 HCI)
I.N. OZEE, b. abt 1840, d. ?; m. Fannie Wall; issue: 2 dau, 1 son, Eddie (d.); son-in-law, James Mott; nieces, Mrs. Charles H. Jackson & Mrs. Charley Frailey; sis, Annie Oxford & Rebecca Curry.(28 Jul & 4 Aug 1921 HCI)
JAMES CARR, husband of Sarah Carr, d.-- ? leaves son, Cela A. Carr and dau, Mrs. Rysdon Dutton. (11 Aug 1921 HCI)
ALTA VINYARD, dau of S.A. & Bettie Vinyard, b. 28 Aug 1892, d. 23 Jul 1921; m. James Spivey 22 Jul 1909; issue:2 sons,1 dau.(11 Aug 1921 HCI)
ADDIE MELLON, dau of Gus & Mary Mellon, b. 5 Mar 1860, d. 13 Aug 1921; m. James M. Ralph, 26 Jan 1876; issue: Willie, Cleave, Walter, Nellie English, Charlie, Myrtle Reed, Mamie Beard, Orval, Manda Dale, plus 3(d.)(08 Sept 1921 HCI)
VIRGINIA WILLINGHAM, dau of the late R. H. Willingham, b. abt 1909, d. last week at g. parents, G. W. Ledbetter. (08 Sept 1921 HCI)
EFFIE LEE, dau of John Lee, b. 18 Jan 1878, d. 1 Sep 1921; m. Shelton Hunter, 02 Oct 1897; issue: Jule & James; leaves husband, parents, and 2 bros, 1 sis. (15 Sept 1921 HCI)
WILLIAM LACKEY, b. abt 1847, d. last night. (15 Sept 1921 HCI)
MILAS CARLISLE, d.,-- ?, son-in-law of D.A.

Ledbetter. (15 Sept 1921 HCI)
JAMES SERVER, b. 15 Mar 1853, d.09 Sept 1921;
leaves wife, Mary; issue: daus, Etta Ward,
Daisy Covington, Mrs.(Minnie) R. A. Ledbetter,
Mary; son, L.D. Server; sis, Mrs. Emma Foshee.
(15 Sept 1921 HCI)
FRED KRIKIE, d. Mon, abt 60 yrs old.(22 Sept 1921 HCI)
HARRY HUMM, d. Mon; leaves parents; bros,
Charles, Mitchell, & Abner Humm.(06 & 13 Oct 1921 HCI)
CHARLES H. LAMB, son of W.R. & Melissa Lamb, b.
Hardin Co., 06 Mar 1860, d. last Tues night;
m. Mary Jane Hall, issue: Mrs Audrey Dale, Mrs.
Lizzie Palmer & Mrs. Bertie Ledbetter.(13 Oct 1921 HCI)
DAVID HURFORD, d. Tues. (20 Oct 1921 HCI)
MYRTLE SWEAT, b. 09 Jun 1880, d. 1 Oct 1921; m.
Andrew Hansen, 17 Jul 1898; leaves husband,
father, chld, 2 sis & 1 bro.(20 Oct 1921 HCI)
JANE CASAD, b. Hardin Co. ILL., 1829, d. last
week; son, M. F. Casad. (20 Oct 1921 HCI)
JAMES M. STACEY, b. 11 Mar 1868, d. 08 Oct
1921; m. Rose Etta Burrough, 09 Aug 1891, (she
d. 20 Dec 1906),issue: 8, 6 survive; m. 2nd,
Laura Mason, 10 May 1914; issue: 2. (20 Oct 1921 HCI)
D.T. WARFORD, d. ?. (27 Oct 1921 HCI)
THEODORE R. TEDFORD, b. 13 Sept 1900 Gallatin
Co., ILL1; d. 21 Oct 1921; leaves, father;
bros, Leslie, Willard & Paul Tedford; sis,
Onita. (03 Nov 1921 HCI)
MARY L. SHAW, wife of John W. Shaw, b. 08 Mar
1870, d. Wed; children: Mrs. Ardes Tate, Elma
Dalton, Mary, Ward, John, Wayne, & Harry Shaw;
bros, Arthur & Morris Price; sis, Mrs. W.P.
Warford. (10 Nov 1921 HCI)
CARRIE DOW SULLIVAN, dau of Charles & Minnie
Sullivan, b. Hardin Co., ILL., 17 Aug 1902,
d. 08 Nov 1921; m. Dewey Ferrell, 07 Aug 1921.
(10 & 17 Nov 1921)
MRS. KATHERINE BERRY, Berry d. last Thur, age
73; son, L. R. Berry. (24 Nov 1921 HCI)
WIDOW GUEDRY, buried last week; sons, George
and Benjamin Edwards. (24 Nov 1921 HCI)
WILLIAM ROSE, d. Salmon, Idaho 16 Nov 1921, age

60 yrs; leaves widow; children: Mrs, Addie Coker, Mrs. Kate Thomas, & William A. Rose; bros, George, Elbert & Charles Rose.(01 Dec 1921 HCI)
ROBERT CLYDE ROSE, son of John and Mollie Rose, b. 16 Jul 1891, d. 25 Oct 1921; leaves mother, 3 bros and 1 sis. (01 Dec 1921 HCI)
ALLIE B. BIRCH, Birch b. Hardin Co. ILL., 03 Jul 1895, d. 31 Oct 1921. (01 Dec 1921 HCI)
EDDIE PRICE, son of Ambers and Dora Price,b. 08 Sept 1908, d. 03 Nov 1921;leaves father, stepson, 3 half bros, & 1 half sis. (01 Dec 1921 HCI)
NAN EDWARDS, dau of George J. Do---, b. 13 May 1875, d. 26 Oct 1921; m. Albert E. Edwards, 14 Dec---; issue: 6, Georgia, John A. & Willa? (01 Dec 1921 HCI)
MRS. J.A. HOLDERMAN, b. Cloverport, Ky. 01 Jun 1866, d. last week in Fulton, Ky.; children: V.A. McClure, Ester, James, & Alva Holderman. (05 Jan 1922 HCI)
PERNETT FERRELL SR., b. Hardin Co. ILL., 09 Jul 1834, d. St. Louis, Mo., last Thur; children: Minerva McCormick, Margaret Woody; sis, Mrs Elizabeth Williams. (05 Jan 1922 HCI)
ROBERT TINSLEY, d. last week at abt 87 yrs.(05 Jan 1922 HCI)
EFFIE CROWELL, d.13 Sept 1921.(05 Jan 1922 HCI)
JOHN CROUCH, age 58, d. in San Antonia, Texas; cousin of R.O. Lacy. (19 Jan 1922 HCI)
R. N. MILES, d. last week. (09 Feb 1922 HCI)
BUELA JACKSON, wife of Fred Jackson, and g. dau of D.A. Ledbetter, d. West Frankfort, last week. She was dau of the late "Bunk" Ledbetter, eldest son of Allen Ledbetter.(09 Feb 1922 HCI)
DAVID KNIGHT, d. last week at abt 70 yrs of age; m. Mahala Justice; issue: E.A., Austin Knight, & Mrs. Lydia Howard; m. 2nd Nettie Mick; issue: 1 son (d). (16 Feb 1922 HCI)
MRS. EDNA LAMBERT, d.last Wed; leaves husband,3 children; sis, Mrs. Perry.(09 & 16 Feb 1922 HCI)
HOSEA DALE, d. Fri; leaves wife, 3 children, & parents. (16 Feb 1922 HCI)
ANNA B. SHERIDAN, b. Hardin Co.ILL., 9 May 1858; d. 27 Jan 1922; m. Samuel Winn in Hardin

Co., 31 Mar 1878;issue: William, Thomas (d.),
Etta, Minnie (d.), Jesse (d.), Cora (d.),
Hepsie, Charlie, & James; leaves husband. (16
Feb 1922 HCI)
JAMES MILLIGAN, d. 5 Mar 1922.(9 Mar 1922 HCI)
MRS. VIRGINIA VINYARD, d. 01 Mar 1922. (09 Mar
1922 HCI)
LOUISA ANN PERRY, b. 06 Sept 1861, Hardin Co.,
ILL., d. 20 Feb 1922; m. Johnie Edwards abt
1884; issue: 2. (d.); m. 2nd Lacey S. Perry,
1889; issue: 5, 1 son, Edgar, survives; sis,
Rosa Wingate, Emma Mott; bro, James Wingate.
(16 Mar 1922 HCI)
MRS. SAM WHITESIDE, d. 28 Feb 1922; leaves
husband & dau, Mary& half-sis, Mrs. James
Robinett. (16 Mar 1922 HCI)
FLORENCE ADAMS, dau of Ben Adams, b. Livingston
ky. 20 Nov 1890, d. 17 Feb 1922; m. Louis
Limbo; leaves 3 children. (16 Mar 1922 HCI)
J.W. FLYNN, d. 17 Aug 1919. (16 Mar 1922 HCI)
WILLIAM TURNER, b. Hardin Co.ILL., 05 Mar 1849,
d. 20 Feb 1922; m. Sarah Graham, 26 Feb 1880;
issue: Willie, John, Anna Belle Lowery,& Lizzie
Hooten. (16 Mar 1922 HCI)
ASAL SHEWMAKER, d. 16 Feb 1922; never married.
(16 Mar 1922 HCI)
EDNA DEVERS, dau of Marion Devers, b. Cave-in
Rock, Hardin Co., 5 Apr 1891, d. 3 Mar 1922; m.
Ray Lambert, 26 May 1911; issue: Arthur Victor
Lambert, Frances Ray Van Lambert, & Edna Hope
Lambert; bros, John, Ordie, Ben, Will(d.) &
George(d.) Devers; sis, Sallie Perry, Phrona
Fraily, Rose Lingnel, Mae Robinson & Pearl
Cleaveland. (16 Mar & 20 Apr 1922 HCI)
MARGARET PATTERSON, sis of William Patterson,
d. last week. (23 Mar 1922 HCI)
L.H.B. MCGINNIS, son of R.J. & Arnett McGinnis,
b. Hardin Co. ILL., 31 Jul 1862, d. 22 Feb
1922; m. Mary C. Cowsert, 13 Jun --; issue:
Mrs George F. Karber, Mrs. Wallace Milligan,
Mrs. Marshall Hughes, Margaret McGinnis, and
Rollin H. McGinnis. (23 Mar 1922 HCI)
HOSEA DALE, son of George Dale, b. 19 Aug 1895,
d. 10 Feb 1922; m. 17 Nov 1917, Maude Ralph,
dau of James N. Ralph; issue: Alma, Luther,
Cecil; leaves wife, parents, 2 bros & 3 sis.

(23 Mar 1922 HCI)
SAM JOINER, b. 16 Apr 1851, d. 09 Mar 1922; m. 1st, Charlotte Vinyard, dau of Phil Vinyard; issue: 16, 6 survive: Phil, Loy, Tracy, Della, Loren, & Essie; m. 2nd, Daisy Cummings; issue; 5, 4 survive. (30 Mar 1922 HCI)
MRS. AUGUSTA HAMP, d.21 Mar 1922.(30 Mar 1922 HCI)
GRANT BELT, son of Hiram & Mariah Belt, d---, at 62 yrs of age; m. --- Joiner; issue: 1 dau; m. 2nd, Eliza Patton; issue: 6; m. 3rd, Maud Kendell; issue: 1 son; 4 sons & 2 daus survive him. (06 Apr 1922 HCI)
E. M. SMOCK, only son of James Smock, b. Hardin Co. ILL., 3 Oct 1876, d. --- 1922; m. Annie Shearer, dau of George Shearer, 05 May 1905;issue: Herbert, Kenneth; leaves wife, parents, & sis. (06 Apr 1922 HCI)
JORDON MORRIS, b. 4 Oct 1863, d. 31 Mar 1922; m. Nora Ball;issue; 7, 6 survive. (06 Apr 1922 HCI)
JAMES K.P. MILLIGAN, b. Tenn., 30 Jul 1845, d. 04 Mar 1922; m. Celia M. Womack, 10 Apr 1866; issue: John A., Abner W., W.H., Lewis N., T.G., Robert G., Nancy L. Hooten, Rhoda E. Modglin. Martha A. Banks. (20 Apr 1922 HCI)
CLAYBORN BELT, d.12 May 1922, 72 yrs old.(01 Jun 1922 HCI)
J.T. SONNEN, b. Crefeld, Germany, 18 Jan 1872. (18 May 1922 HCI)
ROXIE OXFORD, b. 23 Apr 1848. (27 Apr 1922 HCI)
BERT E. SMITH, husband of Nannie Stacey, d. 10 Apr 1922 in Los Angles, Cal. (27 Apr 1922 HCI)
NANCY BEARD nee Womack, wife of William Beard, d.-- ?. (27 Apr 1922 HCI)
JOSEPH M. PALMER, d. 15 May 1922; leaves wife, 8 children, & 3 bros. (08 Jun 1922 HCI)
MRS. MARTHA CRAIG, nee Lee, d. Tue. (08 Jun 1922 HCI)
MRS. HENRETTA STUBBS, wife of T.H. Stubbs, dau of the late W.A. Ralph. (15 Jun 1922 HCI)
BENJAMIN A. NOLES, b. Lincoln Co., Tenn., 15 Mar 1843; children: 6 survive; served in Civil War. (06 Jul 1922 HCI)
HAZEL IRENE ENSLEY, dau of Phoebe Ensley, b. 7 Sept 1909, d. 21 June 1922. (06 Jul 1922 HCI)

ROBERT VENABLE, b. Hardin Co., ILL., d. Thur age 74; children: Mrs. Charles Martin, Fred & Charles Venable. (13 Jul 1922 HCI)
ANNA OXFORD, nee Ozee. b. abt 1847, d. 05 Jul 1922; m. Robert Oxford, 16 May 1866 (he died 11 May 1917);issue; Lucien, Mary, Emma, Elihu Newton(d. abt 30 yrs ago), Dora & Belva; leaves sis, Rebecca Curry & Mary Dunn; bro, J.N. Ozee. (13 Jul 1922 HCI)
MARY SIMMONS, widow of Wesley Simmons, d. Thur. (27 Jul 1922 HCI)
JAMES BEARD, b Ky. 15 Aug 1867, d. 3 Jul 1922; m. Rebecca Lewis, 09 Aug 1867; issue: Henretta, Mrs. Fannie Augusta Underwood, & Mrs. J.R. Oxford. (20 Jul 1922 HCI)
JIM SIMMS, b.05 Aug 1832, d.? (10 Aug 1922 HCI)
DELBERT HOGAN, son of Henry Hogan, d. Sun; bros, Raymon, Fowler, & James.(17 Aug 1922 HCI)
HENRYETTA RALPH, dau of W.A. Ralph, b. 1855, d. 5 Jun 1922; m. T. H. Stubbs; issue: 5.(17 Aug 1922 HCI)
RUBY BISHOP, dau of John Bishop, b. 02 Apr 1903, d. 25 Aug 1922; leaves mother, bro,& grandmother. (07 Sept 1922 HCI)
JOHN MCCLUSKY, b. Swanton, Vermont 21 Jul 1848, d. 27 Jul 1922; m. Lucinda O'Neal,11 Sept 1879; issue: Fred, James, Kate, & Cora; served in Civil War, 3 Reg. 10 Army Corps, New Hamshire (03 Aug & 14 Sept 1922 HCI)
CLARA WILLIAMS, dau of W.J. Hicks, b. abt 1882, d. ?;m. Alonzo Williams in 1906; issue; 2 sons; leaves husband, parents, 2 bros, & 4 sis. (21 Sept 1922 HCI)
JAMES MILLER, son of John & Mary Miller, b. Rutherford Co., Tenn., 06 Jan 1859, d. 17 Sept 1922; child: Mildred, b.08 Nov 1904; leaves sis, Mrs. Anna Reynolds. (05 Oct 1922 HCI)
PAUL CHANDLER KIBLER, son of Wayne and Effie Kibler, b. Kansas City, Mo., 12 May 1916, d.09 Aug 1922. (05 Oct 1922 HCI)
AILEEN MARTIN, dau of Dave Martin, b. Elizabeth town, ILL. 07 Nov 1909, d. 27 Oct 1922. (09 Nov 1922 HCI)
THOMAS JEFFERSON DOUGLAS, b. 16 Oct 1875, d. 27 Oct 1922; m. Nora McDowell 18 Apr 1897; issue: Wayne, Mrs. Sally Edwards, Clyde, Hansel,

Quentin, Eula, Eugene, Marie, & Nora;leaves wife, mother, & 4 sis. (16 Nov 1922 HCI)
MATILDA DENTON, nee Henry, d. 01 Dec 1922, age 85; m. A.M. Denton abt 40 yrs ago; stepmother of William & J.E. Denton. (07 Dec 1922 HCI)
MARY LEZETTE SHIPP, nee Foster, b. 13 Apr 1890, d. 29 Nov 1922; leaves husband,dau, stepmother, & 2 half bros.(14 Dec 1922 HCI)
FLOYD HERBERT MATTHEWS, b. 23 Jun 1873, d. Nov 1922; m.Ethel Cummings, 05 Aug 1914;issue: 3 sons, 2 daus; bro, Henon Matthews.(21 Dec 1922 HCI)
FRANK C. TICHENOR, d. Sat; m. Mattie Birch, dau of the late Richard & Rebecca Birch; issue: 2 sons, 1 dau. (04 Jan 1923 HCI)
MRS. ELLEN HOLDER, widow of A.F.(Finch) Holder, b. 01 Feb 1847*, d. 7 Jan 1923; children; 10, 2 living:Henry & Charles Holder.(18 Jan 1923 HCI)
MRS. EMERT GEE, wife of John T. Gee, b. Hardin Co.ILL., 17 Sept 1866, d. 07 Jan 1923; issue: Mrs. Vinyard, & sons, Solon & Everett Gee; sis, Rachel Sturgill & Jane Ferrell; bros, Joseph, Timothy, Webster, & William. (01 Feb 1923 HCI)
ELIZABETH ANN HOBBS FOSTER, b. Cape Girardeau, Mo., 15 Feb 1835, d. 21 Jan 1923; m. Horace Foster, 09 Dec 1849; issue: 12, 6 survive, Thomas J., John W., I. A., Mrs. M.L. Tyer, Mrs. John Blagg, & Mrs. Wm. Patton.(01 Feb 1923 HCI)
DELZA SHUTT, nee Schroll, b. 1868, d. 19 Jan 1923; m. Jacob Shutt, 1885; issue: Willie, Fred, Virgil, Clyde, Roy, Ezra, & Mrs. Ethel Vinyard; sis, Mara Stubby; bros, John & Louis Schroll. (01 Feb 1923 HCI)
ARZIE SHEWMAKER, son of Milo Shewmaker, b. Hardin Co.ILL., 07 Aug 1898, d. 25 Jan 1923; m.Lillie Healy, 06 Sept 1918; issue: Norman, Dorothy; leaves wife, mother, 2 sis & 4 bros. (08 Feb 1923 HCI)
DOCK PILAND, b. 1859 Monroe Co. Ky., d. 09 Feb 1923. (22 Feb 1923 HCI)
SAMUEL WINTERS, b.----, d. 14 Feb 1923. (22 Feb & 22 Mar 1923 HCI)
ELIZABETH DENT, dau of James and Fannie Dent, b. Alabama, 26 Mar 1848, d. 18 Feb 1923; m. Morgan Bryan 20 Sept 1868; issue: J.W., S.G., Henry, Charles, Davis, Thomas, Bryan, Alice

Hogan, Cordella Rose, Nora Shelton, Mary Lightner(d.), Amanda Wallace(d) and Nettie Thomas (d.).(01 Mar 1923 HCI)
MARY F. RASH, b. 14 Oct 1847*, d. 11 Feb 1923; issue: 7; son, L.T. Rash (15 Feb &08 Mar 1923)
JESSIE FORD, b.Putman Co., V.W.,1850, d. 25 Feb 1923; m. E.J. Baylous, issue: Burnie C.,(d. inf), Mintie Price, Everett, Willie, (wife of Jeff Kilgore). (15 Mar 1923 HCI)
EMMA C. RATCLIFF, dau of George & Eliza Ratcliff b. Crittenden Co., Ky., 20 Sept 1874; d. 01 Apr 1923; m. J.H. Baugher, 21 Aug 1895 at Cave-In-Rock, Hardin Co.; issue: George Alphus, Estelle, Lee Hollas, Horrell Lester, Ollie, & Glenn Baugher, & 2 Infs (d.); leaves father, bro, & 4 sis. (12 Apr 1923 HCI)
E. J. FORD, wife of Jesse Ford, b. Putman Co., West Virgina, b. 02 Aug 1855*, d. 25 Mar 1913; issue: Mintie Price, E.L. Ford, and Willie E. wife of Jeff Kilgore), Everett (d.); leaves 7 or 8 bros.(12 Apr 1923 HCI)
JOHN FERRELL, b.-----, d. 14 Apr 1923; son, H.A. Ferrell. (19 Apr 1923 HCI)
J.N. MILLIGAN, b. 14 Oct 1859, d. 26 Mar 1923; m. Evelyn Parkam ; issue: Cora Stuby, Myrtle Harrison, Gertrude Ledbetter, Bertha Fisher, Maggie Nooks, Maude Partain, & Ila Milligan (son) (19 Apr 1923 HCI)
CHARLES HENRY HOSLER, b. Plymouth, Ind.,03 May 1858, d. 03 Apr 1923; m. Frederaca Karber, 25 Feb 1880; issue: 7, 4 survive: son Louis Hosler killed in WW 1; m. 2nd, Elizabeth Banks, 05 Apr 1913. (19 Apr 1923 HCI)
HOBERT MCDONALD, son of James McDonald, b. Livingston, Ky, 17 May 1896, d. 06 Apr 1923; leaves bros & sis. (26 Apr 1923 HCI)
W.D. DAVIS, d. last Sat, abt 64 yrs old; m. 1st, Flora A. Warford, a dau of David T. Warford, issue: 2 boys (d.), 1 girl; m. 2nd Mary L. Kendricks; m. 3rd to ---Barnard; issue: twins. (03 May 1923 HCI)
E.F. WALL SR., father of G.A. Wall, 82 yrs old (08 Mar 1923 HCI)
MRS. JOHN FERRELL, d. sun; issue: R. A. and Ella Ferrell. (15 Mar 1923 HCI)
LAURA HALE dau of James and Martha Hale, b. 24

Feb 1870, d.09 Apr 1923; m. Jefferson Williams; issue: Elsworth, Virgil, Jeff, James, Theodore, Euls,& Edgar (d);leaves husband, mother,5 bros, & 2 sis. (03 May 1923 HCI)
NOAH FULGHUM, b. 20 Apr 1860, d. 22 Mar 1923, m. Lillie Ferrell; issue; 7.(03 May 1923 HCI)
DR.PARIS, b. 27 Apr 1853, (10 May 1923 HCI)
DR. WOMACK, b. 27 Apr 1860.(10 May 1923 HCI)
H. A. FERRELL, attended funeral services of his parents. (17 May 1923 HCI)
CLARENCE PITTS, son of Alonzo Pitts, b. 03 Oct 1919, d. 16 Apr 1923. (17 May 1923 HCI)
JOHN A. CLARK, b. 23 Mar 1844, Marion, Ky.; m. Mary M. Johnson 26 Feb 1862, m. 2nd Sarah A. Hathorn, 28 Nov 1869 (d.1916); issue: Cora Waggoner, Esther Lane, Cecil Clark, Ruth Travis & Roy Clark. (24 May 1923 HCI)
JULIE IRENE RUSSELL, dau of W. F. Russell, b. 13 Sept 1910, d. 17 May 1923. (24 May 1923 HCI)
CHARLES VINYARD, b. Hardin Co., 09 Sept 1841. d. 26 May 1923; m.1st, Mary Soward (d.10 Dec 1871); issue: Andrew (d.18 Sept 1893) Henry; m.2nd, Mary J. Jenkins 1876; issue: George Vinyard, 3(d.); 5 bros,1 sis (unnamed).(14 Jun 1923 HCI)
W. D. DAVIS, b. Hardin Co.,Il,06 Mar 1861; m. 1st, Flora Warford; issue: 2 sons(d), 1 dau; m. 2nd, Mary Lucinda Kendrick; m.3rd Lizzie Newton; issue: 2 ;leaves 3 bros & 1 sis. (21 Jun 1923 HCI)
MAUDE GRIFFITH, dau of Dr. Griffith, d. last fri; m. Charles Suits. (24 May 1923 HCI)
EARL GARLAND, son of Thomas Garland, d. 10 Jun 1923; m. Stella ---? (14 Jun 1923 HCI)
BENJAMIN J. BROWNFIELD, b. Hardin Co., ILL, Jun 1853 ?, d. 24 June 1923; m. Hannah Oxford (sis of John A., Samuel,& George Oxford);issue: Mrs. E.N. Hall, Mrs. J. E. Denton, James, Mrs. Wiley Leonberger, Mrs. Earnest Oxford, Mrs. James N. Watters & Clarence Brownfield (d.)(12 Jul 1923 HCI)
JOHN S. CURRY, b. 21 Dec 1861, d. 25 Jun 1923; m. Emma Ferrell 5 Aug 1890; issue: Willie(d), Clara Hale, & Minnie Oxford.(12 Jul 1923 HCI)
MRS. BURTON COWSERT, abt. 78 yrs old, d. Thurs; dau, Jane Walker; son, Jake Cowsert, & 5 step-

daus: Kate Jarvis, Jane Ellis, Alice Cowsert, Angie Livers, & Anna Moore. (02 Aug 1923 HCI)
MRS. GEORGE DOUGLAS, d.19 Jul 1923; son, Jeff Douglas, & dau, Mrs James Rash.(02 Aug 1923 HCI)
DAL BELT, son of Jonathan Belt, d. last Fri; son, C.M. Belt. (06 &09 Aug 1923 HCI)
MARCELLUS LEONIDAS TYER, son of John & Rufina Tyer, b. Hardin Co.,ILL.,05 Nov 1858, d.12 Jul 1923; m. Hannah Foster, dau of Horace & Elizabeth Foster, 26 Jul 1885;issue 8.(16 Aug 1923 HCI)
SAMUEL B.WINN, b. Green Co., Ind., 22 Apr 1854, m. Annie B. Sheridan, 31 Mar 1878, Hardin Co. ILL.;issue: W.H. Winn, Etta Johnson, Hepsie Blair, Chas. K., James Winn, 4(d.).(16 Aug 1923)
TRESSIE NICHOLAS BIRCH, dau of Samuel & Jennie Nicholas, b. Elizabethtown, ILL., 05 Jun 1891, d.23 Jul 1923; m. Arthur C. Birch, 29 Aug 1909; issue: Ruby Virginia, Mrs. Arthur Deneen, Annie Marie, Harry Elwood Birch; sis, Myrtle Huff, & g. mother, Elizabeth Lyon. (23 Aug 1923 HCI)
BENJAMIN F. HERRING, d. 28 Feb 1923; Civil War vet, m. Christina ?;.(23 Aug 1923 HCI)
THOMAS J. SIMMS, b. Gallatin Co., ILL., 14 Dec 1853,; m.1st, Henrietta Hamilton 1876; m.2nd, Martha E. Womack 1880; issue: Mrs. Cella Jacob, Rose Simms, & 2 (d.); m. 3rd, Josephine Goins, 31 May--; issue: 2. (23 Aug 1923 HCI)
MAUDIE GRIFFITH, dau of Alexander & Esther Griffith, b.14 Jun 1892, d.18 May 1923; m. Charley Suits, Mar 1910; issue: son;leaves parents, 2 bros & 2 sis. (13 Sept 1923 HCI)
MARTHA J. HINES? b.10 May 1848, d. 07 Sep 1923; m. O.W. Joiner, 04 Jan 1866 ?; issue: Elizabeth Van Biber, William C.(d.) Samuel, John, Issac (d.),Hickman, & James F. Joiner; 2 bros & 2 sis. (13 Sept 1923 HCI)
THOMAS JERRY SMOCK, b. Cave-in-Rock, Hardin Co. 26 Apr 1864; m. May L. Evertson, 09 Jan 1887; issue: 8, 2(d.); bros, James & A.A. Smock; sis, Mrs Noah Hurford. (11 Oct 1923 HCI)
JOHN L. FOWLER, b. Rock Haden, Mead Co., Ky.25 Jul 1897, d.16 Oct 1923; issue: Panzie Arzella & John Robert Fowler; 3 bros,4 sis.(25 Oct 1923

HENRY CLAY FRAYSER, b. Cadiz, Trigg Co., Ky., 02 Apr 1840, d. 25 Oct 1923; m. Nancy Thomas, 22 Oct 1868 (d.18 Dec 1892);issue: Henry H., Fayette S., Eva G., Rose Clark, Eddie,& 3 (d); m.2nd, Rosie D. Wilson, 31 Oct 1894. (15 Nov 1923 HCI)
MARY ELIZABETH COOK, dau of Houston & Lavena Cook, b. Crittenden Co. Ky. 07 Oct 1859; m. George J. Douglas, 1 Jan 1874; issue: 13, 9 survive, Mrs. A. E. Edwards, dau,(d.).(15 Nov 1923 HCI)
CECIL ALVIN MILLIGAN, son of Clyde & Essie Milligan, b. 17 Nov 1916, d. 19 Nov 1923; leaves parents, 2 sis (one named Hildred Bernice Milligan, b. 13 Mar 1922, d. 10 Dec 1923) & 2 g.mothers; (29 Nov,13 Dec 1923 HCI)
HORACE HOBBS, b. 28 Nov 1855, d. 10 Dec 1923; m. Nancy Oxford; issue: 4, Loy & Alonzo Hobbs survive. (13 Dec 1923 HCI)
EARL GARLAND, son of Thomas Garland, d.10 Jun 1923; m. Stella ---(14 Jun 1923 HCI)
BESSIE VINYARD, b. Hardin Co., 17 Feb 1892, d. 15 Dec 1923; m. E. R. Edwards 15 Feb 1911; issue;Robert Wayne & Francis Genevieve Edwards. (10 Jan 1924 HCI)
EEMMA FERAL ASHFORD, b. 30 Jul 1897, d. 08 Jan 1934. (24 Jan 1924 HCI)
WILLIAM H. BOWERS, b. Xenia, Ohio 24 Mar 1902, d.21 Jan 1924; m. Susie Margalin,19 May 1922; issue: William Robert Bowers.(24 Jan 1924 HCI)
JOSEPH MASON, b. Caldwell Co., Ky., 1842, d.11 Oct 1923; m. Nancy Jane Robinson in 1863;issue William Henry, Charles Albert, Mrs. Henry Dossett, Mrs. Joseph Fredrick, & Mrs. Dan Stone m. 2nd, Mrs. Nancy Hufsey; issue: Bryant & Walter Mason; stepdau, Mrs Charley Hess.(24 Jan 1924 HCI)
WILLIAM VOLKERT, son of Antone & Rita Volkert, b. Hardin Co. ILL., 05 Oct 1872, d. 21 Jan 1924; m. Sophia Zimmer, 19 Oct 1896; issue: Mary, James, Leo Volkert, & 4 (d.); leaves bros, George, Antone, John; sis, Mrs. Thomas Zimmer, Mrs. Louis Hamp Jr & Margaret Ginger. (31 Jan 1924 HCI)
MRS. ARTIMISSA REED DOWNEY, b. 04 May 1842,

Hardin Co., d. 20 Jan 1924; m. Henry Clay
Downey, 10 Jan 1871; Issue: Jennie Humm, Mrs.
E.R. Kibbler, Mrs. George Keeling; bro, Louis
Reed; sis, Mrs. Martha Martin.(31 Jan 1924 HCI)
NANCY LEDBETTER, wid of B.L. Ledbetter, d, last
Fri; son, Lee Ledbetter. (31 Jan 1924 HCI)
JESSIE GERHARDT, b.02 Dec 1892, d. 29 Jan 1924;
m. Belle Vaughn, 23 Dec 1911: Issue: 2, 1
survives, Alfred Gerhardt, b.06 Jan 1915.(07
Feb 1924 HCI)
JAMES ALLEN GINGER, son of E.T. Ginger &---?,
(mother was dau of B.L. and Nancy Ledbetter),
b. May 1897, d. 24 Jan 1924; half bros, Loyd &
Earl Ginger; uncles, Thomas Ginger, James G.
Ginger,Richard Ledbetter,John Ledbetter,George
Ledbetter & Lee Ledbetter.(14 Feb 1924 HCI)
ADAM ZEIGLER, b. Germany 01 Apr 1848, d.13 Feb
1924; m.Lucy Schutt,13 Apr 1874; issue: Emma,
Minnie, Walter, John, Maggie(d.), Katie
Mitchell (d.), Mollie (d.), Willie(d.),& inf,
(d.);sis, Mary Herman; bro, Frank Zeigler.(28
Feb 1924 HCI)
ROSA COLLINS, dau of William A. & Mary A.
Collins, b. Hardin Co., 28 Mar 1894, d. 27 Feb
1924; m. Louis Scroggins, 24 Apr 1912; issue;
3, 2 survive: Dorothy & Thelma Scroggins; bro,
James S. Collins. (06 Mar 1924 HCI)
NORMA CORINE HENSON, dau of Alter Henson, b. 03
Jan 1924, d. 27 Feb 1924; leaves 2 bros.(06 Mar
1924 HCI)
MRS. P.J. HOWARD, age 84 d. Wed, wid of Capt.
Philip Howard; issue; P.J., Loren, Harry,
Walter & John Howard. (06 Mar 1924 HCI)
VERNON WILLIAM JR., son of Vernon William, b.
18 May 1923, d. 03 Mar 1924; sis, Gwendoline
William. (13 Mar 1924 HCI)
HENRY "PETE" HILL, son of James A. & Carolyn
Hill, b. Hardin Co., 26 Sept 1864, d. 25 Feb
1924; m. Mattie B. St John, 17 May 1896;(she d.
23 June 1924); leaves Bro, J.A. Hill, plus un-
named bro; sis, Alice Carr, Angie Edmond, &
Cora Turner. (13 Mar 1924 HCI)
JOHN MARSHALL KARNS, son of John L. & Frances
Karns, b. Gallatin Co.ILL,12 Oct 1889;(13 Mar
1924 HCI)
JAMES WELDON PYLES, son of Roy Pyles, b. 31 Aug

1923, d. 06 Mar 1924.(20 Mar 1924)
JOHN FRANKLIN ZIGLER, son of Adam & Lucy Zigler
b. Hardin Co., 29 Dec 1879, d.18 Mar 1924; m.
Izora Partin, 06 Jun 1907; issue: William Otto
Zigler; bro, Walter Zigler; sis, Minnie & Emma
Zigler. (27 Mar 1924 HCI)
EARLENE MELITA GARLAND, b.18 Jan 1918, d.15 Feb
1924; leaves mother & sis. (20 Mar 1924)
MARGARET B.ISHAM, b. middle Tenn., 09 Sept
1837, d.22 March 1924; m.James Isham,17 Feb
1853; issue: 10, 4 survive, J. G. Isham, J. E.
Isham; daus, Mrs. Emmer Vinyard, Mrs. Effie
Gintert; bro, Dan Banks.(03 Apr 1924 HCI)
EVERETT OXFORD, son of Wilmer & Harriet Oxford,
b. 8 Nov 1902, d. 14 May 1923.(10 Apr 1924 HCI)
MARY ZIGLER, b. Hicks, ILL. 6 Dec 1855, d. 3
Apr 1924; m. Franklin Zigler, 20 Apr 1875;
issue: Andy, George, Philip, Katie Oglesby and
Ritta Matheny, (Jacob, Fred, Elizabeth, d.);
bro, Jacob Shutt; sis, Lucy Zigler, and Katie
Pyle. (10 Apr 1924 HCI)
WELDON ANDREW JENKINS, son of Al F. & Ada
Jenkins, b.18 Jun 1912*, d. 19 Apr 1924; leaves
parents & bro, Herbert.(10 & 17 Apr 1924 HCI)
MATTIE ELLIS WILCOX, b. 10 May 1907, d. Apr
1924.(17 Apr 1924 HCI)
GARY EDWARD GRIFFIN, son of William Hardin &
Harriet E. Griffin, b. 18 Dec 1858, d.07 Apr
1924; leaves bro, Roy Griffin & sis, Mrs.
Thomas Hill. (17 Apr 1924 HCI)
J.D. SLAGEL, son of Arthur Slagel, b. 13 May
1922, d. 10 Apr 1924.(17 Apr 1924 HCI)
MRS. D.D. RANDALL b. Hardin Co., 21 Nov 1856,
d. Halstad, Kan.; m. D.D. Randall, 05 Jan 1878;
issue: Daniel G. Randall & Charles W. Randall.
(24 Mar 1924 HCI)
MAE HUFSEY, dau of Dennis Hufsey, b. 07 May
1908, d. 28 Oct 1923. (08 May 1924 HCI)
JIM R. B. RENFRO, b. abt 1849, d. 27 Apr 1924;
wife was dau of Frank Ginger; bro, Norton
Renfro(15 May 1924 HCI)
MISSOURI GILBERT, b.?, d. 07 May 1924; m.1st,
Abe McFarland; m. 2nd, R.F.Taylor.(15 May 1924
HCI)
WILLIAM T. LAMAR, b. Hardin Co., 22 Jun 1851,
d. 21 Dec 1923; m. Elizabeth Jackson, 24 Sept

1872; issue: Louis, Lillie (d. 09 Apr 1910, wife of James Robinett)& Charles Lamar; m. 2nd, Laura E. Staley, 28 May 1884; issue: Staley, Marcellia(d.), Otis,& Mary Lamar (22 May 1924 HCI)
JEANETTE THOMPSON, wife Paul Oxford (d.), son of John C. Oxford, d. 12 Apr 1924, age 32; issue: Hilda Oxford; m. 2nd. Charles Thompson, 27 Oct 1922.(22 May 1924 HCI)
MAUDE M.GRACE,b.13 Feb 1892, d. 23 May 1924; m. John Grace,16 Jun 1915;issue:3.(29 May 1924 HCI)
BELLE LEDBETTER, dau of John T.Ledbetter, d. 11 May 1924; m.1st, Alex Laird; m.2nd. Frank Smith; sis, Ida Sullivan, Kate Hill,Ollie Dale; bros, John J., Quince,& James Ledbetter. (29 May 1924 HCI)
A. C."CAM" FERRELL, b. Hardin Co., 18 Nov 1852, d. Derby,ILL.,25 May 1924.(05 Jun 1924 HCI)
J.R.B. RENFRO, son of D.N. & Nancy Renfro, b. 19 Mar 1852, d. 27 Apr 1924; m. Betsy Ann Ginger, dau of Frank Ginger; issue 6.(05 Jun 1924 HCI)
SHERMAN BROWNING, b. 07 Apr 1865, d. 09 Mar 1924; m. Hannah Rutherford, dau of Arch Rutherford, 1887; issue: Mrs. Moses Suits; m. 2nd, Emma Oxford,dau of Robert Oxford, 1895 issue; 5.(12 Jun 1924 HCI)
VICTORIA SHAD OWENS, b. 1854; m. David Owens, 1884; issue: 2(d.).(26 Jun 1924 HCI)
CLYDE VINYARD, b. 1843. (26 Jun 1924 HCI)
ELIJAH MELLON, son of Gus & Mary Mellon, b.02 Jun 1900, d. Jun 1924. (03 Jul 1924 HCI)
ISSAC N. OXFORD, son of Roxie Oxford, issue: Grace & Aaron Oxford,(10 Jul 1924 HCI)
JOSEPH L. VINYARD, son of Jim Vinyard, b. Hardin Co., 13 Jan 1883, d.14 Jul 1924; m. Aretha Brinkley, 10 Dec 1910; issue: 5. (23 Jul 1924 HCI)
G. W. HILL, d. 24 Jul 1924; leaves son, George Hill. (31 Jul & 7 Aug 1924 HCI)
B. CARROLL TOLBERT, b. 25 Jan 1841, d. 16 Jul 1924; m 1st, --; issue; Will and Rich Tolbert; m. 2nd, --; issue: John Tolbert; m. 3rd, --; issue; Ernest Tolbert, Mrs. Rebecca Roberts, & Mrs. W. P. Irby; B. Carroll Tolbert served in

Co.C,48 Ill. Inf, Civil War.(07 Aug 1924 HCI)
DR. G. W. HILL, b Hardin Co., 08 Apr 1850, d.
24 Jul 1924; m. Rebecca Cathleen Thompson, b.
Webster, Co., Ky. 31 Jan 1879; issue: 7, 2
survive, George Hill & John Warren Hill; dau,
Bessie Cathleen (who d. 08 Feb 1912; sons,
Wellington Hill Gustin & George Warren Gustin.
(07 Aug 1924 HCI)
CHARLES A. GINGER, b. Hardin Co., 11 Oct 1874,
d. 15 Aug 1924; m. Dora Waters, Hardin Co.,
ILL, 1897; issue: Mrs. Hattie Coleman, Mrs.
Nigel Aud, & John E. Ginger(d); half bros,
Omar, Mora, & Roy Patton; half sis, Mrs. Frank
Green, Mrs. Wallace Jennings, & Mrs. Arza
McDaniel; m. 2nd, Emma Black.(28 Aug 1924 HCI)
J.H.KIRHAM, b. Hardin Co., 01 Sept 1844, d. 29
Aug 1924; son, Charles Kirham; dau, Mrs. A.B.
Smith. (04 Sept 1924 HCI)
MRS. J.M. LOWERY d. 13 Aug 1924; son, Gordon;
daus, Mrs. Ed Pernell, & Mrs. Henry Barnard.
(21 Aug 1924 HCI)
MARTHA JANE HODGE, dau of Thomas Hodge, b. 22
Jun 1861, d. Aug 1924; m. J.M. Lowery, 1879;
issue: 6, 3 survive, Mrs. Henry Barnard, Mrs.Ed
Parnell & Gordon Lowery.(11 Sept 1924 HCI)
JANE HOBBS, 82 yrs old, d. 20 Sept 1924; issue:
8. (25 Sept 1924 HCI)
ALLEN & MARY LOVE m. Elizabethtown, 15 Oct
1874. (23 Oct 1924)
HENRY HOGAN, b. 11 Oct 1834, Civil War vet. (23
Oct 1924 HCI)
FREDRICK DONITHAN, Civil War vet, 90 yrs old.
(27 Nov 1924 HCI)
FRANK MAYFIELD, b. Elizabethtown, Hardin
Co.,Ill., 27 May 1890, d.17 Sept 1924; m.
Gertie Patton, 10 Feb 1908; issue: 7, 6
survive. (25 Sept 1924 HCI)
MRS. SIDNEY MCFARLAND, wid of W.P. McFarland,
d ?; bro, Sam Whiteside; niece, Mary Whiteside.
(09 Oct 1924 HCI)
FREDEREKA KARBER, b. Cincinnati, Ohio, 15 Apr
1853; m. Charles Hossler, 30 Sept 1880; issue:
6, 4 survive; son, Louis H. Hossler killed in
France, WW1. (16 Oct 1924 HCI)
MARY JANE LEDBETTER, b. Hardin Co., 06 Nov
1842, d. 20 Sept 1924; m. Allen Hobbs, 18 Feb

1852; issue: Mrs. George Oxford, Josh, George, Arch, John, Riley, Joe & Dock Hobbs.(16 Oct 1924 HCI)
FRANCIS MARION DEVER, b. Lincoln Co., Tenn.,03 Jul 1843, d. 26 Oct 1924; m. Ruth Ledbetter, dau of John & Elizabeth Ledbetter; issue:16, 8 survive: Sallie Perry, Ordway, Rosie Lingal,Mae Robinson, Ben, Pearl Cleveland, Frona Fraily. (13 Nov 1924 HCI)
CARRIE TURNER, dau of Wilmer & Alice Turner, b. Karbers Ridge, Hardin Co. ILL.,02 Feb 1899, d. 17 May 1924, m. J.W. Towery, 26 Jul 1922; mother, Mrs. Dow Moore; aunts, Mrs. Ross Frayser, Mrs. Walter Van Bibler, Mrs. Claude Reddick; uncle, Loren Belford.(27 Nov 1924 HCI)
H. T. FLYNN b. Tenn, 01 Oct 1842, d. 21 Nov 1924; m. Sarah ---; issue: 6, survive: Charley, James, & Frank Flynn. (04 Dec 1924 HCI)
CHARLES E. ROSE, b. Portsmouth, Ohio, 10 Sept 1853, d. 27 Nov 1924; m.Eller Patton, 09 Apr 1873, Rosiclare, ILL.; issue: 6, 4 survive: Walter,Harve,Oliver, Earl Rose.(04 Dec 1924 HCI)
ELLEN STOKES, d. last week; m.--- Patton; sis, Bet Rutherford, Mary Patton; bro, W.E. Stokes. (04 Dec 1924 HCI)
MILLARD LEDBETER, son of "Bunk" & Nancy Ledbetter, b. Hardin Co., d. 22 Nov 1924.(04 Dec 1924 HCI)
VIRGIL OXFORD, son of Mary Oxford, b.18 Jul 1903, d. 02 Oct 1924. (11 Dec 1924 HCI)
WILLIAM JENKINS, d.---1924, son of Henry & Anna Jenkins;leaves, 4 bros (1 bro named Waldo Jenkins); 1 sis, 1 half sis (18 Dec 1924 HCI)
ANGIE MORGAN, b. 21 Mar 1856, d. 07 Dec 1924; m. S.L. Mick, 03 Oct 1878; issue: 8, 5 survive, (1 dau named, Mrs. Floyd Marglin); sis; 2 bros. (18 Dec 1924 HCI)
HOWARD MITCHELL PANKEY, son of John A. Pankey, b. Hardin Co.ILL., 18 Jul 1896, d. 08 Dec 1924; leaves parents, bro, & 2 sis.(18 Dec 1924 HCI)
DR. J. LEDBETTER, d. ----; dau, Mrs. Mary A. Thornton; son, Rev. D. A. Ledbetter; g.sons, Henry Thornton, & John Oxford.(18 Dec 1924 HCI)
SARA J. MIZZELL, b, Livingston Co., Ky. 05 Nov 1852, d. 16 Dec 1924; m. B. J. Jordon, 17 April

1878(he d. 30 Apr 1916), issue: J.H. Jordon,
Mary C. Kaylor; m 2nd, Bill L.Lavander, 05 Jun
1919; leaves bro, Mac Mizzell; sis, Mrs. Lou
Bell.(25 Dec 1924 HCI)
RICHARD LEDBETTER, son of Rev. B.T. Ledbetter,
d. last week. (25 Dec 1924 HCI)
ROSE SHELTER VOLKERT, dau of Anthony & Elizbeth
Shelter, b. 09 Nov 1872, Hardin Co. ILL., d. 16
Dec 1924; m.John Volkert, son of Anthony &
Regius Volkert, 12 Nov 1894; issue: Joseph A.
(d. at 5 mo), Charles F. & Salome Elizabeth
Volkert. (25 Dec 1924 HCI)
MRS. BEN LAVANDER, d. last week; dau, Della;
son, Wiley Lavander. (25 Dec 1924 HCI)
CHARLES GRANDERSON COVINGTON, son of Alfred &
Mary Covington, b. Briensburg, Marshall Co. Ky.
02 May 1852, d.11 Dec 1924; m.Jennie Simpson;
issue: Pearl White, Charles G., Alfred G., Mary
Taylor, Beulah Taylor, Ruth Cosby, J. Hubert,
Esther Barger; bro, John R. Covington, Loyd
Covington. (25 Dec 1924 HCI)
Mrs. H. A. FERRELL, d. Mon; issue: 5, Ruby
Ferrell(dau).(Jan 1925 HCI)
NORA GERHARDT, dau of Henry & Adelia Gerhardt,
b. Hardin Co.ILL., 24 Nov 1888; m. Allen King;
issue: Ruby King; m. 2nd, Henry A. Ferrell;
issue: 5.(15 Jan 1925 HCI)
REBECCA J. REAK, b. 19 Mar 1842, Knoxville,
Tenn., d. 30 Dec 1924; m. Matthew Reak, 29 Nov
1860 (Civil War vet); relatives: W.E. Reak, Roy
Reak, J.D. Reak, Mrs. Tena Foster, Mrs. Janie
Schnell, Mrs. Anna Hayes, Thomas Reak, & Mrs.
Hulda Younger.(15 Jan 1925 HCI)
James W. Lynch, son of Collins Lynch, b. 04
Sept 1904 Gallatin Co., ILL., d.13 Jan 1925; m.
Maude Amsden; leaves wife, parents, 4 bros, & 2
sis. (22 Jan 1925 HCI)
J.B. COWSERT, b. Hardin Co., 06 Aug 1845, d.
12 Jan 1925; m. Lydia Twitchell, 02 Aug 1865
(who d. 20 Oct 1900); issue:9; m. 2nd, Nancy
Cowsert, 26 Jul 1903; 4 bros, 3 sis.(22 Jan
1925 HCI)
PHILIP J. VINYARD, son of Henry & Pinkneyette
Vinyard, b. Hardin Co., b. 08 Mar 1870, d.
Butte, Montana, 13 Dec 1924; m. Sadie
Christenson 1890; issue: 2.(29 Jan 1925 HCI)

ERNEST VINYARD, son of Elmer & Daisy Vinyard, b. 17 Sept 1915, d.29 Jan 1925.(05 Feb 1925 HCI)
SUSAN A. RILEY, b. abt 1829, d. 11 Feb 1925; dau, Mrs. J.R. Palmer.(12 Feb 1925 HCI)
ALFRED SHOWALTERS, Civil War vet, d. Fri; leaves wife & children. (19 Mar 1925 HCI)
BETTY TERR, dau of Curtis ? Terr, b. Crittenden Co., Ky, 25 May 1906, d. 27 Mar 1925 leaves mother, 3 bros, 2 sis.(02 Apr 1925 HCI)
S.A. RILEY, b. Jasper, Tenn., 24 Nov 1828, d. 11 Feb 1925; m. 1st, Asa Foster, 01 Aug 1848; (He d. 9 Nov 1872); issue: Horace Foster, Mary Palmer, & Jodie Palmer; m. 2nd, A.B. Riley, 05 Feb 1874.(He d. 27 Sept 1906)(29 Feb 1925 HCI)
MARTIN MADISON SMOCK, b. Ark, 13 Sept 1836; d. 24 Mar 1925; m. Vina Holleman,04 Aug 1859 (She d. 26 Apr 1898);issue: 10, 4 survive, Henry, John, Bert Smock,& Mary Shelter; Martin served in Civil War, Co. C,48 Ill.(02 Apr 1925 HCI)
MILLARD LEDBETTER, d. Mon, son of James Ledbetter. (23 Apr 1925 HCI)
LILLIE MAY WALKER, dau of Com Walker, b. 02 May 1907, d.11 Apr 1925; m. Howard Derringer, 23 Oct 1925; leaves parents, 2 sis, 4 bros. (23 Apr 1925 HCI)
OPAL OXFORD, dau of Maude Burkhart, b. Cave-in-Rock, Hardin Co., ILL., 11 Apr 1902, d.17 Mar 1925.(23 Apr 1925 HCI)
CHARLES MILLARD LEDBETTER, son of James A.& Dora Ledbetter, b. Elizabethtown, ILL.,07 Sept 1880, d. 20 Apr 1925. m. Lou Lane; 2nd, m. Mae Gregory, 10 Feb 1905. (30 Apr 1925 HCI)
W.J.J. PARIS, b. Crittenden Co., Ky. 27 Apr 1850; m. Elizabeth Lee, 06 Apr 1875 (she was b. Lincoln Co. Tenn, 1856);issue: sons, J.E, A.D., A.G. Paris; daus, Mrs. F.E. Scott, Mrs. C.F. La Grande. (30 Apr 1925 HCI)
ELSIE ROSE, dau of Wiley Rose, b. Saline Co., ILL., 15 Dec 1905, d. 31 Mar 1925; m. Cecil Walker, 09 Sept 1923; leaves, parents, 2 bros, & 5 sis. (30 Apr 1925 HCI)
JUDITH C. MATTINGLEY, dau of Zachary & Judith Mattingley, b. Saline Co., Jan 1841, d. 14 Apr 1925; m. 1st, James Cummings (d.1856);issue: John Cummings; m. 2nd, William Sheldon 1861;

issue:11, 8 survive: Judith(wife of Bill Reak), Oscar, Mary Jane (wife of George Little), Sam, Steve, Willie, Maggie (wife of Arthur Pankey). (30 Apr 1925 HCI)
MISSOURI BLOOMER PALMER, b.03 Apr 1860, d. 22 Mar 1925; m. Calvin Palmer,12 Sept 1880; issue: 5, Mrs. Oma Goble(d. 1923), Mrs. Josie McFall. (30 Apr 1925 HCI)
MARY F. WINDERS, d. Cal, 08 Apr 1925, wid of H.M Winders; daus, Mrs. Morris T. Price,& Mrs. B.P. Weaver. (07 May 1925 HCI)
ORANGE WHITEHEAD, b. Elizabethtown, Hardin Co., ILL.,04 Aug 1887, d. 12 May 1925;leaves wife (Eve), father, stepmother,& 3 bros.(24 May 1925 HCI)
S. GRANT PATTON, son of Samuel & Hannah Patton, b. 27 Feb 1864, d.17 May 1925; m. Alice Treece, 1883; issue: 5; m. 2nd, Mary J. Oxford 1897; issue: 3; leaves 2 sis. (28 May 1925 HCI)
BILL MOORE, b.19 Aug 1844; sons, J.H. Moore, & Charlie; dau, Mrs. J.O. Vinyard, g. dau, Mrs. Charles Jerrells.(28 May 1925 HCI)
TOM SMOCK, served in Civil War; sons, J.W. Smock,(b. abt 1844) & Robert Smock; dau, Mrs. Noah Hurford,(half sis to J. W. Smock) (28 May 1925 HCI)
JOHN TURNER, buried 14 May 1925; son, Edd Turner. (28 May 1925 HCI)
GRANT PATTON, son of Samuel S. & Hannah Patton, nee Oxford; d.?; leaves parents, 3 bros; sis, Rebecca Sutton,Sarah Carr, plus 2 (d.) (28 May 1925 HCI)
EVA PEARSON, dau of H. C. & Mary Pearson, b. Crawford Co., ILL., 08 May 1870, d. 26 May 1925; m. E.T. Scott, 04 Dec 1892; issue: Horatio, Maude, Kate, Edgar, J.M. and Henry E.; leaves husband, 5 sis, 2 bros.(04 Jun 1925 HCI)
MYRTLE HOLLOWAY,b. Union Co., Ky., 19 Feb 1899, m. lester Holloway, 1923; leaves mother, 3 bros,4 sis, one named Julia Grounds.(04 Jun 1925 HCI)
MARY ANN SMOCK, b. 12 Jan 1857, d.17 May 1925, m. W. N. Hurford, 1 May 1881; issue: Aaron,& Mrs. H. B. Riggs. (18 Jun 1925 HCI)
MRS. A. F. ANDERSON, dau of William Hobbs & Amanda Hobbs, nee Page; m.1st, Orin Daymore; m.

2nd, Henry Rose, divorced; m.3rd Joseph M. Anderson,(d); Issue: Alice Morgan; bros; Jeff & William Hobbs; g. son, Tristen Martin; half bros, Marion Hobbs, Dan Hobbs; half sis, Mrs. Lydia Ralph, & Mrs. Ruth Davis; stepdau, Mrs. Mollie Henry. (11 Jun 1925 HCI)
REEDIE HUFSEY, b. 23 aug 1896, d. 09 Jun 1925. (18 Jun 1925 HCI)
JACOB HOWARD PYLES, son of Austin & Katie Pyles, b. 1 Apr 1901, d. 29 May 1925; leaves parents, 4 bro, 1 sis. (18 Jun 1925 HCI)
FRANKIE MCBEE, b. 24 Feb 1905, d. 11 Jun 1925; leaves parents,5 bros,sis,1 dau.(18 Jun 1925 HCI)
ELIZABETH GENTRY, dau of Alexander & Lutitia Gentry, b. Hardin Co. ILL., 18 Mar 1857, d. 29 Mar 1925; m. Wayne Mcdowell, 27 Dec 1875, Hardin Co., ILL.,; (he d. 02 May 1913), issue: Mrs, Nora Douglas, Walter, George Potter (d. 15 Jan 1892), Mrs. Dora---? Perry, Nannie (d. 12 Sept 1897), Wayne, Kell, Mrs. Ida Angelton, & inf son,(d.);bro, John J.Gentry; sis, Mary Locke, Sarah Smith,& Ida b. Clement (25 Jun 1925 HCI)
BONNIE WATSON, 25 yrs old, & Herbert Watson, 19 yrs old drowned in Ohio River.(25 Jun &02 Jul 1925 HCI)
ERMINE JACKSON, b. Elizabethtown, 02 Jun 1904, d. 12 Jun 1925. (02 Jul 1925 HCI)
JOHN W. MILES, b. Covington, Ky., 22 Mar 1847, d, 01 Jul 1925; served Civil War, Co, C. 48 ILL. (09 Jul 1925 HCI)
MRS. THOMAS BAUGHER, d. Sun; son, John Baugher; dau, Mrs. Lawrence Oxford. (09 Jul 1925 HCI).
LLOYD SPEES, d. Okla.; wife, Mollie Ginger, dau of C.E. Ginger. (09 Jul 1925 HCI)
GEORGE FRANKLIN SMITH, son of Charlie & Anna Smith, b. 02 Oct 1898, d. 13 Jul 1925; m. Elsie Lester, 25 Mar 1925. (30 Jul 1925 HCI)
ROBERT LLOYD SPEES, son of Bon Spees, b. 14 Jun 1894, d. 03 Jul 1925; m. Mollie Ginger, 11 Nov 1922; leaves parents, 1 bro,& 3 sis.(06 Aug 1925 HCI)
CHARLES JACKSON, b. Hardin Co. ILL., d. El Reno, Okla., 25 Jul 1925. (06 Aug 1925 HCI)
CHARLES MARION JACKSON, son of William and

Bathsheba Jackson, b. 8 Apr 1851, Hardin Co., ILL., d. 25 Jul 1925; m. Etheinda Gaskill, 24 30 Dec 1869; (she d 24 Nov 1913); issue: E.R. Jackson, Mrs. J.C. Peterson, Mrs. C.G. Baldwin, Mina and Daisy Jackson. (13 Aug 1925 HCI)
MARY C. MOYERS, b. Crittenden, Ky., 19 Sept 1852, 22 Aug 1925; m. William Moyers; issue: 6, Finias, Molly, W.W., J.B., & Maggie Moyers. (27 Aug 1925 HCI)
ADOLPHUS DAVENPORT MCDONALD, b. Ringgold, Georgia, 22 Jun 1854, d. 22 Aug 1925, Ind.; m. Elia ? Hanna, 2 Sep 1885; issue: Katherine & Maude McDonald.(10 Sept 1925 HCI)
JOE HOLBROOK, d. last week; served in Civil War. (17 Sep 1925 HCI)
ISSAC HOBBS, d. last week; m. 1st, Polly Daymond; issue 7; m. 5; total of 15 ? children. (17 Sept 1925 HCI)
LAFAYETTE MOORE, b, Ky; d., at abt 101 yrs of age. (24 Sept 1925 HCI)
MARY LOVE, nee Ashford, b. 19 Oct 1850, d. 06 Sept 1925; m. Allen E. Love, Elizabethtown, ILL., 15 Oct 1874; issue: Martha Susan (who m. Charles Vinyard);she d. 01 Sept 1916), John Allen, Sylvester Britton, James Thomas, Marion Joel (d.Jan 1908), Ollie Clifton (d. inf), Loren Webster, & William Clarence Love.(17 Sept 1925 HCI)
JOSEPH HOLBROOK, b. Hardin Co. ILL., 04 Sept 1842, d. 9 Sept 1925; m. Katie Tolbert (d. 31 Jul 1897): issue: 7, 1 survives; m. 2nd, Mrs Della Rose, 30 Sept 1930; issue: 6, 4 survive; bro, Samuel Holbrook; Joseph served Co. C, 48 ILL., Civil War. (01 Oct 1925 HCI)
LAURA CROWELL, dau of John & Mary Crowell, b. 19 Aug 1880, d. Sept 1925; m. Ira Littrell, 25 Aug 1903; issue: Charles, Willis, Joe, Vernon, & Wilma (male); leaves parents, 2 bros,& 4 sis. (01 Oct 1925 HCI).
JIM LOWERY, b. Hardin Co. ILL., d. Abliene, Texas, 19 Sept 1925; m. Elizabeth -----; issue: Walter, Mary Thom, Edith Ballanger, Frank, Mrs. Frank Olney, and George Lowery; half bro, John L. Lowery, and half sis, Mrs. T. Thornton. (08 Oct 1925 HCI)
HARRY PETERSON,b. Hardin Co.,30 Jan 1896, d.

--; m. Fannie Jane Porter, 25 Dec 1919; issue: Robert Herald Patterson; leaves parents, sis, 3 bros. (8 Oct 1925 HCI)
MRS. HARVE SUITS, dau of Wilmer Oxford, d.(22 Oct 1925 HCI)
AMY OXFORD, dau of Wilmer & Harriet Oxford, b. 7 Jul 1899, d. 15 Oct 1925; m. Harvey Suits, 4 Jul 1918; issue: 2; leaves parents, 6 sis. (29 Oct 1925 HCI)
MICKEY HUGHES, son of William & Mary Hughes, b Weston, Ky., 2 Mar 1898, d. 26 Sept 1925; m. Nelle Isham, 22 Sept 1916; issue: son; leaves wife, mother, sis and bro. (29 Oct 1925 HCI)
RUBY MCFALL, dau of James & Jessie McFall, abt 15 yrs old, d. 12 Oct 1925.(29 Oct 1925 HCI)
MARGARET A. CULLISON, nee Porter, b. 1835, d. 18 Oct 1925; m. 1st James Scarebrough; issue: 1; m. 2nd, James Cullison;issue: Mrs. Georgiana Bascom, Mrs. Tryphene Wingate, & Mrs. Saloma Rose. (29 Oct 1925 HCI)
C.D.M. RENFRO, son of Judge J.H.B. Renfro,& wife, nee McClellan, d. Carbondale, ILL., leaves wife; son, Francis; bro, R.E. Renfro; & half bro, Lacey Renfro. (05 Nov 1925 HCI)
MRS. ANNIE PERNELL, b. 03 Sept 1891, d. 24 Oct 1925; m. James Pernell,1912;issue:2.(12 Nov 1925 HCI)
CHARLES WESTON, b. 01 Apr 1843*, d. 24 Oct 1925; dau, Daisy Leonberger.(12 Nov 1925 HCI)
GERTRUDE LEDBETTER,wife of George Ledbetter, d.03 Nov 1925;dau,Ora Ledbetter.(12 Nov 1925 HCI)
LAURA PEARL JOINER, dau of John & Laura Joiner, b. 21 Oct 1904; d.30 Oct 1925; m. Dewey Baldwin, 22 May 1922; issue: Vern & inf,(d). (12 Nov 1925 HCI)
WILLIAM PRUETT, b. abt 1851, d. 14 Nov 1925; m.--; issue: 4, Hattie & Julius Pruitt survive. (19 Nov 1925 HCI)
ALMA CHARLENE LAGODZINSKI, dau of Joe & Mollie Lagodzinski, b. Hardin Co. ILL., 13 Nov 1913, d. 31 Oct 1925. (26 Nov 1925 HCI)
JAMES OXFORD, 6 sons and 2 daus migrated to ILL., from N.C. abt 1836 along with John W. Oxford, a half bro; James Oxford's sons: Morgan, Elias, James R., Elihu, Samuel C.,&

Isaac Newton, plus 2 dau unnamed; John Oxford's son: Albert Oxford had sons, Clem & Lawrence Oxford.(bio sketch). (17 Dec 1925 HCI)
CHARLES W. WESTON, son of Henry & Sarah Weston, b. Kent Co., England, 11 Apr 1844, d. 03 Nov 1925, Dorrisville, ILL.; m. Margaret Jane Rose, (d. 13 Jul 1902): issue: Lillie Slye, Sarah Twitchell, Charles F., Daisy Leonberger, Ella Ashford, Katherine Weston, son d. at 5 yrs; bro, Thomas Weston; uncle, Frederick Weston. (24 Dec 1925 HCI)
EARL EMERSON SMITH, son of Edward Smith, b. 27 Mar 1918 d. 24 Nov 1925; leaves parents, 2 sis. (7 Jan 1926 HCI)
JOHN P. HOWARD, b. Rosiclare,ILL., 27 Feb 1870, d. 28 Dec 1925; m. Lydia Knight, 04 Apr 1894; issue: Lawrence A., John R., Glenn, Mrs. Jennie Porter, & 1(d); leaves 4 bros. (7 Jan 1926 HCI)
W.L. THOMPSON, b. Ky 24 Nov 1853, d. 13 Jan 1926; m. Mary A. Trimble, 12 Jan 1888; m. 2nd, Lula Lee, 1 Oct 1902; issue: son; leaves sis and half sis. (21 Jan 1926 HCI)
MRS. LOREN VINYARD, nee Shutt; leaves husband & 4 children. (21 Jan 1926 HCI)
JACOB DUNCAN, b. Ky., 29 Nov 1859, d. 28 Jan 1926; m. Josie ---; issue; Mabel Po_ey ? William Duncan; bro,Offa Duncan.(04 Feb 1926 HCI).
CHARLES JESSE ASBELL,b.Pope Co.,ILL.,28 Mar 1887, d. 24 Dec 1925; m. Mary L.Smith, 04 Feb 1911; leaves wife, father,& half sis.(04 Feb 1926 HCI)
THOMAS LEWIS, b. 03 Jul 1859, d.19 Jan 1926; son, Henry Lewis. (04 Feb 1926 HCI)
JOHN H. FERRELL, b. Hardin Co., 29 Oct 1860, d. 09 Feb 1926; m. Sallie R. Williams, 19 Aug 1883; issue: Clifford & Bert Ferrell; leaves wife, 8 bros, & 4 sis; note, John H. Ferrell was son of Joseph Ferrell & Elizabeth Ladd.(18 Feb 1926 HCI)
DR. FRANCIS FOWLER, d. 08 Jul 1925, m. Josie Vinyard, dau of John Vinyard, 29 Aug 1889; issue; none survive; bro, H. Robert Fowler, (d. 05 Jan 1926, m. Mary Griffith, sis of A.S. Griffith, issue: Roberta Fowler, wife of R.V. Willis; bros, Newton M. Fowler (d. 07 Mar

1894), John C & Joe A. Fowler.(18 Feb 1926 HCI)
JOHN L. FRITTS, b. Rome, Co., Tenn, 05 Oct 1850, d. 04 Feb 1926; m. Bettie Ginger, dau of D.V. Ginger, 1871; issue: Mrs. George Septer, William, George, & Mrs. Clyde Duvall; bro, S.L. Fritts & sis, Mrs. J.A. Clark.(18 Feb 1926 HCI)
LEWIS VINYARD, d. last week, son of Elmer Vinyard; served in Co., C, 48 Ill., Civil War. (18 Feb 1926 HCI)
OFFA DUNCAN d. 20 Feb 1926. (18 Feb 1926 HCI)
CHARLES VINYARD, son of John Vinyard, d. Paducah, Ky., last week; sis, Mrs. Dr. Fowler; 4 sons, 1 dau. (04 Mar 1926 HCI)
LEWIS ALLEN VINYARD, son of George and Alice Vinyard, b. 04 Aug 1844, d. 18 Feb 1926; m. Mrs. Lucretia Gullett (mother of J. G. Gullett), 27 Feb 1870;issue: Rachel(d), Elmer E.,& Lora Hughs. (04 Mar 1926 HCI)
CHARLES VINYARD, son of Dr. John Vinyard, b. Pleasant Hill, Hardin Co. ILL., 08 Jun 1865, d. 23 Feb 1926; m. Mollie Page Feb 1887; issue: Hosie, Edward, Nate, Mrs. W.H. Birch, Howard (d), Mrs. Bessie Ewards; bro, W.H. Vinyard; sis, Mary Jenkins, Mrs. John Hubbard, Mrs. F.M. Fowler & Mrs. A.A. Gustin.(04 & 11 Mar 1926 HCI)
JOHN OLDHAM, d. last week; served in Civil War. (11 Mar 1926 HCI)
NANCY HOBBS, dau of Marsh Angleton, d. last week; m. --- Hobbs; bro, Isaac Hobbs; sis, Mrs. A.F. Anderson. (11 Mar 1926 HCI)
MARTHA FRANCES O'HARA, dau of Samuel Ray, b. Jackson Co., Tenn., 08 Apr 1850; m. William O'Hara, 06 Apr 1873; issue: 9, 5 survive, Maude Renfro, Laura Rushing, Sadie Bramlett, Nora Heri, Lillie Sheldon; bros, Logan & John Ray. (18 Mar 1926 HCI)
LOREN LESTER SHELDON, son of M.L. Sheldon, b. Hardin Co. ILL., 26 Nov 1886, d. 11 Mar 1926; m. Lillie O' Hara, 16 Mar 1910;issue: Katherine Sheldon; leaves wife, parents; bros: Alsworth, Clyde, & John Sheldon, & sis,Alice Cummings. (18 Mar 1926 HCI)
MATTIE J. WOLRAB, dau of John & Elizabeth Wolrab, b. Hardin Co. ILL., 13 Oct 1859, d.16 Mar 1926; m. John C. Oxford, 13 Oct 1886;issue:

Grover (d), Paul (d), Owen S.; sis, Maggie Lambert (d.1887), Mary Kenney & Clara Giintert; bro (d. inf). (18 Mar 1926 HCI)
ELIZABETH WILLIAMS, b. abt 1846, d.1926; sons: John, George,& Pete Williams. (18 Mar 1926 HCI)
ELIZABETH FERRELL, b. 25 Aug 1844, d.18 Mar 1926; m. John N. Williams, 1870;issue: John, George & Pete williams; bro, Pernett Ferrell. (01 Apr 1926 HCI)
MARY ANN THORNTON, 84th birthday, 27 Mar 1926; daus, Rebecca Aaron, & Ida Shearer; son, J. A. Thornton. (01 Apr 1926 HCI)
MARTHA SMOCK, dau of Cornellus & Sarah Smock, b. Hardin Co. ILL., 01 Dec 1860, d. 03 Mar 1926; m. W. L. Davis, 11 Nov 1879; issue; Nora(d), Lizzie(d); sons, T.A. & Edgar Davis (08 Apr 1926 HCI)
ALLEN HOBBS, son of Ezekial Hobbs, b. Hardin Co. ILL., 02 Mar 1882, d. 21 Mar 1926; m. Hannah A. Miller; issue: Luther, Oral, Thelma, Violet, Vernon, Eula, Marjorie, & Aline Hobbs; bros, Solomon, Elmer, & Andrew Hobbs; sis, Mrs. Julie Hardin, & Mrs. Fannie Vaughn. (08 Apr 1926 HCI)
----REINER, dau of John Reiner, d. last wk; m. J.E. Isham, son of J.M. Isham. (08 Apr 1926 HCI) DR. J. A. HART, b. Pope Co. ILL., abt 1859, d. 13 Apr 1926; leaves wife, 2 daus, 2 sons. (15 Apr 1926 HCI)
JAMES SMITH, Civil War vet, d. last Tues; dau, Mrs. Claude Martin. (15 Apr 1926 HCI).
JIM DAVIS, b. abt 1846, d. last week; served in Civil War.(22 Apr 1926 HCI)
MARY E. VINYARD, dau of John & Eliza Vinyard, b. Hardin Co. ILL., 04 Dec 1846, d. 15 Mar 1926; m. Mathew Jenkins, 04 Oct 1873;issue: John, C.A.W., Clarence, Alice, Mrs. William Patterson, Mrs. J.J. Leigh, Chalon (d. male), & Inf,(d.); leaves 1 bro, & 3 sis. (15 Apr 1926 HCI)
PINKNEY MCFARLAND, dau of William Pinkney & Druailla Morris McFarland, b.08 Jan 1850; m. Henry Vinyard, 03 Mar 1869;issue: Loyd C., William P., Mrs. J.J. Schyett, Mrs. Charles Christensen, Mrs. Albert Luster, Mrs. W.R. Ledbetter, & 6 (d.); half sis, Mrs. John

Johnson; B.P. McFarland, bro of William Pinkney Mcfarland. (15 Apr 1926 HCI)
WILIAM RALPH, son of John Ralph, b. Hardin Co., 18 Sept 1874, d. 30 Mar 1926; m. Mrs. Lydia Patton, 2 Nov 1907; issue:2.(08 Apr & 13 May 1926 HCI)
S.G. PATTON, b. 27 Feb 1864, d. 17 May 1925. (13 May 1926 HCI)
ASBERRY MCFALL, b. Tenn., 09 Sept 1850, d. 21 May 1926; m. Eliza Bruntly, 1873 (she d. 03 Dec 1896); issue: Fleety Price, John, George, James McFall, & Mollie Birch.(03 Jun 1926 HCI)
WILLIAM PATTERSON, b. Mayfield, Ky., 20 Dec 1853; m. Rebecca Smith, dau of Reddick & Mary A. Smith; issue: James & John Patterson.(03 Jun 1926 HCI)
JOHN L. SMITH, b. 20 Jul 1851, d. 21 May 1926; m. Anna Moore; issue: Nellie Goodrich, Harry Smith, Bursie Buckhanon, & Mrs. Pearl Owen.(03 Jun 1926 HCI)
F.L. DAVIS, b.20 Aug 1871, d. 24 Mar 1926; dau ?, Zena Davis.(01 & 22 Apr & 10 Jun 1926 HCI)
JAMES OLLIE MCDOWELL, son of James McDowell, b. Carrsville. Ky, 01 Jun 1892, d. 03 Jun 1926; m. Maude Isham, 25 Jul 1915; issue: 6, 5 survive; leaves wife, father, 5 bros, & 2 sis. (17 Jun 1926 HCI)
JAMES F. SMITH, b. Union Co., Ky., 01 Feb 1843, d. 07 Apr 1926; m. Anna Keeses, 04 Dec 1868; issue: 11, Mrs. Sudie Hurford, Charles, Edward, Mrs. Claudie Martin, Mrs. Maude, Olive Ball, & Roscoe Smith; Civil War vet (17 Jun 1926 HCI)
MALINDA JOSEPHINE PATTERSON, dau of William Groves, b. Hardin Co. ILL.,05 Oct 1855, d.08 Jun 1926; m. Norman Patterson, 16 Feb 1863 (He d. 13 Jul 1907);issue: William & Ishmael Patterson. (24 Jun 1926 HCI)
FREDRICK DONATHAN SR., 91st birthday, 27 Jun 1926; dau, Mrs. Ollie Story. (01 Jul 1926 HCI)
SARAH STACEY, b. Hardin Co. ILL., 05 Dec 1866, d. 04 Jul 1926; m. William Maple, Nov 1887.(15 Jul 1926 HCI)
JANE LOWERY, dau of A.L. & Daisy Douglas, b. Hardin Co. ILL., Feb 1866, d. 29 Jun 1926; m. E. Thornton, son of John & Augustus Thornton; Hardin Co., 13 Aug 1881; issue: Henry &

Clifford Thornton. (15 Jul 1926 HCI)
CHARLES L. DOUGLAS, b. near Cave-in-Rock, Hardin Co. ILL., 31 Mar 1904, d. 02 Apr 1926; leaves father, sis, 2 stepsis,& stepmother. (22 Jul 1926 HCI)
MARY KENNEDY, wid of Scott Kennedy, dau of J. C. Wolrab; issue: Mrs. Milas Ferrell, Grace Kennedy, Fred & Harry Kennedy; sis, Mattie Oxford, & Clara Giintert. (22 Jul 1926 HCI)
D. ALLEN LEDBETTER, son of Dr. Ledbetter, b. Hardin Co. ILL., 12 Jan 1851, d. 26 Jul 1926; m. Mary Oxford, dau of Elihu Oxford; m. 2nd, ----Morris;issue: Bunk Ledbeter; m. 3rd, Sarah J. Gullett, dau of Pomp Gullett;issue; Della, Ollie, Robert, Adrain, Emma, Ray & James Ledbetter. (05 Aug 1926 HCI)
CHARLES F.LAMAR, son of Luther Lamar, b. Rosiclare, Hardin Co. ILL., 24 Aug 1893, d. 26 Jul 1926; m. Verda Hoffner, 22 Oct 1920; issue: son (d); mother, Sula Lamar; sis, Mrs. R.C. Meisenheimer, Mrs. Marie Adams, Mrs. Arne Karraker; bros, Edd Lamar & Roy Lamar (half bro) & Anna Hurford, half sis.(12 Aug 1926 HCI)
JOHN H. OXFORD, son of J.A. Oxford, b. Hardin Co. ILL., abt 1876, d. Oakland City, Ind., 12 Aug 1926; leaves, father, stepmother; bros, Cecil & Fowler Oxford. (19 Aug 1926 HCI)
ELSIE TUCKER, dau of W.M. Tucker, b. 23 Sept 1908, d. 10 Aug 1926. (19 Aug 1926 HCI)
THJOMAS J. SMITH, son of Isaac & Mary Smith, b. Elizabethtown, Hardin Co. ILL., 08 Apr 1870, d. 23 Aug 1926; m. Mrs. Della Foster, 08 Jan 1901; stepsons, Grover & Owen Foster; bros, Henry & Charles Smith; sis, Mrs. Serens Spivey. (02 Sept 1926 HCI)
MARY CORNELIUS DAVIS, b. 19 Jul 1898, Hardin Co., ILL., d. 27 Aug 1926; m. Olin Talmadge Davis; issue: Mary Virginia & Olen Davis Jr. (09 Sept 1926 HCI)
AMANDA RIGGS, b. 2 Feb 1848, d. 20 Jul 1926; m. Robert Fraily, 12 Dec 1875; issue; Oscar(d), Charles, Mrs. Media Rose, Mrs. Ella Vaughn, Anna Foster, Elva Garland, John & Joseph Frailey. (09 Sept 1926 HCI)
MRS. HENRY GERHARDT, d. 11 Sept 1926. (09 Sept 1926 HCI)

CHRISTINIA HERMANN, 86th birthday,19 Sept 1926. (23 Sept 1926 HCI)
JAMES A. LEDBETTER, 50th wedding anniversary, 17 Sept 1926. (30 Sept 1926 HCI)
W. M. ENSLOW, 50th wedding anniversary, 12 Sept 1926. (30 Sept 1926 HCI)
A.S. GRIFFITH, son of James & Catherine Griffith, b. Spencer, Co., Ind., 6 Jun 1850, d. 29 Aug 1926; m. Sarah Esther Miller, 03 Nov 1888; issue: Maude (m. Charles Suits), Claude, Leniel (m. George Edwards), Paul, Golda (m. Edgar Davis, Alice (m. Earl Austin); sis, Tula Baldwin, Mary Fowler,& Edwinna Warford. (23 Sept 1926 HCI)
ADELIA PATTERSON GERHARDT, b. 4 Jan 1858, d. 11 Sep 1926; m. Henry Gerhardt, 21 Mar 1883; issue: 7, 5 survive; dau, Nora Ferrell, d. 5 Jan 1925. (30 Sept 1926 HCI)
JOHN POTTS, son of Edd Potts, b. 02 Mar 1908, d. 30 Sept 1926. (14 Oct 1926 HCI)
SARA ROSETTA LAXTON, b. Jackson Co., Tenn., 21 Oct 1857, d. 9 Oct 1926; m. James W. Spivey, 25 Aug 1873; issue: 6, 3 survive, Maggie Joiner, Rosa Swaggart, & Howard Spivey; 2 sis, 2 bros. (14 Oct 1926 HCI)
JAMES C. MILLIKAN, Fredonia Ky., 14 Nov 1867, d. 10 Oct 1926; m. Nora Hoskinson, 1890; issue: 3, 1 living, Robert Millikan.(22 Oct 1926 HCI)
WILLIAM GROSS, son of Jacob & Barbara Gross, b. 1 Jun 1861, d. 9 Oct 1926; m. Lydia Decker, 9 Dec 1888; issue: Edith Joyner, Ethel Joyner, Orval, Barbara Betts, Sylvia Leonberger, Blanch Clifton, Orin, Anna, & Olivia Gross. (21 Oct 1926 HCI)
RUTH ENOCH, dau of Millard and Belle Enoch, b. Crittenden Co., Ky., 1900, d. 31 Jul 1926; m. Burnett Belt, 14 Apr 1918; issue: Thomas Burnett & Robert Belt(d). (28 Oct 1926 HCI)
VERNON HENSON, son of Morgan Henson, b. Rosiclare, ILL., 02 Mar 1896, d. 26 Oct 1926; m. Vida Shaw Fulgham, 28 Jan 1917; bros, W.H. & John Henson; sis, Milley Hanuss, Anna Joiner, Rosa Belt, Murble Shaw, & Beula Hansen. (11 Nov 1926 HCI)
I.A. FOSTER, b. Rock Creek, Hardin Co.ILL., 04 Oct 1862, d. --. (09 Dec 1926 HCI)

JOHN JACOB SHEARER, b. 30 May 1851, d. 08 Nov 1926; m. Alice McDowell; issue; G. C. Shearer, & dau (d); bros, G.W. Shearer, plus 1 unnamed; 1 half sis. (16 Dec 1926 HCI)
EMMA MARTIN WILLIAMS, b. Hardin Co. ILL., 09 Feb 1876; m. Elijah Williams, 20 Mar 1901; issue; Roena Barger, Ethel Cummings, Dan, Heloise, Travis, & Louise Williams; 2 sis, 1 bro. (23 Dec 1926 HCI)
J. W. NASH, age 47, d. Mon; children: Gladys, Lottie, Mabel, Eva Lee, & Ecalyn (twins), Vernon, Theodore, Elton Nash; sis, Mrs. H.E. Hargett & Mrs. Fred Whal; bros, George Locke & C.H. Nash; stepfather. W.W. Locke. (23 Dec 1926 HCI)
GEORGE WINTERS, son of Daniel Winters, b. abt 1860, d.---. (30 Dec 1926 HCI)
VIRGINIUS FRAYSER, b. Ford's Ferry, Ky., 27 Feb 1847, d. 30 Nov 1926; m. Ellen Mitchell, dau of John Mitchell; issue: John, Lenard, Angie (d), Herbert, Robert, Ross; m. 2nd, Nancy Cronkrite, 11 Sept 1911. (13 Jan 1927 HCI)
REV. D. ALLEN LEDBETTER, b. Hardin Co. ILL., 12 Jan 1851, d. 26 Jul 1926; issue: Bob, Adrain, Emma, Ray, & Pompey. (20 Jan 1927 HCI)
DANIEL LAWRENCE, b. abt. 1849, d. Golconda, ILL; bro, Abram Lawrence; nephew, Clyde Vinyard; bro-in-law, W.R. Martin. (20 Jan 1927 HCI)
INDIA GINGER, dau of D.V. Ginger; m. Issac N. Oxford;issue: Grace, Aaron; m.2nd, Allen Bernard;m.3rd, Frank Hardesty.(20 Jan 1927 HCI)
SARAH BURNS GREEN, b. Scott Co., Mo.,13 Aug 1842; m. Isaac Green; issue: Lela Hobbs, James, Mrs. Jesse Lowery, Martha Bishop, & W.C. Green. (27 JAN 1927 HCI)
HENRY "BOOZE," FERRELL, son of Joseph Ferrell, d. last week; bros, Edd and Milas Ferrell. (27 Jan 1927 HCI)
GIDEON B. MAHAN, b. Tenn., 29 Jul 1847, d.11 Jan 1927; m. Nancy Ann Severs, 04 Oct 1866 (She d 25 Jan 1896); issue: William, Alexander, Charley(d), John, Gideon, Thomas(d), Harvey J., Nancy Ann(d), Ben A. (d), Samuel A. & Ancen L. Mahan; m. 2nd, Ollie Caldwell (who d. 27 Aug 1903); issue: 1 dau,(d); m. 3rd, Elizabeth

Ledbetter, 23 Jan 1906; bro, Isaac Mahan.(27 Jan 1927 HCI)
HARRY F. SNOW, b. Lola, Ky, 23 Mar 1901, d. 17 Jan 1927; sis, Mayme McDonald; bro, Henry, Allen, & Vernon Snow. (27 Jan 1927 HCI)
HENRY FERRELL, b. Elizabethtown, Hardin Co., 02 Nov 1873, d, 18 Jan 1927; m. Elizabeth Lambert, 1896; dau. Mrs. Roy Johnson; bros, Edd & Milas Ferrell. (03 Feb 1927 HCI)
ELIAS OXFORD, b. abt 1820, d. 04 Jul 1862. (27 Jan & 3 Feb 1927 HCI)
MRS. LOU EDMONDS, b. Posey Co., Ind., 16 Jun 1862, d. 27 Jan 1927; m. John G. Hathorn; issue: Maude Vinyard, Lena Peterson, Goldie Joiner, Ethel Newton, Myrtle Yates, J. W. Hathorn, plus, 2 (d.). (17 Feb 1927 HCI)
NANCY J. MOTT, b. 23 Mar 1824, d. 28 Jan 1927; m. Charles Bloomer; issue: 3, 1 survives, Lillie Mott; 2nd, m. John Mott; issue: Ada (d), Gracie, Clifford, Millard, Gertie, Robert, & Myrtle. (17 Feb 1927 HCI)
DICK FRAILY, d. 10 Feb 1927; m. Mary---, 1865; served in Civil War. (17 Feb 1927 HCI)
CHARLES E. GINGER, son of John F. Ginger, b. 13 Jan 1876, d. 24 Feb 1927; m. Laura Foster, dau of Horace Foster;issue: dau, Ollie; m. 2nd, Lizzie Smith, dau of John & Jane Smith; issue: Clifford, Mollie, Riley, Hettie Ferrell,Maxene, John, Orveta Ginger. (10 Mar 1927 HCI)
WILLIAM BLACK, b. 17 Feb 1849, d. 16 Feb 1927; m. Margaret Williams, 25 Mar 1873 (she d.16 Feb); issue: Joanah, Luellar, Martha, & Samuel Black; bros, Issac & James Black; sis, Mrs. E.J. Warford (10 Mar 1927 HCI)
DORA REED, dau of James & Drusilla Herod, b. Elizabethtown, Hardin Co. ILL., 24 Jul 1860, d. 4 Mar 1927; m. James A. Ledbetter, 13 Sept 1876; issue: James H. (d. 9 Dec 1920), and Charles Ledbetter (d. 1923).(10 Mar 1927 HCI)
SAMUEL OWEN SHERIDAN, son of James & Elizabeth Sheridan, b. Crossville, ILL., 2 Apr 1853; m. Maggie Bennett, 13 Feb 1890; issue: Oasis (dau, d. inf) Edith (wife of Clarence Fleener), Eona (wife of Millard Smith), Myrtle (wife of Henry Keller), Owen Sheridan; m. 2nd, Rose Wilkerson; issue: Ruth (wife of Morris Grant), Eugene, &

Francis. (17 Mar 1927 HCI)
MRS. JAMES GOINS, dau of Henry Gerhardt; m.
James Goins, 1888; issue: Minnie Aldridge, Mary
Cowgill, Edna Waggoner, Frank, Luke, George,
Amiel Goins, Joseph,(d.), plus inf son, (d.)
(17 Mar 1927 HCI)
VITTRICE SINGHI, dau of F.A.D. Singhi, b.
Rockland, Maine, 8 Oct 1842, d. 21 Mar 1927; m.
A.B. Thomas, 26 Nov 1869. (24 Mar 1927 HCI)
JOHN SCROLL, son of George Schroll, b. 15 Feb
1869, d. 02 Mar 1927; m. Mary Reiner, 22 Sept
1889; issue: Freeman, Wayne, Essie, Gertie
Winters(d.), and Effie Vinyard,(d.); leaves bro
& sis. (24 Mar 1927 HCI)
MARGARET GRACE, b. 13 Apr 1850; m. Benjamin F.
Hall, 1874; issue: Nicholas (m.-- Lane), Jessie
(m. Charles Rogers), Wittie (m. John Rogers).
(24 Mar 1927 HCI)
CYNTHIA WOMACK, dau of W.W. Womack, b. Hardin
Co. ILL., 14 Jul 1858*, d. 25 Mar 1927; m.
Marion W. William, (d. 1918); Bros: J.T., J.H.,
W.L., Dr. J.A. Womack, plus 3 bros, (d), & 4
sis, (d). (07 Apr 1927 HCI)
GEORGE HOBBS, d.--, m. Flossie Page, dau of
W.R. PAGE. (07 Apr 1927 HCI)
MALINDA KATHERINE WHITESIDE JACKSON, b.
Edwardsville, ILL., 07 Aug 1862, d. 06 Apr
1927; m. S. L. Jackson, 22 Sep 1903; sis: Mrs.
Philip Morse, Mrs. J.C. Thompson; bros: Thomas
& A.B. Whiteside; stepdaus: Roda & Thelma
Jackson. (14 Apr 1927 HCI)
LEWIS K. JOINER, b. Hardin Co. ILL., m. Sarado
Oxford, dau of Rev. E. Oxford; issue: Ivy &
Vernon Joiner. (14 Apr 1927 HCI)
J.W. FERRELL, son of James K. Polk & Betty Hill
Ferrell, b. 05 Sept 1867, d. 04 Feb 1927; m.
Belle Vinyard, 14 Apr 1895; issue: Homer(d.),
Bert (d.) Randall(d.), Eunice, Ralph, Nolan,
Gladys, Ural; bros: Charles, Arnold, Grover,
Vernon, & Evert; sis: Julia Cox, Nora Milligan.
(21 Apr 1927 HCI)
JOHN J. LEDBETTER, son of John T. Ledbetter,
b. Hardin Co. ILL., abt 1867, d. ---; issue:
Alvin, Jack Ledbetter, Margaret; sis, Mrs.
Ollie Dale, Mrs. Ida Sullivan, Mrs. Kate White;
bros: J.A., Quincy, Herbert Ledbetter; uncle,

Allen Ledbetter; aunts; Mary Lowery (d),& "grandma " Thornton. (21 Apr 1927 HCI)
JOSEPH COCHRAN, b. Carresville,ky., 25 Nov 1866, d. 08 Apr 1927; issue: 5; step dau, Mrs. Dan Flanery. (28 Apr 1927 HCI)
INEZ OXFORD, b. 09 Feb 1906, d. 15 Apr 1927; leaves parents,& 5 sis. (12 May 1927 HCI)
SAMUEL FRITTS, b. Crittenden Co., Ky., 10 Jun 1853, d. 26 Apr 1927; m. Mary b. Laxton; issue: Mary B. Laxton, Loren & Clarence Fritts; sis, Linda Clark. (12 May 1927 HCI)
SEBARY CASAD WATSON, b. 27 Sept 1852, d. 08 May 1927; m. Thomas S. Watson, 17 Aug 1873 (d. 23 Jul 1901);issue: James A., Harry F., Marion (d), Mabel Jackson, Florence, Gertrude Wakeham, Ethel Patton, Thomas S., Bessie Ferrell (d. Feb 1911), Bruce, Gladys Galloway; 1 bro, & 2 sis. (19 May 1927 HCI)
MARTHA J. MARTIN, b. Hardin Co., 19 Aug 1839, d. 20 Apr 1927; m. Daniel P. Martin, 20 Dec 1863; issue: 8, 3 survive. (02 Jun 1927 HCI)
MALINDA STORY WILLIAMS, b. 22 Jun 1872, d.---; m. D.W. Williams, 1898; issue; Eva Bell, Nora, Earl, Claude, Otis, dau (d); 4 bros. (26 May 1927 HCI)
MARTHA J. BALDWIN, b. 27 Sept 1848, d. 30 Apr 1927; m. Richard Palmer; issue: Wiley(d.), Mary Casad(d.), Dora Gregory(d.), Etta Tyer(d.), Mrs. Gregory;m. 2nd, Edward Baldwin (02 Jun 1927 HCI)
MIRANDA LOWERY, b. Hardin Co. ILL., 03 Jun 1866, d. 20 May 1927; m. James Lowery, 26 Apr 1885; issue: Wilburn, Henry, Marion, 2 daus(d); sis: Mrs. George; bro, James B., Omega Lowery.(23 Jun 1927 HCI).
MARY HERRMANN, b. Germany abt 1846, d. 24 Jun 1927; m. Franklin Hermann (Civil War vet), 1868; dau, Mrs. Fred Humm. (30 Jun 1927 HCI)
MALINDA STORY, dau of Thomas Story, d. 27 Apr 1927; m. D.W. Williams; issue: 6, dau, Eva Bell. Thomas Story was son of Jordon Story,& Polly Jones, dau of Jimmie Jones. (30 Jun 1927 HCI)
FRANK ZEIGLER, b. Germany, 14 Jul 1841*, d. 17 Jun 1927, m. Mary Schutt, 20 Apr 1875; issue; 8, 5 survive. (30 Jun 1927 HCI)

EDD VINYARD, son of the late Charley Vinyard, visited sis, Mrs. India Birch.(07 Jul 1927 HCI)
MORGAN OXFORD, d. last week; son, Charles Oxford. (14 Jul 1927)
ROMA AVICE FRAYSER, dau of Ross & Millie Frayser, b. 04 Aug 1917, Hardin Co. ILL., d. 30 May 1927. (14 Jul 1927 HCI)
W. M. BALL, b. Rising Sun, Ind., 17 Feb 1855, funeral, 12 Jun 1927; m. 1st, Sarah Shewmaker, (d. 1895) abt 1876 (She d. 1895);issue: 7, 6 survive; m. 2nd, Mrs. Annie Miller(d. Mar 1921) issue: 5, 4 survive; children at funeral: Walter, Myrtle, Elsie, Ruea, Orvil, Bertus, Donald. (14 Jul 1927 HCI)
LUCY ZEIGLER, nee Schutt, b. 08 Sep 1854, d. 03 Jul 1927; m. Adam Zeigler, 1874; issue: 10, 3 survive. (14 Jul 1927 HCI)
Mrs. J.W. GORE, d. last week; leaves, husband & 4 stepchildren. (28 Jul 1927 HCI)
WILL MILES, son of J.W. & Elsie Miles; m.---; issue: 3; bro, A.A. Miller; sis, Hannah Howard, Bird Carlisle; half sis, Mrs. S.E. Miller, & Mrs. Kate Hill. (28 Jul 1927 HCI)
JAMES A. ROSE, son of James H. Rose, d.---; m.---, issue: son; bros, C.A. Rose, & J.M. Rose. (11 Aug 1927 HCI)
GEORGE HOBBS, son of Allen and Jane Hobbs, b. Hardin Co. ILL., 25 Nov 1868, d. 25 Jul 1927; m. Flora Page;issue: 11, Gracie (d Jan 1919), Seba (d. 1918), Ernest Hobbs (d. Mar 1925). (11 Aug 1927 HCI)
HARVEY MARTIN, son of Charles Martin, b. Marble Hill, Ark., 04 Mar 1905, d. 03 Aug 1927. (01 Sep 1927 HCI)
SARAH J. GERHARDT, dau of Henry &Mary Gerhardt, b. Ind,. 21 May 1869, d. 03 Feb 1927; m. James Goins; issue: Joe(d.), Mrs. Sherman Aldridge, Mrs. Arthur Cowgill, Mrs. Jesse Waggoner,Frank, Jake, luke, & Amiel Gerhardt. (11 Aug 1927 HCI)
CLARENCE CALVIN PATTON, b. 13 Dec 1896, d. 16 Aug 1927; m. Eva Radford, 1921; issue: 2, 1 survives; bro, Granville PLatton, plus 3 unnamed sis. (25 Aug 1927 HCI)
MRS. DORA PALMER, b. 11 Sept 1870, d. 25 Aug 1927, m. W.G. Gregory, 11 Dec 1894. (08 Sept 1927 HCI)

JAMES LAVANDER, d. last week; bro. Ben Lavander; sis, Mrs. Harve Hill; nephew, Wiley Lavander. (29 Sept 1927 HCI)
ELIZABETH BYNUM, b. 22 Feb 1841*, d. 14 Sept 1927, m. Richard F.Bynum (d. 22 Dec 1883), 1867;issue: Josh, (d.1881), W.T., Mrs. T.B. Ginger, Mrs. Richard Williams; bro, Miles Hicks; sis, Jane Carlisle. (13 Oct 1927 HCI)
GEORGE HUFSEY, b. 17 Nov 1848*, d. 28 Sept 1927. (13 Oct 1927 HCI)
JOHN DUMONT, son of John Dumont, b. 1917, d. 1927. (06 Nov 1927 HCI)
THOMAS STORY, son of Jordon & Susanna Story, b. Pope Co. ILL., 21 Feb 1850, d. 13 Sept 1927; m. Mary Jane Jones: issue: Clarence, Ollie, Bert, James, & dau?; bros, Gren & Milo Story. (10 Nov 1927)
WILLIAM KENNETH RICHESON, son of Herman? & Fannie Richeson, b. 03 Dec 1909, d 16 Oct 1927; bros, Herman, Clifford, Albert, Walter; sis; Etta Curry, Dortha Walters, Virgie Davis,& Glenn Vickery. (17 Nov 1927 HCI)
MATTIE LANE, b. 25 Sept 1913, d. 28 Oct 1927; parents, 3 bro, 1 sis. (17 Nov 1927 HCI)
GEORGE PILAND, (Civil War vet) d. 20 Nov 1927; m. ---; issue: 7; bros; J.B. & John Piland. (24 Nov 1927 HCI)
ISABEL ANN CLARK, b. Crittenden Co., Ky., ---, d.08 Nov 1927; m.William H.Edmonds,1869;issue: Fred Edmonds, Norah Verson.(24 Nov 1927 HCI)
NANCY J. MILES, nee Garland, b. Elizabethtown, ILL., 13 Feb 1862, d. 21 Nov 1927; m. 1st, John Cook 1881; issue: Walter, Howard(d.,twins, Myrtle, (she m. James Lamb), Gertie, (she m. Burrel Hobbs); m. 2nd, Frank Foreman(d); m. 3rd, William Farmer (He d. 30 Mar 1912); m. 4th, John W. Miles; sis, Mary Shearer, Lizzie Frayser; bros, Thomas, John, William, Henry Garland. (08 Dec 1927 HCI).
PERRY DAVIS, son of Marion & Lethia Davis, b. 26 Jun 1907, d. 25 Nov 1927.(08 Dec 1927 HCI)
JESSIE ALEX OLDHAM, son of Jessie & Delaney Oldham, b. 13 Nov 1883, d. 10 Dec 1927; m. Lucy Hindall, 26 Sept 1906; (she d. 26 May 1910) issue: Mary Marie Oldham; bros, Elisha, Joseph, Charley, Alex Oldham; sis, Martha,

Sarah. (22 & 29 Dec 1927 HCI)
RACHEL WILLIAMS, dau of W.P. & Opheldia Williams, b. Hardin Co. ILL., 29 Dec 1856, d. 22 Nov 1927; m. Jobe Twitchell; m. 2nd, Jack Inman. m. 3rd, W.R. Sturgill.(29 Dec 1927 HCI)
RUTH CLARK, dau of J. A. Clark, b. Hardin Co., ILL., 13 May 1881, d.13 Nov 1927; m. Frank Travis, 21 Jun 1907. (29 Dec 1927 HCI)
MARCUS L. WALKER, son of Aaron & Patsy Stilley Walker, b. Saline Co., ILL., 22 May 1838; m. Sarah Malcome 1857; issue: 11, 6 survive, Mrs M.L. Shelter, others unnamed; m.2nd Mrs. Malinda Jane Hayes, 1916; served 29 ILL. Inf., Civil War. (29 Dec 1927 HCI)
ELMER WOOTTON, son of A.H. Wootton, d. 21 Dec 1927 (05 Jun 1927 HCI)
LAWRENCE DEWITT SERVER, b. Rosiclare, Hardin Co., ILL., 10 Aug 1880, d. Jan 1928; sis, Mrs. Charles G. Covington, Mrs. Frank Ward, Mrs. Robert Ledbetter, Mrs. L.D. Dusch; mother, Mary A. Server. (19 Jan 1928 HCI)
SUSIE FORD, b. Hardin Co. ILL., 1888, d. 22 Oct 1927; m. John Tolbert 1906; issue: Clifford, Cecil, Ruthie, Lacy, James Walter, inf (d), G.C., John Logan , Milas C., Marguerette, & Molly Tolbert; m. 2nd,---Belt?(26 Jan 1928 HCI)
ALBERT DOUGLAS SWEAT, b. Hardin Co. ILL., 19 Aug 1882; m. Dena Jones, 06 May 1907; issue: Loy Sweat; leaves father, 2 bros. (09 Feb 1928 HCI)
DORA MAE LEDBETTER, dau of Riley Ledbetter, b. 18 Jun 1910, d. 06 Jan 1928. (09 Feb 1928 HCI)
MATTIE FRICKER, dau of F.E. Fricker, b. 29 Jan 1915, d. 13 Jan 1928; leaves parents, 4 bros, 4 sis. (16 Feb 1928 HCI)
THOMAS FULLER JARVIS, b. England, 04 Jul 1842, m. Rachel Joiner; issue: Jentie Jarvis. (16 Feb 1928 HCI)
THOMAS B. GINGER, son of Eli & Jane Ginger, b. 17 Apr 1871, d. 28 Jan 1928; m. Melvinia Bynum; issue: Sylvia Kagner, Clarence, Sereda, Nellie Donithan; half bro, James C. Ginger. (23 Feb 1928 HCI)
RICHARD FRAILY, b. Hardin Co. ILL., 1 Jul 1845, m. Julie Lackey, 15 Feb 1865; issue: Elizabeth Hess, Lelia Gustin, Nancy (d), Frank (d),

Charley (d), Henry (d); bro, Frank Frailey. (01 Mar 1928 HCI)
RUTH CELESTINA LEDBETTER, b. Hardin Co. ILL., 29 Nov 1853, d. 7 Feb 1928; m. F.M. Devers, 24 Sept 1867 (He d. 26 Oct 1924); issue: John M., Ordie, Ben, Rose Leingel, Mae Robinson, Pearl Cleveland, Sally Perry, & Phrona Frailey, (01 Mar 1928 HCI)
LETTA DUTON, dau of James S. Dutton, d. 1928; m. Oxford; issue: Arlee Oxford.(08 Mar 1928 HCI)
CICERO PATTON, son of James & Sarah Patton, b. Hardin Co.ILL., 1857, d. 07 Jan 1928; m. Miranda Rutherford?, sis of Arch Rutherford; issue: Cicero; m. 2nd, Dora Davis, 1875 (She d. 19 Jul 1886), issue: William R., Daniel, Edgar, Effie, & Warren Patton; m. 3nd, Rebecca Hobbs, 12 Jul 1886; issue: Savannah Decker, Alonzo, Hiller, Oral(d.), Earl(d.), Alta Frailey. (15 & 22 Mar 1928 HCI)
BESSIE WINTERS, dau of W. H. Winters, b. 29 Oct 1894, d. 25 Mar 1928; m. Walter King, 24 Sept 1913; issue: 2, 1 survives, Virginia King; leaves parents, 2 bros &4 sis.(05 Apr 1928 HCI)
JOSEPH DENGLER, b.Bengin Germany, 16 Oct 1846* d. 31 Mar 1928; m. Ricka Schutt, 06 Sept ---; issue; August Dengler. (12 Apr 1928 HCI)
MARY ELLEN OLDHAM, b. 17 Nov 1869, d. 05 Apr 1928; m. Dow Boyd, 14 Mar 1889;issue: Nora (d), Sarah (d.), Earl (d.), Alonozo (d.), Mrs. T.J. Bonefield, Mrs. C. Collins, Mrs, H. Taylor, Harold,Frank Boyd; bro, 4 sis.(19 Apr 1928 HCI)
EDWARD ROSCOE FERRELL, b. Metrpolis, ILL., 17 Jan 1880, d. Detroit, Mich.,13 Apr 1928;leaves widow, parents, stepson. (19 Apr 1928 HCI)
HERBERT CLYDE SMOCK, son of Everett & Anna Smock, b. 30 Jan 1908, d. 14 Apr 1928; bro, Kenneth Smock; grandfather, G.W. Shearer.(19 Apr 1928 HCI)
"TOM THUMB" OZEE will be 78 yrs old 01 May 1928. (26 Apr 1928 HCI)
SAMUEL C. OXFORD, son of James Oxford, d. last week; son, Elmer Oxford; bro, James A. Oxford. (10 May 1928 HCI)
MARGARET NAVE LAIRD, dau of Richard Laird, b. Sparks Hill, Hardin Co., 15 Oct 1859, d. 02 May

1928; m. James K. Nave (d. 05 Mar 1925); Issue: Ora, Emma, Averett; m. 2nd, Frank Seavers, 05 Sept 1927.(10 May 1928 HCI)
SCOTT PARIS, b. abt 1860, d. El Paso, Texas, 1928; bro, Dr. W.J. Paris; son. Ezra Paris. (17 May 1928 HCI)
VELVIA IZORA PRATHER, dau of James & Ambie Prather, b. 21 Dec 1902, d. 29 Apr 1928; m. George Koster; issue: 4, 3 survive; bro, Gilbert Prather; half bros, Melvin Wallace, Herbert & Hulbert Prather; half sis, Hattie Banks, Mattie Jennings, Gertrude Holbrooks.(24 May 1928 HCI)
GROVER F.LEDBETTER, son of Frank & Mary Ledbetter, b. 17 Jun 1888, d. 10 May 1928; issue: 7. (30 May 1928 HCI)
LOUIS HAMP SR, b. Hanover, Germany, 05 Jul 1847, d. 01 May 1928; m. Elizabeth Seiner, 1870; issue: 9, 7 survive, Louis, Henry, Kattie Catt, Maggie Smee, Jacob, John,& Nicholas Hamp; sis, Reckie Hubbs, Amanda Hogan; bro, Henry Hamp Sr. (30 May 1928 HCI)
ELIZABETH STEINER, dau of Wentlin Steiner, b. Germany, 21 Oct 1849, d. 11 May 1928; m. Louis Hamp 1870; issue: Louis, Kattie Catt, Henry, Maggie Smee, Jacob, John, Nicholas Hamp; sis, Mrs. Peter Zimmer. (30 May 1928 HCI)
MORGAN OXFORD, d. 1845-1850, migrated to Illinois from N.C. 1833, dau, Mary Patton, abt 85-90 yrs old. (30 May 1928 HCI)
BEN LAVANDER, 84 yrs old, 05 Jun 1928. (30 May 1928 HCI)
HENRY GERHARDT, b. 14 Dec 1857, d.17 May 1928; m. Adela A. Patterson, 21 Mar 1883;issue: John, Nora Ferrell (d. 05 Jan 1925), Lizzie Dixon, Bessie Simmons, Charles H., Daisy Hawkins & inf (d.). (07 Jun 1928 HCI)
MARGARET NAVE SEAVERS, b. Hardin Co., 15 Oct 1859, d. 02 May 1928; m. J.K. Nave, in Indiana, 25 Mar 1875; issue:?, O.E. Nave; m. 2nd, --- Seavers; issue: Emma Everett. (07 Jun 1928 HCI)
DELLA MAE HOLLOMAN, dau of Jesie Holloman, b. 12 Nov 1898, d. 02 Apr 1928; m. Willie Ashford, 11 Feb 1915; issue: Clifford Ashford; sis, Annie Jennings; half sis, Cora Oxford, Hattie Hobbs, & Rosie Smith . (21 Jun 1928 HCI)

JERUSHA CLARY, dau of Henry & Lue Clary, b. Hardin Co., 31 Jul 1868, d. 22 May 1928; m. John Foe Jr., 25 Dec 1890; issue: Mrs. James T. Love, Mrs. Clay Downey, Mrs. Ebb Little, Mrs., Doland Patterson, Lawrence Foe; 3 sis, 1 bro. (21 Jun 1928 HCI)
SARAH JENKINS DOUGLAS, b. Rising Sun, Ind., 25 Dec 1833, d. 12 Jun 1928; m. Tho. Douglas, 25 Nov 1851; issue: 8, 4 survive, Ida Renfro, Nora Winn, Cora Beavers & Lula Threlkeld. (28 Jun 1928 HCI)
MILES HICKS, b. 05 Nov 1839, d.12 Jun 1928; m. Rebecca Megill,23 Apr 1858 (He d. 1 Dec 1914) issue: Josie McMurphy, Albert, Frank Hicks; m 2nd, Myriah Ginger (d. 19 Jan 1928);Civil War vet (21 & 28 Jun 1928 HCI)
JOBE DECKER, b. White Co., ILL., 17 Apr 1849, d.17 Jun 1928; m. Nancy Ellen Irby, 1888; issue: Mrs. Freeman Taber, Effie Cubley, Riley, Henry, Sara, Maria Decker; 4 bros, 2 sis. (12 Jul 1928 HCI)
BETTY ANN VINYARD, b. Karbers Ridge, Hardin Co. ILL., abt 1840, dau of George & Mary Vinyard; m. --- Morrow. (09 Aug 1928 HCI)
JOSEPH W. WAGGONER, son of George Waggoner, b. Lewiston, N.Y., 12 Jan 1854, d. 18 May 1928; m. Mrs. Cora Bennett, 28 Feb 1898?; issue: Ruby Irene (d 18 May 1918), Mae Presley, George, William, Velma Hale, Thelma Vinyard, Robert, Abner Waggoner; bro, Charles Waggoner. (16 Aug 1928 HCI)
ROBERT FRANKLIN MARGLIN, son of James & Nancy Jane Marglin, b. Gallatin Co., ILL, 23 May 1861, d. 16 Aug 1928; m. Eulalia Jackson, 02 Jul 1899; issue; 6. (23 Aug 1928 HCI)
THOMAS HILL, son of Harve Hill, d. 16 Aug 1928; m. Lucinda J. Martin, 27 Aug 1885; issue: Pearl Hill (male); m. 2nd, Gradie White, 14 Jun 1891; issue: Herbert, Goolie Hill; stepson, Loren White; bros, Jack, Walter, Otto, Roy Hill; sis, Elizabeth Jones, Hester Garland,& Minnie Garland. (23 Aug 1928 HCI)
HENRY JETT RIGGS, b. Hardin Co. ILL., 28 Mar 1860, d.12 Aug 1928; m. Sarah Elizabeth Vaughn, 15 Feb 1882; issue: 7, 4 survive, Joseph W., John H., Jerdie Cole Riggs, Virgie Keeling; 3

sis, 2 bros. (06 Sept 1928 HCI)
ROSE ANN HURFORD, b. Hardin Co. ILL., 08 Dec 1860; dau, Melissa Morgan; son, Ollie Cochran; bro, Tom Hurford. (06 Sept 1928 HCI)
WILLIAN RALPH GARLAND, son of John and Hester Garland, b. Hardin Co. ILL.,12 Feb 1896, d.31 Aug 1928; m. Mona Brownfield, Jan 1923; issue: Billy Garland; sis, Mrs. L. C. Brewster; bro, Wiley Garland. (06 Sept 1928 HCI)
ELIZABETH A. FERRELL LYNN, b. Hardin Co., 01 May 1840, d. 09 Sept 1928; m. Jonathan Franklin (d 1887);issue: 4, Fannie L. Simmons, Virginia Nicholas (d.).(13 Sept 1928 HCI)
LOUISA J. BANKS, dau of F.M. & America J.Banks, b.Lynchburg, Tenn.,14 Mar 1860; m. J.J. Luster, 27 Dec 1877; issue: sons, R.C. Luster, H. A. Luster, L.G. Luster. (13 Sept 1928 HCI)
ANDREW J.SWEAT, b. 16 Mar 1861, d. 15 Aug 1928; m. Mary K. Dixon, 1879; issue: Mrs.Eller Conkle & Mrs. Martha Tyree; m 2nd, Zodie Anderson; m. 3rd, Mrs. Daisy Joiner; issue: Millie Pauline Sweat. (20 Sept 1928 HCI)
JONAS SPIVEY, b. Hardin Co. ILL., 1867, d.1928; m. Mollie Ginger, 1855; issue: 8, 4 survive, Dora, James, Lucy, Maude; m. 2nd, Mollie Miller 1906; 2 bros, 1 sis. (27 Sept 1928 HCI)
BESSIE FELLOWS, dau of J. W. & Fanny Fellows, b. Hardin Co. ILL., 06 Jan 1895, d. 21 Sept 1928; m. Eschol Gross; issue: 1; m. 2nd, William Davis; issue: 2. (27 Sept 1928 HCI)
GEORGE HENRY GOINS, son of James & Sarah Goins. b. 19 Sept 1899, d. 11 Sept 1928; leaves father, 3 bros, 3 sis. (11 Oct 1928 HCI)
THOMAS ERNEST BYRAN, son of Morgan & Elizabeth Byran, b.7 Oct 1885, d. 02 Oct 1928; m. Emmeretta Joiner, 26 Dec 1908; issue: 7; 3 sis. 5 bros. (11 Oct 1928 HCI)
MARGARET REINER, 81 yrs old, widow of Goatlieb Reiner, Civil War vet. (18 Oct 1928 HCI)
MAUDE ISHAM, dau of J. G. & Sarah Isham, b. Saline County,ILL., 28 Jul 1891, d.11 Oct 1928; m. Ollie McDonald, 25 Jul 1915; issue: 6, 5 living;parents, 3 sis, 2 bros.(25 Oct 1928 HCI)
MARY GRAHAM,b. Hardin Co. ILL., 01 May 1862, d. 20 Sept 1928; m. William Graham, 09 Oct 1881; issue: 9, 8 survive; Willie Graham, d. 29 Oct

1922; others unnamed. (01 Nov 1928 HCI)
JOSEPH FRANKLIN CRABB, b. 03 Mar 1856*, Miss., m. Mary E. Arbel, 19 Dec 1878; issue: 10, 7 survive; 3 bros, 1 sis. (06 Nov 1928 HCI)
CASSENOR STORY, son of Ollie & Connie Story, b. Hardin Co., 2 Sept 1912, d. 10 Oct 1928;leaves parents, 3 bros, 3 sis. (06 Nov 1928 HCI)
ETHEL EDMONSON, dau of Henry & Mary Edmonson, b. 04 Feb 1897, d. 30 Mar 1928; m.Charles McDowell; issue: Mora, Herbert, Treva, Geneva, Prentice, Mary Galena; bro, Bee; sis, Connie Edmondson. (06 Nov 1928 HCI)
WILLIAM MORRIS, b. Gallatin Co., ILL., 04 Dec 1842; issue: William B., George G., David Howell, Will Smith (stepson), Mrs. Arthur Ready (dau); served Co. C., 31 Ill., Civil War. (06 Nov 1928 HCI)
EDWARD FERRELL, bro of Frank Ferrell, d. last summer. (15 Nov 1928 HCI)
MOLLIE GINGER, dau of Archibald & Polly Ann Ginger, nee Patton, b. Hardin Co., 22 Oct 1866, d. 03 Nov 1928; m. 1st, Marshall M. Miller 28 May 1885 (he d. May 1905); issue: Joseph, John, Ernest; m. 2nd, Jonas Spivey, 04 Nov 1906 (He d. 04 Sept 1928). (15 Nov 1928 HCI)
THOMAS M. OZEE, son of James & Mary Ann Ozee, b. Boone Co., Ky., 01 May 1850; m. Eliza Ann Clevenger, 23 Apr 1870; issue: William J., Lillian Lee(d.), Martha T., Stanley, Mary A. Jones(d.), James A., Joseph(d.), Tom, Walter, & Nellie Lee Ozee. (22 Nov 1928 HCI)
JOSEPH WALKER LEDBETTER, son of Henry & Mollie Ledbetter, b. 13 Mar 1899; m. Callie June Hetherington, dau of John L. & Sidney Hetherington, B. 01 Sept 1905; issue: Herbert, June, Kenneth, Nellie, Virginia, Ruth, Dorothy, John & 1 (d.). (22 Nov 1928 HCI)
HARRINGTON S. FERRELL, d. 09 Dec 1928. (20 Dec 1928 HCI)
SARAH ANN HAWKINS MCTYRE, b. Elizabethtown, ILL., 29 Jul 1859, d.24 Dec 1928; m. Alfred McTyre, 16 Oct 1889; issue: William A. & Mrs. Clay R. Usleaman. (10 Jan 1929 HCI)
MAE OLDHAM, dau of Alex and Lucy Oldham, nee Hindall, g. dau of Joseph Hindall, b. 01 May 1908, d. 27 Dec 1928; m. George Fletcher, 15

Jun 1928. (03 & 17 Jan 1928 HCI).
WILLIE A. PATTON, b. Hardin Co., ILL., 20 Apr 1853, d. 12 Jan 1928; m. Sarah E. Grice, 04 Mar 1880, (She was b. Hardin Co.,ILL.,06 Sept 1860, d. 12 Jan 1928);issue: Arza,James,plus 2(d).(24 Jan 1929 HCI)
WILLIAM J. CULLUM, son of John & Sarah Cullum, b. 03 Jan 1867, d. 08 Jan 1929; m.---,issue: Walter, Julius, Clyde, Ira, Cecil, Mrs. Oscar Rains, Mrs. Ollie Johnson, Loren(d.); bros, Theodore, Thomas Cullum; sis, Mary Cumminger, Cora Rose, Minda Webster. (24 Jan 1929 HCI)
J. B. PILAND, 73 yrs old, 27 Jan 1929. (31 Jan 1929 HCI)
WILLIAM J. HOGON, son of Henry & Jane Hogon, b. Pope Co., ILL., 22 Sept 1875, d. 22 Jan 1929; m. Alice J. Bryan, 12 Jan 1895; issue:Ray Hogon & Opal Hogon Winters. (31 Jan 1929 HCI)
FRANCIS "DOCK" PARMER SPIVEY, b. Jackson Co., Tenn., 1843, d. 07 Feb 1929; m. Harriet Ginger; issue: Candas Jones, Milas, Pink, Halpa?, John, Leona Sneed, Grace Oglesby, Pearl Tobenski; bros; Thomas & Jonas Spivey(d.); sis, Josephine Suits. (14 Feb 1929 HCI)
FRANCIS MINNIE HARPER DEWESEE, b.29 Nov 1847, d.03 Jan 1929; m. Robert Dewesee, 1874; issue: Nannie(d.), Amberes? (inf, d.), Bettie Casby (d. 1908), Minerva Burton,& Leona Cowsert.(14 Feb 1929 HCI)
CHRISTINIA HERRMAN, dau of Sebastine & Mary Josephine Shelter, b. Germany, 21 Sept 1840, d. 20 Jan 1929; m. John Herrman(d 1908);issue: Catherine Siedler (d. May 1927), Mary J. Rubenacker, Sallie, Antone, Mrs. Frances Reif, Michael, Andrew, Regiana Sherres, Elizabeth Joiner. (14 Feb 1929 HCI)
WILLIAM J. CULLUM, son of John G. & Sarah Cullum, b. 03 Jan 1867, d. 08 Jan 1929; m. Elmira Baldwin (d. Mar 1898); issue: Walter, Bertha M. Rains, Loren(d.), Clyde, Julius, Everett (d.); m 2nd, Elizabeth Baldwin, 1898; issue: Ira, Oma Cecil, plus 2 (d.); sis, Nancy M. Ramsey (d.). (14 Feb 1929 HCI)
CAROLINE JOSEPHINE BATH, dau of Henry Bath, b. Germany, 05 May 1862, d. 31 Jan 1929; m. Antone Volkert, 02 Jan 1883; issue: Antone, Henry,

Frank, Thomas & Hattie Volkert, plus 3 (d.); bros, Henry, John Taylor, Herman Volkert; sis, Emma Shelter, Minnie Wallace, Lizzie Parkinson, & Amelia Dixon. (14 Feb 1929 HCI)
FRANK COWSERT, son of Robert & Maria Kelly Cowsert, b. Pope Co., ILL., 07 May 1864, d. 21 Jan 1929; m. Ellen Wyatt, 30 Dec 1886 (She d. 1887); m. 2nd, Mattie Hobbs, 22 Oct 1903;issue: Frank Hobbs Cowsert;sis, Mary McGinnis; nieces, Mrs. George Karber, Mrs. Wallace Milliken, Mrs. F.J. Dowding & Margaret McGinnis; nephew, Rolling H. McGinnis. (21 Feb 1929 HCI)
CORA LANE FERRELL, dau of M.S. Lane. b. 14 Aug 1898, d. 11 Feb 1929; m. James S. Ferrell, 25 Jul 1915; issue: Viola & Geraldine Ferrell; bros, Hugh and Albert Lane. (28 Feb 1929 HCI)
FREDERICK DONATHAN, b. Boone Co., Ky., 28 June 1835; m. 3 times; issue; 11; dau, Connie Story. (07 Mar 1929 HCI)
MARAGRET EMELINE VINYARD, dau of George & Sarah Vinyard, b. Hardin Co., ILL., 18 Nov 1861, d. 20 Feb 1929; m. J.A. Womack, 1883; issue: Mrs. W.T. Warford, Mrs. George Hale, Mrs. J.L. Guard, Mrs. Ted Lewis, Mrs. Earl Brannon; bro, George A. Vinyard; sis, Mrs. Henry Frohock.(07 Mar 1929 HCI)
WILLIAM SIAH HENSON, b. Pulaski Co., Ky., 26 May 1855; m. Mary Brooks; issue: Otto, Lessie Davis & Helen Henson,& 4 (d). (07 Mar 1929 HCI)
WILLIAM DRUMM, b. Elizabethtown, ILL., 28 Aug 1861, d. 01 Feb 1929; m. Mary Gilliam, 02 Apr 1882; issue: Elmer, Myrtle, Lydia, Willie, Harry, Carrie, Ray, Lanie & Gladys Drumm, plus, 4 (d.). (14 Mar 1929 HCI)
JONATHAN MILO JONES, son of F.M. & Susanna Jones, b. 19 Dec 1871, d. 29 Nov 1928; m. Marcy C. Spivey, 29 Apr 1898; issue: Nellie Fricker, plus 1 (d.); bros, F. M., Tom and John Jones; sis, Joshie Davis. (14 Mar 1929 HCI)
ARVETTA BANKS, dau of Henry Banks, b. Hardin Co., 01 Apr 1900*, d. 09 Mar 1929; m. Lacy Vinyard, 15 Mar 1922; issue: Marjorie Laverne Vinyard; sis, Mrs. Homer Simpson, Mrs. Earl Hornbeck, Irene Banks, & Gladys Banks.(21 Mar 1929 HCI)
R.J. REED, son of Wesley & Sarah Reed, b.

Hardin Co., ILL., 26 Aug 1859, d. 23 Feb 1929; m. Alice Dean Steward, 03 Sept 1881; issue: 10, 5 survive. (21 Mar 1929 HCI)
MARTHA J. HALE, dau of Henry & Malinda Ginger b. 01 Jan 1844, d. 13 Feb 1929; m. James Hale; issue: Mrs. Jeff Williams(d), Alvin, William, Robert, Walter, Tom, & Mrs. Everett Anderson; m. 2nd, Jacob Drumm, 1914; m. 3rd, Samuel Winters, 25 May 1920; 2 bros, 2 sis. (21 Mar 1929 HCI)
FANNIE HOLBROOK RALPH, dau of P.D. Holbrook, b. Hardin Co. ILL., 27 Apr 1887, d. 5 Mar 1929; m. W.J. Ralph, 12 Apr 1905, Elizabethtown, ILL.; issue: Deneen(d.), Mrs. Delbert Gangbare, Dorothy Josephine, Evelyn, Walter Jr, Robert; bros, Dee, Harry, Cap Holbrook; sis, Mrs. James Rutherford, Mrs. Clifford Riggs. (28 Mar 1929 HCI)
SARAH JANE DAVIS, dau of Abraham & Elizabeth Davis, b. Hardin Co. ILL., 18 Jul 1853, m.1st, John Stone; issue:? m. 2nd, John b. Lawrence, 1872; issue: ?,9 survive. (04 Apr 1929 HCI)
EDWARD ROSCOE FERRELL, d. Detroit, Mich., 13 Apr 1928. (18 Apr 1929 HCI)
LEONA DEWESE, dau of Bob Dewese, b. Pope Co., Ill., 30 Sept 1885, d. 18 Mar 1929; m. William Cowsert, 21 Apr 1903; issue: Ulysis, Julius & Harry Cowsert. (04 Apr 1929 HCI)
ANNA L. MADDEN, dau of "Buck" and Virginia Madden, g. dau of John T. Madden, b. Hardin Co. ILL., d. 4 Apr 1929; leaves, mother, husband, son, sis & bros. (11 Apr 1929 HCI)
T. JEFFERSON VINYARD, age 91, d. 7 Apr 1929; Civil War vet; m.--- Colbert (11 & 19 Apr 1929 HCI)
CLIFFORD C. RIGGS, son of J.M. Riggs, b. Elizabethtown, ILL., 7 Jun 1892, d. 22 Mar 1929; m. Mattie Holbrook, 18 Aug 1911; issue: Kenneth, Ralph, Electa, Twila, Cassiday, Edward, Charlotte; sis, Hattie Carr, Nema forman, Rose Fergus. (11 Apr 1929 HCI)
J.L. BEDFORD, b. Pope Co., ILL., 10 Dec 1852, d. 10 Apr 1929; issue: dau, Mrs. Doy Moore, Mrs. Ellen Redick, Mrs. W.W. Vanbibber, Mrs. Ross Frayser; son, Loren Bedford. (25 Apr 1929 HCI)

HARRY DEWEY IRBY, b. Potts Hill, Ill., 02 Nov 1899; m. Lena Day, 1916; issue: Carlos Lee, Alice Geraldine Irby; bro; Earl Irby, plus 5 unnamed bros.(25 Apr 1929 HCI)
MOLLIE ELIZABETH DOWNEY, dau of Henry C. & Artimissa Downey, b. 16 Aug 1874, d. 26 Apr 1929; m. Edward R. Kibler, 03 Jun 1896; issue: 5; leaves 3 bros, 3 sis. (02 May 1929 HCI)
DELLAR FRANKLIN WATSON, b. 08 Oct 1895, d. 10 Apr 1929; m. Ethel Riley, 18 Feb 1923; issue: Allene Watson, plus 1 (d.); leaves 1 bro, 2 sis. (30 May 1929 HCI)
ROSETTA SHERIDAN BRAZELL, b. 29 May 1875. d. 27 May 1929; m. Charley Brazell, 1895; issue: 6, 5 survive. (13 Jun 1929 HCI)
WALTER H. HENSON, b. 01 Mar 1891, d. 24 May 1929; m. Shella Ferrell; issue: 5; leaves wife, 4 sis, half sis & bro. (13 Jun 1929 HCI)
ALFRED VAUGHN, b. 04 May 1911, d. 07 Nov 1928; leaves mother, bro, sis. (02 May 1929 HCI)
BEN BASCOME, b. 31 May 1859, d. 08 Jun 1929; leaves wife, dau & bro. (20 Jun 1929 HCI)
APPIE ROBINSON, b. 18 Mar 1848, d. 19 Oct 1928; issue: 8; leaves wife. (20 Jun 1929 HCI)
CHARLES SOWARD, b. Hardin Co. ILL., 21 Sept 1853, d. 16 Jun 1929; m. Mina Crusen, 28 Dec 1878; issue: Mantie(d.), Clarence E., Millie McCue, Clyde B, Mable(d), Vernon B. & Fern Patton. (27 Jun 1929 HCI)
JOHN BIRCH, son of Richard & Rebecca Birch, b. Hardin Co. ILL., 19 Dec 1877, d. 06 Jun 1929; m. Mollie McFall, 26 Apr 1902; issue: 8, 7 survive; 3 sis, mother, grandmother.(04 Jul 1929 HCI)
JANE BIRCH, dau of Benjamin & Elizabeth Birch, b. Rising Sun, Indiana, 24 Sept 1848, d. 14 Jun 1929; m. Lewis Conn, 1872; issue:9; 2 bros, 2 sis. (11 Jul 1929 HCI)
CLARA HANNA SHELBY, dau of Jacob & Polly Ann Shelby, b. 06 Sept 1869, d. 30 Jun 1929; m. John R. Baldwin, 20 Dec 1885; issue: ?; bros, James Shelby, Grant Shelby, Reece Shelby; sis, Martha Vaughn, Anna Vaughn, Harriet Rotes, Anteline Ledbetter, Edith Ledbetter, Margaret Ledbetter, Elizabeth Carter, Mary Allen, Sarah Christy. (11 Jul 1929 HCI)

ENOCH LOGAN, b. 10 May 1883*, d. 18 Jun 1929; m. Francis Parker, 1908, Paducah, Ky., issue: James Clarence, Charles Franklin, Carl Harvey, William Robert Logan(d.). (11 Jul 1929 HCI)
EWING STANLEY, b. 23 Jul 1858*, d. 07 Jun 1929; m. 1st, Sarah Vaughn; issue; Edward Stanley & dau (d); m. 2nd, Florence Ozee, 1896, issue: 9, 7 survive. (18 Jul 1929 HCI)
WARDEN PANKEY, b. Hardin Co., 05 Sept 1906, d. 30 Jun 1929; leaves, parents; bros, Lucian, Everett, Dal, Iley Pankey; sis, Mary, Etta, Agnes Pankey. (25 Jul 1929 HCI)
LILA MAY COWSERT, dau of Alvin Cowsert, b.26 Nov 1915, d.16 Jul 1929. (01 Aug 1929 HCI)
JAMES H. WINGATE, son of Edward & Sidney Wingate, b. 06 Mar 1863, d. 20 Jul 1929; m. Triphena Cullison, 31 Jan 1887; issue; E. Wingate (son); sis, Emma Mott, Rosie Wingate. (08 Aug 1929 HCI)
MARY ELIZABETH FRAILEY, dau of Richard & Mary Fraily, b. 12 May 1866, d. 15 Aug 1929; m. Edward Hess, 02 Oct 1897; issue: Richard & Mrs. Cecil Smith. (05 Sept 1929 HCI)
KATE PARROT, dau of Joe & Mintie Parrot, b.13 Sept 1864, d. 09 Sept 1929; m. John Shadowens, 1881; issue: Oliver, Charlie, Johnie, Elvie, Narlie, Lee Hess; sis, Nan cowsert.(26 Sept 1929 HCI)
W. MORAN BELT, son of Dallas & Minnie Belt, b. Hardin Co. ILL., 06 Jun 1884, d. 21 Jul 1929; m. Lillie May Foster, dau of Horace & Mary Foster, 24 Sept 1905; issue: Robert, Milas, Howard, Wendell, Albert Dean(d.), Mary Virginia, Helen Belt; bros, Charlie, Brownie, Chester Belt; sis, Gracie Belt.(19 Sept 1929 HCI)
GOLDIE BANKS, dau of Henry Banks, d. 14 Sept 1929; m. Earl Hornbeck; issue: Charles, Henry Hornbeck; sis, Gussie Simpson, Irene, Gladys Banks. (26 Sep 1929 HCI)
GEORGE W. MCDOWEL, b.Hardin Co. ILL., 16 Feb 1857, d. 17 Oct 1929; m. Cinthia Burklow, 19 Jan 1879; issue: 10. (24 Oct 1929 HCI)
JOHN PAGE, age 87, Civil War vet; bro; W.R. Page, 83 yrs old. (24 Oct 1929 HCI)
REBECCA HOBBS, b. Hardin Co. ILL., 21 Sept

1860, d. 31 Oct 1929; m. Cicero Patton, 10 Jul 1886; issue: Oral(d.), Savannah Decker, Alonzo Patton, Hillas Patton, Alta Frailey.(07 Nov 1929 HCI)

MABEL E. WEATHERINGTON, dau of Harry & Elva Weatherington, b. Pope Co. ILL., 22 Aug 1903, d. 30 Oct 1929; m. J.T. Joiner, 10 Aug 1924; issue:dau(d.); sis, Alice Floyd, Lula Joiner, Muriel Gullett,Stella; bros, Harrison & Herbert Weatherington. (07 Nov 1929 HCI)

DRUARD BELL, son of James Bell, b. Carrsville, Ky., 14 Dec 1903; m. Helen Jennings, 1923; issue: Druard, Charles Bell; m 2nd Nellie Catella, 30 Jul 1929; bros, Joe, Issac, George, Ernest, Orval; sis, Maude Owens, Junie Downey. (07 Nov 1929 HCI)

VELMA RUTH PERRY, dau of Thomas & Sallie Perry, b. Cave-In-Rock, ILL., 05 Nov 1906, d. 02 Nov 1929; sis, Edith & Esther Perry; bros, Ralph & Eschol Perry. (14 & 21 Nov 1929 HCI)

HOWARD SIMPSON, b. 10 Feb 1876, d. 27 Oct 1929; m. Minnie Brookmier, 18 Dec 1898; issue: Oral (d.) & Henry Simpson. (28 Nov 1929 HCI)

HESTER SMITH, dau of ---Moore, b.---, d.---; m. Elmer Smith, 1924; issue: 2; leaves 4 bros, 2 sis. (28 Nov 1929 HCI)

GUSSIE MAYFIELD, son of Charles Mayfield, b. Elizabethtown, ILL., 30 Jul 1890, d. 15 Nov 1892; m. Dema Rose, 15 Oct 1915; issue: Glen, Helen, John Mayfield; bros, John, & Alfred Mayfield; aunts, Mrs. Bill Yates, & Mrs. Dave Martin. (05 Dec 1929 HCI)

INDIA GINGER, dau of Dan Ginger, b. abt 1871, d. 28 Nov 1929; m. Isaac Oxford, son of Roxie; issue: Grace & Aaron Oxford; bro, Bill Ginger. (05 & 19 Dec 1929 HCI)

JOHN S. FRAYSER, son of Virginius and Ellen Frayser, b. Hardin Co., 05 Nov 1877, d. 20 Jun 1929; m. Kate Okeron, Evansville, Ind., 08 Nov 1895; bros, J.l., Robert M., & R.V. Frayser; 1 bro(d.) & 1 sis (d.) (12 Dec 1929 HCI)

ELIZABETH S. LANIER, b. 30 Jan 1840, d. 8 Aug 1929; m.--Taylor; issue: Mrs. Charles Stevens, & Mrs R.T. Bascom, plus 4(d.).(12 Dec 1929 HCI)

BELLE RICKETTS, mother of George Ricketts, d. 01 Dec 1929.(19 Dec 1929 HCI)

G.T. SHEARER, Golden Wedding Anniversary.(12 Dec 1929 HCI)
LELA VERONA BURKLOW, b. Hardin Co., ILL., 27 Dec 1912, d. 18 Nov 1929. (02 Jan 1930 HCI)
WILLIAM EVERETT CRUSE, son of Anna Pennell, b. 18 Jan 1901, d.15 Dec 1929; m. Mrs. Phoebe Hobbs, 16 Sept 1922; bros, Loyd Cruse; sis, Gertie Grounds, Ethel McDowel, Phene Richeson, Lois Hobbs & half sis, Seba Pennell. (09 Jan 1930 HCI)
BARBARA GROSS, b. Switzerland, Canton Schaffhausen, 19 Jan 1828; m.----; Louisville, Ky, 30 Oct 1856; issue: 7. (2 Jan 1930 HCI)
SAM LATHAM, b. Hardin Co., ILL., abt 1879.(09 Jan 1930 HCI)
BARBARA HUMM, b.Germany, 05 Jan 1846(came to U.S. in 1847); m. Reif; issue:? (09 Jan 1930 HCI)
HENRY MORGAN, b. 10 Oct 1830*, d. 25 Jan 1928; m. Mrs. Jane Harper; m. 2nd, Mrs. Jane Gable; m. 3rd, Melvinia Joiner; m. 4th, Mrs. Amanda Osman. (09 Jan 1930 HCI)
MAGGIE BELT, b. Hardin Co. ILL., 26 Mar 1883, d. 18 Nov 1929; m. Mila Belt, 26 Aug 1902; issue: Floyd(d.), Dewey, Roy, Lloyd, Esther Trint, Mrs. Bonnie McMillian, & Ruby Beltz.(09 Jan 1930 HCI)
RUTHIE LAMBERT, b. 01 May 1848, d. 01 Jan 1930; m. Joseph M. Lane, 29 Dec 1872; issue: Mattie Harison, Mollie Hicks, Jeff, John, Pete, Mack, & Riley Lane, plus 4 (d.); bro, William Lambert. (16 Jan 1930 HCI)
MARGARET SEINER, dau of Wendlin & Elizabeth Seiner, b. Maikammer Bavery, Germany, 21 Dec 1846, d. 02 Jan 1930; m. Jacob Eichorn, 30 Oct 1876 (who d.18 Apr 1917); issue:John, Elizabeth (inf. d.), Christian (d. 14 yrs old), & Willie Eichorn; sis, Mrs. Peter Zimmer.(16 Jan 1930 HCI)
JAMES A. WATSON, b. Elizabethtown, ILL., 1874 (30 Jan 1930 HCI)
MARGARET HURFORD, dau of R.T. Hurford, b. Hardin Co., ILL., 29 Dec 1876, d.08 Feb 1930; m. James Hobbs, 01 Jan 1902; issue: Catherine Shelter, Wiley, Ruth Gillispie, Tom, James, Robert,William Hobbs; bros, Ben & Otto Hurford.

(13 & 20 Feb 1930 HCI)
GEORGE H.DOSSETT, son of James & Nancy Dossett, b. 28 Feb 1847, d. 06 Feb 1930; bros, Ila(d.) & Elbert Dossett. (13 Feb 1930 HCI)
CHARLOTTE HENSON, dau of Job & Frances Henson, b. eastern Ky., 21 Jan 1864, d. 04 Feb 1930; m. David J.Dixon, Hardin Co.,ILL, 26 Nov 1879; issue: James J. Dixon, plus 5 (d.).(27 Feb 1930 HCI)
A.B. THOMAS, b. Thomaston, Main. 14 Apr 1846, d. 20 Feb 1930. (27 Feb 1930 HCI)
PHILIP J. IRBY, b. Hardin Co., ILL., 16 Sept 1876, d. 12 Feb 1930; m. Alice Birch, 1899; issue: Arnold, Wayne, Eva Moore, Wilmetta, & Evelyn Irby. (06 Mar 1930 HCI)
MRS. WILLIAM GLORE, b. 25 May 1891, d. 19 Feb 1930; leaves husband, 5 children. (27 Feb 1930)
WILLIAM HARRISON GARLAND,son of William & Nancy Garland, b. 27 Dec 1866, d. 11 Feb 1930; m. Mrs. Rhoda Dutton, 10 Apr 1893; m. 2nd, Mrs. Minnie Goebel; issue: Dora Aleene Garland; sis, Mrs. J.W. Miles(d.), Mrs. Harriet Hoskinson(d), Mrs. G.W. Shearer, & Mrs. Elizabeth Frayser; bros. Henry(d.), Thomas, & John Garland; stepdaus, Mrs. A.K. Wheller, Mrs. Quorumfox & Mrs. McGill. (20 Mar 1930 HCI)
MARY MATILDA HAMP, dau of Louis & Elizabeth Hamp, b. near Golconda, Pope Co., 20 Feb 1860; m. L.A. Karber, 08 Dec 1879; issue: John, Fred Clarence, Ada Miles, Freda Hale, Mrs. Roy Vinyard, plus 3 infs(d.). (27 Mar 1930 HCI)
THOMAS LESLIE HUGHES, son of T.A. Hughes, b. near Marion, Ky., 30 Sept 1889, d. 30 Mar 1930; m. Lora Hill, dau of Walter Hill, 27 Feb 1921; sis, Eva Hodge,Sadie Hughes; bro, Ilie & Elsie? Hughes. (17 Apr 1930 HCI)
DEE HOLBROOK, b. 25 Feb 1882, d. 21 Mar 1930; m. Grady Aaron(d.29 Feb 1920),21 Mar 1910; issue: W.D. Holbrook; m. 2nd, Rachel Jackson, 08 Dec 1920; bros, Loren & Otto Holbrook?, & 2 sis. (01 May 1930 HCI)
GUY GRIFFITH, b. Cohill, Ky., 08 Feb 1910, d. 21 Apr 1930; m. Marie McCoin, 03 June 1929; bros, Edward & Tony Griffith; sis, Ora Tonny, Millie Oliver, Louise Lawlers, Evelyn, Beatrice & Elizabeth Griffith (01 May 1930 HCI)

MARGARET SPEILLER REINER, wid of Gottleib Reiner, b. abt 1848; issue: Fred(d.),Willie (d.), Henry(d.), John(d.), Mrs. John Osman, Mrs. Will Cox, Mrs. John Ledbetter, Mrs Hathryn ? Jones & Mrs. Caroline Irvin.(08 May 1930 HCI)

CHARLES MAYFIELD, b. Hardin Co., Ill., 16 Nov 1864; m. Margaret C. Gaines, 1887; issue: 4 sons. (29 May 1930 HCI)

MRS. JAMES BEARD, dau of Charles & Charlotte Lewis, b. 10 Nov 1848, d. 22 May 1930; m.James Beard, 19 Aug 1867; issue; Henrietta(inf,d), Mrs. Augusta Underwood & Mrs. Belle Oxford; bro, Brown Lewis. (29 May 1930 HCI)

ARTHUR PRICE, son of Thomas Price, b---, d.---; bro, Morris T. Price; sis, Mrs. W.P. Warfield. (29 May 1930 HCI)

JAMES PARKER FERRELL, b. Hardin Co., ILL., 31 Dec 1848; son, Omar Ferrell;uncle, C.M.Ferrell. (18 May & 05 Jun 1930 HCI)

DAN FLANNERY, m.---Taylor, sis of R.F. Taylor; issue:7; bros, Drue & John Flannery. (05 Jun 1930 HCI)

NANCY JANE MINOR, b. Gallatin Co. ILL., 11 Apr 1849, d. 05 Jan 1930; m. James M. Marglin, 1865; issue: Robert F. Marglin. (12 Jun 1930 HCI)

LUCIAN PATTON, son of John Patton, b. abt 1893, d. Mon. (26 Jun 1930 HCI)

MABEL BOTTEN, dau of Milas Botten, b. 26 Jun 1909*; m. Roscoe Woods, 31 Dec 1928; issue; dau. (03 Jul 1930 HCI)

ANDREW JACKSON, d. last week; m. Mrs. Rhoda Lard; issue: ?; bro, William Jackson; sis, Mrs. J. A. Barnerd. (17 Jul 1930 HCI)

TOM FOSTER, d.---; bro, I.A. Foster. (12 Jun 1930 HCI)

LOY SHOCKLEY, son of James W. & Julia Shockley d. 11 Jul 1930; m. Lottie Turner; issue: 7. (12 & 19 Jun 1930 HCI)

JERRY M. ROSE, b. Pope Co. ILL., 1850; m. Mollie sisk; issue: Lena, Martha J. Clement, Nell Hardesty, Mabel & Mollie.(19 Jun 1930 HCI)

JAMES P. FERRELL, son of Capt. John H. & Nancy V.J. Ferrell, b. Hardin Co. ILL., 31 Dec 1847; m. Elizabeth Hayden, Metropolis,ILL., 26 Jun

1872; issue: Rella(d.),Benjamin d.),Harvey(d.), Edward Roscoe(d.13 Apr 1928),Charles F., Mrs. W.S.Hosick,& James Omar Ferrell.(19 Jun 1930 HCI)
JOHN L. ASHFORD, son of Frank Ashford, b. 06 Sept 1881, near Shelterville, ILL., d. 24 May 1930; m. Ella J. Weston, Eichorn, ILL., 03 Apr 1928; bros, Lon, Louis, Carrol. Harry, Will, Arlie; & Russell; sis, Julia Jackson & Bertha Holloman. (19 Jun 1930 HCI)
FRANCIS FANNIE JOYNER, b. 18 Oct 1854, near Cumberland River; m. James Joyner, 1878; issue: 7, 6 survive. (03 Jul 1930 HCI)
SIDNEY VERNON JENKINS, age 21, d. 22 Jun 1930, Redland Cal., son of Ernest Jenkins & g. son of G.W. Patrick. (03 Jul 1930 HCI)
TROY DUNCAN, son of Ezra Duncan, b. 1 Feb 1917, drowned 5 Jun 1930. (03 Jul 1930 HCI)
GEORGE R. BALDWIN, b. 24 Mar 1865, d. 19 Jul 1930; m. Sarah Crabb, 10 Apr 1890; issue: 13, 9 survive; 3 bros, 2 sis. (24 Jul 1930 HCI)
JOHN BARNERD, d. 31 Jul 1930; Civil War vet, (07 Aug 1930 HCI)
MARY ELIZABETH BAUGHER, dau of William Baugher, b. Hardin Co. ILL., 06 Oct 1887, d. "last week"; m. George Kaegi. (07 Aug 1930 HCI)
WILLIAM THOMAS SCOTT, b.03 Sept 1858, d. 02 Aug 1930; m. Laura Friston, 03 Nov 1881; issue: Henry, Lee, Howard, Willis, Charley, Frank, Harrison, Scott, Susie Jones, Eva Stacey, plus 2 (d.); 2 bros, 1 sis. (07 Aug 1930 HCI)
MARTHA ISABELLE FOWLER, b. 09 Apr 1859, near Eddyville, ILL.,; m. Fields Rumsey, Dec 1876; issue: Alice King (d.22 Jul 1930), Burt (d.), J.M., Robert L., Lillie M. Randolph, D.F., George L., Della McDonald, sis; Sarah Lockerbsy; bros, Joe E.& John Fowler. (14 Aug 1930 HCI)
WILLIAM DOWNEY, b. 18 Sept 1840, d. 03 Aug 1930; m. 1st, ?; m. 2nd, Emma Dimmick; issue: Charles Downey & dau(name unknown); Civil War vet., Co. C, 48 ILL. (23 Jan 1930 & 14 Aug 1930 HCI)
JOHN T. LEDBETTER, m. Mary Lowery; issue: 7; m. 2nd, Julie Foster, (sis of Isaac & Sam Foster); issue: Henry & Mary Ledbetter.(14 Aug 1930 HCI)

ROBBIE BALDWIN, dau of John T. Baldwin, b, abt 1885, d. 21 Aug 1930; m. Charles R. Green;issue Maria & Beatrice; sis, Mrs. Silas Stacey & Mrs. R.E. Santy; bro, C.S. Baldwin.(28 Aug & 11 Sept 1930 HCI)

ELBERT G. ROSE, son of Henry & Elizabeth Whiteside Rose, b. 10 Oct 1844, d. 01 Sept 1930; m. Adaline Ayers, dau of W.N. Ayers, 13 Jan 1871; issue; 2 sons; m. 2nd, Nora Janet Steel; issue: Eugene & Albert Chaney Rose? (04 Sept 1930 HCI)

JAMES A. HILL, Hardin Co., ILL., 15 Sept 1832, d. 15 Mar 1917; m. --- Smith, 1 Jan 1871, (She was b. Saline Co. ILL., 29 Apr 1838), dau of Giles Smith (b. Wythe Co., Va.) & Lucinda Smith (b. Tenn); issue: Elmer Hill, b. 09 Jun 1870; James Hill's mother b. NC; father b. 04 May 1812, Georgia; g. uncle of James was Jesse Hill. (28 Aug 1930 HCI)

WILEY J. DAYMON, b. Hardin Co. ILL., abt 1850; sons, John and Issac Daymon. (28 Oct 1930 HCI)

MARTHA A. VINYARD, dau of John & Eliza Vinyard, b. Hardin Co.ILL., 05 Dec 1849, d. 12 Sept 1930; m. John F. Hubbard, 1863; issue: Sallie (d), James, Charles, Henry, Edward, Fred, Etta, Minnie Boaten, Ivy Hubbard; bro, W.H. Vinyard; sis, Josie Fowler, & Mrs. Alice Gustin. (18 & 25 Sept 1930 HCI)

MARY JAMES WILLIAMS, dau of William Perry Williams, b. 25 Oct 1855, d. 16 Oct 1930; m. H.E. Ferrell, 10 Jan 1911; bros, 4 (d); sis, 4. (30 Oct 1930 HCI)

ALLEN BELT, b. 2 Jul 1877, d. 27 Oct 1930; m. Alice Lard, 10 Aug 1902; issue: Noah, Lillie, Porter, Viola, Palmer, & Lucy Patton. (30 Oct 1930 HCI)

SAM BAUGHER, d. Fri; half bro of Tom Baugher; sons, Gilbert & Jack Baugher. (06 Nov 1930 HCI)

WILLIAM RICHEY, son of W.H. & Bettie Richey, b. Golconda, ILL., 1 Jan 1858, d. 16 Oct 1930; m. Drucilla A Reak, Elizabethtown, ILL., 21 Sept 1884; issue: W.C. Richey, E.R. Richey, Ethel Brown, Mary Elliott, plus 2 infs,(d); half sis. Belle Martin. (06 Nov 1930 HCI)

MILT MARTIN, b. abt 1871, d. 8 Nov 1930; m.---; issue: Irene & Ruth Martin; sis; Clara Oxford;

half sis, Emma Woods, Mae Davis, Ella Rose & Ida Stuart. (13 Nov 1930 HCI)
DAISY CRONKRITE, nee Miller, d. last week; bros, Charley & Loren Miller.(13 Nov 1930 HCI)
ERNEST OXFORD, son of J.H. Oxford, b. 14 Apr 1884, d. 15 Nov 1930; m. Nora Brownfield, 31 Aug 1904; issue: Eva & Adriel Oxford; sis, Nora Berwick & Phoebe Oxford. (20 Nov 1930 HCI)
JOHN F. HINES, b. 27 Sept 1844, d. 11 Nov 1930; m.?;issue: John, Allen, George, Walter, Marion, & Lula Jackson. (27 Nov 1930 HCI)
DAISY MILLER, dau of Chas. Miller, b. Elizabeth town, Ill., 31 Jan 1868; m. George Cronkrite; bro, Orin Miller. (04 Dec 1930 HCI)
NORA WILLIAMS, dau of D.W. & Malinda Williams, b. 09 Sept 1906, d. 03 Nov 1930; leaves father, sis, 3 bros. (04 Dec 1930 HCI)
SUSAN NANCY DAVIS, dau of George & Mary Ann Davis, b. 20 Feb 1857, Hardin Co. ILL., d. 22 Oct 1930; m. Ross Goble, 1878; issue: Della Hill, Polly (inf,d), Ora (d), Ruey (d), Gracie Watkins, Aaron, Noah, & Hattie Hill; step-children Sammie, Laura, Charle, & Willie Goble? (Oct 30 & 04 Dec 1930 HCI)
MRS. ODIE RAMAGE, nee Ashford ?, d.--; mother, Mollie Ashford; sis, Anne Ashford,& Mrs. Barger (25 Dec 1930 HCI)
RUTH IRONS, dau of Clint Irons, b.17 Jan 1913, d. 7 Nov 1930; m. Luther Sheridan, 21 Jul 1930. (13 & 20 Nov 1930 HCI)
STEWART TAYLOR, b. Metropolis, ILL., 27 Oct 1909, d. last Thur; bro, Claude Taylor; sis, Ruth Lippert, & Marie Crain. (27 Nov 1950 HCI)
KATIE ASHFORD, dau of James & Mollie Ashford, b.---, d. 21 Dec 1930; m. Odie Ramage. (01 Jan 1931 HCI)
WALDO JENKINS, b. 26 Jul 1879, d. 22 Dec 1930; m. Nannie Ingram, 15 Mar 1903 (she d. 31 Aug 1918); issue: George, Cecil, Ivy, Opal, and Phoebe Jenkins. (01 Jan 1931 HCI)
ANDY VANBIBER, b. 09 Dec 1865, d. 10 Nov 1930; m. Elizabeth Joiner, 1885; issue; W.W., J.O., Anna Bell Stacey, Mina May Hubbard, Sadie Jane(d), Francis(d), Murtle & Andy Vanbiber. (01 Jan 1931 HCI)

RICHARD EVANS, Civil War vet, 85 yrs old;leaves widow, dau, Mrs. Smock. (01 Jan 1931 HCI)
PHOEBE PYLES, b. 13 Nov 1844, d. 29 Dec 1930; m. John Reiner, 18 Sept 1898; issue: Carrie Klinger, Elmer, Dora (d.),Bertha Ledbetter(d.); stepchildren, Sopha Hines, Mary Schroll, Louis Reiner; bro, Austin Pyles; sis, Mary Jane Vinyard. (01 Jan 1931 HCI)
MELVINA JENKINS, b. 08 Apr 1856, d. 11 Nov 1930; m. George Partain, 18 Dec 1877; issue: Milas, Willie, Grover, Minnie Schutt, Ollie, Etta Ferrell, Anna Shewmaker, plus 2 (d); half bros, Nathaniel, Thomas, Ernest, Loren Jenkins; half sis, Clara Crabb, Ida Angelton; George Pyles, son from 1st m. ?.(01 Jan 1931 HCI)
RICHARD EVANS, Civil War, d. 21 Dec 1931 HCI)
SAMUEL GRINDSTAFF, son of Sarah Grindstaff, b. Hardin Co. ILL., 29 Oct 1875*; m.--; issue: Irvin & Mira Grindstaff; bros, Henry & Andy Grindstaff. (22 Jan 1930 HCI)
WILLIAM MCDOWELL, son of Dora & Kell McDowell. b. Hardin Co. ILL., 12 Nov 1895, d. 21 Jan 1931; bro, Edward McDowell; sis, Mae Rankin. (29 Jan 1931 HCI)
E. SMITH HOSICK, son of Joseph & Elizabeth Hosick, b. Hardin Co., ILL., 27 Jan 1844, d. 31 Jan 1931; m. Mary J. Vinyard, 03 Sept 1865 (She d. 14 Jun 1900); issue: Annie Bell Hosick (b. 26 Mar 1873, d. 15 Sept 1877); m. 2nd, Salina Eads(She d. 20 Dec 1917),Smithland, ky., 27 Jan 1902. (05 Feb 1931 HCI)
MRS. MOLLIE COCHRAN, b. 1869, d. Jan 1931; m. --- Cochran; issue: Reason, Charlie, Mrs. Will Walker, & Mrs. Joe King. (05 Feb 1931 HCI)
MARY ANN CATT, b. White Co., ILL., 29 Aug 1851, d. 02 Feb 1931; m. Jobe Catt, 1871; issue: Asa M. Catt, & Agnes McWade; sis, Florence Gullett, Melissa Lasater, Lydia Gross; bros, Asa Decker, & John Decker. (05 & 12 Feb 1931 HCI)
JOHN A. PATTON, b. 05 Jul 1865, d. 03 Mar 1931; m. Annie Sneed, 12 Feb 1886; issue: 8,6 living. (05 Mar 1931 HCI)
LESLIE HUGHES, d. 30 Nov 1930; wife, Lora Hughes. (05 Mar 1931 HCI)
JOHN A. THORNTON, son of John & Mary Thornton,

b. 01 Mar 1871, d. Mich., 03 Mar 1931; m. Rinda Lowery; issue: Willis, Erma, Lloyd, & Electa (d.) Thornton; bros, D.F. & Henry Thornton. (12 Mar 1931 HCI)
LURLINE SPIVEY, dau of Howard Spivey, age 19, d. 14 Mar 1931. (2 Apr 1931 HCI)
SILAS JOINER, son of Samuel & Ruth Joiner, b. 7 Dec 1901, d. ---; m. Mollie Ferrell; issue: Mildred; m. 2nd, Lula Weatherington; issue: Eugene & Wanda; bro, Sol Joiner; sis, Stella Hamp, Lula Calbert, & Bessie Partain. (02 Apr 1931 HCI)
LILLIE ANN STACEY, dau of Sidney & Georgia Stacey, b. 04 Apr 1905, d. 17 Apr 1931; bros, Edd, Raliegh, Orval, Ezra Stacey; sis, Arvetta, Mrs. Howard Spivey, Mrs. Leslie Lewis,(02 Apr 1931 HCI)
JOHN T. DOWNEY, son of John T. & Elizabeth Downey, b. Massac Co. ILL., 20 May 1853, d.04 Apr 1931; m. Katie McAlister; issue: Herbert, plus 6 (d.); bros, William, Henry, Commodore,& Pell Downey; sis,Levisa Jones(d.), Nancy J.(d.) & Margaret Alice Downey(d.).(09 Apr 1931 HCI)
JAMES J. JOINER, b. Hardin Co. ILL., d. 02 Feb 1862; m. Frances F. Rollins, 1878; issue: 8, 7 survive. (16 Apr 1931 HCI)
FRANCES ADELINE LACKEY, dau of Archie M. and Nancy M. Lackey, b. N.C., 16 Oct 1842, d. 08 Mar 1931; m. Charles Wesley Quellen (who d. 1870); 16 Oct 1860; issue: Mary H. Allen, Albert W., Archie L., John (d), William W. Quellen; m 2nd, M.M. Belt, 1874; issue: Chas. M. Belt, Minnie Lane, Inez Belt(d. at 8 yrs). (16 Apr 1931 HCI)
MARTHA TINSLEY, b. abt 1843, d. last Tues; dau, Mrs. Charles Dence. (23 Sept 1931 HCI)
WILLIAM PYLE, son of Nicholas & Mary Jane Pyle, b. Hardin Co. ILL., 24 Oct 1862, d. 7 Apr 1930; m. Lucy Shell, 12 Oct 1884; issue: John W., Maude (d), Lucy Engles, Elmer, Robert N., and Anna Meyers; bro, Nichols Pyle; sis, Jane Curtis(d). (23 Apr 1931 HCI)
JEFF B. DAVIS, son of Ludwick & Nancy Davis, b. Hardin Co. ILL., 24 Dec 1863, d. 15 Apr 1931; m. Elizabeth Graham, 20 Mar 1884; issue: Van,

Minnie Crow, Lydia Blakley, Effie Dell, Louise & Hannah Davis; sis, Josie Wenton, & Matilida Thomas. (30 Apr 1931 HCI)
NANCY E. OKERSON, dau of Albert & Mary Okerson, b. 25 Jul 1855, d. 18 Apr 1931; m. Charles Hufsey, 1872; issue: Mrs. Orval Hess; m. 2nd, Joseph Mason; issue: E.B. & Walter Mason; bro, C.A. Okerson; sis, Ann Hufsey, Lottie Shearer, & Kate Frayser. (30 Apr 1931 HCI)
NELL ISHAM, dau of Edd Isham, b. Karbers Ridge, Hardin Co.ILL., 6 Jul 1897, d. 8 May 1931; m. Mickey Hughes; issue: Robert Hughes; bro, Howard & Jess Isham; sis, Mrs. Lonnie Bateman, & Mrs. Ernest Glenn. (14 & 21 May 1931 HCI)
WILLIAM HARVEY HILL, b. Hardin Co. ILL., 21 Jul 1838, d. 13 May 1931; m. Mary Jane Lavander, 7 Aug 1859; issue: Elizabeth Jones, Jack, Mrs. John Garland, Otto, Minnie Garland, Walter, Rev. R.E., Tom, & Nora Rich. (21 May 1931 HCI)
JOSEPH STONE, b. Union Co. Ky., 23 Apr 1863, d. 1930; m. Martha Drake, 14 Jul 1886; issue: Clifford, Lawton, Mina Lane, Mayme Rowan, plus 3(d). (25 Jun 1931 HCI)
JOHN ALBERT LEWIS, b. Tenn., 8 Jan 1859, d. 18 Jun 1931; m. Harriet Pogue, 1891; issue: Sadie Powe, Edd Lewis & Leslie Lewis; m. 2nd, Elizabeth Ledbetter, 30 Oct 1904; issue: John A. & Charles W. Lewis. (25 Jun 1931 HCI)
ALLEN PAGE, son of William R. Page, b. abt 1868, d. Sulpher Springs, Ark.; bro, S.M. Page. (25 Jun & 2 Jul 1931 HCI)
GLADYS DOUGLAS, dau of Thomas Douglas,b. Hardin Co. ILL., 7 Oct 1907, d. 21 Jul 1931 m. Walter Oldham, 1 Nov 1923; issue: Norma Gwendolyn, and Theora Fay; leaves mother and 2 sis. (30 Jul 1931 HCI)
JOHN R. OXFORD, b. Hardin Co. ILL., 1 Jan 1867, d. 24 Jul 1931; m. 1st, Julia Angelton; issue: Effie Weber & inf(d); m. 2nd, Mrs. Mary Jane Paris; issue: Eschol & inf(d); m. 3rd, Viloa Bell Beard, 28 Jun 1898; issue: ?; "following children survive him, Eschol, Paris, Raymond, & Mrs. C.A. Flannery";half sis, Betty Rutherford, Nancy Hoover, & Mrs. Isabella Lane; half bro, James Oxford. (13 Aug 1931 HCI)
MOSE QUENTIN BARKER, b. 25 Jul 1856, d. 29 Jul

1931; m. Lilly Ann Crus, 22 Jan 1869 (She d. 12 Feb 1892); issue: May McKinney & Minnie Duncan. (13 Aug 1931 HCI)
CHESTER A. HUBBARD, b. 20 Nov 1866, d. 15 Aug 1931; m. Anna Cunningham, 1880; issue; Mrs. Jess Shewmaker, Lora Hicks & Otto Hubbard; m. 2nd, Amanda Goins;issue: Bessie Hubbard. (20 Aug 1931 HCI)
HENRY RITTENHOUSE, b. Switzerland Co. Indiana, 14 Oct 1840, d. 13 Aug 1931; m. Charlotte Persinger 16 Sept 1863; issue: Rosa Lee, Laura Peyton, William A., Hattie,& Permington Rittenhouse; leaves 2 bros, sis ?. (20 Aug 1931 HCI)
BERT DALE, b. abt 1870, d. Aug 1931; son, Arzie Dale. (27 Aug & 03 Sept 1931 HCI)
GEORGE W. OXFORD, son of Elias & Nancy Jane Oxford, b. Hardin Co. ILL., 20 Aug 1858, d. 11 Aug 1931; m. 1st, Belle Stathem; m 2nd, Julia Hobbs, 25 Dec 1884. (27 Aug 1931 HCI)
MARGARET E. GULLETT, dau of Waltman & Emma Gullett, b. 30 Mar 1864, d.--; m. James R. Patton, 02 Oct 1881; issue: Grace Wall, plus 2 (d). (03 Sept 1931 HCI)
JAMES BURTON DALE, son of John & Jane Dale, b. Livingston, Ky., 11 Feb 1870, d. 21 Aug 1931; m. Laura Alice Oxford, 11 Aug 1889(She d. 08 Nov 1903), issue: Arza, Raymond, Roy, Celia, Hancil, Ruby, Evelyn, Lora Bessie & Alice; m. 2nd, Ollie Canmpbell, 26 Oct 1907.(03 Sept 1931 HCI)
ANDY GRINDSTAFF, son of Sarah Grindstaff, d. 03 Sep 1931; leaves wife, 3 children & bro, Henry Grindstaff. (10 Sept 1931 HCI)
BEN HURFORD, b. Hardin Co. ILL., 11 Mar 1862, d. 15 Sep 1931; m.--; issue: Hiram, Catherine, Alma, plus 4 unnamed. (17 Sept 1931 HCI)
ELMER EDDIE HILL, son of James & Carolyn Hill, b. Hardin Co. ILL., 09 Jun 1870, d. 13 Aug 1931; m. Maggie M. Moore, 29 May 1910; issue: Allan A., Claude D., & Carolyn Hill; bro, Rev. J. A. Hill; sis, Alice Carr, Anzie Edmonson, Cora Turner. (17 Sept 1931 HCI)
J. BRUCE MILLER, b. Elizabethtown, Ill., 07 May 1853, d. 17 Sept 1931; m., Alice---; issue: Bertha, Oliver, Glover & Gordon Miller. (24 Sept 1931 HCI)

KATE ROBINETT, b.---,d.---; m. O.E. Nave; issue: James Nave. (01 Oct 1931 HCI)

ANDREW GRANDSTAFF, b. Hardin Co. ILL., 30 Jun 1888, d. 04 Sept 1931; m. Pearl Briles, Tolu, Ky., 20 Aug 1917; issue: 3; leaves, mother, bro, & 3 sis.(01 Oct 1931 HCI)

FRANK MCCOIN, son of Jim McCoin, b. Pope Co., ILL., 23 Feb 1880; m. Carrie Lee Dan, 23 Feb 1903; issue: Arthur & Marie McCoin.(20 Aug & 01 Oct 1931 HCI)

WILLIAM DAVIS, b. Hardin Co. ILL, 26 Jan 1877, d. 29 Sept 1931; m. Mag Golsby; m. 2nd, Josie Joyner; leaves 1 child, 2 bros.(01 Oct 1931 HCI)

FURDELA DUNCAN, b. Marion, Ky., 17 Apr 1877, d. 28 Sept 1931; issue: 3. (01 Oct 1931 HCI)

BENJAMIN HURFORD, son of William and Sarah Hurford, b. Hardin Co. ILL., 11 Mar 1862, d.15 Sept 1931; m. Annie L. Jackson, 17 Nov 1885; issue: Isaac, Wiley, Thomas, Austin, Hiram, Alma & Catherine; bro, Jesse & Noah Hurford; sis, Mary Coffee. (01 Oct 1931 HCI)

JOHN CONKLE, b. Hardin Co. ILL., 02 Jul 1863, d. 13 Oct 1931; m. Annie Packey, 03 Mar 1888;issue: Thomas, Fannie Martin, John, Bessie Decker, Sidney Mott, Sam & Christopher Conkle; bros, Tom & Isaac Conkle. (15 Oct 1931 HCI)

ERNEST MONTGOMERY, son of Theodore & Elizabeth Montgomery, b. Gibson Co. Ind., 19 Dec 1872; m. Etta McCleary, 6 Jun 1896; issue: Burtis Edward, John Wesley, Charles C., Paul Theodore, Mrs. W.W. Kemper, Helen Ruth, Mary M.; bro, 1; sis, Mrs. Sam Gladish, Mrs. George Koupas & Mrs. Joseph Carithers. (26 Nov 1931 HCI)

MAUDE JONES (male), 57 yrs old, d. ---; leaves 9 children. (03 Dec 1931 HCI)

JAMES BUCHANAN MCGLOTHLIN, son of Jahn & Maragaret Mahan McGlothlin, b. Hardin Co. ILL., 6 Mar 1856, d. 07 Dec 1931; cousins: John Garland, Thomas Garland. Lizzie Frayser, & Mrs. George Shearer. (10 Dec 1931 HCI)

WARREN LOWERY, son of J.M. & Miranda Lowery, b. 28 Aug 1892, d. 17 Dec 1931; m. Marie Swaggart, 4 Jul 1928; issue: Alma Irene, & Edna Marie Lowry; bros; Wilburn & Henry Lowery.(24 Dec

RACHEL BROWN, b. Franklin Co., ILL., 20 Oct 1873, d. 4 Dec 1931; m. 1st, ---; issue: Ella Henson; m. 2nd, Robert Merrill, issue: 10, 6 survive; m. 3rd---; m. 4th, Turner Brown; issue from all marriages:Hattie Summers, Elmer, Seth, Claude, John & Edith. (24 Dec 1931 HCI)
VIRGINIA MCNUTT, ex wife of Pernett Ferrell, d. 4 Jan 1932; issue: Anna , Margaret & Minerva Ferrell. (07 Jan 1932 HCI)
JOHN J. GENTRY, son of Alexander & Lutitia Gentry, b. 01 Sept 1851, d. 26 Mar 1934; m. Mary Thomas Adkins, 1872; issue: Minnie Gagnon, Tom Eunice Oxford & Ben Gentry; step dau, Grace Gentry; m. 2nd, Clara Stevens, 1900; issue; Richard Gentry; other issue:? Howard Gentry, Anna Monroe, Robert Gentry, Doris Garland, Ida Steber & Grace Gentry; sis of John J. Gentry; Sarah Smith & Ida Clement. (29 Mar & 12 Apr 1934 HCI)
ARAHABLE RUTHERFORD, son of Arahable "Arch" & Rebecca Oxford Rutherford, m. Lydia Wilkerson; issue: Joseph, James, Hannah (wife of Sherman Browning); bros, James, Joseph(d.),& Thomas Rutherford; sis, Miranda Ingram (wife of Ben Ingram) (12 Apr 1934 HCI)
RILEY TURNER, b 13 Mar 1864, d. 06 Apr 1934; m. Mary Tensley, 1 Jul 1883; issue: Ed, Bertha, Ollie, Cora, Etta, Ella, Loren, plus 3 (d.). (12 Apr 1934 HCI)
JOHN CALVIN OXFORD, son of Sam & Patsy Oxford, b. 28 Jan 1858, d. 17 Apr 1934; m. Mattie Wolrab, 1886; issue; Owen Oxford, plus 2 sons (d.). (19 Apr 1934 HCI)
WILLIAM PARKINSON, b. Shelterville, ILL., 1874, d. 16 Apr 1934. (19 Apr 1934)
MALINDA JANE GINGER, dau of Daniel & Ann Ginger b.02 Sept 1846*,d.02 Apr 1934; m.John H.Sneed, 01 Mar 1864; issue: Alice Stone, Billie Sneed, Annie Patton, Lucaine Sneed, Lillie Green, Izora Lawrence, Alfred Sneed, Clara Deatta, & James Sneed; bro, Joe Ginger. (19 Apr 1934 HCI)
NANCY C. JARRELLS, b. 08 Jan 1861,d. 17 Apr 1934; m. Thomas Jarrells, 05 Oct 1884; issue: Alma Russell, Mary Scarborough & Anna Collins. (26 Apr 1934 HCI)

WILLIAM VINYARD, b. Hardin Co. ILL., 1854, d. 08 May 1934; issue: Milas Vinyard; Mrs. Josie Fowler & Mrs. Like Gustin. (10 Mar 1934 HCI)
MAZRIAH H. RONDEAU, wife of C.A.F. Rondeau, b. 7 Nov 1862*, d.--. (07 Jun 1934 HCI)
FRANK GOINS, b. Hardin Co. ILL., 1894, d. last Sun; m. Myrtle Fulghan; issue: May, Mary, James & Bobbie Goins;3 bros & 3 sis.(07 Jun 1934 HCI)
JOHN P. PAGE, b. Hardin Co., ILL., unmaried; bro, Walter Page & Adli Page; half sis, Mrs. Charles Hubbard. (07 Jun 1934 HCI)
FRANCIS REIF, dau of John & Christina Hermann, b. Pope Co. ILL., 25 Nov 1871, d. 28 May 1934; m. George Reif, 29 Oct 1894, in Hardin Co. ILL. issue: Mitchell Reif & Mrs. Frank Zilk; sis, Mrs.George Ruebenachker, Mrs.Theodore Scherrer, Sally Hermann,& Mrs. Hickman Joiner; bros, Andrew, A.F. & Michael Hermann.(07 Jun 1934 HCI)
NAOMI RUTH TINSLEY, dau of James Tinsley, b. Rock Creek, ILL., 10 Jan 1902, d. 09 Jul 1934; m. Cephus W. Kinney; sis, Myrtle Reed, Mattie Slagel, Alliam, Theda, & Cowne Tinsley; bro, Archie Tinsley. (12 Jul 1934 HCI)
ANNA BELL, dau of Bill & Anna Ozee Winters, b. Hardin Co. ILL., 1871, d. thurs; m.--; issue: son & dau; m. 2nd, Joshua Pennell; bro James & Robert Winters; sis, Myrtle Sutton.(14 Jun 1934 HCI)
EMMA CURRY GINGER, b. 1864; m. Siegel Curry; m. 2nd, --- Ginger:issue:? Minnie Curns & Clara ---? (21 Jun 1934 HCI)
NANCY COWSERT, b. abt. 1855, d. last Tues; m. Ben Cowsert; issue: Alice Gertrude, Rose, John, Willie & Lonnie Cowsert. (21 Jun 1934 HCI)
EARL BARGER, b. Pope Co. ILL., d.--; m. Della Sneed; issue: Nonette, Bernard Barger, plus son,(d.). (28 June 1934 HCI)
SARA EMMA FERRELL, dau of Joseph & Elizabeth Ferrell, b 17 Apr 1864, d. 19 Jun 1934; m. J.S. Curry, 5 Aug 1880; issue: William H.(d. 06 Feb 1918), Minnie Davis & Clara Hale; bros, 6; sis, 2. (28 Jun 1934 HCI)
MARY LACKEY, dau of Archibald and Nancy Lackey, b. N.C., 03 Dec 1847, d. 20 Jun 1934; m. Richard Frailey, 15 Feb 1865; issue:

Lizzie(d.), Nancy (d.), Lela, Henry(d.), Charlie(d.) & Frank Frailey. (05 Jul 1934 HCI)
PENN V. TROVILLION, b. Pope Co. ILL., 07 Apr 1855; issue: son, 2; dau, Madge Trovillion.(05 Jul 1934 HCI)
ARTHUR COFFEE, son of A. B. Coffee, b. White Co. ILL., 24 Sept 1856; d. 06 Jul 1934; m. Mary A. Hurford, 1896. (12 Jul 1934 HCI)
DAISY SERVER COVINGTON, dau of Mary A. Server ?, b. Elizabethtown, ILL., 1886, d. Wed of last week; m. -- Covington; issue: Daisy Server Covington; sis, Mrs. L.D. Dusch, Mrs. Frank Ward & Mrs. Robert Ledbetter. (19 Jul 1934 HCI)
MRS. C.H. DUTTON, b.---, d. 09 Jul 1934; issue: sons, Newlin, Lester, Ewell, Arles (son by earlier marriage; dau, Hester.(19 Jul 1934 HCI)
LOUIS DUSCH, b.Indiana, 1851, d. Wed;issue:L.P. & Maurire Dusch. (19 Jul 1934 HCI)
WILLIAM BANKS, son of Joseph & Alice Banks, b. Marshall, Texas, 28 Jan 1882, d. Jul 1934; m. Edith Moore, 1916; issue: James, Dorthea, Opal, Georgia, Mae, Everett & Jean; sis, Lucie Ralph, & Nellie Suits. (26 Jul 1934 HCI)
MRS. A.T. GARLAND, dau of James H. Beavers, b. __, d. last Sat; m. A.T. Garland; issue: Mrs. Robert Frayser, Joe, Charles, Arthur & Ray Garland; bros, John, Joe, Pete, Ross & Walter Beavers; sis, Mattie Walker.(26 Jul 1934 HCI)
EMORY WILLIAMS, son of Mrs. J. C. Williams, Hardin Co. ILL., 1875, d. Mon; m. Bertha Lawrence, 1907; issue; Fern Kindler, Joe, Tom, Naomi Robb, Sue, Vera, Marjorie & Dean; bro, R.H. Williams; sis, Blanche Brown. (26 Jul 1934 HCI)
RICHARD HOLLOWAY, son of Thomas & Miley Holloway, b. 04 Jul 1892, d. 24 Jul 1934; m. Hettie Lewis; issue:?; bros: John, Lee, Millard & Lester; sis: Nora Austin, Mattie Oldham, & Nellie McDowell. 26 Jul & 02 Aug 1934 HCI)
HENRY LEDBETTER, son of Millington and Mary Ann Ledbetter, b. Hardin Co., 09 Apr 1881, d.19 Jul 1934; m. Gertrude Banks, 28 Jul 1903; issue: Orval(d), Howard, & John Ledbetter; bros: William R.,David W.,James M.& Philip Ledbetter. (09 Aug 1934 HCI)

PHARIS ANN FELLOWS, b. Hardin Co. ILL., 02 May 1847, d. 19 May 1934; m. Isaac Oxford, 1871; issue: William(d), Ida Jane (inf,d.), Minnie (Mrs. Charles Sullivan). (23 Aug 1934 HCI)
L.A. LEZYNISKA, b. Rosiclare, ILL.;leaves son, mother, widow, bro, & sis. (23 Aug 1934 HCI)
CLAUDE TANNER, son of Virgie & Lora Tanner, b. Porterville, Cal., 25 Jun 1915, d. 11 Aug 1934; bros: Henry M. & George Tanner; g. fathers, A.W. Milligan & G.W. Tanner. (23 Aug 1934 HCI)
GEORGE DOUGLAS, b. 1854, d. last Tues; m---; issue: Nora Mason, Dave, Jeff, Grover, Mabel Tedlock, Cora Rash, & Emma Jenkins. (30 Aug 1934 HCI)
JOHN PILAND, b. Hardin Co. ILL., d. this week; m. ---;issue: Robert, Joseph, James, Pearl & Kitty Piland;bro, Joe Piland.(06 Sept 1934 HCI)
MARY MATILDA KARBER, dau of Frank Karber, b. Hardin Co. ILL., 16 Mar 1876, d. Roseburg, Or., 27 Aug 1934; m. John Ewell, 16 Oct 1904; 1904; issue: Frank Ray Ewell(d. 1918); bros: George, Ezra, Henry, Will; sis: Junie(Mrs. Ray Howard), Lucy(Mrs. Clyde Soward?) & Eula(Mrs. Mac-- Bauman ?)   (30 Aug & 06 Sept 1934 HCI)
MYRTLE EWELL, b. Hardin Co. ILL., 1889, d. San Diego, Cal, 1932; m. Jack Ridley; bro, Arland Ewell. (06 Sept 1934 HCI)
HELEN BEAVER, wid of Hugh McConnell, b. Hardin Co. Ill., abt 1846; issue: Alma Dowdy, Mary Yeaky, Zoa Ledbetter & Richard McConnell; bro, Judge Beaver. (20 Sept 1934 HCI)
GEORGE JACOB DOUGLAS, son of Jeremiah & Nancy Douglas, b. Hardin Co. ILL., 10 Sept 1857, d. 28 Aug 1934; m. Mary Elizabeth Cook, 01 Jan 1874; issue: Mrs. Albert Edwards(d), A.L. Douglas, Nora Mason, D.A. Douglas, Grover C. Douglas, S.J. Douglas, Mrs. Bert Ingram, Mrs. J.E. Rash, Mrs. Nathaniel Jenkins & Mrs. Charlie Tadlock; m. 2nd, Mrs. Lora Bebout. (20 Sept 1934 HCI)
EPHRAIM SHAW, b. 1868, d. last Mon; issue: Clarence & Lavada Rickets.(13 Sept 1934 HCI)
HARRY PATTERSON, b. Hardin Co. ILL., 30 Jan 1896, d.01 Oct 1925; m. Fanny Jane Porter, 25

Dec 1919; issue: Robert Herald Patterson. (25 Oct 1925 HCI)
GEORGE S. LILLARD, b. Calhoun, Ky., 1872, d. Oct 1934; m. Laura Bell Layoff; issue: 2 dau. (11 Oct 1934 HCI)
BLANCHE CASAD, dau of Thomas L. & Eliza Casad, b. Hardin Co. ILL., 16 Jun 1873, d. 09 Jul 1934; m. Charles H. Dutton, 12 Dec 1903;issue: Arlen, Newlin, Lester Dutton & Hester Satterfield; bro, Otto Casad; sis, Vina Womack. (20 Sept 1934 HCI)
EARL SHEWMAKER, son of Charles Shewmaker, d. Tues. (25 Oct 1934 HCI)
OLLIE WALKER, b. Tolu, Ky., d. Tues; leaves wife & 4 children. (25 Oct 1934 HCI)
MRS. JOSEPHINE SMEE, b. Hardin Co. ILL., abt 1862, d. Mon; issue: Harve Smee, unnamed dau, plus 3 (d.). (25 Oct 1934 HCI)
MARY RUDD, wife of Lorenzo Rudd, b. Crittenden Co. Ky, 1897; m.--; issue: Anna & Mariah Rudd; leaves bro & sis. (25 Oct 1934 HCI)
GEORGE TAYTON, b. Madison Co. Ky., 06 Sept 1834. (01 Nov 1934 HCI)
GRACE MARTIN, dau of Eugene & Hettie Martin, b. 23 Sep 1912, d. 1 Oct 1934; m. Virgel Douglas, 23 Oct 1930;issue: Virgil Ray Douglas; sis, Gold Rigsby, Josephine & Imogene Martin. (01 Nov 1934 HCI)
PHOEBE WATKINS, b.01 Jan 1842, Hardin Co.,ILL., dau of Daniel Watkins,(b. near Louisville, Ky., & Susan Walston (b. Saline Co., ILL.); m. Henry Hoewischer;issue: Harry, Philip, Maude (d.at 5 yrs); m. 2nd, Thomas Oldham, 10 Oct 1878;issue: C. Fleetwood Oldham; bro, D.W. Watkins. (03 Jan 1935 HCI)
HARRIET GREGORY, b. 28 Dec 1834; m.-- Gregory; issue: John, W.C. Gregory & (03 Jan 1935 HCI)
ELIZABETH CAROLINE GINTERT,dau of Frank Gintert b. 22 Sept 1888, d. 27 Dec 1834; m.Ezra Karber, 10 Oct 1909; issue: Dorothy,Bertis,Paul; bro, Fred Gintert.(03 Jan 1935 HCI)
SUSIE SCOTT, dau of Thomas & Laura Scott, b.15 Oct 1893,Hardin Co.,d.28 Dec 1935; m.Noah Jones,19 May 1917; bros,Henry,Harrison,Frank Howard, Lee,Willis Scott; sis,Eva Stacey.(03 Jan 1935)

SARAH ELIZABETH BAKER, dau of Calvin & Frances Baker, b. 05 Nov 1851, Hardin Co., ILL.; m. William Rose, 1869; issue: Francis (d. 1914), Mrs. J.G. Gullett; bro, Morgan Baker; sis, Lucy Baker, Mary Baker. (10 Jan 1935 HCI)
RICHARD NATHANIEL COLE, son of James & Martha Ann Cole, b. 1845, Bowling Green Ky.; m. 1st, Maravilla Wilson, New Madrid, Mo., issue: 3, Ada Dederick (2 d.); m. 2nd, Jennie Carroll; issue: Olivia (d. at 17), Dewey (d. at 2 yrs), & R.C. Cole, b. Cardsville, Ky. (17 Jan 1935)
MAGGIE FRAILEY, dau of Tobe Frailey; m. Tommie Austin, issue; Henry, Roy & Luther Austin.(17 Jan 1935 HCI)
MARY E. GARLAND, dau of William and Nancy Jane Garland, b. 22 Sept 1856; d. Jan 1934; m. G.W. Shearer, 01 Dec 1879; issue: Mrs. Lilbern Farmer, Mrs. Annie Laura Smock, G.F. Shearer, Mrs. Robert Mair, Robert Shearer; bros, Tom, John Garland; sis, Mrs. R. V. Frayser (17 Jan 1935 HCI)
HARRY WHITEHEAD, son of Harry & Rebecca Whitehead Brown, b. Culpepper, Va., 29 May 1840; m. Melia Austin, (dau of Edmund and Nancy Austin), 1869, Elizabethtown,ILL.; issue: George, Henry, Orange, Edd, James, Jessie, Mrs. Lula Duncan; m. 2nd, Mrs. Anna Johnson, 1907; bros, George, Lemon, Phil, Orange; sis,? Tilde, Lou. (24 Jan 1935 HCI)
ESCHOL RUTHERFORD, son of Joesph & Ethel Rutherford, b. 13 Feb 1899, Hardin Co.,ILL., d. 15 Jan 1935; m. Maida Hambrink, 23 Aug 1924; bros, Harry & Virgil Rutherford; sis, Gladys Adams. (17 & 24 Jan 1935 HCI)
ASA FOSTER, son of H.B. & Sarah Foster, b. 09 Dec 1874, d. 8 Jan 1935; m. Anna Frailey, 26 Mar 1899;issue: Noah (d. 25 Dec 1899), Opal Foster (b. 01 Oct 1903); bros, Clarence, Henry, Wallace, Marion, Horace Foster; sis, Etta Hart (half sis), Lilley Finnley, Mrs. Frank Holt. (10, 17 & 24 Jan 1935 HCI)
HANNAH ISABEL LANE, b, 23 Nov 1870; m. H.G. Lane, 1886;issue: Hester, Edith (inf. d.) Edward(inf. d.), Stella (d. Aug 1905); half bro, James A. Oxford; half sis, Nancy Hoover (24 Jan 1935 HCI)

JAMES RILEY PATTON, son of Samuel & Lucinda Shell Patton, b. 05 Jan 1861, Hardin Co.,ILL., d.29 Jan 1935; m. Margaret Gullett,02 Oct 1881; issue: 3, (2 inf d.) Grace Wall, survives. (31 Jan 1935 HCI)
ZACHARIAH EDMONDSON, son of Gracen & Jane Riley Edmondson,b.17 Mar 1848, Martin Co., Ind., m. 1st, Sarah Elizabeth Pruett,dau,of Thomas & Margaret Pruett, 1868, Daviess Co.,Ind.;issue; John T., W.H., Newt, Mrs. Bell Scott, & Julia Cochran; m 2nd, Emma Richards; m.3rd, Mrs. Mary Butler, 1883 (who had children by 1st marriage, Thomas Butler & Josie Yates;issue: by Edmondson) 4, none survived. (31 Jan 1935 HCI)
MRS. CLEMENT MCDOWELL, dau of Walter Rutherford; leaves son and dau; bros, Ewing, Clement Rutherford; sis, Mazie Edwards, Elva Blair.(07 Feb 1935 HCI)
EMMA CAROLINE GREGG, dau of Hugh & Stacey Skelton Gregg, b. 22 Sep 1851, Hamilton Co., ILL.; m.1st, John N. Hubbard, son of Presley & Jane Hubbard, 1871; issue: Florence, Dora, Jennie, Hugh, & Mary; m. 2nd, Thomas L.Jenkins; issue: Thomas Jenkins; bros,James, William, Frank, John; issue by Hugh Greggs 3rd, marriage were Albert Gregg, & Mrs. Anna Abney. (07 Feb 1935 HCI)
FRED RALPH, son of George & Laura Ralph, d. Feb 1935; m.--- ?; issue: Mrs. Carl Frayser; bro, Gilbert Ralph; sis, Nellie Baker, & May Simmons. (07 Feb 1935)
VIRGIE RUTHERFORD, dau of Walter & Laura Rutherford, b. 16 Apr 1909, d. 03 Feb 1935; m. Clemens McDowell, 23 Oct 1926;issue: Norma Ferrol, Betty Alice & Gary Ewing McDowell; sis, Mazie Edwards & Elvia Blair; g. Father, Thomas Rutherford. (07 Feb 1935 HCI)
SAMUEL DOUGLAS MILLER, son of Samuel Douglas & Kate S. Miller, b. 1 Nov 1884, Elizabethtown, Il.; issue; Mrs. Fred Frazier and Samuel D. Miller. (14 Feb 1935 HCI)
WILLIAM J. BIRCH, son of Benjamin & Elizabeth Jones Birch, b. 16 Aug 1854, Cincinnati, Ohio; m. Hyremetty Lyons, dau of John & Nancy Belt Lyons, 11 Jan 1874, Hardin Co., ILL.; issue: Cora E. Cowsert, Alice Irby, Lula Ellis, Eva

White, Benjamin, Daisy Barnard, W.H., Dewey; bros, Richard, John, Benjamin, George, & Al Birch; sis, Martha Jane Conn, Laura Ralph; half sis, Ollie Sanders. (14 Feb 1935 HCI)
ELLEN HOLLOMAN, wife of S.A.D. Holloman, b.19 Jun 1866, Bay City, ILL.,d.09 Feb 1935; m. 1st, T.J. Vinson (d. 02 Dec 1904); issue: 9, Gurtie McElvrly, Bertha Cassick, Meltin, Rella Foe, Tom, Rheba Clark & Ruby Wright; m. 2nd, S.A.D. Holloman. (14 Feb 1935 HCI)
LEO R. SHELTER, son of Andrew Shelter, b. 02 May 1903, d. 03 Feb 1935; m. Cecilia Koch, dau of M.J. Koch,07 Oct 1925;issue:Noveda,William, Joseph, Bonnie Lou Shelter; bro, Richard & Bernard Shelter; sis,Barbara Zimmers.(14 Feb 1935 HCI)
ALBERT TAYLOR WINN, b. 22 Oct 1854, son of William Wayland Winn & Nancy Gibbons Winn, (who was b. Rising Sun, Ind); m. Sonora Belle Douglas, 26 Mar 1878; issue; Sadie McDowell, Will, Nan S. Barger, & Nora Matheny; bro,Perry Winn; sis, Mary Kaigi. (21 Feb 1935 HCI)
WILLIAM JACKSON HILL, age 61, son of William Harvey & Mary Jane Hill, d. 15 Feb 1935. (21 Feb 1935 HCI)
MRS. Savannah A. Daniels, b. 28 Aug 1864; m. Will Daniels(d); issue: Cora McGoin; g. dau, Marie Burke; g. son, Arthur McGoin (21 Feb 1935 HCI)
WILLIAM GILLESPIE JENKINS, son of Nimrod & Margaret Jenkins, b. 5 Oct 1849, Rising Sun, Ind., d. 15 Feb 1935; m. Mary Willie Edwards, 24 Sep 1871; issue; Charles. John, & Josie Ainsworth, Ella Grace Ames, Maude Hastie, Myrtle Herrin; bros, Zedick & John Jenkins; sis, Martha Belle Jenkins. (21 Feb 1935 HCI)
LURINDA CATHERINE JACKSON, dau of Tyra & Elizabeth Jackson, b.14 Aug 1850, Hardin Co., ILL., m. John Allen Barnard, 1867; issue: Dock, Mallie Holbrook, Allan, John, Spence, Walter, Alda Barnard, and Mollie Holbrook; bros, John, William, Andy, Stephen Jackson; sis,Sara & Liza Jackson. (28 Feb 1935 HCI)
S.D. MILLER, son of S.D. Miller & Katie Steel Miller (S.D & Katie were Married 26 Mar 1870), b. 01 Nov 1884, d. 10 Feb 1935; m. Anna

b. 01 Nov 1884, d. 10 Feb 1935; m. Anna
Hetherington, Apr 1905; issue;Geraldine Frazier
& S.D. Miller. (28 Feb 1935 HCI)
BARBARA HUMM, dau of Fredrick & Anna Barbara
Humm, b. 05 Jan 1846, Malkanner, Rhinefaltz,
Germany; m. Nicholas Reif 1869; issue: Saloma
& Catherine (Mrs. George Hermann.(07 Mar 1935
HCI)
ROSS BEAVERS, b. abt 1884, d. Mar 1935,
Blythesville, Ark., bro. Walter Beavers; sis,
Mrs. Horace Walker, Mrs. Perry Winn,& Mrs.
Harriet Garland. (28 Mar 1935 HCI)
WILLIAM HURFORD, son of David & Jemima Hurford,
b. 10 Jul 1881, d.10 Mar 1935; m.Ellen Wallace,
15 Jan 1905; issue; Vernon, Herbert, Wallace
Hurford, & Virgie Pabst, plus half bros & half
sis. (14 & 28 Mar 1935 HCI)
LUCIAN PANKEY SR., son of James & Mary Jane
Vinyard Pankey, b. 10 Sept 1866, Hardin Co.
ILL., d. 20 Mar 1935; m. Edith Burton, 01 Mar
1893; issue: Agnes, Dal, Iley, Mrs. James
Spivey, Mrs. Orval Irby, Everett, Lucian,
Ward(d), Ray(d); bros, John Andy, George,
James, Arthur(d); sis, Mary Jane Burton.(04 Apr
1935 HCI)
HALLIE WILLINGHAM, d. 31 Mar 1935, Sullivan,
Ky., m. Edward Ferrell; issue: 3; bro, R.H.
Willingham. (04 Apr 1935 HCI)
MOLLIE ROSE, age 85, wid of Jerry Rose, d. 5
Apr 1935, Gainsville, Fla.; dau: Nell Hardesty,
Martha Clement, Mabel Rose, Lena Rose, Mollie
Barner. (11 Apr 1935 HCI)
BEULAH IRENE OLDHAM, dau of Frank Oldham, m.
"Cap" Holbrook; issue: Cappie & Pete; sis,
Mrs. Jack Orr & Mrs. Dick Mueller. (11 Apr 1935
HCI)
JOHN B. MOYERS, son of W.C. & Mary Moyers,
b. 02 May 1887, Crittenden Co. Ky., d. 10 Apr
1935; m. Minnie Vaught, 18 Jul 1912; issue:
sons, Glenn and Gathal Moyers. (11 & 18 Apr
1935 HCI)
JOHN ROBERTSON DECKER, son of Asa & Lydia
Patrick Decker, b. 20 Jun 1854, Gallatin Co.,
Il.; m. Susan Holbrook; issue: Elizabeth (d.
inf), Owen(d), Asa, Myrtle Tolbert, Lydia
Young, John Jr., C.C., Gordon, Goldie Hurford;

sis, Florence Gullett, Milissa Lasater, Lydia Gross; bro, Asa Decker. (25 Apr 1935 HCI)
JAMES A. TADLOCK, son of John B. and Fidelia Tadlock, b. 13 Jun 1854, Grundy Co. Mo.; m. Martha Whitaker, 1877; issue: George, Clarence, Richard, Charley, Freeman, Laura Douglas, Ollie Crowell, Ida Burman & Ettie Littrell. (02 May 1935 HCI)
WILEY DAYMOND, age 85?; m. Lucretia Frailey; issue: 7, Issac, John Daymond & Mrs. Harry Frayser; m. 2nd, Anna Adams; issue; none; m. 3rd, Della Jackson; issue: 5. (02 May 1935 HCI)
LOREN Z. HUBBS, d. Mar 1935; bro, Riley Hubbs; stepbro, John b. Holloman; wife, unnamed; son, unnamed. (09 May 1935 HCI)
SARAH STANLEY, dau of Jimmie and Sarah Ellas Stanley, b. 02 May 1864, Gallatin Co. ILL.,; m. J.B. Stayton (who d. 24 Jan 1892), 13 Aug 1882; issue: 6, Ethel Dutton, Minnie Davis, & Gertie Patton, survive; m. 2nd, Samuel Gibbs (who d. 12 Jun 1911), issue: 4, Bennie & Harry Gibbs, survive. (09 May 1935 HCI)
HORATIO G. LANE, b. 1847; m.--?,; issue: W.M., J.A., G.E., Mrs. Ed Ferrell, Mrs. Add Kellen, R.H., Mrs. Henry Bascom. (16 May 1935 HCI)
WILLIAM KING, son of William King, b. 22 Mar 1885, d. 12 May 1935; m. Corda---; issue; Mrs. Audrey Cowsert, Mrs. Clyde Cowsert, Wallace & Jewell King. (16 May 1935 HCI)
IRVING MCCLUSKY, b. 17 Dec 1905, Rosiclare, ILL., d. 02 May 1935; m. Esther Tucker, 19 Mar 1927; issue: Denny McClusky; sis, Loren McClusky & Mrs. Dean Davis; g. Father, John McClusky. (23 May 1935 HCI)
WILLIAM WINTERS, son of John & Margaret Rex Winters, b. 29 Oct 1845, Ripley Co. Ind.; m. Susan Delph Ozee, 1865, Hardin Co. ILL.,; issue: Robert, James, Ernest, Myrtle Patton, Della Oxford, Annabell Pennell, (5 d.); bros, John, Dan, George, Owen & William Winters; sis, Carolyn (d,12 yrs), Catherine Rucker & Mahala Jane Bruner. (23 May 1935 HCI)
FLOYD MARGLIN, b. 1888, Gallatin Co. ILL., d. 2 Jun 1935; issue: James Gordon, Billie, and Katherine Marglin. (06 Jun 1935 HCI)
MARY E. PAGE, dau of John & Harriet Page, b. 14

Apr 1866, Hardin Co. ILL., d. 06 Jun 1935; m. Charles Vinyard, 13 Feb 1897;issue; Hosea, Nat, Edward, India Birch, Howard(d), Bessie Edwards (d 1925). (13 Jun 1935 HCI)
JESSE BARNES, son of Emmanuel Barnes, b. 05 Sept 1885; issue; Charles Bennett, Wyoma Louise Barnes; bro, Ollie Barnes; sis, Ora Vick. (13 Jun 1935 HCI)
RICHARD FULKERSON TAYLOR, son of James Pinkney Taylor & Catherine Formault Taylor, b. 05 May 1855, Pope Co. ILL.,; m. Mollie Ledbetter, dau of J. Nelson & Rebecca Ledbetter, 1884; issue: Rebecca, Eunice, Richard Fowler, Benjamin Herrin, Paul(d), Mary(d), Jack(d) & Floyd; m. 2nd, Mrs. Lillian B. Clark, 17 Feb 1925; bros, Jonathan, Spencer, Caleb, William Francis; sis, Priscilla. Richard Fulkerson Taylor was g. son of Aaron & Mary Lee Taylor, g.dau of Lighthorse Harry Lee. (20 Jun 1935 HCI)
INDIA VINYARD BIRCH, m. W. H., Birch, 1920; issue: Marion, William, & Jeanette Birch. (27 Jun 1935 HCI)
JOHN SAMUEL HUFSEY, son of Samuel & Matilda Sawyer Hufsey, b. 01 Oct 1854; m. Anna Okerson, dau of Albert & Mary Winn Okerson, 04 Feb 1885; issue:5,Mamie Crow, Eunice Gibbs & John Hufsey. (27 Jun 1935 HCI)
JOHN T. SULLIVANT, age 78, d. 14 Jul 1935; m. Mariah Barnes; issue; Mrs. John Quertermous, Mrs. C.A. Breeder, Hobart, Willard, Ray & Bruce Sullivant. (18 Jul 1935 HCI)
SARAH GENTRY,age 68, dau of Alexander & Lutitia Gentry, d. 02 Jul 1935; m.Horatio Douglas,1882; issue: 5, Jesse Douglas, survives; m. 2nd, George H. Smith; issue: 6, Lillie Pennell, Dewey, Pearl Seagraves, Radford & Reed Smith, (1 d.). (18 Jul 1935 HCI)
ELIZA HUGHES, age 97, wid of Lycurgus Hughes (Civil War vet), d. 21 Jul 1935.(25 Jul 1935 HCI)
ANNA PATTON, age 83, wid of Lewis Patton, d. 22 Jul 1935;issue: Will Patton; bros: Buck, George & Richard Moore; half sis: Sarah Skelton, Kate Clifford & Nora. (25 Jul 1935 HCI)
SARAH A. PATTON, dau of Samuel & Hannah Patton,

m.--- Carr; issue: Lottie Richardson, Leslie Hodge & dau, (d.). (25 Jul 1935 HCI)
HARRIET BELT, dau of Jonathan & Mary Belt, b. 28 Dec 1843, d. Jul 1935; m. John Gregory; issue: Willian G., John, Mrs. I.A. Coltrain & Mitty Hill(d.). (01 & 8 Aug 1935 HCI)
L.T. GOETZMAN, son of J.R. Goetzman, b. Shawneetown, ILL., m. Lucille Burton, dau of E.E. Burton. (01 Aug 1935 HCI)
BELLE FLORENCE WILLIAMS, dau of T.L. & Harriet Williams, b. 05 Sept 1870, d. 25 Jul 1935; m. Alvin Hale, 27 Mar 1887;issue: Thomas(d), Laura Etta(d), Charlie, Guy & Lolene Hale.(01 Aug 1935 HCI)
JOSIE BELT, age 73, dau of Joel & Sarah Belt, d. 03 Aug 1935; m. William Bascom; issue: Daisy, Bessie Wingate, Nola Smith, Grover & Henry Bascom;half bro, Frank Oldham; sis,? Rose Vick, Mrs. Dill Shoemaker & Nell Boyd.(08 Aug 1935 HCI)
THELMA WAGGONER, dau of Joseph & Cora Waggoner, b. 10 Jun 1902, d. 08 Aug 1935, m. Ora Vinyard, 17 Feb 1920; bros, George, A.H., Abner, Robert, Presley & William Waggoner; sis, Mae Ward, Velma Hale & Ruby Waggoner. (15 Aug 1935 HCI)
GRACE GREENLEAF, dau of H.A. & Mary Greenleaf, b. 1869, Vevay, Ind., d, Aug 1935; issue: Katherine Robinson, Mary, Pauline & Ann---?; bros, Carol & Joe W. Greenleaf. (22 Aug 1935 HCI)
JOE KEELING, son of James Keeling, b. 1851, Hardin Co. ILL., m. Emma Hodges, 1875, Hardin Co. ILL., dau of James Hodges; issue: 10, Ada, Tate, Ellen Riggs, Ed & Fred Keeling Virgie Bengall,& Eva Morris,survive. (29 Aug 1935 HCI)
FRANCES HARDESTY, b. 15 Sept 1861, d. 25 Aug 1935; m. John H. Goodwin, 30 Mar 1878;issue: Mrs. Walter Dimick, Mrs. Harve Renfro, Ross & Robert Goodwin. (29 Aug 1935 HCI)
LILLIE MADDOX, dau of John T.& Margaret Maddox, b.13 Nov 1858, Hardin Co. ILL., m. John V.Lee; issue: Effie Hunter, Walter Lee, Clifford Lee & Daisy Olwin.(05 Sept 1935 HCI)
ED ROSE, son of Mollie Rose & --? Rose d. 21 Aug 1934; bros, Clifford Rose & William Rose; sis, Mrs. Otto Ledbetter, Mrs. Freeman Hubbs,

Mrs. Virgie Schutt, Mrs. Joe Shelter & Eula Rose. (26 Sep 1935 HCI)
JOHN LEWIS NEWMAN, son of John & Catherine Newman, b. 09 Mar 1844, Monroe Co., Va., m. Elizabeth Ogden; issue: Edward F. & George W. Newman; m. 2nd, Maria Xander; bro., George W. Newman. (27 Sept 1935 HCI)
MAGGIE CREAMER, dau of Johnnie Creamer, b. 11 Mar 1870, Cadiz, Co. Ky., d. 2 Sep 1935; m. E. P. Shaw, 05 Jun 1890;issue: 7, Mrs. Ramona Ricketts & Clarence Shaw, survive; bros, Alley, Charlie, Tommy, & Johnnie Creamer; sis, Minnie Foxx. (27 Sept 1935 HCI)
RICHARD MCCONNELL, son of Hugh & Helen Beavers McConnell, b. 11 Oct 1867, Hardin Co. ILL.; m. Lucy Alice Bently; issue: 4, Gladys, Ellis, Cyrus & dau(d at 3yrs); m. 2nd, Olive B. Alexander; issue: Everett, Mary Pearson, & Richard McConnell. (27 Sept 1935 HCI)
SHERMAN VAUGHN, m. Essie---; issue; Oleda Jewell: bros, Oscar, McKinley, Loren, & Miles; sis: Ollie Johnson, India Hardin, Pearl Vaughn & Iva Vaughn. (10 Oct 1935 HCI)
LAURA MCAMOS,? b.? 1863;m. James b. McFarland: issue: James T. & Mattie McFarland Lucas; m. 2nd, John Newman. (10 Oct 1935 HCI)
WILLIAM HENRY BASCOM, son of Gais & Sarah Tinker Bascom, b. 23 Jun 1855, East Enterprise, Switzerland Co. Ind; m. Josie Belt, dau of Joel & Sarah Belt, 05 Jan 1882; issue; 5, Daisy, Grover & Nola Smith Bascom, survive. (17 Oct 1935 HCI)
HUBER DEMONT DALTON, son of Charley Dalton, b. 21 Dec 1897, Livingston, Ky., d. 09 Oct 1935; m. Pearl Keeling, 12 apr 1919; issue: Willina Fay(d) & Marcella(dau); bros: John, Charlie, & Reed Dalton; sis, Opal Dalton.(17 Oct 1935 HCI)
JOHN F. HUFSEY, b. 11 Oct 1854; issue: John & Dennic Hufsey. (17 Oct 1935 HCI)
FRED MCCLUSKY, son of John & Lucinda O'Neal McClusky, b. 6 Apr 1881, Hardin Co. ILL.; m. Anna Cruson, 29 Mar 1903; issue: Gordon (who m. Della Wamack), Rodney & Irene Pruett McClusky. (24 Oct 1935 HCI)
JOHN BOATRIGHT, age 66, d. 23 Oct 1935; m.

Hattie ---; issue: Ray, Fred & Anna McDowell; bros, Macki, Louis, Lenard, Allen & Charles. (31 Oct 1935 HCI)

JENNIE HOWARD, dau of W.P. Howard, b. 13 Nov 1902, Rosiclare, ILL.; m. Henry Lane, 01 Nov 1930; bros, Marvin & Loren Howard. (31 Oct & 07 Nov 1935 HCI)

JOHN LEWIS KING, b. 1844, Hardin Co. ILL., d. 28 Oct 1935; m. Charlotte---; issue: Harold, Velma, Doris & Norma King; sis, Daisy Volkert. (31 Oct 1935 HCI)

GEORGE ROBERT MOYERS, son of William & Catherine Moyers, b. Jan 1879, Sheridan, Crittenden Co. Ky., d. 21 Nov 1935; m. Ora Ferrell, Jan 1912; bro, Wesley Moyer; sis, Maggie Carnahan. (28 Nov 1935 HCI)

IDA CLEMENT, d. 23 Nov 1935; m. John Clement; Issue: Clarence & Ivy McLean. (05 Dec 1935 HCI)

MARY JANE EVANS, dau of Mary Ann Evans, b. 27 Oct 1865, Hardin Co. ILL., d. 18 Nov 1935; m. Jim Simms; issue: Andrew Simms, 2(d.); m. 2nd, S.R. Holbrooks; bro, Jim Evans. (05 Dec 1935 HCI)

MORGAN TUCKER, b. abt 1852, d. 21 Nov 1935. (05 Dec 1935 HCI)

WILLIAM ALEXANDER RALPH, son of W.A. & Mary Ralph, b. 26 Aug 1868, Hardin Co. ILL., d. 30 Nov 1935; m. Emma Russell, 14 Jan 1896; issue: Elmer, Henrietta Patterson, Mary Hardin, Ben, Dora Bass Ralph & 2 (d); bro, McClellan. (05 Dec 1935 HCI)

MRS. ANNA BIRCH, b. ? 1860, d. Dec 1935; sons: Arthur, Roy & Oscar. (05 Dec 1935 HCI)

WILLIAM HARVEY HERRIN, son of George & Elizabeth Curry Herrin, b. Webster Co. Ky.; m. Flora Hunter; issue: O.T. Herrin & W.C. Herrin; m. 2nd, Mrs. Elsie Brown; issue: James Harvey (d. at 9 yrs), Wilford Horace, Clara Bernice, Walter Erlo & Ethel Ruth Herrin; bros, James & Benjamin Herrin. (12 Dec 1935 HCI)

SARAH JANE MASON, dau of Caswell Mason, b 11 Dec 1835, Princeton, Ky; m. Shephard Frailey, 1852; issue: 4, Robert & Dan Frailey, plus 2 daus(d); m. 2nd, Joel Oldham, 1891. John Frailey was son from Shephard Fraily's 1st, Marriage. (12 Dec 1935 & 16 Apr 1936 HCI)

DAVID CORNELL, son of Edward & Laura Cornell, b. 10 Feb 1890, Pope Co. ILL., d. 21 Dec 1935; m. Rachel Joiner, 1911; issue: Freda Potts, Meredith Cowsert, Vercie, Millard, Margie, Garcie, Archie, Wilburn, Nora, Cleoma(inf,d.); Bros: Alonzo, George & Frank Cornell; sis: Carrie Lackey & Minnie Harrison.(2 Jan 1936 HCI)
LOU CROW, age 76, d. 20 Dec m. Albert Crow; issue: Vida Millikan, Thomas, Willis, Howard, Charles & Russell; sis, Mary Matson.(02 Jan 1936 HCI)
CHARLES LEDBETTER, son of Arthur & Mary Ledbetter, b. 06 Mar 1875, d. 03 Jan 1936; m. Maggie --; issue: Carol Virgil, Katherine Carrie,& Charline Ledbetter; g. father, Samuel Hufsey. (09 Jan 1936 HCI)
MRS. JAMES LEDBETTER, b. 16 Jan 1882, d. Jan? 1936; m. James Ledbetter, 31 Aug 1901; issue: Charles, John, Viola, Virgie, Frankie(dau) & Mary Turner. (09 Jan 1936 HCI)
MARY JANE LAMB, dau of W.R. & Malisia Lamb, b. 16 Jan 1864, d.08 Jan 1936; m. Thomas Belt, 05 Mar 1882; issue: Willis, Clara (d. 9 yrs.), Ida Brittain; bros: Willis, George, James, & John Lamb; sis: Sophronia Finley. (16 & 23 Jan 1936 HCI)
TRIPHENA LITTLE KING, b. 30 May 1864, Hardin Co. ILL., d. 08 Jan 1936; m. Joseph A. King, 1887; issue: Charles, Allen, Loren, John L. King & Daisy Volkert. (16 Jan 1936 HCI)
NANCY E. BOYD, b. 21 Nov 1857, d. 08 Jan 1936; m. Dow Boyd; issue: Bessie Oldham,Effie Pearson & Otto Boyd. (16 Jan 1936 HCI)
JOHN ROWLAND, son of James Rowland, b. 08 Sept 1900, Crittenden Co. Ky.; m. Golda Hall; bros: Bill & Raymond Rowland; sis: Mrs. E.V. Young. (16 Jan 1936 HCI)
WILLIAM TUCKER BYNUM,son of Richard & Elizabeth Bynum,b. 22 Mar 1876, Hardin Co., ILL; bros: J.A. Bynum; sis: Margaret Ginger & Myrtle Williams. (23 Jan 1936 HCI)
CHESTER JONES, d. 26 Jan 1936; mother, Belle Jones; bro, Neal Jones; half bro, Charles Day. (30 Jan 1936 HCI)
WILLIAM NOAH HURFORD, age 76, d. 25 Jan 1936;

bro, Jesse Hurford. (30 Jan 1936 HCI)
LENORA HOSKINSON, dau of I.R. and Nancy, b. Hardin Co. ILL., d. 9 Feb 1936, Dallas, Texas; m. J. C. Millikan; issue: Robert Millikan; bros: Logan & Willburn Hoskinson; sis: Mrs. Charlie Stephenson. (13 Feb 1936 HCI)
WILLIAM CALVIN PALMER, age 71, d. 16 Feb 1936; son; Cecil Palmer. (20 Feb 1936 HCI)
ANDREW JACKSON WINN, age 65, son of James & Ellen Winn, d. 16 Feb 1936; m.--; issue: Willie Winn. (20b Feb 1936 HCI)
CHARLES W. SMITH, b. 1861, d. 22 Feb 1936; son, Loren Smith. (27 Feb 1936 HCI)
MRS. FRED JACKSON, dau of Frank Tabor, b. 14 Dec 1909, Mexico, Ky., m. Fred Jackson, 29 Aug 1928; issue: Yvonne Lee, Peggy Sue, William Eugene Jackson. (27 Feb 1936 HCI)
WILLIS ALLEN COX, son of Soloman & Jane Cox, b. 09 Oct 1870, Saline, Co. ILL.; m. Elizabeth Reiner, 1889; issue; Fred, Raliegh, Cecil, Allen, India Calbert, Audrie Ferrell, Elizabeth Hobbs; bros, D.N. Cox; sis, Anna Belle Joyner. (27 Feb 1936 HCI)
CLYDE EDWARD MAYFIELD, son of Frank & Ruby Mayfield, b. 8 Mar 1921, Elizabethtown, ILL., d. 01 Mar 1936; bros, Charles, James, Frankie; sis, Juanita & Mrs. Roy Leonard; stepsis, Beulah Holton. (11 Mar 1936 HCI)
MARY E. MANHART, b. 22 Jun 1850, d. 14 Mar 1936; m. Thomas Fowler; issue: Robert Fowler & Thomas (who d. in Inf), m. 2nd, G.W. Manhart. (19 Mar 1936 HCI)
JAMES A. STEEL, son of Alexander A. & Sarah Steel, b. 05 May 1864, d. 13 Mar 1936; m. Mrs. Adelaid Rush, 16 Nov 1894; issue: Alexander, Frederick, Rodney, Charles; sis, Jennie Rose, Della Caldwell, plus 2 (d.). (19 Mar 1936 HCI)
SARAH ESTHER LEDBETTER, b. 18 June 1873 *, Hardin Co, ILL.; m. A.S. Griffith; issue: Maudie, Claude, Lenel, Alice, Paul & Golda; m. 2nd, George Ledbetter. (09 Apr 1936 HCI)
ROSA SPIVEY, dau of James Spivey, b. 24 Jun 1877, Fairview, Fulton, Co. ILL.; m. Wiley Swaggirt, 19 Apr 1896; issue: Jewell & Vevith; bro, Howard Spivey; sis, Ollie Joiner. (23 Apr & 7 May 1936 HCI)

CLEVE VINSON, b. 24 Feb 1885, Mayfield Ky., d. 26 Apr 1936; m. Myrtle Clark, 09 May 1908; issue (inf d); bro, Hershel Vinson. (30 Apr 1936 HCI)
ROBERT EUGENE GINGER, son of James b. & Lizzie Ginger, b. 04 Dec 1904, d. 16 Mar 1936; bros: John, Walter(d), Warden(d); sis: May Smith, Eva Pyles,Shuah Mick & Lucille Ginger. (30 Apr 1936 HCI)
SARAH JANE MCDOWELL, dau of Eli & Rachel McDowell, b. 7 Apr 1860, Hardin Co. ILL., d. 22 Apr 1936; m. James Burklow, 04 Jul 1879, Shawneetown, ILL., issue: Jack, Otto, Robert, Ray, Annie Conditt, Kate Lampert, Alice Winters & Bessie Pennell. (30 Apr & 21 May 1936 HCI)
VIRGINA JOINER, dau of Clint Joiner, b. 04 Jan 1918, d. 19 May 1936; m. Goethal Moyers, 25 Apr 1936; bro: Glen Joiner; sis: Helen Threlkeld, & Ernesteen. (28 May 1936 HCI)
ROXIE WINDERS, dau of J.W. & Susie Winders, b. 11 Jul 1905, Hardin Co. ILL., d. 28 May 1936; m. Harvey Suits, 21 Sept 1928; issue: Harlan, Eugene, Herschel, Lavern Suits; bros, ?; sis: Nora, Belva, Mae & Marie Winders.(04 Jun 1936 HCI)
CHARLES S. WINN, b. abt 1870, d. 30 Apr 1936; m. Lee ---; issue; Thelma Louise, Irene Winn; step son, Clyde Foster. (07 May 1936 HCI)
AMARIAH ALPHEUS GUSTIN, son of Isaiah Gustin & g. son of Amariah Gustin; b. 2 Feb 1849, Rising Sun, Ind., ILL., d. 06 May 1936; m. Alice Vinyard, issue; Em (son), Ada Lee Kornstein, Bill; sis, Betty Pell. (14 May 1936 HCI)
MARY ELIZABETH WINN., dau of William Wayland & Nancy Gibbons Winn, b. 03 Sept 1861, Hardin Co. ILL., d. 8 May 1936; m. Henry D. Kaegi, 1885, Lawrence, Kan.; issue: George, Omer, Will,Roy, Charles, Bernard, Loren, Herbert; bro, Albert Taylor Winn. (14 May 1936 HCI)
JOE SANTY, son of Frank Santy, b. 30 Apr 1899, d. 24 Apr 1936; dau, Helen; bros, Clarence, Ruie & Earl; sis, PearL Wallace. (21 May 1936 HCI)
ANNA HETHERINGTON, dau of Richard & Jane Little Hetherington, b. 06 Jan 1864, d. 7 May 1936; m.

George Morris, 1885;issue: Mrs. Hatchett Smith, George, William, Overton(d.), Herbert(inf.d); sis, Mrs. Norton Renfro. (21 May 1936 HCI)
T.A. DUNN, age abt 80, d. 14 May 1936; sis, Mrs. Dutton. (21 May 1936 HCI)
HARRY WHITEHEAD, b. 29 May 1840, Culpepper, Va; m. Melia Austin, 1869, Hardin Co. ILL., (26 May 1936 HCI)
BILLY WINTERS, son of John Winters, b. 1845, Riley Co. ILL., m. Susan Delph Ozee,1865. (26 May 1936 HCI)
EZEKIEL HOBBS, son of Arch Hobbs; m. Frances Ann Keeling, 15 Aug 1877, Harding Co. ILL.; issue; 10, Andrew, Julia Hardin, Fannie Vaughn, Sol & Elmer Hobbs. (28 May 1936 HCI)
JOHN FRAILEY, step-son of Sarah Jane Oldham, born abt 1851, d. May 1936, Ind.; son, Alex Frailey; daus: Anne Perry, Ora McLean & Gusta Jones. (04 Jun 1936 HCI)
WILLIS COWSERT, b. 25 May 1860, d. 24 May 1936; m. Mindy Vaughn, Feb 1881; issue: W.L., Green, Aaron, Ulysses Cowsert & Anna Irons. (11 Jun 1936 HCI)
AL JENKINS, age 63, b. Hardin Co. ILL., d. 28 Jun 1936; m. Ida ---; Issue: Herbert Jenkins. (05 Jul 1936 HCI)
DANIEL PATTON, d. 25 Jun 1938; m. Anna ---; issue: 4; bros, Warren & Hillis Patton. (05 Jul 1936 HCI)
DAVID WINTERS, son of George & Margaret Winters b. 28 Jan 1861, Hardin Co. Ill.,d. 30 Jun 1936; m. Bettie Gustin, 1888; issue: 6, Alice, Dell, Phoebe, 2 (d.); m. 2nd, Della Dunnaway, 1907; issue; Opal, Millie, George, David & Charlie; bro: William Winters; sis: Anne Dale & Finney Austin. (02 & 16 Jul 1936 HCI)
JACOB SCHUTT, age 74, d. 5 Jul 1936; sons; Willie, Virgil, Ezra & Clyde. (9 Jul 1936 HCI)
TRICE CLARK, son of Lester & Elizabeth Clark, b. 12 Aug 1918; sis: Gladys Birch, Helen Cochran, Hazel Ashford, Anice Allen; bros, Roy & Bobby Clark. (16 Jul 1936 HCI)
JAMES LEONARD FRAYSER, son of Virginnium and Ellen Frayser, b. 1876, Hardin Co. ILL., d. 14 Jul 1936, St. Louis, Mo.; son: Leonard Frayser; dau: Maisie Dixon & Rosella Frayser;

bros: Ross & Bob Frayser. (23 Jul 1936 HCI)
NANNIE E. STACEY, dau of Jordan & Betty Stacey, b. 21 Mar 1856, Overton Co. Tenn., d. 20 Jul 1936; m. R.L. Girvan, 10 Jun 1877; issue: Mrs. Alpha Jackson, Myrtle Hyatt, Georgia Miles, Vera Thomas & Raleigh Girvan; bro: W.B. Stacey. (23 Jul 1936 HCI)
RICHARD NATHANIEL COLE, son of James & Martha Cole, b. 1845, Bowling Green, Ky.; m. Marvilla Wilson, New Madrid, Mo.; m.2nd, Jennie Carroll; issue: R.C. Cole. (30 Jul 1936 HCI)
WILL SEINER, age 66, d. Fri, West Plains, Mo.; sis, Mrs John Rotes & Mrs. Michael Herrmann.(06 Aug 1936 HCI)
LEONORA GRIFFITH, dau of Thomas & Cynthia Griffith, b. 18 May 1867, Carrsville, Ky.; m. John T. Kibler, 16 Feb 1886, Elizabethtown, ILL.; issue; Eddie (inf,d.), Daisy M., Wayne P, Weldon G.;sis; Sula Lamar, Emma Hoke. (27 Aug 1936 HCI)
THOMAS COWSERT, son of Willie & Sarah Cowsert, b. Oct 1865, d. 01 Sept 1936; bros: Charles & Ben Cowsert; sis:Betty Peas & Mary Jane Henson. (03 Sept 1936 HCI)
JAMES F. COX, son of William Cox, b. 24 Apr 1869, Salem, Ky., d. 5 Sept 1936; m.--; issue: Gilbert, Clinton Cox & Mrs. Alley Minner. (10 Sept 1936 HCI)
ABRAM LAWRENCE, son of J.B. & Sarah Lawrence, b. 15 Mar 1873, Hardin Co. ILL.; m. Willie Lofton,31 Oct 1901; bros: J.D., Elic, Addison, Sylvester, & Lawrence; sis: Ada Vinyard, Agnes Mott, & Bertha Williams.(24 Sept 1936 HCI)
ETHEL RICHEY, dau of G.S. Richey, age 39, d. 24 Sep 1936; m. Fred Brown; issue: Wilfred Brown; bros: William G. & Elliot Reak Richey; sis, Mary Lee Elliott. (01 Oct 1936 HCI)
MARY A. KEELING, dau of James L. & Elizabeth Keeling, b. abt 1856, Hardin Co. ILL., d. Sept 1936; m. Henry Hans; bros: J.W., T.F., & J.H. Keeling; sis, Frances Ann Hobbs; stepson, Fred Hans; stepdau, Mrs. G.H. Sheridan. (01 Oct 1936 HCI)
NORA EDITH RICHEY, dau of W.S. & Drucillia Reak Richey, b. 22 Nov 1896, Paducah, Ky., d. Sept 1936; m. George Frederick Brown, 05 Sept 1913,

Shawneetown, ILL.; issue: Winfred, Mary Emma, Hazel,Beatrice; bros: William Clifton & Elliott Reak Richey; sis, Mary Lee Elliott. (01 Oct 1936 HCI)
JOHN PERRY, age 61, d. 17 Oct 1936, Anniston, Mo.; bro, Tom Perry; sis, Elvira Tadlock. (22 Oct 1936 HCI)
WILLIAM JACOB RICE, b. abt 1863, Saline Co., Il., d. 03 Oct 1936; m. Denie---; issue: Cecil C., Kenneth & Oscar Rice; bros: Louis & John Rice. (08 Oct 1936 HCI)
MARY ANN JACKSON, dau of Thomas & Lucy Ann Glace Jackson, b. 15 Aug 1856, near Smithland, Ky.; m. Aaron S. Johnson, 11 Nov 1874; issue: Charlie (d. 21 yrs), Ewing (d. 19 yrs), George (d 12 yrs), Francis (dau, d. 24 yrs), Laura (d. 2 yrs), Ella Blais, Eva Price, Ida Obermark, Pearl Barton, Mrs. Joe Frailey, Aaron, & Frank Johnson. (08 Oct 1936 HCI)
EDDIE LOCKLAR, age 58, son of John and Barbara Locklar, d. 23 Oct 1936; bros, George Locklar; half bro, Frank; sis, Florence McBee. (29 Oct 1936 HCI)
ABE SLUPSKY, b. 26 Jun 1861, London, England, d. 23 Oct 1936; m. Caroline Fischer, 16 Feb 1896; St.Louis, Mo.;issue: Edward, Abe, Morris, Armedee & Mrs. Orval Duke. (05 Nov 1936 HCI)
SALLIE HERMANN, dau of John & Christine Hermann b. 26 Dec 1867, d. 11 Nov 1936; bros, A.F. & Michael Hermann,plus 1(d); sis,Lizzie Joiner, Mary J. Ruebenacker, Regina Scherrer, plus 2 (d). (19 Nov 1936 HCI)
BLANCE MAY FORD, dau of T.J. Ford, b. 1904, Desoto, ILL., d. Nov 1936; m. Granville Tichenor, issue: Vernon Tichenor; sis, Mrs. John Pate. (03 Dec 1936 HCI)
MARY ELIZABETH JOHNSON, age 98, wid of A.B. Johnson, d. Nov 1936; issue: John, Louis, Arch Johnson, Lula Combs, Martha Newton and Laura Ledbetter. (03 Dec 1936 HCI)
LAURA TOLBERT, b. abt 1876, d. 30 Nov 1936; m. Will Tolbert; issue: Bennie, Thanor Tolbert, and Annie Joiner. (03 Dec 1936 HCI)
FREDERICK KINNEY, b. abt 1850, d. 20 Nov 1936; unmaried. (03 Dec 1936 HCI)
MRS. CARRIE WARFORD, d. 28 Nov 1936, Marion,

Ky.; issue; Roy & George Warford, Mrs. Toy Watson & Mrs. Arza Oxford. (03 Dec 1936 HCI) THOMAS CURTIS, son of Broad Curtis & Elizabeth Barton Curtis, d. 6 Dec 1936; m. Anna --, issue: Fowler Curtis, Madelin Grandstaf, Ethel Margaret Porter & Katherine Nelson. (10 Dec 1936 HCI)
JAMES BURKLOW, son of John & Martha Susan Cook Burklow, b. 29 Aug 1854, Hardin Co. ILL.; m. Sarah Jane, dau of Eli & Rachel,McDowell, 04 July 1879,Shawneetown, ILL.; issue: Robert, Annie Conditt, Kate Lampert, Andrew Jackson, Otto, Alice Winters, Bessie Pinnell & George Raymond Burklow; bros,Sam & Charlie Burklow; sis, Eliabeth Needham. (10 Dec 1936 HCI)
DELILAH TERRELL, wid of Joseph Eli Terrell, d. 08 Dec 1936; issue: Mack, Commodore, Walker, Hugh & Edna Terrell Durham. (10 Dec 1936 HCI)
NANCY REYNOLDS, dau of Alex & Amerine Reynolds, b. 05 Apr 1872, Hardin Co. ILL., d. 09 Dec 1936; m. F.M. McDowell, 1891; issue: Charles, Robert, Grace Needham, Rose Griggs, Pearl Hobbs; m. 2nd, Aaron Pinkey McDaniels, 27 Dec 1936; half bros, Otis, Henry, Richard Brittain, Wallace Dixon; half sis, Pearl Morrison; aunts, Mary Brown, Emma Brown; step children, Flossie Gregory, Hazel Grancy & David McDaniel. (17 & 24 Dec 1936 HCI)
GEORGE RICKETTS, b. 15 Jan 1885, Hardin Co, ILL., d. 09 Dec 1936; issue: Raymond, Walter, Mrs. Oscar Crabb, Charles & Mrs. Floyd Hill. (17 Dec 1936 HCI)
EUEL THOMAS SCOTT, son of Aaron Freeman Scott and Elizabeth Bell Scott, b. 10 Feb 1851, Livingston, Ky.; m. Eva Pearson, 04 Dec 1892, Hardin Co., ILL., issue: Edgar, Matt, Henry, & Haratio Scott; sis, Maude Swaggert and Kate Scott. (24 Dec 1936 & 14 Jan 1937 HCI)
ROSE STILL, b. Saline Co., ILL., d. Dec 1936; m. R.R. Givens;issue: Pearnus "Red" Givens,& Lealie Vinson; m. 2nd, Ross Threlkeld; bros, Oliver, Arthur & Virgil Still; sis, Rosa Simmons. (31 Dec 1936 HCI)
BEN LAVANDER, son of Thomas Lavander, b. May 1844, New Albany, Ind.; m. Cassander Rose, 1869, issue: Wiley Lavander & Mrs. Tyer. (31

Dec 1936 HCI)
EZEKIAL HOBBS, b.04 Jun 1844, d.05 Jan 1937; m. Frances A. Keeling, issue: Sol, Andrew, Elmer, Julie Hardin, Fannie Vaughn & 3(d.) (7 Jan 1937 HCI)
MARY REINER, dau of John Reiner, b. 06 Feb 1871, d. 13 Dec 1936; m. John Schroll, 22 Sept 1899; issue: Freeman, Wayne, Essie, Gertrude Winters, & Effie Vinyard. (20 Jan 1937 HCI)
MARTHA JONES, b.19 Feb 1851, Pope? Co. LL., d. 26 Jan 1937; m. Thomas Cochran; bro, John Jones. (11 Feb 1937 HCI)
ROBERT GOODWIN, son of John Goodwin, b. 1884, Rosiclare, ILL., d. 26 Jan 1937; bro, Ross Goodwin; sis, Mrs. W.H. Renfro & Mrs. W.E. Dimick. (11 Feb 1937 HCI)
EARL ED BURKE, b. 27 Jan 1860, d. 23 Jan 1937; issue: Carroll, Raymond, Betty Thompson, & Ora Davis Burke. (11 Feb 1937 HCI)
ASROE OWENS, son of C.V. & Emily Owens; m. Mabel Austin; issue: Wanda Ruth & Geraldine Owens; bros, Adiel, Roscoe & Orba Owens; sis, Beulah Walker, Prudie Wasson & Seretha Brown. (11 Feb 1937 HCI)
DORA JACKSON MCDOWELL, 67, wid of Kell McDowell d. 25 Jan 1937; son, Ed McDowell; dau, May Rankins; sis, Betty Hutchinson & May Collom; bros, George & Ed Jackson. (11 Feb 1937 HCI)
MRS. ADDIE GAINES, d. 29 Jan 1936; sons, Earl, Nemo & Ura Gaines. (11 Feb 1937 HCI)
YULEE HARDIN, son of Cam & Sarah Hardin,b. 30 Jan 1904, Lola, Ky., d. 05 Feb 1937; dau, Milodeen; sis, Mrs. Zelpha Wilson; bros, Reed, Jess, Ray & C.D. Hardin. (11 Feb 1937 HCI)
RICHARD REED, Son of R.J. & Alice Dean Reed, b. 01 Jun 1879, d. 01 Feb 1937; m. Eva Dale, 12 Oct 1912;issue: Mildred, Ruth & A.C. Reed; bros, Robert, Riley & James Reed; sis, Ethel Cook.(18 Feb 1937 HCI)
PAUL H. THRELKELD, age 41, d. 09 Feb 1936 (37?), Owensboro, Ky.; m. Ruth; issue: Paul Threlkeld. (18 Feb 1937 HCI)
L.A. KARBER, d. 18 Feb 1937; m.---; issue: Ada Miles, Mrs. Charlie Hale, Mrs. Roy Vinyard, John & Fred Karber. (25 Feb 1937 HCI)
BERTA UNDERWOOD, dau of J.M. Underwood, b. 18

Mar 1898, Hardin Co. ILL., d. Feb 1937; m. Enos Austell; issue: son; bro, Millard Underwood; sis, Docia Sturgeon, Viola Lindsey, Addie Mann, Effie Muellar & Tressie Steele.(4 Mar 1937 HCI)
FRANK GENTRY, age 64, son of James and Ollie Gentry, unmarried; bros, James, & Henry Gentry; sis, Eliza Herrington & Mrs. Willis Lamb. (04 Mar 1937 HCI)
JOHN WESLEY WATKINS, son of William & Linda Watkins, m. Grace---;issue: Gilbert Watkins; step dau, Mrs. Herbert Smith. (04 Mar 1937 HCI)
MOLLIE JENNINGS, b. Hardin Co. ILL., d. 26 Feb 1937. (04 Mar 1937 HCI)
BILL WALLACE, son of Tom Walker, d. 1 Mar 1937. (04 Mar 1937 HCI)
CHARLES ANDERSON OXFORD, son of James & Florence Oxford, b.12 Aug 1881,Hardin Co. Ill., d.09 Mar 1937; m.1st, Maude Patterson; issue: Opal Oxford; m.2nd, Belvia Patton; issue: Mildred Oxford; m.3rd, Eunice Gentry; issue: Charles Eugene Oxford & Mary Thomas;bros, S.E., Herbert & Arza Oxford. (11 Mar 1937 HCI)
BESSIE CONKLE, dau of John & Annie Conkle, b. 28 Dec 1898, Hardin Co. ILL., d. 4 Mar 1937; m. Henry Decker, 03 May 1927; 4 bros, 3 sis. (11 Mar 1937 HCI)
CARROLL HOLBROOK, son of Samuel & Betsy Ann Holbrook, b. Hardin Co. ILL., 29 Oct 1868; m. Mollie Barnerd; m. 2nd, Catherine Shanks; dau, Thelma Wilson; sons, unnamed. (11 Mar 1937 HCI)
ED PATTON, d. Mar? 1937; bros, Walter, Enos Patton;sis, Mrs. James Porter.(11 Mar 1937 HCI)
IKE F. ROGERS, b. 11 Apr 1852, Tenn., d. 22 Feb 1934; m. Mary J.C. Russell,28 Sept 1873; issue: George W., Anna Smith, Charles D., Ellis,Isaac, Louella & Almedia Black, Elmer Alvin, Lottie Cowsert, Lucy Rutherford, John(d), plus, 2 inf, (d.). (18 Mar 1937 HCI)
NORA FERRELL, dau of James K.P. Ferrell & Elizabeth Hill Ferrell, b. 03 Mar 1876, d. 28 Feb 1937; m. Henry Milligan, 29 Jun 1893; issue: Leslie, Ray, Orval, Opal(d.), Pearl (son?), Mrs. Frankie Moore & Mabel Partain; bros, 5 (unamed) (04 & 25 Mar 1937 HCI)
ANTONE VOLKERT, son of Antone & Rittie Volkert b. 7 Mar 1857, Hardin Co.ILL., d.1 Mar 1937; m.

Caroline, 2 Jan 1883; issue; Antone, Henry, Frank, Thomas, Hatttie Hurford (3 d.?); bros, George & Jesse Volkert; sis, Maggie Ginger.(01 Apr 1937 HCI)
GEORGE LEWIS LAVANDER, son of Lewis & India Lavander, b. 1854; sis, Catherine Lavander(b. 1850, d. Apr 1937), Addie (age 74); bro, J. Mack & Charles Lavander. (15 Apr 1937 HCI)
MRS. M.C. RUSSELL, 87, b. Hardin Co. ILL.; dau, Jane & Mrs. James A. Hunter; bro, W.P. Warford. (15 Apr 1937 HCI)
ANNA PEARL BROWN, age 25, dau of Mark Brown, d. 09 Apr 1937; m. Earl Vaughn, 18 Aug 1932; issue: Ida Louise Vaughn; bro, Bill Brown; sis, Imogene & Mrs. Tom Creamer. (15 Apr 1937 HCI)
CHARLES MARION DAVIS, b. 14 Feb 1853, d. 06 Apr 1937; m. Martha A. Holbrook, 07 Aug 1873; issue: George Davis, & (4 d); m. 2nd, Mary Mott, 4 Jul 1885; issue: Otto & Noah Davis & (1 d); m 3rd, Martha A. Burkhart, 05 May 1894; issue: Leonard Davis, (2d); m. 4th, Leslie L. Hinson; issue: Sylvia Bryan, Herpie Davis & (7 d.) (15 Apr 1937 HCI)
JAMES A, OXFORD, son of James Russell Oxford, d. 21 April 1937; m. Florence---; issue: S.E., Herbert, Arza & Charlie Oxford(d); sis, Nancy Hoovan. (29 Apr 1937 HCI)
FLORENCE BELLE RAMSEY, dau of Charlie & Mary Ramsey, b. 07 Mar 1882, Crittenden Co. Ky., d. 31 Mar 1937; m. James Melin Roberts; issue: 9, Joyce Capps, Mrs. John Ginger, Mrs. Wesley Moyers, Mrs. Ellsworth Vinyard, James & J.D. Roberts; bros, William Ramsey.(29 Apr 1937 HCI)
JESSE VAUGHN, age 59, d. 24 Apr 1937; m. Nancy Singleton, 1907; issue; 10, Mrs. Casadine McDowell, Mrs. Phinias Chanceller, Mrs. Howard Creamer, Reba, Marvin, J.W., Betty Jean & Joe Ann Vaughn. (29 Apr 1937 HCI)
LAFE TWITCHELL, son of Franklin & Mary C. Twitchell, b. 30 Oct 1875, Hardin Co. ILL., d. 30 Apr 1937; m. Sarah ----; issue; Charles Twitchell; bros, Jake, George & Joe Twitchell; sis, Alice Stone. (06 May 1937 HCI)
THEODORE SHELDON, d. 02 may 1937; m. Martha Cowsert; issue: (sons) Loy & Arley Sheldon. (06 May 1937 HCI)

HENRY JACOB ROHOOF, son of Thomas & Sarah Rohoof, b. 1880, d. May 1937. (13 May 1937 HCI)
JESSE GREEN ISHAM, b. 07 Sept 1869, Hardin Co. ILL., d. 08 May 1937; m. Sarah Raymer, 10 Oct 1887;issue:Mrs. Lon Bateman, Mrs. Ernest Glenn, Howard, Jesse Isham; sis, Mrs. John Gintert, & Mrs. Lucian Vinyard. (13 May 1937 HCI)
ESSIE MAY WATKINS, dau of James B. & Elizabeth Jones Watkins, b. 15 Feb 1886, Elizabethtown, ILL., d.12 May 1937; m. Charles M. Johnson, 12 Oct 1912; issue; Gordon, Buster, Robert, Marcel Emma, & Mrs. Noah Lacey; bros, William, Harry & James Watkins; sis, Alta Gobel & Bessie Ralph. (20 May 1937 HCI)
THOMAS WASHINGTON BAUGHER, son of Jesse & Elizabeth Frailey Baugher, b.19 Mar 1861,Hardin Co, Il.; m. Margaret Brown, 1879;issue: William (d.inf)& Martha Marshall Lucas(d.11 Jan 1937), Jeff, Fred,John, Minnie Oxford,Lizzie Milligan, Clara Beavers;half bros, William Winters, Frank Price & Samuel Baugher; bro, Jesse (d. inf); half sis, Mary Dale(d. 1901). (27 May 1937 HCI)
JOHN HENRY GREGORY, son of John & Harriet Gregory; m. Georgia---; issue: Gwyn (son),John, Mrs.David Jones;bro, William G.Gregory; sis, Mrs. I.A. Coltrin.(27 Mar 1937 HCI)
VIRGIE VAUGHN, dau of Joe Vaughn age 19, d. 21 May 1937; m. Millard Conkle. (27 May 1937 HCI)
MELVINA LEE, dau of Charles & Mariah Lee, b. 05 Jan 1867, Elizabethtown, ILL., d. May 1937; m. Charles William G. Gerhardt, 01 Jul 1867; issue: Lora Irby, Hazel Thompson & Clarence Gerhardt, bros, Charles & John Lee; sis, Lula Thompson (27 May 1937 HCI)
CHARLES SUTTON, age 43, son of America Sutton?, d.31 May 1937;bro,John Sutton.(03 Jun 1937 HCI)
ETHEL WATSON, dau of Thomas & Sebary Casad Watson, b.04 May 1887, Hardin Co.ILL.; m.James Patton, 17 Apr 1907, Nashville, Tenn; issue: Roy (inf d.), Mary Addis Abbott,Paul,Tom,Peggy & Bob Patton; bros,James, Harry, Thomas & Bruce Watson;sis,Mae Jackson,Gladys Galloway,Gertrude Wakeham,& Florence Watson.(10 Jun 1937 HCI)
LILLIE B. PIERCE, dau of George & Lucretia Pierce, b.07 Oct 1871, St.Louis,Mo.;m. R.F. Taylor, 30 Apr 1936 ; bro, Harrie Pierce; step-

son, Ben Taylor; step-dau, Eunice Taylor.(10 Jun 1937 HCI)
BESSIE JANE JOINER, dau of Samuel & Ruth Joiner b. 30 Aug 1904, d. 04 Jun 1937; m. Tom Partain; issue: Deneen(son), Marjorie Ruth Partain; sis, Lela Colbert & Stella Hamp; bro, Sol Joiner. (10 & 24 Jun 1937 HCI)
DODDRIDGE GRAHAM GIBSON, d. Jun 1937, Webster Grove, Mo.; son, Dodd Gibson; daus, Mrs. Oliver Horn & Mrs. Richard Jones; 4 bros, 1 sis. (17 Jun 1937 HCI)
MINERVA HOBBS, dau of Jefferson Hobbs (who d. abt 50 yrs ago), d. Jun 1937; m. John Burklow; issue: William Burklow; m. 2nd, Tommy Walton; bros, Sherman & Charlie Hobbs.(24 Jun 1937 HCI)
OVERTON EUGENE WATSON, son of Alva Troy Watson, b. 25 Jan 1914, d. 10 Jun 1937; bro, Douglas Watson; sis, Deneen Birch, Donna Joe & Patty Rhea. (1 Jun 1937 HCI)
ED SMITH, b. Union Co. Tenn., d. 03 Jul 1937; m.Lila --;issue: Harley Smith.(08 Jul 1937 HCI)
JOSEPH GINGER, son of Arch Ginger, b. 1870, Hardin Co. ILL., d. Jul 1937; m. ---; issue: Mrs. Vinyard, Alice Lane, John, Fannie Vinyard, Mrs.Nevil Vinyard,Bryan,Mrs.Jesse Schoggine; sis, Hattie Ricketts, Rosa Leonberger & Roxie Ledbetter. (22 Jul 1937 HCI)
WILLIAM JOSEPH WHITEAKER, son Mark & Elizabeth Whiteaker, b.11 Jan 1872, New Burnside, ILL., d.17 Jul 1937; m. Alice E.Mathis, Nov 1900; issue: Hall Whiteaker; sis, Astra McElroy, Martha E. Burris, Geneva Brown, & Gertrude Compton. (22 Jul 1937 HCI)
BERTHA BANKS, dau of Daniel & Nancy Banks, b. 28 Aug 1855, Hardin Co. ILL.; m. Silas Sneed, 1902; issue; Gertrude Gore, Howard, Effie Carman, Stella Foster, Janie Vaughn, Ina Lane, Carl, Lorene Sneed & (4 d.); bros, Clyde, Ezra, william, Edward K., Oatis E., Otis D., & John J. Banks; sis, Mrs.Allen Chancey, Nellie Mott & Effie Grice. (29 Jul 1937 HCI)
GEORGE W. LEDBETTER, son of James & Polly Ledbetter, b. 07 Dec 1858, Hardin Co. ILL., d. 09 Aug 1937; m. Rachel ---; issue: Mora(son), Charles, Harry, Ora Ramshaw, Mrs. W.P. Pell; bros, Henry(d.) & John Quincy Adams Ledbetter.

(12 Aug 1937 HCI)
JACOB G. GULLETT, son of Jacob & Lucretin Gullett, 19 Jan 1864, Tenn, d. 28 Jul 1937; m. Forence Decker, 09 Dec 1863 (1883 ?).(12 Aug 1937 HCI)
JAMES LEDBETTER, son of James Anderson & Polly Ledbetter, b. 28 Oct 1856, Hardin Co.ILL., d. 20 Aug 1937; m. Dora Herod, 1876; issue: 2 sons(d.); m. 2nd, Mrs. Zoa Curry, 09 Jan 1938; step-dau, Helen Curry; bros, George & Henry Ledbetter. (22 Aug 1937 HCI)
MRS. W.P. IRBY, dau of Carroll Tolbert, b. 26 may 1880, Hardin Co. ILL.; m. William Irby; issue: Orval Irby. (02 Sept 1937 HCI)
VIRGIL HOLLOMAN, age 36, son of George Holloman, d. 30 Aug 1937; m. Pearl Conrad, 26 Apr 1926; issue:---; bros, Evertte Holloman; half bros, Luther, Frank, James & Charlie Hicks; half sis, Cora Beabout & Ruth Hogg.(02 Sept 1937 HCI)
JIMMY BURKLOW, b. Aug 1854; m.Sarah Jane issue: ?. (02 Sept 1937 HCI)
KATHERINE E. KERR, dau of Clarence C. Kerr, g. dau of Tony Kerr & Mrs. Tony Kerr (who was dau of John F. Hombrick), & g. dau of Asa McDonald & Mrs McDonald(who was dau of J.E.Y. Hanna). (09 Sept 1937 HCI)
ALBERT DUTTON, age 75. d. 11 Sept 1937; issue: Joe, Arlo, Luther & Stella Leonberger.(16 Sept 1937 HCI)
MAGGIE ROWLAND, wife of Al Rowland, d. 16 Sept 1937; issue: Mrs. Ab Richerson, Mrs. Harry Gibbs, Mrs. Lowell Boyd & Mrs. Jessie Tite. (23 Sept 1937 HCI)
OSCAR C. BAUER, son of O. Bauer, d. 15 Sept 1937; issue: Arma & Jack Bauer; sis, Mona Brown. (23 Sept 1937 HCI)
PEARL COLLINS, dau of B.F. Collins, b. Carmi, ILL., d. 23 Sept 1937; m. Ed Crider; issue: Helen, Earl, Don & D.F. Crider; bro, Frank Collins; sis, Mrs. Milberry Littels. (30 Sept 1937 HCI)
PLEAS GIBBONS, age 65, son of Elijah Gibbons; m. Minnie Wallace,28 May 1892, Hardin Co,ILL,?; issue: Elmer,Ora Thorne,Maggie,J.B.,Roper,Earl & Mrs. Goldey Hudson. (30 Sept 1937 HCI)

WASH LEDBETTER, age 64, d. 09 Sept 1937;issue: Burlin & Joe Ledbetter. (30 Sept 1937 HCI)
JOHN COOK, age 42, d. 01 Oct 1937;issue: 10. (07 Oct 1937 HCI)
OREN RANDALL PENNELL, son of William & Lottie Pennell, b. 13 May 1923, d. 16 Sept 1937. (07 Oct 1937 HCI)
Mr. & Mrs. Frank Santy (She was dau of Wilson Partain); m. 03 Oct 1880, Pope Co. ILL.; issue: Earl, Mrs. Pleas Wallace, Ruery & Clarence Santy. (14 Oct 1937 HCI)
SUSAN ADELLA WINTERS, dau of William Winters, d. 13 Oct 1937; m. Armstead Oxford. (14 Oct 1937 HCI)
CLAURA LURETTA SHELBY, dau of Reece & Katherine Shelby, b. 22 May 1879, d. 17 Sept 1937; issue: Mrs. Essie English, Pearl Butler, Loyd Freeman, Bertie Shelby; sis, Sarah Belford. (14 Oct 1937 HCI)
SARAH MOORE SHELTON, age 67, d. 03 Oct 1937; son, Austin Bernard; bros, Dick & Charlie Moore; sis, Nora Parker & Kate Clifford. (21 Oct 1937 HCI)
MARY ETTA FOSTER, dau of Asa & Susan Foster, b. 18 Jul 1849, Hardin Co. ILL., d. 20 Oct 1937; m. John Palmer, Mar 1866;issue:Bertha Thornton, Dora Riggs, W.H. Palmer;sis, Mrs. Jodie Palmer. (21 Oct 1937 HCI)
JAMES TINSLEY, m.---, 24 Oct 1897; issue: Myrtle Reed, Mattie Slagel, Alonzo, Charles, William & Theda Watson; sis, Marie Dinse & Minnie Dubois. (28 Oct 1937 HCI)
JOHN A. KERR, son of Stanley & Susan Kerr, b. 27 Aug 1868, d. 18 Oct 1937; m. Ada Garrett, 16 Oct 1887; issue: Mrs. R.H. Crawford, Mrs. O. C. Trail, Mrs. W.H. Capron, Stanley, Garrett, Leslie & Mildred Kerr; bros, E.S. & A.T. Kerr; sis, Rosinia Golightly; uncle, Tony Kerr. (21 & 28 Oct 1937 HCI)
BILLIE J. GARLAND, son of Ralph & Mona Garland, b. 8 Dec 1924, Hardin Co. ILL., d. 25 Oct 1937; g. parents, John & Hester Garland;uncles, Wiley Garland & Marvin Brownfield. (04 Nov 1937 HCI)
BAKER FINNEY, b. 17 Mar 1862, Pope Co. ILL.; m. Majenta Jarvis, (who was b. 05 Mar 1870) Hardin Co. ILL.; issue: Duke Finney & Mrs. Clarence

Rose. (11 Nov 1937 HCI)
SARAH ELIZABETH BAKER, dau of Calvin & Francis Baker, b. 05 Nov 1851, Hardin Co. ILL.; m. William Rose, 1869. (11 Nov 1937 HCI)
WALTER OZEE, d.last wk; bros, Simon, Tim, Will Ozee; sis, Mrs. Lee Foster & Florence Stanley. (18 Nov 1937 HCI)
THOMAS ERNEST HENRY, age 70, b. Union Co. Ky; bros. George & John Henry; sis, Ellen Frayser. (25 Nov 1937 HCI)
MARY ODIUM, dau of William Odium, b. 19 Jan 1846, Marion, ILL.; m. William A. Sheretz, 1863; issue; dau; m. 2nd, H. Kibby, 1916; issue: Mrs. Joe Butler, Mrs. James Closson, & Mrs. Walter Pearson. (25 Nov 1937 HCI)
WILLIS SHUFFLEBARGER, son of David & Angie Shufflebarger, age 68, b. Hardin Co. ILL., d. 25 Nov 1937; m., Minnie Hastie, dau of James Hastie; issue: Charlie(d.), John(d.), Gladys(d.), & Mrs. Cleta Lewis; m. 2nd, Anna Hobbs, dau of Isaac Hobbs; issue; (sons) Charles, Cleo, & Mora Shufflebarger; bros, Hiram, Charles, George & Will Shufflebarger; sis, Minnie Thoms & Laura Radcliffe. (02 Dec 1937 HCI)
SARAH CRABBE, dau of Thomas W. Crabb, b. 05 Sept 1868, Pope Co. ILL., d. 29 Nov 1937; m. George Riley Baldwin, abt 1889; issue: Elmer, Edith Colbert, Willie Archie, Gertrude Cox, Arza, Dewey, Ida Reins & Hattie Elliot. (02 Dec 1937 HCI)
IDA BELL TURNER, dau of Louise Turner, b.19 Apr 1882, Hardin Co. ILL., d. 24 Nov 1937; m. Frank E. Fricker, 21 Aug 1900; issue: Howard,Freeman, Fred, Stella Davis, Marshall?, Ethel, Emma, Mayme; bro, Willie & Fred Turner; sis, Stella Sinanes. (02 Dec 1937 HCI)
JULY ANN FERRELL, dau of Jury & Alice Ferrell, b. Livingston Co. Ky., 03 May 1863;m. J.H. Bell; issue: Maude Owens,Junie Downing, Joe, John, Isaac, David, Ernest, George & Orvil Bell. (09 Dec 1937 HCI)
GEORGE WASHINGTON BREWER, age 88, son of Ambrose & Amanda Brewer, b. Hardin Co. ILL., d. last wk; issue: Lula & Fred Brewer (16 Dec 1937 HCI)

HATTIE SADLER, dau of Samuel Sadler, b. 26 Sept 1872, d.18 Dec 1937; m. Pleas Rose;issue:Ray & Clarence Rose; sis, Mollie Rose; half sis Mrs. Mary Thompson. (23 Dec 1937 HCI)
LEONIDAS E. VICK, age 65, b. Carrsville, Ky., d. Dec 1937; m. Mrs. Rose Frayser; issue; Mrs. Ethel Claxton,& son & 2 daus.(30 Dec 1937 HCI)
LAURA LAYOFF, dau of Philip & Betty Layoff, b. 29 Mar 1873, Rosiclare, ILL; m. George Lillard, 14 May 1904; issue: Martha & Maybell; father-in-law, Z.T. Lillard. (30 Dec 1937 HCI)
ETTA FRIEZE, age 76, b. Hardin Co. ILL., d. Denver, Col.; bro, R.C.Tyer. (30 Dec 1937 HCI)
ELLA E. FRAYSER, age 78, b. Hardin Co. ILL.; m. --Parsons;bro,Richard Frayser.(08 Jan 1938 HCI)
ELIZABETH OXFORD,dau of Wilmer & Harriet Oxford b. 19 Nov 1896, d. 5 Jan 1938; m. Harry Rutherford; issue: Randall Rutherford; m. 2nd, Escol Patton, 02 May 1921; sis, Mrs. Ulys Mason Mrs. Ray Richgels & Mrs. Bryan Rutherford. (13 Jan 1938 HCI)
WILLIAM J. RENFRO, age 88, son of Duncan and Nancy Enoch Renfro, b. 02 May 1849, Lincoln Co., Tenn., d. 8 Jan 1938; m.Ida M. Douglas Simpson, 13 Apr 1879; issue: Thomas b., Ray, Anna, Broadway (d.) & Roscoe Renfro. (20 Jan 1938 HCI)
ROSE OLDHAM, dau of James & Sally Oldham, b. 17 Oct 1873, Hardin Co. ILL., d. Jan 1938; m. Eddie Eugene Frayser, 1893; issue: Stella Kaegi & Carl Frayser;bro, Frank Oldham; m. 2nd, Lee Vick; sis, Nellie Boyd & Della Shewmaker. (20 Jan 1938 HCI)
THERESA POST, 71, dau of Frank Joseph & Theresa Kercher Post, b. Baden, Germany;m.John Eichorn Feb 1889, Hardin Co. ILL.;issue: Martin, Mrs. George Humm; bro, Anton Post. (20 Jan 1938 HCI)
CHARLETON LAMB, age 22, son of James Lamb, d. 15 Jan 1938; bro, Thurlow, Randall, Tommie & Arthur; sis, Myrtle Lamb. (20 Jan 1938)
SARAH ELIZABETH LEONBERGER, age 82, wid of Fred Leonberger, d. Jan 1938; issue; Mrs. S.B. Love, Sarah Denton, Charles, Willey & George. (27 Jan 1938 HCI)
JERDIE RIGGS, dau of Sallie Riggs, d. 3 Feb 1938; m. B.C. Cole: issue; Genevieve, Mrs.

Herbert Kaegi & Mrs. Gilbert Cox; bro, Joe & John Riggs; sis, Mrs. Ray Keeling. (27 Jan 1938 HCI)
LULA ANN PARROTT, dau of Daniel and Lucinda Parrott, b. 17 Aug 1869; m. Jesse Hurford, 22 Jun 1890; issue: W.D., Samuel, Arthur, Mrs. Ernest Young, Mrs. Loyd Boulden, Mrs. David Asbell & Mrs. Jim Volkert. (03 Feb 1938 HCI)
SARAH ELIZABETH DAVIS ?, dau of Mrs. Josie Davis, b. Hardin Co. ILL.; m. Mitchell Humm, 1918; issue: Quentin Allen, Luciene, Thomas,& James Humm, bro Frank Davis?; sis, Mrs. Addie Davis. (03 Feb 1938 HCI)
GEORGE PATRICK, age 77, b. Shawneetown, ILL.; leaves wife, son, 2 dau. (03 Feb 1938 HCI)
JERDIE RIGGS, dau of Sallie Riggs, d. 3 Feb 1938; m. B.C. Cole; issue: Mrs.Herbert Kaegi, Genevieve & Mrs. Gilbert Cox; bros, Joe & John Riggs; sis, Mrs. Ray Keeling. (10 Feb 1938 HCI)
CHARLIE BOWDEN LACKEY, son of William & Minerva Lackey, b. 28 Sept 1888, Hardin Co. ILL., d. 01 Feb 1938; bro, Frank Lackey; sis, Mrs. Neal Northern; uncle, E.B. Hughes. (10 Feb 1938 HCI)
THERESA ROST, dau of Frank & Theresa Rost, b. 06 Apr 1868, Baden, Germany, d. 13 Jan 1938; m. John Eichorn, 1890; issue: Martin and Maggie Eichorn. (17 Feb 1938 HCI)
PERNETT FERRELL, son of Henry & Augusta Ferrell b. 20 Apr 1872, Elizabethtown, ILL., d. Feb 1938; m. Mrs. Annie Williams, 12 Sept 1923; step children, Roland Williams, Mrs. Alpha Esterves; bros, Ed Ferrell; sis, Mrs. Wiley Lavander & Mrs. Tom Jackson. (24 Feb 1938 HCI)
MRS. LOU RALPH, dau of Fanuel & Mary Hines, b. 20 Apr 1870, d. Feb 1938; m. Jesse Holloman; issue: Annie Jennings & Della Ashford; m. 2nd, Grant Ralph; issue; Mattie Hobbs, Cora Oxford, & Rosie Sisco; bros, Obe & William Hines. (24 Feb & 03 Mar 1938 HCI)
JOHN YARBER, son of Robert & Betsy Yarber, b. 28 Mar 1872, d. 17 Feb 1938; m. Etta Smith, 4 Jul 1902; Issue: Mrs. Vada Hayes & Loretta Turner & 5(d.) (24 Feb 1938 HCI)
HARRIET G. SHEWMAKER, dau of David & Nance Shewmaker, b. 27 Nov 1854, Hardin Co. ILL., d. 16 Feb 1938; m. Jim Winn, 1877; issue: Minnie

Keeling; m. 2nd, George Hufsey; issue: Melinda Hobbs, Maude Rash, Loren, Nellie Hopkins,& Lennie Hufsey. (24 Feb 1938 HCI)
EDNA HAMBRINK, dau of P.H. Hambrink, age 43, b. Hardin Co. ILL., d. 20 Feb 1938; m.--- Kaiser; issue: Clifton Martin Kaiser?; bros, Byran, Orval & Clarence Hambrink; sis, Ota Stanley, & Maida Hambrink. (03 Mar 1938 HCI)
DAVIS SUITS, age 80, b. Hardin Co. ILL.; m. ---?; issue; Mose, Charlie, Orval, Milas,Harve, John, Olen Suits, Mrs. Alonzo Patton, & Mrs. Ed Lampert. (10 Mar 1938 HCI)
WILLIAM DENTON, age 65, son of Allen Denton, b. Hardin Co. ILL., d. 13 Mar 1938; m. Sarah Leonbarger; issue: 2 ; bro, James E.Denton(d.). (17 Mar 1938 HCI)
JESSE HURFORD, son of William & Sarah Williams Hurford, b.18 Jul 1851, Hardin Co. ILL., d. 9 Mar 1938; m. Lula Ann Parrott, 20 Jun 1890; issue: Ellen, Eva, Samuel, William, Daniel, Gertrude H. Young, Arthur, Katie H. Boulden, Viola H. Asbel, Helen H. Volkert; bros, Joe (d. inf), Davis, Ben, Noah; sis, Martha H. Chaney, & Mary H. Coffee. (17 Mar 1938 HCI)
LYDIA WILKERSON, age 94, dau of J. & Sylvia Jordan Wilkerson, b. Hardin Co. ILL., d. 19 Mar 1938; m. Arch Rutherford; issue: Joe & James Rutherford. (24 Mar 1938 HCI)
MARY MAY GRACE, age 51, wid of Robert Grace, d. Mar 1938; dau, Ethel. (24 Mar 1938 HCI)
JOHN WILLIAM HENSON, age 54, d. 23 Mar 1938; m. Lee Alice Shockley, 1903, Marion, Ky.;issue Mrs. William Williams; bro, Andrew Henson. (31 Mar 1938 HCI)
ELLEN IRBY, dau of William & Katie McFaden Irby b. 21 Aug 1870, Hardin Co. IL., d. 27 Mar 1938: m. John Decker; issue: Mary, Sarah, Addie, Mrs. Clarence Cubley & Henry Decker; bros, Bill & John Irby; half bros, Earl, Fred & Walter Irby; half sis, Ethel Matthews. (31 Mar 1938 HCI)
JOSEPH L. CUBLEY, son of Miles & Sarah Cubley, b. 04 Mar 1865, Mt. Vernon, Ind., d. 28 Mar 1938. (31 Mar 1938 HCI)
ELVA ELLIS, dau of Moses Ellis, b. 30 Mar 1907, d. 09 Apr 1938; m. Clarence Love, 31 Mar 1923; issue: Thurman Love; sis, Iva Marsh, Sophia, &

Sylvia Williams; bros, Arvil & Alvin Ellis. (21 Apr 1938 HCI)
FRED WUTHERMAN, age 63, b. Germany, d. 1938. (21 Apr 1938 HCI)
MINNIE WALTERS, age 67, dau of Garland Walters, d.15 Apr 1938; m. George Jerrells; issue: Charles Jerrells; half bro, James; sis, Helen, Logsdon, Josephine Grace, Mag Robinson. (21 Apr 1938 HCI)
CHARLES WALDEN, age 65, son of John Walden, d. Apr 1938; m. Elizabeth Hicks, Harrisburg;issue; 4; bro, J.J. Walden ?; sis Mrs. Jesse Crabb.(28 Apr 1938 HCI)
MARY PERRY, age 65, d. 24 Apr 1938; m. George Perry; son, Bernard Dunn; half sis, Mrs. Shearing. (28 Apr 1938 HCI)
SARAH JANE GULLETT, dau of Waitman & Julia Emma Gullett, b. 7 Sept 1861, Hardin Co. ILL.; m. D. A. Ledbetter, 11 Jun 1882; issue: Robert, Waitman, Emma Carlisle Dodd, Adrian, Mrs Rae Patton, Della (d.) & Ollie (d.); bro, U.G., Charles, James, Noah & Ben Gullett; sis, Margaret Patton, Mollie Patton, Essie Robinson, & Clara Yandell. (12 May 1938 HCI)
HORATIO LANE, b. 08 May 1847, Tenn.; m.---, 04 May 1870, Princeton, Ky.; issue: W.M., Alva & Mrs. Ed Ferrell, 5 unnamed, plus (2 d.) (19 May 1938 HCI)
JOEL L. GOETZMAN, age 76, d. 14 May 1938; bros, John & Louis Goetzman. (19 May 1938 HCI)
EZRA JACKSON, age 66, d. 11 May 1938, Quincy, ILL.; sis, S. Hosick & Anna Hurford. (19 May 1938 HCI)
MARY LOU KIMBRO, age 37, dau of Cal Kimbro, d. 22 May 1938; m. Jesse Speer; issue: Mrs. Glenn Marland, Virginia & Charles Speer; bros, Earl, Elmer, Hubert & John Kimbro; sis, Anna Gale Rush, Callie Parker & Nellie Little. (26 May 1938 HCI)
ALICE BIRCH, dau of William & Harmetta Birch, b. 26 Jul 1877, d. 3 Jun 1938; m. Philip Irby, 2 Jan 1899; issue: Arnold, Eva Moore, Wilmetta Hawkins, Evelyn Irby? & Wayne irby?; bros, Dewey, Ben & W.H. Birch; sis, Cora Cowsert, Lula? Ellis, Daisy Bernard & Eva White. (09 Jun 1938 HCI)

OSCAR BIRCH, d. Jun 1938; bros, Arthur & Roy Birch. (09 Jun 1938 HCI)
ELLEN HENRY, age 78, dau of James & Fannie Henry, b. Ky., d. 08 Jun 1938; m. Charles b. Frayser; bros, Tom, John & George Henry. (09 Jun 1938 HCI)
R.F. TAYLOR, d. 09 Jun 1938; sons, John, Robert, & Thomas Taylor. (16 Jun 1938 HCI)
C.C. DIMICK, son of Franklin & Amanda J. Dimick b. 01 Sept 1862, Hardin Co. ILL.,; bros, George F.Dimick & 3 (d.); 4 sis (d.).(16 Jun 1938 HCI)
ROBERT HENRY SCOTT, son of William Thomas Scott & Laura Scott, b. Crittenden Co. Ky., d. 17 Jun 1938; bros, Frank, Howard, Harrison?, Willis, & Lee Scott; sis, Eva Stacy. (23 Jun 1938 HCI)
MYRTLE BYERS, age 58, d. 22 Jun 1938; m. Julian Byers; issue: Lizzie Philips, Frances Wallace, J.C., Eugene & Arkle Byers; bro; Ezra Davis; half bro, William Rollo; sis, Mary Doyle. (30 Jun 1938 HCI)
JAMES M. LOWERY, b. 08 Nov 1857, Hardin Co. ILL.; m. Martha Jane Hodges, 04 Jun 1880. (30 Jun 1938 HCI)
CHARLES LAVANDER, son of Lewis and India Lavander, b. 10 Nov 1867, d. 30 Jun 1938; m. Florence Hubard, 1892; issue: Alta (d), Essie (d), Lewis (d) & Mrs. Stone; bro, Mack Lavander; sis, Addie Lavander. (7 Jul 1938 HCI)
MRS. EMMA REED, b. 12 Sept 1864, d. Jul 1938; m. William Henson, 29 Dec 1887; issue: Lula McCaughan, Luna Henson, Mae Harrison & Pearl Clardy; m. 2nd, Able Hardin; issue: Mattie Campbell; m. 3rd, Henry Reed. (07 Jul 1938 HCI)
WILLIAM FRANKLIN CONN, age 68, b. Hardin Co., ILL., son of Samuel & Harriet Conn; m. Etta Roberts; issue: sons, Harold, Claire, Wayne, Edgar, Walter, James, Myril Conn & (1 d.?) (07 Jul 1938 HCI)
REBECCA THORNTON, dau of John R. & Mary Ledbetter Thornton, b. 05 Jan 1861, Hardin Co. ILL.; m. Richard Birch; issue: Dollie Tyer, Mattie Tichenor Walther, Maude Carmen,& Alexander Birch; m. 2nd, W.D. Aaron, 26 Dec 1923; bro, Henry Thornton; sis, Mrs. Sidney Patrick. (14 Jul 1938 HCI)
MARY DAMERON, dau of Richard & Susan Dameron,

b. 06 Mar 1854, d. 9 Jul 1938; m. William Wright; issue: Fred, Hicks & Sallie Vaughn. (14 Jul 1938 HCI)
MARTHA J.VINYARD,dau of William & Mary Vinyard, b.01 Nov 1858, Karbers Ridge, Hardin Co. ILL., d.14 Jul 1938; m. William J.Flynn, 16 Feb 1890; issue:Charlotte,Charles, Walter?,& Clyde L.Flynn; bros, Alex, Charles & Trevis Vinyard; sis, Ella Davis. (21 Jul 1938 HCI)
ANNA ROGERS, dau of Isaac & Mary Rodgers, b. 29 Jan 1878, Hardin Co. ILL., d. 24 Jul 1938 ; m. Charlie Smith,1895; issue:Elvas,Leta Joyce, Isaac, Clifford, Mary, Othel, Lowel (d.5 yrs), George (d.) & (2 d.).(28 Jul 1938 HCI)
CLEM PAGE, son of James & Lucy Woodruff Page, b. 02 Mar 1892, Hardin Co. ILL.; m. Esther---; issue:Mrs.Roy Carr, Mrs.John Carr, Mrs.Hillis Price & Mrs. William McCoy; sis, Mrs. Lon Showalter, Rhoda Hubbard & Flossie Collins; half bro, Ralph Page. (28 Jul 1938 HCI)
NEWLIN DUTTON, son of Charles & Linnie Bain Dutton,b. 10 Aug 1901, Elizabethtown, ILL., d. 16 Jul 1938, Seattle. Wn.; bros,Lester & Hester Dutton. (28 Jul 1938 HCI)
PHOEBE WILLIAMS, b. 25 Dec 1863, d. 29 Jul 1938 ; m. Martin Young, 5 Feb 1879; issue: Ernest, Lewis, Eunice, Vaughn Young & (1 d.?).; m. 2nd, Ed Miller; bro, Thomas Williams; sis, Dora Mayberry. (04 Aug 1938 HCI)
MRS KATHERINE JACKSON BRUNER, b. Gallatin Co. ILL., abt 1853, d. 14 Aug 1938; dau, Mrs. Bill Daugherty. (18 Aug 1938 HCI)
HENRY LEWIS, age 56, son of Thomas & Rachel Lewis, d. 14 Aug 1938; half bros, Jake, Fred, Richard Robinson; half sis, Eva Moore. (18 Aug 1938 HCI)
JAMES LASATER, son of T.J. & Melissa Decker Lasater, b. 14 Nov 1885, Hardin Co. ILL.; m. Sarah Ledbetter, Aug 1904; bro, Robert Lasater; sis, Mrs. W.S. Page, Mrs. Walter Smith & Mrs. V.A. Bizzle. (25 Aug 1938 HCI)
BILLIE PATTON, age 63, d. 24 Aug 1938; issue: Orlie, Horace, Roland & John Patton; bros, Hillas & Alonzo Patton; sis, Mrs. William Burklow, Mrs. James Frailey & Mrs. Asa Decker. (01 Sept 1938 HCI)

HENRY BARNES, son of Henry Barnes, d. Aug 1938; bro, Dave Barnes. (01 Sept 1938 HCI)
IMOGENE PATTON, dau of Hillis & Tressie Patton, b. 21 Dec 1913, d. 30 Aug 1938; m. Bethel Milligan,09 Nov 1935; issue: Rosemary Milligan. (01 & 08 Sept 1938 HCI)
LUCINDA O'NEAL, dau of James & Nancy O'Neal, b.09 Nov 1858, Johnson Co. ILL.; m. John McClusky, 11 Sept 1879; issue; Fred, James, Kate Connell & Cora Shelby. (08 Sept 1938 HCI)
SAMUEL LANIER, age 89, son of Asa & Martha Lanier, b. Hardin Co. ILL., d.07 Sept 1938. (15 Sept 1938 HCI)
JAMES WESLEY SWITZER, son of Wm. & Electiville Switzer, b. 28 Dec 1871, Gallatin Co., ILL., d. 8 Sept 1938; m. Merta Murphy, 26 May 1900; issue: Doris Whipple, Dee Switzer & Ralph Switzer; bro, Andrew Switzer.(15 Sept 1938 HCI)
MARY HENTON, dau of Tom Henton, b. 14 Feb 1906, Tenn.; m.--- Hardesty; issue; Lennie & Jewell Hardesty; m. 2nd, --- Winters; issue; Margaret, Norma & Doris Winters. (22 Sept 1938 HCI)
JAMES SILAS FERRELL, son of Horace Greely Ferrell, b. 09 Nov. 1893, Ozark, ILL.; m. Cora Bell Lane, Carrsville, Ky., 1914; issue: Viola Milligan, Geraldine Smith; bro, Edgar Ferrell. (29 Sept 1938 HCI)
DRURY MORGAN, son of Ray Morgan, b. 11 Dec 1920 Elizabethtown, ILL., d. Sept 1938; bros, Clell, & George Morgan; sis, Laura Karber & Elizabeth Rose Morgan. (29 Sept 1938 HCI)
WILLIAM HENRY BASCOM, age 83, son of Gais & Sarah Tinker Bascom, b. East Enterprise, Ind, d. 01 Oct 1938; m. Josie Belt, 25 Jan 1882 issue: Henry, Grover, Bessie Wingate, Daisy Bascom and Mrs. Noel Smith. (06 Oct 1938 HCI)
HENRY PRUETT, son of Benjamin & Mary Pruett, b. 12 Feb 1880, Hardin Co.,ILL., d. 06 Oct 1938; bros, James, John & Benjamin F. Pruett. (13 Oct 1938 HCI)
ISSAC OMAR SMITH, son of Charlie Smith, d. Oct 1938; siblings, George(d.), Othol, Elvis, Clifford, Leta & Mary Smith. (13 Oct 1938 HCI)
MRS. MARY STUBY, d. 17 Oct 1938;issue; Mrs. Gibbons, Mrs. John Partain & Elmer Stuby. (20 Oct 1938 HCI)

MARY JANE WARFORD, dau of William & Mary Warford, b. 06 Feb 1853, Hardin Co. ILL., d. Oct 1938; m.--- Grace; issue; John Grace; bro., W.P. Warford. (20 Oct 1938 HCI)
MRS. VERNON SNOW, dau of Earl Wayland, d. 12 Oct 1938; m. Vernon Snow; issue: Lois & Alfred Snow. (27 Oct 1938 HCI)
LETHA MARSHAL, age 84, wid of John Marshall, d. 24 Oct 1938; issue: Otto, Clarence, Charles, Ed Marshall & Anna Partain. (27 Oct 1938 HCI)
MRS. MOLLIE JENKINS, age 85, b. Hardin Co. ILL. issue; Charles, John Jenkins, Mrs. R.M. Hastie, Mrs. James Herrin, Josie Arnsworth & Ella Grace Aims. (03 Nov 1938 HCI)
LUM DECKER, son of John & Susie Holbrooks Decker, b. 01 Jan 1889, Hardin Co. ILL.; m. Ota Smith; issue: Wilma Farmer; bros, John, Asa, & Gordon Decker; sis, Myrtle Tolbert, Golda Hurford & Lydia Young. (03 Nov 1938 HCI)
ROBERT LEONARD SISCO, b. 05 Jul 1889, Ky., d.7 Nov 1938; m. Laura Hughes, 1912; issue: Walter, Paul, Earl, John, Jack, Hazel & Pauline Sisco. (10 Nov 1938 HCI)
FANNY HURLEY, dau of Mose & Mary Hurley, b. 28 Nov 1872, Ky.,d. 09 Nov 1938; m. Robert Lawless abt 1888; issue: William, John, Lulie Williams, & Addie Weaver. (17 Nov 1938 HCI)
ANNA PARTAIN, dau of George Partain, b. 27 Feb 1887, d. 08 Nov 1938; m. James Wm. Shewmaker, 13 Jan 1909; issue: Nora Shewmaker; sis, Minnie Schutt, Etta Ferrell; bros, Ollie, Grover, & Willie Partain. (24 Nov 1938 HCI)
KATIE WOOD, dau of Alfred & Sarah Wood, b.11 Nov 1863, d.18 Nov 1938; m.--;issue: Ethel Knight, Audrey Morgan & Emily Mobley. (24 Nov 1938 HCI)
WARREN VAUGHN, age 54, d. 21 Nov 1938; m. Anna ?;issue; William, A.W.,Valier Reed;stepdau,Mrs. Claude Scott& Dorothy Douglas.(24 Nov 1938 HCI)

SARAH ELIZABETH ROSE BAKER

Mrs. Sarah Elizabeth Rose, daughter of the late Calvin and Frances Baker, was born on the Jim Pruett farm, a short distance from Elizabeth town, on November 5, 1851. She was one of nine children of whom four, including her are now living. They are Morgan Baker of Gallatin Co., Mrs. Mary Baker Pearson and Mrs. Lucy Baker Wasson of Harrisburg.

In 1854 her father, together with three other families moved to Gallatin County, going up the Ohio River to Shawneetown in a keel boat. They settled on a farm near Shawneetown. Morgan Baker still lives in the house which was built by his father long years ago.

In 1869 she was married to Wiley Rose, a member of one of the oldest pioneer families of Hardin County. To them were born three children, one of whom died in infancy, Miss Frances Rose died in 1914 and Mrs. D.(?) G. Gullett of Elizabethtown. She has two grandchildren, Mrs. Robert Price of Carbondale and County Judge James Gordon Gullett of Elizabethtown, children of Mrs. Gullett and one grandchild, Rose, small daughter of Mrs. Price.

The house now owned and operated by Mrs. Rose was built in 1817 by James McFarland and was never used as dwelling but was a tavern, then an inn. Mrs. Rose bought the house in 1884 and has operated a hotel there ever since. The Rose House is probably the oldest operating hotel in the state of Illinois.

Mrs. Rose can trace the history of Hardin County from its earliest beginning to the present time. She tells us that three men came from the Eastern part of the United States to this, then far distant western country. Their names were Hardin, Grandpier and Mcfarland. They obtained a tract of land from the government and settled there. After awhile Hardin went away and Grandpier died, but James and Elizabeth McFarland stayed, and from these three families, we have Hardin County, Grandpier Creek, and McFarland Precinct and Elizabethtown, the town getting its name from Elizabeth McFarland.

Mrs. Rose has an excellent memory and is a most interesting conversationalist. Her home overlooking the beautiful Ohio River, is one of the most beautiful sites in Hardin County, and has been a haven for many a weary traveler, who has no doubt pleasant memories of the Rose Hotel and Mrs. Rose.
Sarah Elizabeth Baker, HARDIN COUNTY INDEPENDENT, Jan 10, 1935

C W. BARNERD

C. W. Barnerd the subject of this sketch was born in Hardin (then Pope Co.) County, lllinois July 19, 1831. He died at his home at Dorrisville, Saline County, Illinois on August 26, 1915 at the age of 84 years.

His first marriage was to Elizabeth Hess, a sister to the late David Hess. This union produced eight children. His second marriage was to Riller Wallace, a sister to Levy Wallace of Bald Knob, ? Arkansas and the late W. R. Wallace of this county. This union produced 10 children.

During the later part of the seventies, he and his first wife moved to Kansas and farmed but soon moved back to this county. Soon after their return his wife died, but he soon remarried. He sold his two farms on what is known as "The Mountain," a mile or two southwest of the Rock Creek School where he lived for many years and accumulated considerable property.

C.W. Barnard and his second wife moved back to Kansas in 1881 but stayed for a short time and then returned to the county and state of his nativity.

Soon after his return, he purchased some cheap woodland in the northern part of this county and settled, remaining at that location until 1900 when he moved to Saline County.

The subject was a blacksmith by trade, and his mechanical genius was such that he could do any kind of woodwork that was necessary in his trade. He was also a farmer and farmed somewhat extensively in Hardin and Saline counties.

C. W. Barnerd was known as an industrious,

hard-working, upright, conscientious citizen. He is survived by his wife, children, thirty-eight grandchildren, and twenty-eight great-grandchildren, and a brother, J.A. Barnerd. His funeral was preached by his nephew, A.J. Clanton.
C.W. Barnerd, HARDIN COUNTY INDEPENDENT, Jan 9, 1915.

WILLIAM HENRY BASCOM

A few months ago, Mr. William Henry Bascom, with a sly twinkle in his eye, informed the writer that he had just "come of age." Having been born on the 23rd of June, 1855, he, on the 23rd of last June, passed his 80th milestone. He therefore, became eligible to a place among those aged citizens of Hardin county, who having lived their four score years or more, are included in the list of subjects whose biographical sketches have appeared during the past year.

Mr. Bascom was born at East Enterprise in Switzerland county Indiana, and was the son of the late Gals and Sarah Tinker Bascom. The father was born in one of the eastern states and the mother's native county was the same as her son.

East Enterprise was a town located between Vevay and Rising Sun, Ind. During the latter half of the 19th century there seems to have been a general imigration of families from that part of Indiana to this section of Southern Illinois. Many of these families located in Hardin county.

According to Mr. Bascomls statement, people from the Hoosier state settled on and became owners of the land which is now Mrs. Hannah Tyer's farm and that which surrounds it for a radius of five miles.

The parents of Mr. Bascom were also among those who came here from that section. When he was a lad of eight years, the family came down the Ohio river on a flat boat landing at Cave-in-Rock on Christmas Eve, in 1863. This being his first such trip, it made a very vivid impression on his mind.

At that time there was only one store in Cave-in-Rock stood where the Methodist church now stands and was owned by a Mr. Vermillion and by the late Alex Frayser who is well known throughout this county. The only church was of methodist denomination and was a log building which stood on the hill where the old cemetery now is.

Mr. Bascom states that only two houses are now standing which were here at that time, the one occupied by the family of John W. Blee, and owned by J. W. Hill, and the one owned by Harley Frayser and his mother, Mrs. Dora Lackey. The only two people living who were citizens of Cave-in-Rock at the time of the arrival of the Bascom family were A.A. Gustin, whose home is near that town, and his sister, Mrs. Aaron Pell, of Rosiclare.

Mr. Bascom was the second of three children. The oldest was a sister who later became Mrs. Laura Kimball and who died at Reno, Nevada three years ago. His brother, Ben Bascom, died in Blythesville, Ark., six years ago.

The night that the family arrived an eight inch snow covered the ground. The father left the mother, sister, and little brother in town, but took William Henry and drove out to the home of his uncle, Nim Jenkins, who had already settled on a farm about four miles northeast of Cave-in-Rock. As they rode in an ox cart, it took about two hours to cover a distance which now requires only a few minutes.

The family at first made their home in the village, occupying the house which stood just back of the house now owned by Tom Henry and formerly occupied by the post office. They stayed there until in March, 1864, then moved to a farm about one and a quarter miles west of Cave-in-Rock and just below the Joe Riggs' place. The hardships of pioneer life proved to be more than the father was able to endure and he died during the following October. After his death the mother moved her little family to the Tom Douglas farm, where an uncle then lived. She stayed there two years and then moved back to her own forty acre farm.

With the help of her two young sons, she succeeded in clearing the land and they remained there until the children were grown.

Mr. Bascom attended school in a log house which stood where the house recently purchased from Charles Garland by Joe Frailey now stands. He distinctly remembers using the old Webster's blue backed spelling book which was the chief textbook of those days. He recalls a teacher by the name of Fugat. Rate Mitchell was the name of another and a third was the mother of the late Miss Hattie Rittenhouse.

On the 5th of January, 1882, he was united in marriage to Josie Belt, daughter of the late Joel and Sarah Belt. They were married by Jake Hess in the old log house later owned by Mrs. Sallie Riggs and destroyed by fire a few years ago. They lived for a short time on the Simmons farm which Paris Oxford now owns, but in December, 1883, moved to their own home, a log house on the farm near town where he still makes his home. For fifty three years they lived and worked together. At the time when this history was first recorded death had not yet invaded the home, but since that time Mr. Bascom has suffered the loss of his faithful wife, who passed away on the third of last August.

Five children were born to this union: Daisy, who is still at home with her father, Grover, whose home is near Cave-in-Rock, and Mrs. Nola Smith, of St. Louis. There are twelve grandchildren and one great-grandson, James Henson Wingate, son of Mr. and Mrs. Hanson Wingate.

Mr. Bascom possesses a most remarkable memory and it is interesting to listen as he recalls many things connected not only with the history of Cave-in-Rock but with that of the nation as well. Among his memories are incidents which took place during the early days of the Civil War shortly before the family left Indiana. There were many calls for volunteers, and he well remembers how soldiers played fife and drum and then pled with their listeners to enlist in the service of their country. Fathers and sons would step out as volunteers while mothers and wives wept and even fainted as they were overocome by their fears for their loved ones.

All of his life Mr. Bascom has been honest and industrious. When but a lad he did all that he could to lighten the burdens of the widowed mother who was left alone to support her family in a new and uncleared country. When he came to manhood and became the head of his own family he persisted in his efforts to obtain a living from the soil and did so to the best of his ability.

Now that he is left without his companion of more than half a century, he is still courageously "carrying on" in his own little home, caring for himself and his daughter. His sight and hearing are still active, though he sometimes suffers from the rheumatic pains of old age. He makes frequent trips to town, sometimes walking the distance more than once during the day.

His many friends sympathize with him in his bereavement, but hope that pleasant memories of the past will enable him to enjoy many more happy and peaceful years of life.
Kathreyne McDonald, HARDIN COUNTY INDEPENDENT, 17 October 1935.

ARTHUR BIRCH

Arthur Birch is the oldest son of T.A. Birch of Cave-in-Rock precinct. He was born and raised on a farm among the hills of Hardin, working in the summer and going to school in the winter, during his boyhood days, walking as far as five miles to school. He says," There is no such a thing as failure when one is determined to get an education and there is plenty of room at the top of the ladder for all who will ascend."

Arthur secured most of his common school education at Peters Creek, where he obtained education sufficient to teach. He has earned two diplomas, one from the common schools of Indiana one from Hardin County. He also holds certificates from both Hardin and Saline counties. After teaching he was not satisfied with a common school education and therefore attended two summer drills at Elizabethtown and Southern Normal at Carbondale. INDEPENDENT, 21 May 1908

OTIS BRITTAIN

Mr. Brittain, a native of Hardin County, was born October 8, 1886 in the Bend of the River country, the son of Thomas Brittain. Otis had three known siblings: a sister, Pearl and brothers, Henry and Richard.

Otis Brittain was married twice. His first wife was Mrs. John Byrnes. This union produced 18 children: Mildred, Gladys, Tom, Weldon, Gradie, Beulah, Masella ?, Cora, Rozella, Vada, Wanda Hope, Virginia, Theodore, Harvard, plus four deceased. Apparently, the Brittains were divorced, and he remarried. His second wife Mrs. Hester Reed Patton died last March in the hospital in Shawneetown.

Brittain served four terms as sheriff of Hardin County. His first term of service was in 1930 to 1934.

As Sheriff Brittain, he became prominent all over the county as an officer who helped to solve many murders. His most notorious case was the murder of Earl Austin who was killed with dynamite by his wife and her accomplice. Another case in which Brittain played an important part in was the murder of Eddie Turley by his wife.

Brittain's nerve was proverbial. During his term as sheriff, a bad man from the east end of the county was terrorizing the village of Cave-in-Rock, threatening to kill with the revolver he was flourishing, the first man that came near him. Brittain coolly walked up to him unarmed and saying, "You won't kill anyone". With these words, Brittain knocked the man cold with a blow from his fist.

Otis Brittain suffered a heart attack while coming down the courthouse hill and died in the Rosiclare Hospital in March of 1943. A short time before his death he resigned his job as a guard in Joliet Menard prisons to return to Hardin County to farm.

HARDIN COUNTY INDEPENDENT, 4 March 1943

WILLIAM J. BIRCH

Among the retired businessmen of Hardin county, one the oldest to be found is William J. Birch of Birch's Spring, located on route three, Elizabethtown.

Willam J. is the third child of eight children whose parents were Benjamin Birch and Elizabeth Jones and he was born near Cincinnati, Ohio, on August 16, 1854. His brothers were Richard L., John Benjamin, George and Al, and his sisters were Martha Jane Conn, Laura Ralph, and one half sister, Mrs. Ollie Sanders, of these, George of St. Louis, Mo., Mrs. Coon of Elizabethtown and Mrs. Sanders of Colorado are living.

At the time he was about three years old his parents moved from Ohio to to Illinois in Hardin County, first renting the The Alex Ralph farm, known as the old Doe Ayers' place. While living on this farm, the house burned and all the contents was lost. The family lived in the home of Alex Ralph for about a week. The father walked to Shawneetown to Take up a piece of land of forty acres under the Bit Act. It was government land and was located on Hog Thief Creek, Hardin County. There a shanty was built and the family lived for several years.

Then this land was sold and they rented a farm on Saline Creek for one year, after leaving this farm they came to the place he now owns and rented from an old lady by the name of Cole. They spent several years there and then rented the Ben Lavander farm on Route One, Elizabethtown for two years.

At the age of 19, William J. married Miss Hyremetty Lyons, 14 year old daughter of John Lyons and Nancy Belt. The wedding took place on January 11, 1874, at the home of the bride near Cavein-Rock, Illinois

The late Ben Renfro, county clerk at that time, issued the marriage license. Mr. Birch having been a pupil of Mr. Renfo in the public school in Hardin County and oft times would take an extra onion along with him to give his teacher. One day Mr. Renfro informed "Billy" that he was going to quit teaching and get in the race for county clerk, and promised him that when he got to be a grown man and ready to marry, he would issue him a license free. When William started to pay for his license, Mr. Renfro reminded him of it. Keeping his promise, he issued a free license.

To this union nine children were born, namely namely, Mrs. Cora E. Cowsert, Mrs. Alice Irby, Mrs. Lula Ellis, Mrs. Eva White, Mrs. Daisey Barnard, Dr. W.H., and Dewey, all of Hardin County. Dr. Birch was a twin, his sister living only for about ten months.

Mr. and Mrs. Birch had and old fashioned wedding served in the old fashioned way and prepared by the bride's mother. Among the guests present at the ceremony and now living are "Aunt" Sarah Oldham, Dyke Gustin, Bob and Dan Frailey, all of them lived near Cave-in- Rock. There was no Charivari at their wedding and they spent their first evening together at the M.E. Church on the hill at Cave-in-Rock. Rev. Clanahan was the pastor there at that time and delivered the sermon that evening.

After their marriage they purchased forty acres of land near Peters Creek and built on it, but never lived on it. They moved to Cave-in-Rock on H.J. Belt's farm and lived there one year. They then moved on the place now known as the Jim Rutherford place in 1901 and really started their business life on this forty acre tract of land.

Their first big start was a crop of turkeys which they raised and marketed atShawneetown, there being no market for them here. A wagon load was taken to that place for which they received five cents per pound and the entire lot brought $25.00. They invested that money in a little stock for a family grocery store. They stayed in business at Cave-in-Rock for fourteen years. In 1915 they came to Elizabethtown and he bought the Cheap Store stock from Miss Clara Gullett and operated a store there until he retired in 1929. Now he lives on the old farm where he was principally raised.

Mr. Birch is one of the most successful business men Elizabethtown has ever had. He is a member of the M.E. Church, He belongs to no lodge affilations. He has five children who have passed fifty years of age.

One of the remarkable features about this large family is that they all live in Hardin County, and any of them can reach their parents in thirty minutes or less.

The couple marrying at ages 19 and 14, have lived a happy married life for 61 years together. Mrs. Birch is now 76 years of age and still does all her own work around the home. In the summer she raises chickens and has a nice garden.

JAMES BURKLOW

On the summit of a rugged hill overlooking the old Antioch Church near Lambtown stands a house which has for 56 years sheltered on the aged sons of Hardin County. We refer to James Burklow, familiarly called by his friends, "Uncle Jimmie" Burklow.

He was born August 29, 1854 on a farm later owned by A.A. Gustin and known as the "Henry Rittenhouse Place." For more than 82 years he has participated in the life of this county. His father was John W. Burklow, a native of Boone County Indiana, and his mother's maiden name was Martha Susan Cook. She was born in Kentucky, but brought to Illinois by her parents when but a young child.

He was the oldest one of ten children, having had three brothers and six sisters. All of them lived to be grown, but there are now only two brothers and one sister living. The brothers are Sam and Charlie Burklow, who live in Shawnee Hollow, and the sister is Mrs. Elizabeth Needham. She is blind and her home is at Cereal Springs.

On February 27, 1867, the Burklow family left the Rittenhouse farm and moved to what is now the Alva Lane Place on the Bend of the River. They moved there on account of their father' health. It was thought that a copperas spring located there that would be beneficial to his health. After two years his health was so greatly improved that he brought from John Ray the farm adjoining and cleared it. James Burklow, the subject of this sketch, spent his life from the age thirteen until his marriage on this farm.

He says at that time there were in the country great flocks of wild turkeys and many wild deer. Wolves were plentiful. His father raised sheep. Around the sheep houses he dug trenches. These were filled with rocks to keep the wolves from digging under at night. During the day the sheep were carefully guarded. His mother carded the wool, spun it into thread, wove it into cloth and made garments which the family wore. He remembers the old spinning wheel reel and loom which she used many times, staying up late at night to do the work which could not be done during the day.

There was a big fireplace in the house to which they moved in '67 and there was a chimney constructed of wood and stone. Contrary to the usual custom the chimney was built inside the house. Candles were used for light. Stumps were kept on fire or burning stumps were covered with ashes as a substitute for matches, of which there were none.

"Uncle Jimmie" also recalls the time of the Civil War. He remembers climbing up on a gate and listening to the playing of the fifes and drums by those who were enlisting volunteers.

He helped his father raise the crops of wheat, corn, and potatoes upon which they depended for food. His meager schooling was such as the majority of country children of those days. The school house was built of logs and seats were wooden benches and slates were used instead of blackboards and paper. At the Rittenhouse place the teacher was a man named John Jacks. After they moved to the Bend of the River, he attended the St. John's School.

At the age of twenty five he decided to establish a home of his own and on July 4, 1879 at Shawneetown, he married Sarah Jane McDowell, a daughter of Eli and Rachel McDowell and a native of Hardin County. For a year the young couple lived on the Willis Hamilton farm near

Lambtown which is now the home of Mrs. Otis Brittain. At the end of that time the wife's father deeded to her the land upon which stands the house previously mentioned. There were eighty acres of land and this was cultivated by the young farmer. When the wheat was ready to cut, they cradled it, using a reap hook which took off just the top of the stalks. The wheat was spread on the ground and then rode horses over it or tramp it out. A wheat fan stood near by. The fan separated the wheat from the chaff as it passed through and the wheat came out on a quilt in front of it.

Eight children were born to Mr. and Mrs. Burklow all of whom are living. They are Robert Burklow, sisters Mrs. Annie Conditt and Mrs. Kate Lampert all of whom live near Lambtown; Andrew Jackson and Otto who live with their father; Mrs. Alice Winters whose home is in Gallatin County; Mrs. Bessie Pinnell, near Camp Cadiz, and Geo. Raymond of Caseyville, Ky. There are 19 grandchildren and nine great grandchildren. Until the death of Mrs. Burklow on 20 April 1936, there had never been a death in the family. For several years before her death her health was not good and Mr. Burklow was almost her constant companion.

For twenty five years he has he never spent a night away from home. For five years he has eaten no evening meal. He has never smoked or chewed tobacco and for over 25 years he has used no coffee. He is getting feeble now, but he does what he can, helping to feed the stock and working in the garden during the gardening season. He can still read and he relies solely on his memory to furnish the facts of this biography.

Katheryne McDonald, HARDIN COUNTY INDEPENDENT 10 Dec 1936

ANDREW J. CLANTON

Andrew J. Clanton was born June 14, 1859 in Gallatin County, the son of Thomas Clanton and Mary Barnard.

In his early childhood he moved with his family to Rock Creek where he lived his entire life. In early manhood he chose for his life's companion, Dora Mae Groves. They were married on March 25, 1886. This marriage was blessed with seven children: Martha, Brian, Mrs. Cora Foster of Rock Creek, Mrs. Jessie Farley of Eldorado, Mrs. Charlie Farley of West Frankfort and Thomas A. Clanton, deceased.

When the children were quite small, Andrew became a minister of the Baptist Church. He was a close companion of James Crider, J.B. Tucker J. T. Thornton, Elijah Tinsley and other older ministers who have since died. He has been pastor of most of the General Baptist Churches in Hardin County and Sunday School Superintendent of Rock Creek Church for a great number of years.

He supported his family by working as a blacksmith during the week and preached on Sunday. When his health no longer permitted him to preach, he rang the church bell on Sunday to summon the people to Sunday School.

Andrew Clanton died August 25, 1942. He leaves one brother, Ferrell Clanton of Rock Creek, thirty grandchildren and eight great-great- grand children.
HARDIN COUNTY INDEPENDENT, Sept. 3, 1942

JOHN ALEXANDER CLARK
John A. Clark the subject of this sketch was born March 23, 1844 Near Marion, Kentucky,
 The education facilities at that time were very bad and young Clark obtained but a meager education. He learned the carpenter and cabinet making trade and followed that vocation through out his life.

John came to Illinois in 1861 and on February 26, 1862, he married Mary M. Johnson. She bore one child but it died at 14 months and the mother soon followed.

He married Sarah A. Hathorn on November 26, 1869 by whom he had nine children, namely: Cora Waggoner of Karber's Ridge; Esther Lane and Cecil Clark of Rosiclare, Illinois; Ruth Travis of Carrsville, Kentucky, and Roy Clark of Elizabethtown, Illinois; plus four deceased.

Sarah A. Hathorn Clark died on November

16,1916. John Alexander Clark died on April 23, 1923.

HARDIN COUNTY INDEPENDENT, May 24, 1923

Richard Nathaniel Cole

Richard Nathaniel Cole was born on a farm lying in the forks of the Green and the Barren rivers, near Bowling Green, Kentucky in 1845. His parents, who were of Scotch Irish descent, were the late James and Martha Ann Cole. His father was a native of Virginia and his mother was born in Kentucky. Of a family of eight, R.N. Cole was the seventh child, he having had six brothers and one sister. He and one brother R.F. Cole of Louisville, Kentucky are the only remaining members of this large family.

His father was a successful farmer of pioneer days. He at first owned one hundred acres of land located as above mentioned. This he sold for eight hundred dollars and with that sum purchased acres near the first farm. He developed this land and dealt largely in stock. On this farm the subject of this sketch spent his childhood.

In 1861, Richard N. Cole enlisted in the service of the Union Army under General Shacklefoot at Hartford, Kentucky, but owing to his extreme youth he was not mustered in until the following year. In his first year, he added many recruits to the service of the Union by going at his own risk into dangerous territory, persuading and piloting men back to the ranks of the army for enlistment. These trips were usually made at night and very frequently required swimming of the river.

Three of his brothers were already in the service. It is very remarkable that all served until the end of the war in 1865 and none of them were even scratched in battle. While all except the subject of this sketch have passed on to the Great Beyond, the youngest lived to sixty-five years of age.

"Little Cole" as he was called by his comrades still boasts of having been the most dependable thief in all of Sherman's army, having many times ventured out and brought in a hog, a sheep, or a calf to relieve the hunger of his comrades when others failed.

Cole served under Generals Shacklefoot, Burnside, Logan, Grant, Custer and others of not such great fame. He was with Sherman on his famous march to the sea. He had two horses shot out from under him, one at Bean Station, Virginia and the other at Knoxville, Tennessee. He was captured twice but made his escape both times. He was found unconscious from the effects of freezing on two occasions.

After the war, he returned to the home of his parents, but remained there but a short time. From there he went to Missouri near New Madrid. He there met and married Marvilla Wilson. To this union three children were born of whom only one is living Mrs. Ada Dederick, whose home is in Texas.

During his young manhood his wife died, and he left Missouri and came back to Kentucky. After several years' time he married a second time, to Jennie Carroll of Hillardsville, Kentucky. Three children were born of this union, a daughter, Olivia who died in 1907, at the age of 17; a son, Dewey who died in 1898 at the age of 2 and R.C. Cole, who was born at Cordsville, Kentucky, and with whom his father now resides, as he was left alone a second time on May 8, 1932. There are grandchildren in Texas and three at this place, the daughters of Mr. and Mrs. R.C. Cole. They are Mrs. Herbert Kaegi, and the Misses Martha and Genevieve Cole.

After the war, Mr. Cole's chief occupation was farming. Later he became greatly interested in bees and about the year 1905, he engaged in the raising them at Alzey, Kentucky. In 1912 the family came to Cave-In-Rock and purchased property in Hessville. There he devoted his attention to bees and to truck farming until, on account of the infirmities of age, he was unable to continue at these tasks.

Perhaps some of the readers of this history may be interested in hearing how he won the title of "Dr. Cole" by which name he is often called by his friends here. In his earlier years, he compounded a medicine, his customers began calling him "Dr. Cole."

Mr. Cole is probably the only living man near here who can claim the distinction of having voted for Abraham Lincoln for president of the United States. At the time he did this he walked five miles through mud and rain in order to reach the polls.

While he is almost blind, and is feeble and bent with age, his son tells that his health is better than it has been for twenty years.

After the death of his wife in 1932, he went to live with his son, R.C. Cole, who lives about one and one half mile west of Cave-In Rock. There he receives the best of care. On account of his feebleness, he is now unable to come to town as he did formerly, and his visits are greatly missed by his many friends here.
HARDIN COUNTY INDEPENDENT, Jan. 17, 1935

WILLIAM LENTICUM DAVIS

Mr. Davis was born August 1, 1855 in Hardin county, Illinois on the farm known as the Harry Frayser place, one half mile northeast of Cave-in-Rock. When questioned as to the origin of his somewhat unusual middle name. He said that he was named after his family doctor. Dr. Lenticum requested that the mother name the first born child after him which she did.

"Uncle Bill's" father was George F. Davis, born in Alexander county North Carolina. His mother, before her marriage, was Mary Jane Frailey and was born on the John Tyer place, the daughter of the late Daniel Frailey. His grandfather Davis came to Hardin County early in the century, bringing his wife and four sons. He left another son, the uncle for whom the subject of this sketch was named, in North Carolina. He also left three daughters.

When he arrived in Hardin County, he located on the top of Smyrna Hill and farmed there until the age of 84. He then moved in with his oldest daughter, Mrs. Betsy Simmons until the time of his death four years later. His son, George, married Mary Jane Frailey and located on the farm where William Lenticum was born. At that time it belonged to her father, Daniel

Frailey. Daniel Frailey met a tragic death, while he and his son Phil were cutting wheat a storm came up. They ran to the barn for shelter and were both struck by lightening. It is said that they were buried on the farm where the family of Adiel Douglas lives.

From the above. we note that some wheat was raised in this country at that time, though not in large quantities. Uncle Bill says that it was beaten out of the husks with poles and separated from the chaff by the wind.

Mr. Davis had three sisters and two brothers, but only one brother, Dan Davis survives. He lives near Cave-in-Rock.

William L. Davis was married to Miss Martha Smock, September 11, 1879, at the Rittenhouse farm by John Jacks, a justice of the peace. Two daughters and two sons were born to them. Only the two sons survive, Tot Davis of Chicago and Edgar Davis near Cave-in-Rock. There are only five grandchildren, C.D. Adams of Chicago, Wayne, Pauline, Wanda, and Shirley Davis, children of Mr. and Mrs. Edgar Davis with whom he makes his home.

Mr. and Mrs. Davis began their married life on the Jim Ledbetter farm. Fifteen dollars was the sum he had to furnish his home. For $10 he bought a stove and two bedsteads at $2.50 each. He made a table and put a dry goods box in the corner of the kitchen for a cupboard. His mother gave him 12 pounds of feathers and he bought a tick. He also filled some beds with dry grass.

Later they moved to a box house built by Marion Devers near Oak Grove School. They lived there three years, then moved to the Dr. Dunn place. From there they went to the Eb Dossett place and then to the Bee Edmundson place in the Bend of the River. After a year at Little Saline they moved to the farm recently purchased by the Mahoning Mining Company. There Mr. Davis lived for more than 36 years until the house burned. During all these years he was a farmer. He especially enjoyed handling and trading in stock, having shipped many car loads of animals to Cincinnati and St. Louis.

Mrs. Davis died March 3, 1926; but Mr.

Davis continued to live on his farm until the burning of the house when he moved in to the home of his son. He has been affiliated with the I.O.O.F. lodge of Cave-in-Rock for many years. He served as county commissioner, 1934-1937.

He says he was never arrested or paid a nickel fine. His father took him to see a jail. The sight so impressed William that he determined never to go to jail. His father told him, "If you will be a good and law abiding citizen, you will never have to go there."

Among other memories of his childhood, Mr. Davis recalls his school days. When he was seven years old, he attended school on the second floor of the Hill property now occupied by Everett McConnell, one of the two oldest buildings in Cave-in-Rock. This was only a temporary arrangement while the work was being done on the old school house on the hill. The building is now occupied by Mr. and Mrs. Burtis Douglas and Mr. and Mrs. Ralph Frailey. The first teacher he remembers was a man named Threlkeld. The benches were split logs. There were no desks, slates or black boards. Shelves were placed along the walls. The pupils stood up to write with goose quill pens dipped in pokeberry ink. The text books were few, chief among them being the old Webster's blue-backed spelling book.

In 1867 his father moved across the river to Kentucky, but as the schools over there were hard to reach, Mr. Davis stayed with his grandfather and attended the old Tyer school which stood in the woods almost directly where the road runs in front of the home of Dewey Green. His teacher was named Casad. Other pupils he recalls were Katherine Boyd, Hiram Belt, Mary Wingate, Em Wingate, Bud Cullison, and John and Will Jenkins, none of them now living.

While he was too young to enlist at the time of the Civil War, he remembers hearing the cannon from distant battle fields. No battles were fought near here, but he recalls seeing the soldiers when they came home on furloughs. There was a big barbecue given for these soldiers at the Dunn place west of Dunn Springs near where he now lives.

Once while he and his sister were searching for ginseng near their home in Kentucky, they found a great pile of muskets, carbines and shot guns, evidently left there by soldiers.

He says that ginseng was plentiful in Hardin county then. It was found near Pawpaw growth. Searching for it was a common occupation in those days. It could be taken to Shawneetown and sold for 75 cents or a dollar a pound. He says a man named Hobbs made a living selling ginseng, pinkroot and yellow Puccoon.

Mr. Davis was not a hunter but he remembers seeing trees loaded with pigeons feeding on Chinkapins. These pigeons were probably those known as passenger pigeons, a kind extinct now. He says that the red or fox squirrels that are seldom if ever seen, in the woods, were numerous in the 60's and 70's.

While the early pioneers had to wrest their living from the soil, they enjoyed some forms of recreation. Their social gatherings consisted largely of "wood choppings", "clearings", and "rail maulings", accompanied by dances at night. The music was furnished by old time fiddlers. Mr. Davis thinks that half the county, which was thickly wooded, was cleared by this means. A farmer in need of such work would invite in all the men and boys in the surrounding country. They cut the timber, mauled the rails, and made ties. Some time three or four thousand ties would be split in one day. The men of that generation did not realize the value of the timber and were wasteful to a degree which would be condemned today.

Another sport which furnished amusement then was horse racing. A half mile track lay along the river bank between the two sloughs at Cave-in-Rock. The river bank then was almost straight up and down and ten or twelve feet high. Among those that raced on this track was Riley Barker, an uncle of George Ferry and Mrs. Ella Moore of Cave-in-Rock.

When the farmers had their land cleared, They began to raise Irish potatoes. Enormous quantities were shipped by flat boats to New

Orleans and other cities in Louisiana. At one time in the early 80's, Judge Tyer on what was known as the Tyer place, raised 300 bushels to the acre on ten acres. They sold for from 20 to 25 cents per bushel, sometimes as high as 60 cents. Seven flat boats lay at the landing at one time. They were owned by the late Joe Mason, Judge Tyer, Capt. John Gregory, Johnnie Goodwin, and a man named Hardrick. Ox teams brought the potatoes to town. Those not sold were stored in large cellars in town. At the time when the seven boats were loaded, four cellars were also filled. Sometimes the line of wagons reached from the corner where the Methodist church now stands to the Betty Mahn property. Apples and corn were shipped out on steam boats. The great production of potatoes later made the land infertile.Then farmers turned their attention to the raising of stock. The cattle and hogs were shipped on steam boats which made regular trips up and down the river.

Among the most interesting recollections of Mr. Davis are those concerning the development of the business life of Cave-in-Rock. The first stores he remembers were those in operation during the war. Sam Barley and Ross Lattimore had a store near where Joe Beavers now lives, but as there was a street then on the river bank, the store faced toward the river. Barley at first had a store on a boat. Later he sold it and moved to the John Ledbetter farm near Cave-in-Rock. "Uncle" Dickie Thomas sold whiskey during the war in the building now occupied by the Rigsby's cafe and the family of Ray Lambert. John Goodwin built a large store room where the Methodist church now stands. It was the building torn down when the new church was built. The building where the post office now is was built by the late Capt. John Gregory. W.H. Hill, James Ledbetter, Bill Smith, and John R. Oxford were among those who later operated stores in the building.

Joe Thornton and Jim Simpson owned a store where the Reed grocery is now. The saloon above mentioned owned by Dickie Thomas was later torn down and replaced with a large store building built by John Lowery. The corner adjoining Ab's Cafe was occupied by a store and post office building owned by the late Webb Pell. The late Dr. Hill bought property owned by a Dr. Mozee, moved in from Mt. Zion and built a store on the lot between the home of C.C. Kerr and the Hill property, occupied by Everett McDonald. A store operated by John Thornton burned down and was replaced with the Masonic building. The Hardin County State Bank building was built by John Lowery in 1904. Other names mentioned among former prominent business men were George Shearer, Green, Armstrong, Riley and Holderman.

Among the first physicians who practiced in Cave-in-Rock was a Dr. Binkley. He later went to Shawneetown and then to Chicago, where he died.

Dr. Dunn, father of Mrs Willis Dutton and the late Tot Dunn, moved from Equality to Hardin County and bought the place that is still called the Dunn farm at the head of Big Sink. Squire Henry Hardin also moved from Gallatin and brought what is now the Dan Davis place. These are the ones who were instrumental in the naming of the county.

REBECCA CURRY

Mrs. Rebecca Curry, who will be 92 years old next month, is almost blind, lives in a house in Gallatin County built by her son, Clarence Curry.

She was born May 9, 1852 in Boone county, Kentucky and was brought to Hardin County by her parents when she was six years old. They lived near where the Sparks Hill post office now stands.

She has been married four times. When she was 15, she was married to Louis Lane. They had four children, Nancy who died in infancy, Willie, Robert and Henry. Mr. Lane died when Henry was a small child. Rebecca then married Theodius(Teddy) Corwin. Their son was named Zadock. Her third marriage was to Frank Guidrey. A son named Charles was born. He moved when married to Kansas and died there. One of his children is now in the service. Her fourth marriage was to Owen Curry. He died July 25,

1943, one month before his 96th birthday.

Mrs. Curry remembers when at eight years old, she helped her mother spin thread on the old spinning wheel to make clothing for the family. Her hobby was piecing patchwork quilts, which she made in various designs.

She has been a member of the General Baptist church since she was 18 years old. She has 25 grandchildren living, 12 dead; 50 great grandchildren, 5 dead; and 11 great-great grandchildren.

Except for her eyes, Mrs. Curry is in good health and said if she could see, she would do some work yet.

HARDIN COUNTY INDEPENDENT, April 6, 1944.

JOHN DECKER,

John Robertson Decker was born on a farm near Shawneetown in Gallatin County, Illinois on June 20, 1854. His father, the late Asa Decker of Decker's Springs, was a native of Indiana and his mother, the late Lydie Patrick Decker, was born in New Jersey. He was the sixth child in a family of twelve children. The children now living besides him are Mrs. Florence Gullett of near Decker's Springs, Mrs. Melissa Laster of Joe Catt Mountain, Mrs. Lydia Gross of Harrisburg and Asa Decker of Phoenix, Arizona.

When he was about five years of age, his parents moved to a farm near Herod in Pope County where he attended his first school. He recalls that the school house was built of logs and that it was hearted by a large fire place at one end of the building.

It was while living at this place that the Civil War began and his father became a soldier in the Union Army. Mr. Decker was only a small child at the time, but he has an excellent memory and can relate many interesting stories of the Civil War period. He remembers clearly the day his father rode away to the war on his own horse with about three dozen other men who met at his house. Some of his neighbors at who joined the group were Ben Thacker, Harve Lambert, Aaron lambert, Thomas Crank, Jesse Waggoner, and John Z. Rose. The captain of his father's company was Dr. T.S. Herod of Shawneetown. He also remembers hearing the Battle of Fort Donalson and of going with his father to see Joe Gibbs, one of their neighbor's who was killed for being a deserter in the Union Army.

While his father was away in the army the problem of carrying on the farm work and making the living was left in the hands of his mother, his brothers and sisters, and himself.

"Uncle" John remembers plowing with a yoke of steers. He says that he drove the steers and his mother sowed wheat out of her apron. His father helped cut the wheat and take it to the mill when he came home on his furlough.

Another interesting event that he recalls is that all of the neighbor women used to come to his home and get his mother to read and answer their letters for them during the war. He says that his mother was the only woman in their neighborhood that could write and it became her duty and privilege to assist her friends in carrying on a correspondence with their husbands, sons and brothers while they were away in the army.

From Pope County the Decker family moved to a farm in White County, and sometime later they moved from there to Decker's Springs where they lived for many years. Mr. Decker recalls that the trip from the farm in White County to the new home in Decker's Springs took three days. He says that there were several families of them moving at the same time and that there were thirteen wagons in their procession besides the horses and cows that they were driving.

When Mr. Decker was about thirty years of age he was united in marriage with Miss Susan Holbrook of near Decker's Springs, and to this union were born nine children. The oldest, a daughter named Elizabeth, died in infancy and one son, the late Owen Decker of Rosiclare, died in 1921 from injuries received in the mines where he worked. The other children are Asa Decker of Spark's Hill, Mrs. Myrtle Tolbert of near Grossville, Illinois, Mrs. Lydia Young of Dixon, Illinois, John Decker, Jr., of near Keeling, C. Decker of Elizabethtown, Gordon

Decker of Chicago and Mrs. Goldie Hurford of Rosiclare. He has nineteen grandchildren living and four great grand-children. He and his wife celebrated their fiftieth wedding anniversary in December 18, 1934.

From Decker's Springs "Uncle" John and his wife moved to a farm near Moore's Spring which is about three miles from Elizabethtown, and from there they moved to Rosiclare where they are living at the present time.

When being interviewed by a reporter for his life's story Mr. Decker was very frank to admit that he had not had much schooling during his life time, but is very apparent to anyone who has the privilege of talking with him that he is a well-read man. He enjoys keeping up with the latest government news by reading the daily newspapers and listening to radio broadcasts and is a very enthusiastic reader of history, geography and the Bible. His favorite hobby is discussing history, past and present, with his friends which are many.

HARDIN COUNTY INDEPENDENT, Apr. 25, 1935

JAMES DENTON by Judge Hall

James Emitt Denton was the third son of Allan Denton, who as a young pioneer made his way from the Carolinas Country where he married Mary Ann Patton, sister of the late James, Elias and Grant Patton, and of Mrs. Sarah Carr and Mrs. Rebecca Sutton. He settled what was later known as the W.D. Davis farm near Sparks Hill.

My father had come down the Ohio on a flat boat; had seen the East and the South with quite a little of the Civil War; had married a cousin of Mrs. Dentons and he and Uncle Al could match far-away yarns as few other men could do. They drove over to our house or we to theirs for the week end and had there wild turkey, fat 'possom, wild honey, maple syrup, wine of the wild grape, hoe cakes and all those "good eatings" which people ate before dyspepsia was written in the books or in the stomachs of mankind either.

The Denton children consisted of three boys, Andrew, William, and James Emitt. There were two girls who died young. Emmitt was all nerve and play; an inveterate wrestler, always daring some boy to "dirty his back." Ever genial and jovial in humor, but took no insults big or little without a hard fight. If a boy was too big he took after him with clubs or stones, and Andrew and William often had to interfere to keep him from doing some bad work.

In School he learned easily with time off for amusement, but ever teacher learned to trust him among his best friends. When he discovered a large boy concealing a dangerous stone for the teacher, Emitt spoke up appraising him of the danger but alas, now few of that gay class are left to match such reminiscences.

About this time the Denton home met with an inestimable misfortune. That frugal wife and patient mother died. After a while, Emitt hired out to his uncle James Patton, who found plenty of work for him to do, but saw to it that he continued his schooling, just at the age when a boy is likely to forget his books. His uncle was sort of King Midas; everything turned to money he touched, and if as the Wise Man says:" charity covereth a multitude of sins." James Patton has many notable deeds to his account. When Emitt married rather young, he backed him with a good Harris Creek farm. By some additional help by his father and father-in-law, he was soon marketing products with the rest of those sturdy farmers.

He married Ida Ann Brownfield, daughter of Esq. B. F. Brownfield. By this marriage he became brother-in-law to James Brownfield, the writer, Ernest Oxford, Wiley Leonberger, and James Waters.

He farmed and taught a for years, as did his two brothers. Andrew married Miss Sudie Hess, but died soon after his first child was born. She is Mrs. Phoebe Manhart of Owasso, Michigan. William wedded Sarah daughter of Mr. and Mrs. Fred Leonberger. There was a half sister born about his time or later who is Mrs. Herbert Ledbetter of Elizabethtown.

Soon after after his marriage Emitt and his brother entered Yellow Springs School again, which at this time was raised to Academic proportions and many of the best scholars and teachers in this country took advantage of this some attending both winter and summer. Emitt burnt late oil and soon became a good Latin scholar, with a knowledge of Greek, higher mathematics, history, science, literature and political economics. In a year or two he assumed courage in our literary society to meet the eloquent Judge Schneider in debate and vied with the scholarly J.J. Page as a parliamentarian.

From this school he and his brother William went to Huntington Law School in Tennessee. After finishing the course, William formed a partnership with Att'y John C. Oxford of Elizabethtown, but in about a year he gave his place to Emitt and went out in search of other fields, locating at Golconda, and later Shawneetown, where he still lives and where he has held an honorable status as an attorney and served Gallatin as States Attorney.

After a few years of successful practice, Emitt was elected States Attonery, and under his sane and economical advice and careful court procedure, Hardin County at the close of the term could boast of being wholly out of debt for the first time in her history. Economy has been a chief characteristic of all his businesses. It is generally true that men who are careful and frugal in the management of their own businesses, may be safely trusted with the management of public funds. At the time of his death he was not what we would call a wealthy man, yet he lived within his income and accumulated some valuable farming lands and city property as well as some money.

After the close of his office of States Attorney, he acted as Adjusting Attorney for Labor Claims in West Frankfort and other coal fields. At about the same time his services were called for in other courts in Southern Illinois, and he took and held a wide reputation as a learned attorney dreaded by opposing counsels a "hard fighter." Mr. Denton carefully preserved his reputation and respect of courts by adhering scrupulously to approved legal ethics.

James E. Denton has done perhaps more than any one man, to maintain an enviable reputation of the Elizabethtown Bar Association. Some readers may not know that located in one of the smallest counties of the state, this bar long took and held a reputation as "One of Brainiest Bars in the Southern half of Illinois"

When the Hardin County Court House burned Mr. Denton was one of the major forces in promoting a new building. This was done at a time when Harding County was facing bankruptcy. Mr. Denton has served his county as States Attorney since the completion of the new court house, and with accustomed economy in balancing the county budget did much during his four years in office to pay off our bonded indebtedness.

Virtually all his children were born while he was in his preparatory studies on the farm. These are Loren E., Arzie, Virgil, Olney, Beulah and Rachel. Virgil died in infancy, but the others live to mourn the loss, it seems to me one of most devoted fathers that I have ever known.

All five of his children hold high grade certificates under the laws of Illinois. The sons have had college and university training and all are teaching at present. Beulah became the companion of Mr. Percy Howard, and little Gene Howard is Mr. Denton's only grandchild. Mr. Walter Walker is Rachel's husband in whose home Mr. Denton passed to the beyond.

In politics Emitt was a well-informed, yet liberal politician. He admired many Republican leaders and I doubt that I ever heard him speak reproachfully of any public officer. He held Theodore Roosevelt one of the greatest of men, and believed that the party of Abraham Lincoln died with him.

As well as his family and other relatives there are many friends who will miss his cordial associations, free legal counsel and sane advice in many matters. The Latins spoke of such a loss as "alter ipse amicus" (a friend is a second self). A tribute by Judge Hall to an old friend.

HARDIN COUNTY INDEPRNDENT March 18, 1937

LOREN EVERETT DENTON

Mr. Denton is a son of States Attorney and Mrs. James E. Denton of Elizabethtown. He was born in 1895 in Hardin County, near the Yellow Springs school house. He attended grade school in Elizabethtown, taking both his high school and college work at Carbondale, Illinois, graduating from the latter in 1923. He also has a brother in the teaching profession, Richard Olney, of Deland, Illinois. Denton has another brother, Arza, who is employed in East St. Louis, Illinois, and two sisters, Mrs. Beulah Howard, wife of Mayor P.E. Howard of Rosiclare and Mrs. Rachel Walker, wife of Walter Walker, a merchant in Golconda.

In 1917, Mr. Denton was married to Miss Joey Piland, daughter of Mr. and Mrs. J. B. Piland of Elizabethtown. Mrs. Denton is an accomplished musician and home maker. They have one little girl, Lucille, who is in the second grade of the Rosiclare grade school.

The Dentons live in their own home on McLean Street in Rosiclare. The grandparents of Mr. Denton were the late Allen Denton and wife of Gallatin county and the late Benjamin and Hannah Brownfield, pioneers of Hardin County.

Mr. Denton's first school teaching work was done at Stone Church School where he taught from 1914 until 1916. He then was hired at Steel School and taught there until 1918. Then he went to Corinth School and taught until 1920.

After his experience in these rural schools, he secured a position teaching the intermediate grades at the Elizabethtown public schools. He also taught three years at the Elizabethtown High School. In 1922, he went to Rosiclare where he taught in the eight grade, and has been in the Rosiclare schools since 1922.

He became superintendent of the school he now serves in 1927. He also teaches English and Geography. In his first school, Mr. Denton had one hundred pupils to teach all of the eight grades by himself, and now he has some four hundred pupils with an efficient staff of teachers to help him.

Mr. Denton's hobby is gardening and he is

also fond of doing shop work during his leisure time. He is Junior Warden of the Rosiclare Masonic Lodge and a member of the First Methodist Church of that place.
HARDIN COUNTY INDEPENDENT, Jan 16, 1930 & May 28, 1935.

C. C. DIMICK

    C. C. Dimick was born on a farm one mile north of Rosiclare, September 1, 1862, the youngest son of Franklin and Amanda Dimick. He had three brothers and four sisters; all of whom have died.
    With his brother, George F. Dimick, C. C. Dimick was in the general mercantile business in Rosiclare from 25 to 30 years. He was postmaster there for 17 years.
    Mr. Dimick went to Evansville, Indiana in 1914, where he entered the retail business in 1915. He remained in business until January 1936, when he was "swept out of business by the Ohio River"

WILLIAM DOWNEY

    William Downey was born September 18, 1840 in Hardin County, Illinois and died in Oklahoma City, Oklahoma on August 3, 1930.
    He lived the first thirty years of his life in Rosiclare, Illinois. During this time he was married four times. The first marriage produced two children, but they apparently died in childhood. His second marriage was to Emma Dimmick who bore him two children, a girl and a boy. The girl died before she was grown and the boy, Charles, is still living. The last two marriages were childless.
    William enlisted in Company C. 48th. Illinois during the Civil War. He served four years and returned home in 1865. He lived in Rosiclare until 1900 when he moved to Oklahoma.
    The following is a letter written by "Uncle Bill" Downey to the HARDIN COUNTY INDEPENDENT, January 23, 1930 issue.
    "Well I was born near Rosiclare, Illinois in 1840. I have seen 90 new year days, who can beat that. I have a little inspiration in me. I

can tell when dinner is about ready. I can smell the biscuits cooking and they are good for me.

Well I was reared up a poor boy and had to work hard. I was the oldest child. There were 7 of us that had to eat, and I did my part to provide. Father was a carpenter and I learned the carpenter trade under my father.

I ran away from home when I was about 18 years old. Father sent mother to see me to coax me back home; I had a good mother. Her father was Billy Pell. He started Rosiclare and we lived on the banks (the Ohio River?) of Rosiclare when there three houses only.

I was the oldest grandchild and grandfather gave me lots of things. When I got of age, He gave me 40 acres of land near Shelterville.

Well I went out to the Civil War in 1861. My stepbrother, Henry Downey, went with me. He was only 17 years old. Brother Henry was wounded in Georgia; the breast plate on his cartridge box saved his life. I was lucky; I did not get wounded in all the Civil War.

When the war was over, I came home. I was about 25 years old and I took a notion to marry. I had about 500 dollars, and I bought 80 acres, and I added more. When I sold out, I had 300 acres. I went to Rosiclare in the mercantile business and made a success.

When I came to Oklahoma, I had about a $1000. I went to trading and speculating in about everything and lost out. I am still here. This is a wonderful world. I would like to live a little longer. There will be more to see as the world is progressing."
HARDIN COUNTY INDEPENDENT, Aug.14,1930 & June 16,1938.

DRIVER BROTHERS REUNION (IRA DRIVER)
In compliance with the promise I will try to give some account of a recent trip to north western Missouri. On Tuesday August 18th, wife and I leave home for our son-in-law's Robert McAllister of Saline County.

After an over night visit, we boarded the train for Carmi and there take passage for St.

Louis, reaching that city about 4 o'clock P.M. At ten o'clock same evening, we take passage on the Missouri Pacific for Warrensburg where my brother has made his home since he left Cave-in-Rock in 1854.

We reached his home late in the afternoon of the following day, and he came in from helping a neighbor stack wheat. You can scarcely imagine the scene of that meeting, after a separation of forty-nine years, in which time both passed through a war unsurrpassed in the annals of history in numbers of battles and daring deeds in the short period of four years.

In addition to the ordinary circumstances of long separations and happy reunions, we had each fought the four years on opposite sides, for opposite principals, and to me it was like receiving a lost brother in my arms, as we embraced each other, and hugged and talked and wept.

I thought of the happy days of home, and of mother, and of the breaking up family when mother died in 1853. And then thought of two brothers and two sisters who have died since brother Will and I had parted, and the fact that we two were the only survivors of a large family of eight children, and we had met in love and reasonable health after so strange a separation of 49 years, he being sixty and I being sixty five years old.

It seemed as if a whole three score years were lived in a few moments as I held him and thought how I had pressed him to my bosom when he was a little babe of only a few days old.

Well we stayed a few days with brother Will, visited and stayed with his second married daughter and her husband, and had the company of his elder married daughter and her husband all the time we were at his home, and he and his youngest daughter, Bertha, hauled us over to Levi McMurphy's, six miles south of Warrensburg, where my wife's first husband is buried. The McMurphys now own the farm owned by my wife and her first husband. Levi McMurphy was one of our Hardin County boys, and has become wealthy since moving to Missouri.

My brother served the confederate cause under Senator Cockrell who was his first captain. Afterwards his colonel, and who, I believe, has the honored distinction of being U.S. Senator.
Ira Driver, INDEPENDENT STAR, Sept.16, 1903

ZACHARIAH EDMONDSON

Zachariah Edmondson was born in Martin County Indiana, March 17, 1848. He was the son of the late Gracen and Jane Riley Edmondson. He was the third of a family of eight children, having had five brothers and two sisters, none of whom reside in this locality.

His childhood and youth were spent with his parents in his native state. In 1868, at the age of twenty he married in Daviess County, Indiana, Sarah Elizabeth Pruett, who was the daughter of the late Thomas and Margaret Pruett.

To this union were born four sons and two daughters. The sons were John T. Edmondson, who passed away at Carmi, Illinois some years ago, W.H. Edmondson, of near Cave-in-Rock, Harve Edmondson, of Kuttawa, Kentucky, and Newt Edmondson of Cave-in-Rock. The daughters were Mrs. Bell Scott of Cave-in-Rock who also passed away, and Mrs. Julia Cochran whose home is in Rosiclare. Illinois. There are twenty-four grandchildren and thirty-four great-grand children, many of whom reside in Hardin County.

The early married life of our subject was spent on a farm in Indiana, but as Mr. Edmondson had an inclination toward trapping and fishing, they soon left the farm and commenced a different life on a house boat on the Ohio River. During the fourteen years on the river, he was also employed much of the time working in the timber.

After seventeen years of married life, his wife died at Maunie, Illinois. Following the death of his wife, Mr. Edmondson left the river and moved to a farm about one and a half mile from Dycusburg, Kentucky. He remained there for only a year, then moved to Ford's Ferry, Kentucky, where he carried the mail for some two or three years from that place to Marion.

Kentucky.

In 1887, he was married to Emma Richards, but they lived together for only a short time, when he was again left alone. From Ford's Ferry, he went to Weston, Kentucky where he engaged in the timber business for several years.

In 1883, he was united in marriage to Mrs. Mary Butler, the mother of two children. They are Thomas Butler of Rosiclare and a daughter who is now Mrs. Josie Yates and whose home is near Kuttawa, Kentucky. Four children were born to this union none of whom are living.

About the year 1905 the couple left Weston and came to Illinois making their home on what is known as the Herrin farm not far from Cave-in-Rock. They remained for several years on the Herrin farm, then moved to what is now known as the Lamb farm. At this place a tragic event occurred. His youngest son, "Little Zach," a bright little lad of seven, was instantly killed by a falling timber while at play with other children.

In 1913 the family went to Carrsville, Kentucky where Mr. Edmondson found employment as a carpenter and also as a shoe repairer. After a few years they returned to Illinois where he worked chiefly at the cobbler's trade.

On August 6, 1930, after a pleasant married life of thirty-seven years, the aged man was again separated by death from his companion. Since that time he has made his home on the farm of his son, W.H. Edmondson, near Gentry's landing. Mr. Edmondson has very good health for one of his age. While he is not as active as in his earlier years, he is still a fine shot and takes great pleasure in a good squirrel hunt. He is of a jovial and social nature and greatly enjoys exchanging jokes with his friends and neighbors, all of whom greatly love and respect him.

Zachariah Edmondson died August 2, 1937.
HARDIN COUNTY INDEPENDENT, Jan 31, 1935 & Aug 12, 1937.

ANDREW J. FERRELL

Andrew J. Ferrell, the youngest son of

Clement and Sarah Edwards, was born in Illinois (Pope Co.?) on 29 April 1830. His siblings were probably as follows: William Carrol Ferrell, born about 1815; James Ferrell, born 6 May 1819; Thomas Ferrell, born 6 April 1821; John Ferrell, born 9 March 1825; Joseph Ferrell, born about 1828; Perlina born about 1826; and possibly others unknown.

In 1854 Andrew married Rebecca Lyons, the daughter of Robert Lyons. Rebecca was born on 12 June 1834 in Rising Sun, Indiana.

By 1870 Andrew and his family had moved from Harding County Illinois to Saline County as he appears in the 1870 census for that county. However, he had returned to Hardin County to the Cave-in-Rock area by the time of the 1880 census. Andrew died in 1893, the place of death unknown. Rebecca died on 30 December 1915 in Harrisburg. Their marriage produced the following children: Sarah E. Ferrell, born about 1853; Ollie Ferrell, born about 1855; Martha Ferrell, born about 1857; Clement H. Ferrell, born Dec. 1862; Frank Ferrell, born 25 Oct. 1865; William C. Ferrell, born about 1867; James J. Ferrell, born about 1869; Orval Ferrell, born 11 July 1875

DOCUMENTATION

1. Clement Ferrell and Sarah Edwards were married in Sumner County, Tennessee on 26 April 1811, according to Sumner county Tennessee Marriage Records and Clement's military records (War of 1812)

2. Andrew Ferrell's birth date was given in the William H. Ferrell family Bible. Bible was in the possession of Raymond Ferrell in 1955 in California. William H. Ferrell was a descendant of Thomas Ferrell, born 6 April 1831.

3. Clara Hale, granddaughter of Joseph Ferrell and Elizabeth Ladd, recalls her mother (Emma Ferrell) speaking of Uncles Tom, Jim, Andy, and Clem? Emma also remembers visiting her mother's first cousins: Sarah Ann, Polk, John, Martha, and Charles. These were the children of James and Mary Mott Ferrell. This fact would establish James (born 06 may 1819) and Joseph (born 05 Oct 1828) as brothers. Clara also recalls Perlina as

a sister to Joseph, her grandfather.

   Clement may be a brother to William Ferrell of Fulton County Arkansas as both men served in the same regiment in the War of 1812 (Capt. Henry Hamilton's company of Tenn. Militia) If this is true, then Clement (b.1822) would be a nephew to Clement and Sarah and not a son.

   In the 1830 census for Fayette County, Ill., Clement H. Ferrell is listed with eight males and one female. He may have had other sons or some of the eight males may not have been his sons.

4. James Ferrell family bible gives James's birthdate. A copy of this information has been printed in the SAGA, a publication of the Genealogical Society of Southern Illinois.

5. Thomas Ferrell's birth date was given in the William H. Ferrell bible.

6. John Ferrell' s obituary dated 20 Dec. 1901, was found in the Saline County Register, Harrisburg, Illinois.

7. Rebecca Ferrell's obituary dated 31 Dec. 1915, was found in the Saline County Register, Harrisburg, ILL.& The Hardin County Independent, 6 Jan.1916, Elizabethtown, ILL., gives her place of birth, marriage date, and lists the names of the children.

8. Andrew Ferrell family is listed in the 1880 census for Hardin County, Cave-In-Rock district.

9. The 1900 census, Harrisburg Township, Saline County, ILL., gives Clement H. Ferrell's birth date. He died in 1945, his obituary was dated 4 Dec. 1945, Saline County Register.

10. The 1900 census for Harrisburg gives Frank Ferrell's birth date as Oct. 1866. His obit gives his birth date as 23 Oct. 1865. He died 24 Feb.1905 in Saline County. See Register for obituary notice.

11. Tombstone reads, James J, Ferrell, Sept 9 1872 - Feb 23 1901, located in Sunset Hills Cemetery, Harrisburg, Saline Co. Illinois.

13. Orval Ferrell's birth date is given as 11 July 1876 in the Gaskin Funeral Home Records, Harrisburgh, ILL,

CHARLES M. FERRELL

Charles M. Ferrell was born 30 November 1819 in Marshall County, Tennessee to Elizabeth and Charles (?) Ferrell. Charles M. may have had other siblings, but only one was listed in the 1840 census for Marshall County. This was a brother John H. who moved to Hardin County, Illinois with Charles and their mother Elizabeth in the early 1840s. Charles was listed in the 1850 census for Hardin County, Illinois along with his wife, Martha, and a four-year-old son who was born in Illinois. Charles's father had apparently died by the time the family had removed to Illinois as he did not appear in the 1850 census, and Elizabeth was shown living with her son John H. and her daughter-in-law, Nancy.

Charles M. Ferrell married Martha Adaline Winters, 27 August 1840 in Marshall County, Tennessee. This union produced the following:
Eliza Jane Ferrell, b. 01 Nov 1842 , d. 09 Apr 1843; Charles H. Ferrell, b. 11 Apr 1846, d. 06 Jan 1860; Henry Ferrell b. --, d. 30 Jun 1879; Martha Adaline, b.--, d. 10 Mar 1879.

In 1861 Charles was mustered into the 29th Illinois as a captain and was promoted to colonel in 1862. During the Battle of Pittsburg Landing, Colonel Ferrell's troops turned a Confederate Cavalry charge. General McClernand's report read in part:
"The 29th Illinois Infantry inspired by the courageous example of their commanding officer, Lt. Col. Ferrell, bore the chief part in this engagement...."

In the action at Pittsburg Landing (Shiloh), the 29th lost 100 men killed or wounded out of a force of 400 men.

Col. Ferrell resigned his commission 11 August 1863 due to the ill health of his wife, Martha, and returned to Elizabethtown in Hardin County. His activities after he resigned his commission are somewhat sketchy. He was elected to the Twenty-Eight General Assembly 1872-1874 of the Illinois State Senate. He was mentioned in the 20 April 1877 issue of *The Hardin Gazette* "re-establishing" his business.

In the 1880s, Col. C. M. Ferrell (as he was called in the Hardin Co. newspapers) owned and operated a large general store and produce business. He also owned several river boats that he used to haul potatoes to market. He was active in land and real estate transactions. His name was found many times in Hardin County land records. C. M. Ferrell was one of the most frequently mentioned names in court actions, generally filed by him to collect a debt or to recover property. Charles Ferrell's willingness to stand up and fight was characteristic. The newspapers of that day carried two stories that illustrated this trait.

In one instance, Pleasant Rose entered the store and fired four rounds from a pistol at Ferrell. The Colonel grabbed a whip from the rack and drove Rose from the store. No reason was given for the attack, except Rose had been drinking.

In another instance, Ferrell forcibly ejected an "Irishman" who abused a Mr. Server. The text did not identify Server or the "Irishman"

Riley Oxford relates a story about C. M. Ferrell that shows the Col. in a different light. Riley worked in Elizabethtown in the mining days. He related the following incident. "Hardin County being the first and only mining section in the West, very few knew anything about iron mining. Many Irish workers who understood mining came to our county from the East, and that they were a gay set of fellows. One Saturday pay day a nimble young fellow offered to wager a gallon of good whiskey that there wasn't a man on the job who could hit him with a club. Colonel Ferrell who was in the prime of life and who had been somewhat of a fighter himself accepted the wager.

So, the bully Irishman walked out with a shillalah in hand. A Irish shillalah is a stout cudgel about the size of a large hoe handle, but not so long. The hilarious crew found one for Col. Ferrell, and gathered around the contestants to see the shillalah bout. The Colonel struck and punched at the Irishman rather lightly at first, but each of his efforts was skillfully warded off with the Shillalah of the practiced Irishman.

At length the contest became more spirited and the Irishman caught a rather quick lick of Col. Ferrell which jarred the colonel's hand painfully. Angered, the Colonel came back with a quick stroke intended to knock the bully down. Nevertheless, the practiced shillalah again caught Colonel's club, jerking it from his hand and whirling it over the heads of the bystanders into the bush.

Then rubbing his hand, Colonel Ferrell exclaimed, 'D---n him , draw out his gallon; I'll pay for it; pay for two before I'd fight him again.'"

Charles M. Ferrell was an important and influential man in Southern Illinois. He was appointed to various local, county and state positions. He apparently sold his business interests in the late 1880's or early 90's and moved to Evansville, Indiana and later(?) to Madison, Wisconsin. The 28 September 1894 issue of *The Hardin Republican* mentioned that Col. C.M. Ferrell had returned to his home in Madison, Wisconsin. *The Saline County Register* for 19 ? July 1901 carried a reprint of the Elizabethtown *Star*'s obituary of Col. C.M. Ferrell. It stated that he had gone to Madison, Wisconsin to spend the summer, and died there in a hotel on 08 July 1901.

He left no known descendants, but his brother John H. Ferrell had several children that survived and there should be descendants of that line.

DOCUMENTATION
1. Charles M. Ferrell, Military Records #SC 450797.
2. Marshall Co. Tennessee 1840 census.
3. *Hardin Gazette* 12 March 1880 (obituary of Elizabeth Ferrell mother of Col. C.M. Ferrell)
4. Hardin Co. Illinois census 1850-1880.
5. *Marriage Records, Marshall County, Tenn. 1836-1870*, transcribed by Deane Porch 1976, Louis G. Lynch, Publisher, Franklin, Tenn.
6. Tombstone inscriptions, Price and Methodist

Cemeteries and correspondence with B.G. Ferrell, researcher on Ferrell line (birth and death dates of Charles, Martha, and children).
7. *Report of the Adjutant General of the State of Illinois, Vol. 2 1861-1866*, Revised by Brig. General J.N. Reece, Phillip Bros. State Printers, Springfield, ILL.. 1900 (29th ILL. Regiment).
8. *Blue Book of Illinois 1903*, James A, Rose, Secretary of State (Lists C.M.Ferrell in State Senate, 1872-1874).
9. *Hardin Gazette,* 6 March 1880 edition (Rose shooting incident).
10.*Hardin* Gazette 24 March 1882 edition ("Irishman" incident).
11.*Saline County Register*, 19 (?) July 1901 edition (reprint of Col. Ferrell's obituary).
12. *History of Hardin County,Ill.* Historical Committee for the Centennial. p.23. (shillalah incident).

CLEMENT FERRELL
    Clement H. Ferrell was born 1789, according to his military records. He was probably the son of James Ferrell and Tabitha Hayes who were married in Granville, North Carolina. Thomas is identified in James' military records as a son. William, and Jane Ferrell Martin are also possible children of James and Tabitha Ferrell. Clement's military records show that he was drafted from Sumner County, Tennessee into the Tennessee Militia for approximately six months. He fought in the battle of New Orleans under General Andrew Jackson.
    Clement H. Ferrell married Sally or Sarah Edwards on 26 April 1811 in Gallatin, Sumner County Tennessee. They had removed to Bedford County, Tennessee by 1820 because he appeared in the 1820 census of that county. Later, he was counted in the 1830 census for Fayette County, Illinois and in the 1840 and 1850 censuses for Hardin County, Illinois.
    The marriage of Clement and Sarah produced the following known children: William C. Ferrell, born abt 1815 in Tenn.; James Ferrell, born 6 May 1819 in Tenn.; Thomas A. Ferrell,

born 6 April 1821 in Tenn.; John Ferrell, born 9 March 1825 in Tenn.; Perlina Ferrell, born 1826 in Tenn.; Joseph Ferrell, born 5 October 1828 in Tenn.; Andrew J. Ferrell, born 29 April 1830 in ILL.; male ? Re: 1830 census for Fayette Co. ILL.;

Clement H. Ferrell died on 15 October 1862. In 1871 at the age of 82, Sarah made application for a widow's pension. Her death date and place of burial are unknown.

MARRIAGES

1. William C. Ferrell to Elizabeth A. Ginger, 23 July 1836 in Pope Co. ILL.
2. James Ferrell to Mary Mott, 6 May 1838 in Pope Co., ILL.
3. Thomas A. Ferrell to Mary Jane Hubbard about 1844.
4. Perlina Ferrell to Obadiah Hubbard, 15 June 1846 in Hardin Co. ILL.
5. John Ferrell to Saline Weaver, 25 October 1848 in Hardin Co., ILL.
6. Joseph Ferrell (1) Elizabeth Ladd about 1850 in Hardin Co.; ILL., (2) Elizabeth Shell about 1867 in Hardin Co.; 3) Sarah Elizabeth Moore about 1874.
7. Andrew Jackson Ferrell to Rebecca Lyons about 1854.

DOCUMENTATION

1. Clement H. Ferrell military record, War of 1812, file # WC 1024 1812
2. James Ferrell military record, Revolutionary War. He served in the 9th and 10 regiments of the North Carolina Line. He died in Sumner Co., Tenn. in 1812. His widow was Tabitha Hayes.
3. William Ferrell military record, War of 1812, # SO 20301, SC # 15723, # 13206-160-50. This man served in the same unit with Clement H. Ferrell and was probably a brother. He married Lucy Guinn, 22 May 1822 in Bedford Co., Tenn. He lived in Fulton Co., Ark. 1851-1882, died 1 Nov. 1884 in Bloomer, Sebastian Co., Ark.
4. James Martin military record, Mexican War, pension # 963, Old War Widow 13, 673. His wife, Jane, was probably a sister of Clement Ferrell. *Sumner County Tennessee Marriage Records 1787-*

1838. These records give Clement and Sarah's marriage date.

6. Marshall County, Tenn., 1840 census for Charles Ferrell. This Charles could be a son of James and Tabitha Ferrell.

7. The family of Clement Ferrell and Sarah Edwards has been reconstructed from interviews with their descendants. Clara Hale, granddaughter of Joseph Ferrell and Elizabeth Ladd, and Stella Mae Jones, daughter of Joseph Ferrell and Elizabeth Moore, stated that Perlina was Joseph Ferrell's sister. Clara Hale recalls her mother talking of Ferrell Uncles: Tom, Andy, Jim, and Clem. She was unsure of the "Clem" as there were several Clems in the Family. Clara also remembers visiting her mother's first cousins: Sarah Ann, Polk, John, Martha, and Charles. These were the children of James and Mary Mott Ferrell. Alleta Ferrell Warfield, grand-daughter of Andrew Ferrell, said that Andrew's father was Clement Ferrell. John Ferrell's obituary stated that "his parents brought him to lllinois, settling first in Fayette, County but afterwards moving to Hardin Co. ILL."

8. William H. Ferrell bible.

9. *Marriage Records Book A* for Pope County Illinois.(William C. Ferrell and Elizabeth Ann Ginger)

10. James Ferrell bible.

11. Obadiah Hubbard military records (131st Illinois Vols.) gives marriage date for Perlina Ferrell.

DICK FERRELL

Dick Ferrell, son of Joseph Ferrell and brother of our townsmen, John H. and Edward Ferrell of Evansville, Ind. and "Booze" Ferrell, formerly a resident of Elizabethtown, but now living in Sikeston, Mo., and God only knows how many more of this immediate family according to the *Saline County Register* is now one of the leading Presbyterian preachers of the Northwest. The graphic story of his life as a champion prize fighter and later a missionary worker is told as follows:

The strangest religious congregation in the whole Northwest is that which has as its pastor Dick Ferrell of Spokane, former welter-weight pugilistic champion of the South.

The parish embraces the entire forest-clad portion of Idaho; except the Potlatch holding and includes 5000 lumberjacks to whom no body except Dick preaches the gospel. In the whole wilderness there is no church except the scattered bunkhouses and the nearest approach to organ music is the soughing of the wind in the lofty evergreens. It might well be called "The Parish of the Pines."

Dick Ferrell was born in Harrisburg, ILL. 29 years ago, and began his pugilistic career at an early age.

He has the rare distinction of never having been knocked out in his life, and this despite the fact that he engaged in 14 fights during his four years in the ring. He won 12 of these with knockouts. In beating Billy Mayfield at Peoria, ILL. In 1907 Dick won his welter weight championship. He knocked out the champion in two rounds. His hardest fight was with Jimmie Adams in St. Louis. He knocked out his opponent in the 14th round, incidentally breaking his nose and administering such a bad beating to his face that intimate friends of Adams could not recognize him the next day. Dick himself did not come through unscathed. To use a homely simile his face looked like a hamburger steak.

Bob Fitzsimmons discovered Dick when he was working as a horseshoer in a little Illinois mining town named Herrin. He was then 19 years old and Fitzsimmons told him that if he stuck to the game he would be a champion. "Lanky Bob" later reiterated this prophecy in the columns of the *Chicago Tribune*, and, it undoubtedly would have come true except for one thing. After all that Dick got religion.

It was while he was in training at Chicago in 1908 for a fight with "Knockout Brown" that Dick was converted. He had the reputation in the ring of being a fighter rather than a boxer and, he carried these wholehearted tactics with him into the church. He wired his opponent's manager to call off the fight.

That instead of knocking out fighters he was now fighting to knock out the Devil. Dick thereby lost a $500 purse. He became a stanch member of the Fourth Presbyterian church in Chicago and specialized in boys' club work.

About a year ago some of the lumber companies decided as an experiment to send Dick out to work among the lumberjacks of Idaho. At present the Potlatch Company's men are cared for by a Y.M.C.A. They number about 2000, but the other 5000 men scattered throughout the state have no "sky pilot" but Dick.

Dick makes his headquarters at the Spokane Y.M.C.A. and goes off on trips of several days each week. On his back he carries a 50 pound pack filled with reading matter which the woodsmen are eager for. His clothing is that of the typical lumberjack. While not going out of his way for a fight, Dick is an advocate of muscular Christianity. He knows that, although brain is not despised, brawn is honored, and endurance is the ideal of the lumberjack.

One run in he had was in a saloon of a little town in the Idaho panhandle. A burly French Canadian, the operator of a gambling resort, took offense at Dick's work because it was reducing his profits. Before a crowd of men he accused the missionary of working a bunco game to get the lumberjacks' money.

"I never take a penny from the men," said Dick, "and we are going to settle this question right here."

Both men threw off their mackinaws and went at it with bare fists. It took just half a minute to land a terrific right wallop on his opponent's jaw which crumpled him up on the ground. The missionary was the first to throw water on his erstwhile opponent and when he came to the men shook hands and agreed to let bygones be bygones.

Shortly after the affair in the saloon the sky pilot ran into a bunch of lumberjacks. One big, husky fellow was pretty drunk and shedding maudlin tears. He saw Dick and called out "Why didn't you come around sooner. When I was paid off I had $300 and I wanted you to keep it for me."

So Dick, in addition to his duties as sky pilot, is called on to act as banker for his charges. Sometimes when they don't ask him he volunteers his services as he did in the case of one man who had not been back to his family for five years. The reason was that he always went on a big spree when he got out of the woods and didn't have enough car fare left when he sobered up to pay his way home. Dick conducted him out of the woods, bought his ticket and saw him safely on the train. Today that man is supporting his family and report has it that he is a regular attendant at church.

One graphic story of a conversion is told by Dick. He was trudging out to one of the camps with his heavy pack on his back when the foreman of the gang, just out from town, overtook him. They walked along in silence for a while.

"How's it going?" said Dick finally, although knowing very well that it was going far from well.

"The same old story," said the foreman sheepishly. "I've been off on another drunk and I'm dead broke."

Dick talked to him and got him to admit he wanted to quit booze, but that he didn't have the strength of will to do it.

"Have you ever publicly prayed to become a Christian?" queried the sky pilot.

"No," was the hesitating reply.

"You get right down on your knees in the road and we'll find out whether there's a God or not."

So the two of them knelt in the rough logging road and prayed for power over booze. Since that day the foreman has straightened up.

In the letter writing line Dick is often called on to work overtime. Particularly when he visits the men who have been injured and wish to write to relatives from the hospitals or his services required Dick regularly makes the rounds of the hospitals at Priest River, Sandpoint, Newport, and St. Maries. He says that his most effective missionary work is often done

with the lumberjacks in these places.
HARDIN COUNTY INDEPENDENT, Dec. 30, 1915.

RICHARD TOWNSEND FERRELL

Richard "Dick" Townsend Ferrell was born 25 March 1885 in Elizabethtown, Hardin County Illinois, the son of Joseph Ferrell and his third wife, Elizabeth Moore. On 12 December 1917, Dick married Leone Ziebell. This union produced two children: Miriam Elizabeth Ferrell and Richard Joseph Ferrell.

Dick was a professional fighter, before he left the ring to become a Presbyterian missionary. According to his wife, Leone, the world's champion boxer, Robert Fitzsimmons, refused to fight Dick because of Dick's prowess in the ring. Later, as a minister, Dick met with Fitzsimmons to counsel him on personal and marital problems.

Dick attended the Moody Bible Institute from 1910 to 1913. In 1914 he was sent by the church as a missionary to the lumber jacks of the Northwest.

During WWI, he took leave from his "Lumber Jack" ministry to serve as a Y.M.C.A. secretary at Fort Lewis, Washington. After the war, he returned to the Northwest woods to serve the lumber jacks until the 1950's.

Dick Townsend Ferrell died 15 May 1956 in Spokane, Washington.

Dick's life was featured in *Presbyterian Life* magazine (1949) and on a national T.V. program, *Crossroads* (1956). Dick is also listed in *International Bluebook*(1943) and *Who's Who on the Pacific Coast*(1949-1951).

SOURCES
1. Letter written by Leone Ziebell Ferrell to her sister-in-law, Stella Mae Ferrell Jones in 1965.
2. *Biographical Review of Johnson, Massac, Pope and Hardin Counties* (Chicago: Biographical Publishing Co., 1893), pp. 359-360.

JOHN H. FERRELL

John H. Ferrell, son of Joseph Ferrell and Elizabeth Ladd, was born in Hardin County,

Illinois on 29 October 1860. He lived most of his life in Elizabethtown, Illinois. Shortly before his death, he moved to West Frankfort, Illinois.

John married Sallie R. Williams on 19 August 1883. This union produced two sons: Clifford Ferrell, born Elizabethtown, ILL., 19 June 1887, died in France, 21 September 1918; Bert F. Ferrell, born ? Elizabethtown ?

John H. Ferrell was a Judge and lawyer in Elizabethtown. According to *The Bench and Bar of Illinois Historical and Reminiscent*, he was admitted to the bar in 1896. He was a member of the bar association for over 20 years. This reference lists him as John H. Ferrell Jr. He was elected to the office of county judge in 1906 and reelected in 1910.

Judge Ferrell was active in fraternal and religious organizations. He was a member of the Masons and The Odd Fellows. According to his obituary, he was not a formal member of any church, but he attended the Methodist Church. The Men's Bible Class "sessions were always interesting when he attended."

Judge John H. Ferrell was apparently a colorful character as his name appeared quite often in the *Hardin County Independent*. After Sallie and he had moved to West Frankfort, Illinois, the judge sent the *Independent* a story of how all of Sallie's baby chickens had been caught and eaten by crawdads (crayfish). After the story was printed, Judge Ferrell took great glee in pointing out to the editor that the story was a hoax. John H. Ferrell was a man who came from a very humble background but through hard work and study, he became very successful.

In 1921 he suffered a stroke that left him paralyzed. Judge John H. Ferrell died at West Frankfort, Illinois on 9 February 1926 at the age of 62.

Documentation

1. *Biographical Review of Johnson, Massac, Pope and Hardin Counties 1893* pp. 359-360.
2. "Ferrell" *Hardin County Independent*, February 1926, p.1 (obituary).

3. *Bench and Bar of Illinois Historical and Reminiscent,* P. 803, Chicago: Lewis Publishing Co.
4. "John H. Ferrell Announces his Candidacy for Reelection," *Hardin County Independent*, July 7, 1910, p. 1.
5. "Letter from a Comrade of Clifford Ferrell," *Hardin County Independent*, July 23, 1919, p. 1.
6. "Military Funeral for Corp. Ferrell," *Hardin County Independent*, February? 1920, p. 1.
Note: Clifford Ferrell married Bessie Watson ? 28 August 1906, California?. She died 3 February 1911 in California ?.

JOHN H. FERRELL

John H. Ferrell was born near Chapel Hill, Marshall County Tennessee on 15 April 1823, the son of Charles? and Elizabeth Ferrell, and a brother of Charles M. Ferrell. This family was enumerated in the 1840 census for Marshall County with Charles M. Ferrell as the head of the household.

Apparently, Charles M.? (60-70 year old male?) died between 1840 and 1850 because there are no further record of him. By 1850, the family had moved to Hardin County Illinois, as they were counted in the 1850 census. Charles Sr.? was not listed in the census.

Both sons had established their own homes, and Elizabeth was living with John H.

John H. Ferrell married Nancy Virginia Jane Pillow, niece ? of Civil War general, Gideon Pillow. Nancy was born on 5 January 1826 in Tennessee. The exact marriage date is unknown, but they were probably married about 1845. This union produced the following: James P. Ferrell, born 31 December 1847, died 31 May 1930; Martha Ferrell, born 1849, died ?; John C. Ferrell, born 1851, died ? Josephine A. Ferrell, born 1855, died ?; Nellie A. Ferrell, born 1860.

During The Civil War, John served in the U. S. Navy as a ship's pilot. He received The Medal of Honor for his action aboard the U S Monitor, NEOSHO. The citation reads as follows: "... during the engagement with enemy batteries at Bells Mills, Cumberland River, near Nashville,

Tenn., Dec 6, 1864. Carrying out his duties courageously during the engagement, Ferrell gallantly left the pilothouse after the flag and signal staffs of that vessel had been shot away, taking the flag which was drooping over the wheelhouse, made it fast to the stump of the highest mast remaining although the ship was still under heavy fire from the enemy."

After the war, John and the family moved to Massac County and were counted in the 1870 census for that county. How long they remained in Massac County in unknown. John and his wife may have returned to Hardin County as they are both buried in the Price Cemetery in Elizabethtown. John died on 12 April 1900; Nancy died in Paducah, Kentucky in July of 1914.

MARRIAGES

James P. Ferrell to Elizabeth Hayden at Metropolis, ILL. on 26 June 1872.
Josephine A. Ferrell to John ___ of Madison, Indiana at Hardin County on 19 July 1894.

DOCUMENTATION

1. Marshall County Tenn., census for 1840.
2. *Marshall County Tennessee Tax Records 1839-1841*. William H. Ferrell and Charles M. Ferrell are listed in the tax records. The William H. Ferrell is unknown,
3. Hardin County Illinois census for 1850.
4. Massac County Illinois census for 1870
5. *America's Medal of Honor Recipients Complete Official Citation*, Highland Publications, Minn. 1980, p. 768.
6. *Hardin County Marriage Records*, Josephine A. Ferrell.
7. John H. Ferrell obituary. " Died at his residence north west of this city, Tuesday afternoon, Apr. 17, 1900 at 4 o'clock, Capt. John H. Ferrell after an illness of nearly three weeks duration of Pneumonia fever. He will be buried by the I.O.O.F. order at this place Thursday evening. Extended notice next week.(unidentified source but probably *Hardin County Independent*)
8. James P. Ferrell obituary. "James P. Ferrell was born near Richland school house December 31, 1847; died May 31, 1930 aged 82 years and 5

months. He was the oldest son of Capt. John H. Ferrell and Nancy V.J. Ferrell. He married Elizabeth Hayden at Metropolis, ILL. on June 26, 1872 to this union seven children were born, three of whom Rella, Benjamin, Harvey died when small and Edward Roscoe died April 13, 1928.

He leaves to mourn him his aged wife, a son, Charles F. Ferrell, a daughter, Mrs. W.S. Hosick of Elizabethtown, a son, James O. Ferrell, of Oakland, California, a niece, Mrs. Violet Fritts of Metropolis, a nephew, Marsh Ferrell in Florida, nine grandchildren, four great grandchildren, besides a niece of his wife whom they raised from infancy and loved as their own." (unidentified source, but probably *Hardin County Independent*)

9. Death notice: "Mortal remains of Mrs. John Ferrell, mother of Capt James Ferrell of this town was brought here from Paducah ... She was accompanied by her son, Mr. John T. Ferrell of Metropolis and Miss Joe Ferrell of Paducah. *Hardin Co. Independent*, 23 July 1914.

10. Price Cemetery inscriptions. Members of the Charles M. Ferrell family and members of the John H. Ferrell family are buried there. The cemetery is located in Elizabethtown, Illinois.

JOSEPH FERRELL

Joseph Ferrell, son of Clement Ferrell and Sarah Edwards, was born in Tennessee on 5 October 1828, possibly in Bedford County as Clement was listed in the 1820 census for that county. His siblings were probably Thomas, Andrew, William, James, Perlina, and Clement(?).

By 1830, Clement and Sarah had moved to Fayette County Illinois as he was enumerated in the 1830 census. James Ferrell was also listed in the Fayette County census for that year. This was probably a brother. The next move was to an area in Pope County that later became Hardin County. Clement and Sarah remained in Hardin County for the rest of their lives.

Joseph appeared in the 1850 census for Hardin County, Illinois along with Isabel, age 15. The "Isabel" was probably his first wife, Elizabeth Ladd who was born on 2 January 1834.

Elizabeth would have been 15 years old at the time. According to the *Biographical Review of Johnson, Massac, Pope and Hardin Counties Illinois*, Joseph's first wife was Elizabeth Ladd whom he married about 1850. This union produced eight children, all of whom were born in Hardin County: Nancy, born about 1852; Sarah Emma, born 17 April 1864, died 19 June 1934; James, born 23 April 1853, died 22 June 1955; William L., born 15 February 1855, died 30 September 1855; unidentified male, born 1857, died--; John Harve, born 29 October 1860, died 9 February 1926; two unidentified.

Elizabeth Ladd Ferrell died on the 14th of April 1866 and was buried in Pleasant Hill Cemetery, Hardin County.

Joseph then married Elizabeth Shell, daughter of Solomon Shell. This union produced three children: Milas, born 11 November 1867; Edward, born 24 August 1869; Henry, born --, died 18 January 1927.

Elizabeth shell Ferrell died on 22 June, 1873 and was buried in Pleasant Hill Cemetery.

Joseph then took as his third wife, Sarah Elizabeth Moore. This union produced 12 children: Ella, born 1875; Robert, born 1877; Thomas Jefferson, born March 1878; Laura, born August 1880, died 6 June 1960; Fred, born October 1882; Richard Townsend, born 25 March 1885, died 15 May 1956; Hedley, born--; James Harvey, born 10 February 1886; Harry Grover, born 11 September 1888; Stella Mae, born 16 June 1892; Frankie, born --; Mary, born--.

Joseph and his family moved from Hardin County in the late 1880's to Saline and later to Williamson County. Very little is known of Joseph and his three wives. He was involved in politics and religion as his name occasionally appeared in the Hardin County newspapers under those topics. He was apparently a deeply religious man. His obituary described him as "a soldier of the Lord for 50 years." According to his son Richard Townsend, Joseph's last words before he died were the ones he sang from the hymn, "O Happy Day." When he completed the verse, he sank back on his bed and died. Joseph died on 9 April 1904 and was buried at Marion, ILL. Elizabeth Moore Ferrell died two years later on 24 July 1906, and she was also buried at Marion.

MARRIAGES

Sarah Emma Ferrell to John Curry, 5 August 1880; Nancy Ferrell to Charles Hubbard; Milas Ferrell to Annie Kenney,16 December 1894; Edward Ferrell to Mabel Clark, 8 November 1893; Henry Ferrell to Elizabeth Lambert, 23 December 1896; Stella Mae Ferrell to Homer Hindman; James H. Ferrell to Carrie Ann Johnson, 30 July 1910; Fred Ferrell to Melissa E. Bell, and Vera Reese Riggs; Richard Ferrell to Leona Ziebell, 12 Dec.1917; Laura Ferrell to Ira Martin, --? and to Charles A. Turner, November 1914

DOCUMENTATION

1. Clement Ferrell military record, War of 1812,# W.C. 1024 1812.
2. *Sumner County Tennesse Marriage Records 1787-1838.*
3. The family of Clement and Sarah Edwards Ferrell has been re-constructed through inter-interviews with descendants of Joseph Ferrell. Clara Hale, daughter of Emma Ferrell Curry who was the daughter of Joseph Ferrell, and Elizabeth Ladd, and Stella Mae Ferrell Jones daughter of Joseph Ferrell and Elizabeth Moore Ferrell. Clara said that Perlina was Joe's sister and an aunt of her mother, Emma Ferrell Curry. She also remembers her mother, Emma, speaking of Ferrell uncles: Tom, Andy, Bill, and Jim , and perhaps a Clem. She was not sure of the Uncle Clem as there were several Clems in the family. She recalls visiting her mother's first cousins: Sarah Ann, Vida, Polk, John M., Martha, and Charles. These were the children of James Ferrell and Mary Mott.
4. Joseph Ferrell obituary, 15 April, 1904 edition of the *Herrin News*, Herrin, Illinois.
5. *Biographical Review of Johnson, Massac, Pope, and Hardin Counties.*(Chicago: Biographical Publishing Co., 1893) pp. 359-360.
6. J. Gray, *Obituaries From Hardin County Illinois.* (DAR).

7. Tombstone inscriptions, Pleasant Hill Cemetery, Hardin Co., Illinois: James, son of E.J. and J. Ferrell, b. April 23, 1853, d. Jan 22,1855; William L., son of E.J. and J. Ferrell, b. Feb. 15, 1855, d. Sept.30, 1855; Elizabeth, wife of Joseph Ferrell d. April 14, 1866.
8. *Hardin County Illinois Marriage Records* (Henry, Edward, and Milas Ferrell)
9. Henry Ferrell death certificate, Bureau of Vital Statistics, Jefferson City, Mo.
10. *Hardin County Independent*, 30 Dec. 1915 issue: " Dick Ferrell, son of Joseph Ferrell and brother of our townsmen, John H., and Edward Ferrell and also a brother of Milas Ferrell of Evansville, Indiana And " Booze" (Henry) Ferrell, formerly a resident of Elizabethtown, but now living in Sikeston, Missouri... "
11. *Who's Who On The Pacific Coast*, entry for Richard T. Ferrell.
12. Laura Ferrell Turner obituary, undated and unidentified, but probably Whitefish, Montana newspaper. Mrs. Laura Turner passed away at a Whitefish hospital on June 6, 1960... Laura Erline Turner was born August 14, 1879 at Elizabethtown, Illinois.
13. Sarah Emma Ferrell Ginger obituary, unidentified and undated. "Sarah Emma, daughter of Joseph and Elizabeth Ferrell, was born April 17, 1864, was married to J.S. Curry Aug.5, 1880. To this union one son and two daughters were born. Mr. Curry died June 25, 1923, later she was married to Daniel Ginger who preceded in death. William H., only son, passed away Feb.6, 1918. Deceased is survived by two daughters, Mrs. Minnie Davis of Marion, ILL., and Clara Hale of Lincoln, ILL., six brothers, two sisters ... also survive... She expired at her home ...June 19, 1924."
14. Story carried in Hardin County newspaper, unidentified and undated. "The Late Uncle Joe Ferrell's children who were born and partly reared on hill south of Pleasant Hill school house met Sunday, June 22, at Fairy Cliff, Thacker's Gap picnic Grounds. Uncle Joe Ferrell married a third time and reared a large family out of 23 children, there are only 11 living. By

the first marriage were Nann Hubbard (deceased), Mrs. Emma Summers of Elizabethtown, John H. Ferrell(deceased). By his second marriage were Milas of Evansville, Ind., Edd of Rosiclare, Henry (dec). By the last marriage were Thomas of Herrin, ILL., Fred of Bearden, Ark., Dick of Spokane, Wash., Harry of Benton, ILL., James H. of Herrin, ILL., Mrs. Bert Turner of Sandy, Montana, Mrs Homer Hindman of Herrin...."
15. Hardin County census, 1850-1860, Joseph Ferrell
16. Saline County census, 1900, Joseph Ferrell
17. John A. Ferrell obituary, *Saline County Register*, 20 December 1901 issue.
18. *Hardin Co. Illinois Birth Records, V0l 2.*
19. Gallatin Co, census. "James Ferrell," should ? be Joseph Ferrell.
20. Carrie Ferrell obituary, dated 1959, Murphysboro paper ? " Mrs. Carrie Ann Ferrell, 79, of ...Murphysboro, died Monday.... She was born Aug. 5, 1889 in Murphysboro, the daughter of Henry and Betty Henson Johnson. She married July 30 1910, in Murphysboro to James H. Ferrell who died in 1951. Mrs. Ferrell leaves a daughter, Mrs. R.O. Harris, of Sarasota, Fla., and a son, T.Y. Ferrell of Mt. Clements, Mich., ... a brother, Joseph W. Johnson of Murphysboro, and a sister, Mrs. Ivy M. Connelly of Murphysboro...."
21. Joseph Ferrell obituary, *Herrin News*, 15 April 1904.

LAURA BELL STACEY FERRELL

Laura Bell Stacey, the daughter of James Byram Stacey and Mary Ann McMurphy, was born 20 December 1872 in Hardin County, Illinois near the historic iron furnace.

She attended Richland School for her early education and later she attended summer sessions at Elizabethtown, Illinois where she studied physics, botany, zoology, other sciences and practice, and theory of teaching. She taught school for seven terms at Richland and Pinhook and apparently gave up teaching when she married Volentine Ferrell on 9 December 1894.

But she had a life-long interest in

education, and visited her old schools and others on various occasions.

Laura also had other interests. She was talented in music: she played the accordion, mandolin, and organ. However, she gradually lost her hearing as a result of a typhoid infection and was forced to give up music. She was deaf at the age of twenty-five, but she learned to lip read and was able to lead a very productive life in spite of her handicap. During World War I, she was an American Red Cross chairwoman for her district. She organized and registered 16-year-old girls to serve as nurses in World I in the event they were needed. Laura also knitted gloves and socks for the Red Cross to send over seas.

Laura was active in the Social Brethren Church. Often she would cook for 40 to 50 people as they attended conferences. These functions would often last for several days. She taught Sunday School, worked with the Ladies Aid, and raised funds for a new Baptist Church building.

Like many women of her generation, Laura Bell took great pride in homemaking. She was an excellent cook. She canned fruit, vegetables, and made jellies. Laura made clothes for the family and did all kinds of fancy work and stitching. She loved flowers. Many pictures of Laura show her in her garden tending flowers.

Laura Bell Stacey Ferrell on 25 April 1940.

DOCUMENTATION

1. Biographical information supplied by Norman Ferrell and Hattie McDaniels, children of Vol and Laura Bell Ferrell.

2. *Hardin County Illinois Past and Present*, Turner Publishing Co., Paducah, Ky. 1987.

THOMAS FERRELL

Thomas A. Ferrell, son of Clement and Sarah Edwards Ferrell, was born in Tennessee on 6 April 1821, probably in Bedford County as Clement was enumerated in the 1820 census for that county.

The family arrived in Illinois between 1830

and 1840 because Clement was counted in the 1830 census for Fayette County and in the 1840 census for Hardin County. Clement and Sarah lived out the remainder of their lives in Hardin County.

Thomas A. Ferrell was shown in the 1850 census for Hardin County, along with his wife, Mary Jane Hubbard who was born 10 December 1825. Thomas probably married Mary Jane about 1843-44, as her first child was born in 1845. This union produced the following: Missouri, born 10 June 1845, died 14 February 1888; Mary Jane, born 5 January 1847, died--; Sarah Elizabeth, born 6 April 1850, died 29 June 1884; Thomas A., born 23 December 1853, died 11 September 1854; Malissa Ann, born 29 April 1855, died 16 July 1855; Margaret Josephine, born 26 October 1856, died 13 January 1947; William H., born. 6 April 1861, died--.

DOCUMENTATION

1. William H. Ferrell Bible gives the birthdates of Thomas A., Mary Jane, Andrew J. and Elizabeth Jane Ferrell. William H. Ferrell married Mary B. Epperson on 15 Oct 1883. She was born 25 Oct 1862, died 31 Aug 1911. Issue: Thomas J., born 19 Mar 1885, d. Dec 1941; William H. b., 10 Jan 1887?, died 24 Apr 1901; Ruth, born 13 Aug 1889, died--; Raymond D. born, 2 Sept 1891, died--; Mary, born 26 Jun 1895, died 28 Feb 1896; Floyd A. born, 27 Dec 1898, died---; Fred A., born 14 Nov 1902, died 5 May 1908. Sarah Elizabeth Ferrell married a Mr. Ferguson and she died 29 June 1884. William C. Turk married Mary J. Ferrell, 12 November 1868.
2. *Saline County Illinois Marriage Records* 1847-1880), complied by Bernard Moore).
3. Rose Cemetery in Hardin County Illinois. "Thomas A. Ferrell, son of Thomas A. and M.J. Ferrell Dec 23, 1852-Sept 17 1853."
4. *Gaskin's Funeral Records Saline Co. Illinois* complied by Bernard Moore. "Josephine Seagrave, b. Oct. 14, 1858, Shawneetown, ILL., d. Jan 13 1947...Husband, Samuel Seagraves. Father, Thomas Ferrell, born Tenn. Mother, Jane Hubbard, born Hardin County., ILL. Informant; Tony Racine, Harrisburg."

5. Tom Ferrell obituary, *Saline County Register* 20 March 1906. " Uncle Tom Ferrell was buried at the city Cemetery Monday afternoon... of late he made his home with his son-in-law, Sam Seagraves... His daughter Mrs. William Turk came up from from Paducah."
6. Sam Seagraves Family, 1880 Saline County census, page 127, line 145. Seagraves, Sam 38, Josie 23, wife; Sallie 6, dau; Emma 3, dau; William 1, son; Sallie, 57; mother.
7. Samual Seagraves married Josie Ferrell, *Saline County Illinois Marriages 1847-1880.*
8. Samual Seagraves b. 1845, d. 1906, Josephine b. 1857, d. 1947. *Saline County Cemeteries Vol. VI*, published by John Murphy.
9. Josephine Seagraves, born 16 October 1858, Shawneetown, Ill., died 13 January 1947. Buried Ingram Hill Cemetery. Husband Samual Seagraves. Father Thomas Ferrell. Mother Jane Hubbard, born Hardin County Illinois. *Gaskin Funeral Records.* Saline County Illinois.
10. William Ferrell Family, 1900 Census, Linton, Indiana, dist # 37, line 42.Ferrell, William head, b. Apr 1871 (1861?) Bell, wife, b. 1862; Thomas Jr., son, b. Mar 1885; William Jr., son, b. Jan 1887; Ruth dau, b. Aug 1889; Raymond,son, b. Sept 1891; Floyd, son, b. Dec 1898; Thomas Sr., father b. Apr 1821.

Volentine Ferrell

Volentine Ferrell was born 29 my 1867 near Karber's Ridge in Hardin County, Illinois, the son of William Carroll Ferrell and Sarah Pyle.

Volentine or "Vol" as he was often called, grew up in Hardin County, and attended various rural schools in that county. He received a good education for his day. In his twenties, he attended Teachers' Institute, a summer course that would probably be equivalent to a modern college class. Volentine then taught two sessions of school at Richland and Pinhook schools between 1887-1889. He was paid an average of $30.00 per month.

In March of 1889, he saw an opportunity to go into business and he subsequently bought a stock of goods and rented a store building in

Hicks, Illinois. By April of that year, he had paid in full for the merchandise, and soon (1890) purchased 1/2 acre of land and the store building.

He married Laura Bell Stacy, daughter of James Byram Stacey and Mary Ann McMurphy on 9 December 1894. This union produced the following: Mable, born 24 April 1896; Otis M., born 5 June 1898; Mollie, born 3 June 1901; Hattie Blanche, born 8 January 1904; Harry Roosevelt, born 12 August 1906; Hazel, born 7 September 1909; James Randall, born 8 March 1912; Norman, born 16 April 1914; Russell Gordon, born 15 October 1917.

In addition to his business interests, Volentine was a minister of the Social Brethren He pastored Green Valley, Cedar Bluff, Mt. Pleasant churches, and possibly others. All these churches were in Southern Illinois. However, due to a throat condition, Vol was unable to fulfill the speaking requirements of a full-time ministry, and consequently he limited his pastoral duties to memorial services, special sermons, and the performing of marriages.

Volentine was a man of varied interests. He served as county clerk of Hardin County in 1894-1898, county commissioner for several terms, justice of the peace, school director, notary public, and postmaster. He was a member of the Odd Fellows, and Karber's Ridge Masonic Lodge # 974. He obtained the degree of Past Master at his lodge.

In the 1920's, Vol bought a clothing store in Elizabethtown and a store in Rosiclare. He eventually sold his store in Elizabethtown and located in Rosiclare where he remained active in business, church, and community. He died 20 May 1959.

DOCUMENTATION
1. Biographical information supplied by Norman Ferrell and Hattie Ferrell McDaniels.
2. *Hardin County Illinois Past And Present*, Turner Publishing Co., Paducah, Ky. 1987.

WILLIAM CARROLL FERRELL

William Carroll Ferrell, the son of James Ferrell and Mary Mott, was born 15 February 1847 near Elizabethtown, Hardin County, Illinois.

In 1865, he enlisted in the 49th Regiment of the Illinois Volunteers, and he was sent to Paducah, Kentucky for garrison duty. He remained at this post until he was discharged in September of 1865.

William married Sarah Pyles on 05 July 1865; Sarah was born 25 November in Hicks, Illinois, the daughter of John Pyles and Phoebe Lyons. This union produced the following: Volentine Ferrell, born 29 May 1867, died 20 May 1959; Susan Ferrell, born January 1870, died 16 July 1932; Willie Ernest Ferrell, born October 1881, died September 1961; Estella Ferrell, born 25 November 1879, died 10 January 1898.

Sarah Pyles Ferrell died on 20 April 1908, and William married Nancy Pellen on 13 May 1912. She was born in Franklin County Tennessee on 10 January 1848. Nancy had been widowed several times previously to her marriage to william Carroll Ferrell. There is no record of any children from her previous marriages.

Shortly, before his last marriage, William had moved to Campbell, Missouri where he died on 7 October 1930. Nancy's time and place of death are unknown.

MARRIAGES
1. Volentine Ferrell married Laura Bell Stacey, 09 December 1894.
2. Susan Ferrell married Thomas Estes.
3. Willie Ernest Ferrell married Ollie Banks, 8 December 1902.

DOCUMENTATION
1. Military records give date and place of birth for William C. Ferrell, marriage dates for both of his marriages, and birth dates for his children.
2. James Ferrell Family Bible also gives birth date of William Ferrell.

FOWLER BROTHERS

Through the urgent request of Mrs. Josie

Fowler, widow of the late Dr. F. M. Fowler, that we write an obituary proper of the Fowler brothers is our excuse for giving a brief history of their lives in one brief write-up.

Three of the brothers, H. Robert, Francis M. and Newton L. came to this county 40-odd years ago, when they were poor, struggling young men, seeking a location from which to determine on a life calling or profession.

When they first came here, they all taught school, and engaged in any other gainful occupations that did not interfere with their studies, until each chose his life profession, and because of their intelligence and industrious and hustling dispositions, they made a favorable impression on our people generally, and therefore had many friends here, who gladly extended aid and comfort to all of them in their life professions.

The oldest H. Robert chose the law as a profession, which naturally led to politics and as a Democrat was elected and served four years as State Attorney of Hardin County, and later was elected to both houses of the State Legislature. Still later he was elected to two terms to the Lower House of Congress. He continued untiring the study and practice of law.

He was widely known in Southern Illinois as a criminal lawyer and Democrat politician, but with few equals as a lawyer and perhaps no superiors. He was nearing his 75th year's end when death claimed him January 5, 1926.

Francis M. and Newton I. each chose medicine as a profession, and both seemed to be headed for a brilliant and useful career, when Dr. N.L. Fowler met an untimely and tragic ending on March 7, 1894.

The life of Dr. F.M. Fowler, however, was spared until July 8, 1925, when a long and useful life suddenly came to a end while he and his wife were taking treatment at a sanitarium in Tennessee. He had spent many years relieving suffering humanity, and ranked high among our best physicians; and that kindness of heart and the great sympathy and anxiety he always manifested toward his patients, had a great therapeutic effect on them. When Dr. Fowler answered a sick call and entered the home of many Hardin County families, his presence gave immediate relief.

Soon after Fowler reached his majority, he was married to miss Josie Vinyard, daughter of Rev. Dr. John Vinyard, August 29, 1889. She had been a school teacher and taught 12 terms of school, 3 terms after her marriage. Suffice to say their married life was very pleasant, and very successful from a financial standpoint. One daughter, Roberta, blessed this union, who is intelligent and highly educated. A short time ago she became the wife of Mr. R.V. Willis, a fine portly looking man with whom Mrs. Mary Fowler(?) will hereafter make her home at Christopher, ILL.

Senator and Dr. Fowler are survived and mourned by their wives, (and the former by one daughter) and two brothers, John C. of Tenn. Joe A. (a lawyer) of Denver, Colorado, and three sisters, Mrs. Nancy Walters, Mrs. Sarah Lockaby and Mrs. Bertha Rumsey (mother of D.F. Rumsey, the late senator's law partner).

All three of the subjects of this sketch were Masons and each had the honor and distinction of burial by that order. Dr. N.L. was buried at Eddysville, Pope County and the other two at Sunset Cemetery, Saline County. J.A. Oxford, HARDIN COUNTY INDEPENDENT, 18 Feb. 1926.

ELLEN HENRY FRAYSER

She was a native of Kentucky, but her parents, the late James and Fannie Henry moved to Hessville, near Cave-in- Rock when she was 16 years of age. Two years later when she married Charles B. Frayser. They moved to Cave-in-Rock and the remaining 60 years of her life were spent there.

They established the Frayser Hotel, which for over 50 years has been one of the landmarks of this section of the country. When Mr. Frayser died 25 years ago, Mrs. Frayser's brother, Tom Henry came from Kentucky to assist her in operating the hotel. Upon his death, a second brother, John Henry came, but due to her declining health and his advanced age, they were unable to carry it on, and with her death the hotel has passed out of existence.

The Frayser Hotel was almost the last link between Cave-in-Rock of old whose chief connection with the world at large was the slow and uncertain traffic upon the river.

In those former days, A lodging place for the traveling salesman, stockmen, and others "who were waiting for the boat" was a necessity, and for many years, Mrs. Frayser served the public by providing them with food to eat and a place to "stay at night."

Ellen Henry Frayser died in her home on June 9,1938. She is survived by only two brothers, John who is still making his home at the former hotel and George Henry of Henshaw, Kentucky. There are several nephews and nieces in Union county, Kentucky.
HARDIN COUNTY INDEPENDENT, June 9, 1938.

RICHARD GARVIN

Richard Garvin, aged 87, last November 20th is a resident of Rosiclare who has left his mark on most of the buildings in Hardin County and most of the picket boats on the river in the last half century.

He is a painter by trade and did commercial sand papering for his father at the age of eight. He has painted houses and business places in Cave-in-Rock, Elizabethtown, Rosiclare, in Tolu and Caseyville, Kentucky. He painted packets and excursion boats dry docked in Paducah. He also painted the John S. Hopkins, the boat which the river dry docked on Hurricane Island for six months in 1906.

Mr. Garvin was born in North Carolina, November 20, 1841, but his parents moved to Baton Rouge, Louisiana when he was a baby. In his early youth he was busy store boating on the Mississippi River with his father, trading with Negroes who were then slaves. "They had money" he said of the slaves. " They got their Saturdays off, and had truck gardens of their own and chickens and brought groceries and goods from us. Lots of them were better off during slavery then they are now," he said.

"I saw Jefferson Davis a number of times after the Civil War," he said. " Davis weighed about 165 pounds, always dressed in gray, and had one artificial eye."

Mr. Garvin was too young to fight during the war. When Mr. Garvin was 21, he saw the famous race of the two river boats, the ROBERT E. LEE and the NATCHEZ which was won by the ROBERT E. LEE. He said the ROBERT E. LEE was a new boat, and they sawed every other timber on her, so the timbers would give with the water to win the race.

Mr. Garvin was married in Tennessee and came to Kentucky on the other side of the river from Rosiclare to visit his wife's relatives. They decided to settle in Rosiclare. That was February 2, 1877. He said the mines were shut down when he moved there, but that Howard and Kirk of Pittsburgh were getting rock out of the Wood quarry, later the Howard quarry for jetties in New Orleans Mr. Garvin's wife died soon after he moved to Rosiclare, and he was married a second time. His second wife died two years ago. They had nine children. Garvin now lives with his daughter, Mrs. Georgia Miles.

He first rented a house when he moved to Rosiclare, near the house in which Mrs. Stella Davis died a few years ago. Mr. Garvin's house which he built about 40 years ago is about a block from the Rosiclare Hospital.

Rosiclare had been incorporated and there had been a town board before Mr. Garvin moved there. " But the board members had all gone away and there was no ruling board then", he said. " So we had an election and I was one of the board elected. I served 12 years. The village board served free to keep order, etc", he said.

Mr. Garvin said many's the time, he arose early and pulled his skiff three miles up the river to Elizabethtown for a day of painting. "And many's the time that my feet nearly froze and I had to land on the way and jump up and down to get my circulation going."

Mr. Garvin hunted and fished in his spare time. He said there used to be plenty of catfish, Buffalo, carp, hackleback, eels, turtles, blue cat and channel cat in the river. He remembers Barnett Lake in Kentucky, opposite Elizabethtown was another good fishing spot. Hardin County was the place for quail and rabbits. Mr. Garvin is in excellent health and takes long walks every day, though he doesn't hunt anymore.

"I haven't done much of anything lately, only painted one house, Johnson's since Christmas", Mr. Garvin said." I worked regularly until three years ago when they turned me out with the stock to pasture. Because I have a few gray hairs, the Democrats don't think I should work", he laughed.
HARDIN COUNTY INDEPENDENT, Feb. 16, 1939

L.T. GOETZMAN

When L.T. Goetzman Rosiclare's leading merchant came to that city early in 1918 and started a ready-to-wear store in the building next to the Y.M.C.A. Few people in Hardin county realized that he was to become one of Southern Illinois' outstanding merchants, attracting trade from many miles throughout Southern Illinois and Northern Kentucky.

Mr. Goetzman was born in Shawneetown, Illinois, his parents being Mr. and Mrs. J.R. Goetzman of that city, his father having been in business there for than fifty-two years. His grandmother, Mrs. Ulmsnider, who is now past ninety years of age, came to America when only twelve years of age.

With a modest beginning, Mr. Goetzman built his business on the foundation of service and fair dealing to a high position among mercantile enterprises in this section of the state.

On June 24, 1918, just previous to coming to Hardin County, Mr. Goetzman married Miss Lucille Burton, of Newton, Illinois, daughter of Dr. and Mrs. E.E. Burton of that city. They are both prominent in social affairs in Rosiclare and live in an elegantly appointed home of their own on Walnut street of that city.

In 1932 Mr. Goetzman built the building which he now occupies, a fire-proof structure on the main business street of Rosiclare and one of the finest retail mercantile buildings to be found anywhere.before coming to this section of the state, he was employed for ten years by Howell and Waller of Shawneetown, Illinois.

During the construction of the large dam at Golconda, Mr. Goetzman also owned and operated a store in that city, closing it at the completion of the dam.

Mr. Goetzman and his wife have traveled extensively in both in this country as well as Mexico, Cuba, South and Central America.

"Buddy" Goetzman as he is affectionately called by his innumerable friends, is considered to be one of the best business men in this section of the county and one may tell from a look through his store that he is familiar with modern business procedures.

Note: Louis W., Joseph, L., and John R. Goetzman were brothers and owned Goetzman Brothers Grocery store in Shawneetown.

Louis W. Goetzman ran for representative from Hardin County. In his newspaper ad he stated: "I came to Shawneetown in 1871. Two years later my brothers Joseph L. and John R. and myself established the grocery firm of Goetzman brothers, which proved to be a successful venture that is still in business after a period of more than 50 years." Louis W. also served in various political offices: City Clerk, 1883; Shawneetown Mayor, 1888, State Board of Equalization, 1912. He also ran for Congress in 1916.

HARDIN COUNTY INDEPENDENT Aug. 1, 1935, Jan 13, 1936.

EMMA CAROLINE GREGG JENKINS

Emma Caroline Gregg was born in Hamilton County, near McLeansboro, Illinois on September 22, 1851. She is a daughter of the late Hugh and Stacey Skelton Gregg.

Her father was married three times, his three wives preceding him in death. To the first union were born four children, all of whom are now dead. His second marriage was to Stacey Skelton and to this union were born seven children. Mrs. Jenkins was the fourth child and the only one that now survives. To the third union were born two children, Mr. Anna Abney of Evansville, Indiana and Albert Gregg of Broughton, Illinois.

Her father the Hon. Hugh Gregg was a member of Illinois State Legislature for several consecutive terms.

He signed the charter for the first street car operated in Chicago. This car was drawn by mule. He was a prosperous farmer, having owned large farms in both Hamilton and Williamson counties.

Mr. Jenkins remembers attending the political rallies held for Abraham Lincoln when he was running for the presidency, and the tragedy of his assassination. Two of her brothers, Frank and John fought in the Civil War and an uncle was killed in that war. The first negro she ever saw was an escaped slave. He ran across their yard, and was pursued by officers. She remembers distinctly that, one afternoon, on coming home from school she found a crowd of men at her home. She, with the rest of the children, was very frightened. Neighbor women had been called in to help her mother cook for them. They proved to be Union cavalrymen on the hunt for deserters. They had closed all roads leading to McLeansboro. A neighbor lady and her daughter, who had been called to McLeansboro on account of the illness of her mother, was held at the Gregg home until after midnight when the soldiers were ready to leave. They then preceded into town.

She saw her first train at Carbondale when she was about fifteen years old, She attended the school at Cherry Valley in Williamson County. Those were the days when they wore lindsey dresses and studied the blue back elementary spelling book, Wilson's history, etc.

After the death of her father, she lived with her half-brother, Albert Gregg, until her marriage in 1871 to John N. Hubbard. To this union were born five children: Florence, Dora, Jennie, Hugh and Mary. Of this number only two survive. They are Mrs. Charles Lavander and Mrs. T.M. Mott both of Rosiclare,

John Hubbard was the son of the late Jane and Presely Hubbard. Presely was an old steamboat pilot. He made many trips up and down the Ohio River, piloting the boat called the "Jeanette."

During the early married life of Mrs. Jenkins, then Mrs. Hubbard, she and her husband moved to Missouri in a covered wagon, on their way there they crossed the river at Chester. Mrs. Hubbard was dissatisfied and they remained in Missouri only a few months. On their return trip they crossed the Mississippi River at Cape Girardeau. It was the last trip that the ferry boat made because the river was soon blocked with ice. After their return Illinois they lived on a farm near Eldorado until the death her husband on September 19, 1884.

Two years after the death of her first husband, she married Thomas L. Jenkins, a Civil War veteran. To this union was born a son, Thomas Jenkins, now of Rosiclare.

Shortly after their marriage, they moved to Rosiclare, where they resided until his death on November 7, 1901.

Many old settlers will remember her brother James M. Gregg, successful lawyer, who practiced law in Elizabethtown and Harrisburg. He died in Colorado in 1885.

Another brother, William M. Gregg, was president of the First National Bank in Harrisburg for many years. He was forced to go California for his health, but died there about ten years ago.

Mrs. Jenkins has three living children, eleven grandchildren and five great grandchildren.

She has been a member of the Christian church since her arrival in Rosiclare, some years ago. Her eye sight has been failing for several years, and now she is practically blind. In spite of this handicap, she remains very cheerful, recognizing her friends by their familiar voices. She makes her home with her youngest daughter, Mrs. T.M. Mott of Rosiclare. HARDEN COUNTY INDEPENDENT, February 7, 1935.

MARGARET GREEN HOWSE

Margaret Green was born in Hardin County, the daughter of Mr. and Mrs. W.C. Green of Cave-in-Rock. She has one sister, Mrs. Raymond Rose and one brother, Dewey Green, superintendent of the Cave-in-Rock Community High School.

From her autobiography, we learn that while a small child she obtained from her grandmother many interesting bits of family history. The father of her great grandmother was a Methodist circuit rider, his home being a plantation in the state of Virginia.

The family crossed the river into Illinois, locating in Hardin County. A grand-daughter, Miss Mary Austin became the wife of William C. Green, who had come to Illinois from Tennessee with his mother and several brothers and sisters, his father having died several years previously.

In writing of her birthplace Mrs. Howse continues: "Like Abraham Lincoln I was born in Hardin County, of which Elizabethtown was the county seat, but Lincoln had been dead for almost thirty years when I was born. Yet I believe my first home was almost as crude as his. Mother has told me about the small log house with its old fashioned fireplace which had to be piled high with logs to warm the air that came through the cracks."

"The next year" she says. " We moved into a cozy home of our own."

The January following her third birthday was unusually cold and she took ill. Up to this time she had been a healthy and happy child. The day before she had learned to turn door knobs and go alone from one room to another, she writes: "I wearied at last of my play and was put to bed early. I did not rest properly and by morning has a high temperature. The physician who came for the first few days evidently failed to diagnose the case properly, because he advised my parents that there was no cause to worry, and left only medicine to make me rest.

Relying entirely upon his confidence, my parents gave me the medicine and I continued to lie in a stupor without any apparent change until the days grew into weeks. Finally another physician was summoned. He knew at once that I had inflammatory rheumatism, and that my optic nerve had been so affected that I would never see again. He threw away the sleeping potion and gave me instead medicine that woke me up, and I began to gain strength."

When she was well again, she had to begin life all over again but was soon able to recognize people by their voices, hands by touch and flowers by smell. One or twice a week she was taken in a buggy twenty miles to an oculist, but to no avail.

In a few years, a friend told the parents of the school at Jacksonville where blind children were taught. The mother wrote to the superintendent of the school, Frank H. Hall, inventor of Hall Braille Writer, requesting books. Mr. Hall replied that the books were not for sale but insisted that Margaret attend the school.

In September 1901, accompanied by her father, Margaret set out on the 230 mile journey to Jacksonville.

She soon adapted herself to her new surroundings and by the end of the first year was determined to remain in school until she completed her course. Nine years she studied and then she stood, as she says, "one beautiful June morning in a class of eight
receiving my diploma from high school." During this time her mother learned the braille system in order that she could correspond with Margaret.

After her graduation, Miss Green was at home for a few years, but upon learning that the school at Jacksonville was giving a business course. She returned to the school and in six months had completed the course which included typewriting and the use of the dictaphone.

Soon after completing the course, she

secured a position as dictaphone operator in the office of Illinois Glass Company of Alton, Illinois where she remained for several years.

In 1926 she left the office and traveled for two years, collecting money for the erection of a home for aged blind women.

At the end of that time, she became an employ in the state civil service and has since taught blind adults in 12 counties. She visits these people in their homes in order that they may not sit in darkness, but may be, with the things she teaches them, be busy and happy.

The active and useful life of Mrs. Howse has not been without its romance. While at Jacksonville, she became acquainted with another student who was almost entirely blind, Frank Howse of Mowequa. Later, they were married and live happily at Mowequa.

Mrs. Howse is an accomplished woman. She is qualified to give instruction in music. She knits, weaves leather, cuts and makes garments and writes. In addition to all of these, she is a model housekeeper.

As she wishes no commendation for her efforts, perhaps we should only say as she requests, that her "efforts have been blessed." HARDIN COUNTY INDEPENDENT, Mar. 2, 1939.

HARRIET BELT GREGORY

Mrs. Harriet Gregory was the daughter of the late Jonathan and Mary Belt. She was born on December 28, 1842, and departed this life July 28, 1935, her age being therefore ninety-one years and seven months. Until the time of her death she was the oldest living member of the Belt family who took an active part in the early history of Hardin county, her father being a well-known physician.

She was the second of eleven children, she having five brothers and five sisters, all of whom preceded her in death. Mrs. Gregory was a native of Hardin county, her birthplace having been a farm ten miles northeast of Cave-in-Rock. Two weeks after her birth her parents moved across the river and located on a farm which lay near Marion, Kentucky. There she spent her girlhood and there on March 14, 1860, she became the wife of John Gregory, the son of a General Baptist preacher.

Soon after their marriage the Civil War commenced, and as her husband enlisted in the Union Army, she was left during the time with her parents. Not long after the beginning of the war, the Belt family returned to Hardin County and when they came Mrs. Gregory accompanied them.

When the war was over and lieutenant Gregory was mustered out he joined his wife and they established their home on a farm near Cave-in-Rock which is still known as the Gregory farm.

To this union three sons and and three daughters were born. The first child, a son and the sixth a daughter, died in infancy. The first daughter, the late Mrs. Mitty Hill, passed away at Commerce, Texas in 1891. The second daughter is Mrs. I.A. Coltrin of Cave-in-Rock. The two sons are Dr. William G. Gregory of Cave-in-Rock and Dr. John Gregory of Eldorado, Illinois. There are also four grand children, eleven great grandchildren and several nieces and nephews left to mourn her loss.

When the children were about grown the family moved to Cave-in-Rock. After the marriage of the sons and daughters, the aged couple lived happily together until death separated them on May 24, 1914.

Until about six years ago Mrs. Gregory continued to be active and well, and looked after household duties herself, but after the destruction of their home by fire, her health and eye sight began to fail. She had several serious falls the last one which occurred July 23, being the immediate cause of her death.

Mrs. Gregory united with a Baptist church in Kentucky in her early youth, but later transferred her membership to the Methodist church in Cave-in-Rock. She attended the services of the church until her failing health made it impossible for her to do so. But even after she was unable to attend she retained a great interest in the church, and gave of her means to its support.

She was a woman of many virtues, a loyal citizen, a scrupulously neat housekeeper, a faithful friend, and above all, a loving and devoted mother. HARDIN COUNTY INDEPENDENT

DR. A.S. GRIFFITH

A.S. Griffith, oldest child of James M. and Catherine C. Griffith, was born in Spencer County, near Gentryville, Indiana, June 6, 1850, and died in Hardin County, August 29, 1926. He was the oldest of 7 children of which Mrs. Mary Fowler of Champaign, Illinois and Mrs. Tula Baldwin of Los Angeles, California survive.

The family left Indiana and moved to Carrsville, Kentucky in 1865 and lived there until 1885 or 86 and then moved to Elizabethtown, Hardin County, Ill. The eldest daughter, Edwinna, married Dr. J. D. Warford at Elizabethtown, but she lived only a few years after marriage. Tula married A. M. Baldwin, and Mary, the other sister, married Senator H. Robert Fowler who died a short time ago.

Dr. Griffith attended medical college in Louisville, Kentucky in 1873 and later the University of Tennessee, the Nashville Medical College in the sessions of 1880-81. He came to Elizabethtown some time prior to his parent's move there and began the practice of medicine. His practice covered a large part of the north part of the county and some areas of Gallatin County.

While living at Sparks Hill, he married Miss Sarah Esther Miller on november 3, 1888, and as a result of this union six children were born to them, namely: Maude, Claude, Leniel, Alice, Paul and Golda. Maud married Charles Suits and died in California some years ago. Claude a chiropractor, married in Henderson, Kentucky and he and his wife live in Florida. Leniel married George Edwards, Alice married Earl Austin, and Golda married Edgar Davis, and they all live near Cave-In-Rock, Illinois.

Dr. Griffith bore the distinction of being a kind and generous hearted man, honest in his dealings with his fellowman as related by his

neighbors, Asa Reynolds and A.E. Love. They also said that the doctor traveled in all types of weather to treat his patients, in many instances without pay. He felt he had a moral obligation to treat the sick.
J.A. Oxford, HARDIN COUNTY INDEPENDENT, Sept. 23, 1926

BARBARA GROSS

Barbara Gross who died in her home at Grossville, May 11, 1900 wrote the following biography of herself in 1887, and it was printed in the Cave-in-Rock *Register*.

"Editor of *Register*, according to promise, I send you a history of my past life. I was born January 19, 1823 in Switzerland,Canton Schaffhausen, on the Rhine.

I came to Louisville, Kentucky in 1854, but was not satisfied with the country. I had $17 and I hired out to get enough to take me back home. When I had $50, I took the chills and spent the last cent to get them stopped.

I then thought to try again, but the doctor advised me to get a position where I would not have to work so hard, so I obtained a position to take care of six children and made $30.

By that time I became acquainted with my husband, and we married October 30, 1856 at Louisville, Ky. in Avangarish Reformed Church. My husband had $50 and I had $30. This we spent next day for the things needed to go into housekeeping with.

We moved to Nelson Furnace, 39 miles from Louisville and lived there one year and then moved back to Louisville where we staid sixteen months, and from there moved to Illinois furnace which was run by Wolf & Co. We staid there one year and in March 1860, we bought forty acres of land from Robert Howard for which we paid $215 in gold.

My husband raised three crops on it and on Dec. 14, 1862, he went into the war and left me with four little children, the youngest being three months old and the oldest five and a half, that was all the help I had.

In the spring of 1863, I rented the land to Mr. Neel for half. I had 100 bushels of old corn when he commenced, and I boarded some of his children that summer and in the fall I had 120 bushels altogether. I thought that would not do, so the next year I hired hands by the day for which I had to pay 75 cents a day for common farm work, and in the fall when I counted up, the expense was more than the crop was worth.

In September 1864, news came that my husband died in Andersonville Prison, then all my hope was gone. But I afterwards received a pension of $6 a month for myself and $2 for each child.

I kept on farming, waiting for the boys to become large enough to take charge of the farm, but when the oldest boy was 10 years old, he died. The next was a girl and I had to wait for the two youngest.

I was compelled to hire hands for 10 years. You can guess what a time I had. I made nothing by farming, but at that time there was good range in the Coalings and I raised horses and cattle by this means and got along tolerably well and bought 120 acres more land, making 160 altogether.

I am now 64 years old, my children all grown, the daughter married and left me and my two sons, the youngest of whom is twenty five, are now running the farm.

I thing I have done my share of the work and would like to rest, but under present circumstances, I must still do the house work but am willing to give up for some one to take the lead as I have plenty to keep myself as long as I live without looking to some one else for support, and have long since learned that a good name is far better than riches".

HARDIN COUNTY INDEPENDENT, Jan. 2, 1930

HENRY W. GUSTIN

Henry W. Gustin is the son of ex-sheriff A.A. Gustin of Peters Creek and son-in-law of Dr. G.W. Hill of Cave-in-Rock. He attended the common schools of Elizabethtown, Peters Creek, and Cave-in-Rock.

At an early age he attended for six months Leclare College, and industrial school founded by N.O. Nelson, the St Louis millionaire.

He graduated from Valparaiso University, receiving a Bachelor of Science Degree. Such was his standing in his graduating class that he was permitted to enter as a regular student without examination, the Harvard University Law School.

In addition to his work at Valparaiso University, Mr. Gustin completed work at the University of Indiana, College of Liberal Arts, doing work in the departments of Political Economy, Literature, History, German, Philosophy and Ethnology. THE INDEPENDENT, Apr. 14, 1910.

ELIHU HALL

Elihu Hall, age 39, was born and reared in Hardin County. In the early part of his life, he determined to have an education. After qualifying himself as a teacher and having taught his first term, he entered Oakland City College of Oakland City, Indiana. This he continued to do as his means afforded until he graduated in the courses of Bachelor of Science and Bachelor of Divinity. He has taught several terms of school in Hardin and other counties.

Mr. Hall is a farmer, owning and controlling a small farm in the northern part of the county.

Within the last six years, he has devoted a very large portion of his time to the study of law and has covered practically the grounds required by the State Board of Examiners for admission to the Bar. Mr. Hall is eminently qualified to interpret the legal intendment of the various propositions of law that so commonly comes before one acting as a County Judge.
THE INDEPENDENT, July 7, 1910 (political ad)

L. T. HERCHMER

L. Theodore Herchmer was born in Feruna, California, in 1875. His mother, who was 84 years old when she died, had been born in a covered wagon, when her parents, the Lindleys, were on their way from Oregon to California. The Lindley family had 12 children. Mary

Fuller, L.T. Herchmer's aunt, is the only survivor of his mother's family.

Herchmer's father's people had gone to Oregon from Herchmer, New York.

When Mr. Herchmer was three years old, his parents left California for Fort Spokane, Washington, where his father had a saw mill for several years. Later they settled in Colville, Washington. Mr. Herchmer's father died when he was 16 years old and his mother married again later.

Mr. Herchmer got the wanderlust and went to British Columbia. There he enlisted and went to South Africa where he fought in the Boar War. He was wounded there, and a silver plate was put on the top of his head. Several years later this had to be removed.

He went to London after four years in South Africa and located there for a year before returning to this country. He has been drawing a pension from the British Government. Mr. Herchmer was married to Jean Tilly in Spokane, Washington in 1906. This union produced a son, Ted Herchmer.

After their marriage, Mr. and Mrs. L.T. Herchmer Sr. went to Northern Ontario where he prospected for gold in the Porcupine District. Mrs. Herchmer remembers walking into the district, a distance of 50 miles, with a pack on her back.

Later they went to South America where they located at Sierra De Pasco, Peru for 10 years.

After their return to the United States, Mr. Herchmer mined in Nevada and Canada again before being employed by the Aluminum Ore Company at Bauxite, Arkansas. They were located there for a few years and 17 years ago moved to Rosiclare where Mr. Herchmer has been general superintendent of the company's works.

Mr. Herchmer was a good miner. He was credited with having installed the underground system at Bauxite, Arkansas for the Aluminum Ore Company, before being sent to Rosiclare.

Of old pioneer stock, Mr. Herchmer had lived a life of adventure as a soldier of

fortune, a miner, a prospector, and a traveler. He has told many an anecdote of his adventures and travels. His only regret was that he had not stayed in Northern Ontario which has become one of the great gold fields in the world.
    L.T. Herchmer, general superintendent of the Fluorspar Division of Aluminum Ore Co. of America died in the Rosiclare Hospital,Saturday night after a short illness.
HARDIN COUNTY INDEPENDENT, July 23, 1941

JOHN HENNING JR.
    John, or "Mr. Kroger" as he is called by his friends was born on a little farm five miles west of Harrisburg on September 7, 1911, his father and mother being Mr. and Mrs. John Henning.
    John's grandparents on both sides were early pioneers in Indiana, coming to Saline county and making their home there henceforth. His father still operates the farm where John was born and where he grew to manhood.
    When John was only two years of age he had the great misfortune of losing his mother.
    After attending the county school near his home and graduating from the eight grade, he went to Harrisburg to obtain his high school education, graduating from the Harrisburg High School with the class of 1932.
    While attending high school, John spent most of his leisure time clerking for the Kroger stores in that city, so when he had completed his high school curriculum, the Kroger Company was only too glad to avail itself of the full time services of this energetic and well-liked young man. It was not long until he was promoted to the position of Relief Manager of the Kroger store in this district in 1934, soon after which he came to his present position in Rosiclare.
ROSICLARE REGISTER ? June 4, 1935

WILLIAM HARVEY HERRIN
    Mr. Herrin is the son of the late George and Elizabeth Curry Herrin. His father was a native of Tennessee, his mother a Kentuckian. He was born in Webster County, Ky., on the farm

owned and cultivated by his father. The principal crop raised on this farm, as on others in that section, was tobacco.

Mr. Herrin may well be termed a "self made man" as when he was a lad of only eleven years, the father died leaving the mother and four children. In addition to Mr. Herrin there was an older brother, James, also a well-known citizen of Hardin County, another younger brother, the late Benjamin Herrin, and a sister Rissie, who later became the wife of John Tyer, and who is now deceased.

The death of the father placed the burden of the family's support on the two older brothers and they responded nobly to the task. Necessarily the amount of schooling which they were able to obtain was somewhat limited. They acquired an education by contact with the world which enabled them to stand on an equality with those who may possibly have received a greater amount of academic education.

They remained on the farm in Kentucky until they were fifteen and seventeen years of age. A half sister Kathleen was the wife of the late Dr. George Warren Hill, who at that time was conducting a drug business in Cave-in-Rock. As Dr. Hill owned a farm near the village, he informed the boys that he would give them work, so they packed their few clothes into a suitcase and started for the Cave.

They crossed the river at Caseyville and set out on foot across rough country roads. Putting a stick through the handle of the suitcase, they took turns carrying it as they trudged on toward the village destined to play so important part in their future.

At this time which was about the year 1889, the men engaged in business here were Webb Pell, father of W.A. Pell, Dr. Green, Dr. H.A. Greenleaf and a man named Simpson and his son.

For several years the boys worked at various occupations in Cave-in-Rock. Later they sent for their mother and she made her home here until at the age of 88, she passed on to the Great Beyond.

At the age of twenty,"Harve" Herrin wed

Flora Hunter. Two sons were born to his union, O.T. Herrin who is a traffic policeman and lives at Elizabethtown, and W.C. Herrin, who with his uncle, James Herrin, conducts his business known as the farmers' Implement Company,

For a time after his marriage, Mr. Herrin clerked in J.L.Lowry's store, but he soon went into business for himself and purchased a small store and grist mill at Casade, Ky. He not only sold merchandise, but bought stock and grain. His trade grew, until he was able to erect the larger building, now know as Easly's Store.

After remaining in this business for six years, he married his present wife, Mrs. Elsie Brown in November, 1908. They lived on her farm in Hardin County for two years then purchased the Henry Dossett farm now owned by W.C. Green. For two years they lived at that place, then bought from Bob Hill his place in Cave-in-Rock, twenty two acres with a dwelling overlooking the Ohio River.

To their union were born five children: James Harvey,who died at the age of nine years; Wilford Horace,who was married and has his home near his parents;Clara Bernice,who is a student at the Business University at Bowling Green,KY. ;Walter Erio, who is also married and now at Peoria, Ill.; and Ethel Ruth, who is still at home.

Together Mr. and Mrs. Herrin have changed this place into a beautiful home equipped with modern improvements. Mrs. Herrin with her love for flowers and her knowledge of their cultivation, has added to the attractiveness of their already beautifully located home. She also has by her business ability and ingenuity made it a profitable as well as lovely place, as during the past few years it has become popular as a hotel.

About twenty years ago, Mr. Herrin bought an interest in the implement store, but after 10 years gave the interest to his son, Clarence.

In 1918, he and his brother James purchased which they afterwards sold Naylor and Company of New York, and which was then developed into the Benson Flour Fluor Spar Mining Company.

About ten years ago, He purchased a half merchandise with Charles Lavander. Later Mr. Herrin sold his interest to Mr. and Mrs. Blee.

At present Mr. Herrin owns a half interest in the grain elevator at Shawneetown and assists in conducting its business at that place. He also owns a third interest in the St. Thomas Coal Mines in Gallatin County.

He has filled various positions of trust in the county, having been elected County Commissioner in 1926. He was thus in office at the time of the construction of the new court house. In Cavein-Rock he has more than once served on the Board of Education. About eighten years ago, he united with the Methodist Church of Cave-in-Rock and ever since been one of its most loyal members. For about ten years he has been the efficent teacher of the men's Bible Class of the Methodist Sunday School. He is also chairman of the Board of Trustees of that church. His staunch and liberal support has contributed largely to the erection of the new church building. Mr. Herrin has won for himself a large measure of respect and esteem in the communities in which he lives and works.
Katheryne McDonald, HARDIN COUNTY INDEPENDENT, December 12, 1935

LEWIS HICKS
Lewis Hicks was born on Hicks Branch in Hardin County, Illinois, December 18, 1832. He married Margaret Patton on March 27, 1850. This union was blessed with 5 children, 4 boys and 1 girl of which all died in infancy except for Mrs. Sarah Ferrell who still survives. Mrs. Hicks died October 15, 1863.

Lewis married again on August 5,1868 to Mary Johnson. This union produced 10 children: Charles, Ben, Marion, (he died October 19,1891) Henry, Milo, Fannie, Loy, others ?.

Lewis was afflicted with blindness for the most of his life and confined to bed the last 5 years of his life. He died May 1, 1907. He leaves one brother, Milas Hicks of Hicks, ILL., and two sisters, Mrs. James Carlisle and Mrs. Richard Binum of Rosiclare.

Loyd C. Vinyard, HARDIN COUNTY INDEPENDENT, May 23,1907.

Dr. G. W. HILL

Dr. G. W. Hill was one of the best known physicians in Southern Illinois, passed away at his home at Cave-in-Rock, July 24 1924.

He was a man favorable and well known over quite a large part of the Mississippi Valley, was known as a man of a big heart, a brilliant mind. He was a thinker of rare attainments, things scientific, and he was of an inventive turn, having perfected many inventions which however is usual with inventors did not result in gain in dollars and cents still he lived to see some of them in use.

He was born near Cedar Point, one mile east of Cave-in-Rock, Illinois, April 8, 1850, on a store boat owned and operated by his father which plied between Louisville and New Orleans.

He was raised to manhood on a farm in Union County, Kentucky. After which he educated himself as a teacher, and while teaching several terms of school he studied medicine. Finishing his studies, he began the practice of medicine in 1878 in Cave-in-Rock.

Since then he has been engaged in many business enterprises, General Merchandise at both Rosiclare and Cave-in-Rock, also was in the floor mill business for a while at Cave-in-Rock. He, in the olden days, bought large quantities of potatoes and shipped them by flatboat from Cave-in-Rock to New Orleans.

He was instrumental in helping many prominent men to start up the ladder. Dr. W. G. Gregory of Cave-in-Rock studied under him before entering Rush Medical College. Robert Rogers of the Delker Buggy Company was one of his boys. C.C. English, for many years, treasurer of the Hargadine Dry Goods Company of St. Louis, started with him in his store at Cave-in-Rock. L.E. Thomas, a well known real estate dealer of Erick, Oklahoma trained under him. P.C. Frazier, a wholesale paint manufacture trained as a pharmacist by him. James and Harve Herrin, prominent business, men owe much of their success to his personal interest in them.

He was married to Rebecca Cathleen Thompson in Webster County Kentucky, January 31st, 1879. To this union was born 7 children, four boys dying in infancy, an only daughter, Bessie Cathleen Gustin, died February 8, 1912, leaving two sons, Wellington Hill Gustin and George Warren Gustin. G.W. Hill's sons are all that are living of his children, George L. Hill of Greenville, Ky., and John Warren Hill of Cave-in-Rock, Ill.

He established the manufacture of his private formula preparations, some of them 35 years ago, adding to his line until he owned a large line of preparations which are in use in many sections of the United states.

He retired from active business of all kinds in 1922, living on his stock farm one mile north of Cave-in-Rock, which place he had been stocking with pure bred cattle, until at the time of his death, he had established one of the best herds of Hereford Cattle in the country.
HARDIN COUNTY INDEPENDENT, August 7, 1924

EZEKIEL HOBBS
Ezekiel Hobbs was born June 4, 1844 near his present home, the son of Mr.and Mrs. Arch Hobbs.

He served during the entire period of the war and was wounded twice. He was struck on the head by a "minnie ball," and another time he was wounded in the knee. He contracted chronic diarrhea, as so many soldiers did during the war. He served under G.B.McClellan, fought in the Battle of Shiloh, and was with Sherman in his March to the Sea.

After his return to Hardin County, on August 15, 1877, he was married to Frances Ann Keeling, the ceremony being performed by John Waldon, justice of the peace. They had 10 children, five of whom are living: Andrew, who served during the World War; Julie Hardin, Fannie Vaughn, Sol and Elmer, who live in Hardin County.

Mr. Hobbs will be 92 next Thursday. He is unable to tell of his service during the war-- papers were accidently destroyed some years ago.

So, it is impossible to learn where he served and his experiences during the war. A picture of him was not available this week's paper. HARDIN COUNTY INDEPENDENT, May 28, 1936.

P. E. HOWARD

Mr. Howard was born in Rosiclare thirty six years ago and is the son of Mr. and Mrs. W. H. Howard, now living at Neely's Landing, Missouri, on of the oldest and best known families in Hardin County. His wife was the former Miss Beulah Denton, the daughter of State's Attorney and Mrs. James Denton of Elizabethtown. Mayor and Mrs. Howard have a daughter, Miss Jean who attends the Rosiclare grade school.

Mr. Howard is chief electrician at the Rosiclare Mine which position he has held for a number of years. He was elected to the Rosiclare City Council and served one term when he became mayor at the following election.

During his term in office, he coordinated the planning and construction of the Rosiclare water works project. This undertaking was probably the largest project that has ever been started in a city the size of Rosiclare. Much of the success of that project is due to Mayor Howard. He also arranged for the paving of Main Street in Rosiclare, which will soon be under way.

Mr. Howard received his schooling in the Rosiclare public schools and is a genial and well-liked individual. He is a 32nd degree Mason and a Shriner.
HARDIN COUNTY INDEPENDENT, April 1935

HOWARD BROTHERS

The Howards a family of captains, one of the oldest families of Rosiclare, held a reunion Easter Sunday in the Y.M.C.A. and celebrated the golden wedding anniversary of Loren and Lillie Howard and the 49th wedding anniversary of Philip and Annie Howard.

The heads of these families are sons and grandsons of Capt. Philip J. and Sarah J. Howard, who at one time owned the Rosiclare Mines and nearly all the business houses, residences, and vacant lots in the village. They also owned a farm lying east of town, owned and operated the stone quarries along the river front.

Captain Phillip Howard was a partner in mining with Hopkins Loudon, who was connected the McLeans of Cincinnati, Ohio and Washington.

Captain Phillip Howard was veteran of the Civil War. He volunteered as a private and rapidly advanced. He was commissioned a captain in Co., C. 29th Regiment, Illinois Volunteers. The captain and his wife are buried in the cemetery near the Christian Church.

Captain Loren is the oldest of the five sons, who are also called captain. Captain Loren for more than 25 years was interested with his father in the stone quarry business.

By directing the movement of boats and barges he earned the title as captain. With his wife, Capt. Loren lives in El Paso, Texas. They are in Rosiclare for their first visit in 15 years. In Texas the captain manufactures barber supplies for men and beauty supplies for women.

Capt. Philip J. is the second son and twice earned his title. He was an officer at the Southern Illinois prison at Menard where he was always saluted as captain. For many years he superintended one or more of the Barrott quarries on the, Cumberland, Mississippi and Ohio rivers. In this work he was addressed as captain. He and his wife, Anna, live near Smitherland, Kentucky.

Captain John R. was the third son. He died in 1925. His widow, Lydia, lives in Rosiclare.

Captain Harry is the fourth son. He owned and operated stone quarries near Rosiclare on the Ohio River but for the past 15 years has superintended large quarries on he Mississippi River. As is customary for men in his position, he is addressed as Captain by his associates and employees. With his wife he lives at Neely's Landing, Missouri.

Captain Walter, the fifth and youngest son, has earned the title for his work in the mining and quarry business. For many years he was foreman for the Hillside Mines. Later he became engaged in quarrying stone Missouri and Kentucky. With his wife, Pearl, he now lives in Smitherland, Kentucky.

Those from out of town who attended the party included Mr. and Mrs. Wesley Howard, Neely's Landing, Missouri; Mr. and Mrs. Marvin Howard, Cape Giradeau; and Mr. and Mrs. Glen Porter of Harrisburg.

April 21, 1938 HARDIN COUNTY INDEPENDENT

OBEDIAH HUBBARD.

Obediah B. Hubbard was born in Pope County in 1823. According to family members, he was the son of Richard Hubbard.

Obediah married Perlina Ferrell on 15 June 1846, the daughter of Clement Ferrell and Sarah Edwards. This union produced: John Franklin Hubbard, born 28 January 1846, died 10 July 1935; Charles Hubbard, born 1849,; Sarah Jane Hubbard, born 17 April 1852, died 31 December 1939; Hillis Albert Hubbard,; Missouri Hubbard, William Carroll Hubbard; and Chester Hubbard, born 1865.

On 12 August 1862, Obediah answered the call to arms during the Civil War. He served in the 131st and the 29th Illinois regiments, the latter commanded by Col. Charles M. Ferrell. Colonel Ferrell was probably related to Perlina Ferrell, possibly a cousin. Obediah served until 6 November 1865. The 131st and the 129th engaged the enemy in several actions.

As was the case of many Civil War soldiers, Obediah suffered from exposure which developed into chronic illiness, and he was discharged. In 1867, he made application for a pension, stating: " ... He is broken down in health and constitution and is greatly disqualified for performing manual labor."

Obediah died on 16 April 1876, leaving Perlina to rear a large family. She applied for a widow's pension in 1890 and received 12 dollars a month.

According to family members Perlina was red headed and talked with a Irish brogue. She could neither read nor write. Perlina Ferrell Hubbard died on 21 February 1913.

MARRIAGES

John Franklin Hubbard married Martha A. Vinyard in 1863, born 5 December 1849, daughter of John and Lizzie Shell Vinyard and had issue: James A. Hubbard, born 27 February 1870; Charles Franklin Hubbard, born 8 August 1874?; Thomas Edward Hubbard, born 1877; Sara Jane Hubbard, born 1 August 1876, died 10 April 1889; Henry Hubbard, born September 1879; Etta Hubbard, born 1 March 1881; Ada Hubbard, born 16 August 1885, died 27 Jan 1887; Alpha Hubbard, born 26 January 1887; Minnie Hubbard, born 19 Feb 1889; Leonard Ivy Hubbard, born 23 January 1891; male child, born 23 Jan 1891, died 23 Jan 1891; William Hubbard, born 11 May 1893; T. Fred Hubbard, born 11 May 1893.

Charles H. Hubbard married Mrs. Nancy J. Barton, 15 July in Gallatin County, Illinois and had issue: Annie Hubbard, born October 1879; Blanche Hubbard, born June 1882; Edna Hubbard, born April 1884; Bertha Hubbard, born July 1888; Charles Hubbard was living in Gallatin County Illinois in 1900. James Matthew McMurphy and Sarah Jane Hubbard married in 1872 (?)) and had issue: Emma McMurphy, born 7 February 1873, died 21 March 1940, Bozeman, Mont.; Samuel McMurphy, born 14 Sep 1874, died 9 October 1874, Hardin Co. ILL.; Etta McMurphy, born 8 August 1875, died Butte, Mont.; Maggie Mcmurphy; born 10 October 1877, died 1947; Silas McMurphy, b. 20 September 1879, died 17 February 1928 in Califorina; Noah McMurphy, born 13 April 1882, died April 1917; Tom McMurphy, born 19 April 1884, died 30 June 1952, West Frankfort. ILL.; Henry McMurphy, born 28 January 1886, died 19 October 1944; Katherine McMurphy, born 25 June 1888, died 6 October 1966; Chloe McMurphy, born 5 September 1893, died 26 August 1976; Jennie Blanche, born 25 December 1905.

Note: Sarah Jane bore her first child in 1873 and the last one in 1905, 32 years of child bearing. This is very unusual. Some of the birth dates could be in error.

Hillis Albert Hubbard married Elizabeth Ginger and had issue: Alice Hubbard, born 1881; Lacey Hubbard, born 1885; Cora Hubbard, b. 24

October 1886; Maude Hubbard, born 17 Apr 1888.
William Carroll Hubbard married Nancy Jane Ginger and had isue: Clara L. Hubbard, born October 1884; Effie Hubbard, born 7 December 1886; male, born 31 March 1891, died 31 March 1891; James Hillis Hubbard, born 12 June 1895; Bertie Hubbard, born 21 September 1895, Missouri Hubbard had two children out of wedlock. As one descendant observed " Missouri was not a bad girl, just poor" She worked as hired girl for several families. Some of men she worked for took advantage of her. Missouri's children are as follows: Dora --, married John Jennings; George--, born 31 July 1878, m. Arabell Palfreeman, b. 4 August 1885.

Chester Hubbard married Ann Cunningham, 1 December 1890. She was the daughter of Willis Cunningham and Mary S. Corton?. Children of the first marriage: Jesse Hubbard Shewmaker, Lora Hubbard Hicks, Otto Hubbard, Chester married a second time to Amanda Goins. One child was born to this union: Bessie Hubbard.

DOCUMENTATION

1. Minnie Hubbard, daughter of John Hubbard and Martha Vinyard wrote Verbie Hubbard Isley, a researcher on the Hubbard line, that Richard Hubbard was the father of Obediah Hubbard, There is a Richard Hubbard listed in the 1840 census for Hardin Co.,ILL.
2. Obediah Hubbard Military Record, file # WC 278-844.
3. Obediah Hubbard Family, 1850 census for Hardin Co., ILL.
4. Obediah Hubbard Family, 1860 census for hardin Co., ILL.
5. Martha A. Hubbard Obituary, *Hardin County Independent*, Sept 18 and 25 1930. Abstracts as follows: Martha A. Vinyard, daughter of John and Eliza Vinyard, b. Hardin Co., ILL., 5 Dec 1849, d.12 Sep 1930; m. John F. Hubbard, 1863;issue: Sallie(d), James, Charles, Henry, Edward, Fred, Etta, Minnie Boaten, Ivy Hubbard; Bro, W.H. Vinyard; sis, Josie Fowler and Mrs. Alice Gustin.
6. Charles H. Hubbard Family, 1900 Census ? Gallatin County, ILL.

7. Sara Jane Hubbard McMurphy Obituary, Hardin County, Il., 4 Jan 1940. Abstracts as follows: Sarah Jane Hubbard, age 88, d. 31 Dec 1939, dau of Obediah Hubbard, widow of J. Matt McMurphy; issue; Henry, Tom, Emma Fiddler, Etta Pankey, Maggie Hayes, kate Tucker, Clo Ferrell, Blanche Jones; bros, William and Hillis Hubbard.
8. Noah McMurphy Obituary, Hardin County Independent, 12 Apr 1917. Abstract as follows: Remains of Noah McMurphy, killed in explosion at West Frankfort was brought here for burial. He was the son of Matt Mcmurphy. He leaves a wife and two children.
9. Birth and death dates were supplied by Bernard Ferrell (deceased) and Verbie Hubbard Isley. Mrs. Isley apparently contacted members of her family to obtain the information on the Hubbards. From context of Bernard Ferrell's letters to me (Ed Ferrell), it appears that he based his information on tombstone inscriptions census and Hubbard family members. The information that I have been able to check has been accurate. Some of the dates have varied from those found in obituaries.

JOHN SAMUEL HUFSEY

John Samuel Hufsey, who was born in and spent his entire life in the vicinity of Cave-in-Rock. Mr. Hufsey was born on the 11th of October, 1854 and hence within a few months will pass his eighty first milestone. He comes from one of the sturdy pioneer families who settled in this part of Illinois during the early period of her history. His great grandfather was a German sailor who left the sea with the adventurous spirit which characterized our forefathers, made his way across the wilds of a new country and sought a home in the hills of what is known now as Hardin County. Among the prize possessions of some of the members of the Hufsey family are relies from the ship on which he sailed.

Here his children were born and here they made their homes and raised their families. One of the sons was Samuel who was born on the farm which is now the home of Mr. and Mrs. John Tyer.

It was the family home for a time and on it the old grandfather lies buried.

Samuel Hufsey became the husband of miss Matilda Sawyer, who was a native of Georgia, but who was brought by her parents to Illinois when a small child. To their union were born ten children, the fourth one being John Samuel Hufsey, the subject of this narrative. Of these ten children, two brothers and one sister died in infancy and another sister at the age of four. One brother, Charlie, died in his early manhood and another one, George, passed away about eight years ago. There are two brothers and a sister still living. They are W.F. Hufsey, who lives about four miles north of Cave-in-Rock, Dennis Hufsey, who is seventy-six years of age and who lives on what is known as the Sam Winn farm, and Mrs. Mary ledbetter who lives near Cave-in-Rock with her son, Charles. All of the family have spent their years in the county to which their grand father came so many years ago.

When John Hufsey was a little lad of four, his parents moved from the farm on which he was born to Honey Creek, below the Charlie Ledbetter place and five miles northeast of Cave-in-Rock. After a short time, they moved again to a new home at which place, they built on the hill which is now Mr. Ledbetter's home and where they remained for the greater part of their married life. He attended the old Round Top school now known as the Martin school and recalls the old Webster Blue Backed Spelling book which was the chief text book of those days. He also well remembers the men who were the teachers of the school. Perhaps some of these names are familiar to some of older readers of this sketch. His first instructor was John T. Simmons. Another one was Wm. Jackson, father of Mrs. Dora McDowell, of Cave-in-Rock, John Jenkins who was mentioned as a brother to the late Wm. Jenkins in the history recently published was also included in this list, and still another was Henry Winders.

He also remembers that his father worked in the old paper mill at Seller's landing. One morning on his way to work, the father found a wolf among the sheep, and after killing it came back to tell his boys about it. In those days deer and wild turkey were plentiful and the family owned a pet deer.

Mr. Hufsey helped his father clear the land, remaining with him until he was past thirty years of age. He recalls the old time log rolling which the neighbors gathered at those days. He and his father raised potatoes which they shipped on the boats which plied the river, furnishing the chief means of transportation.

On February 4, 1885, he married miss Anna Okerson at the home of her parents who were the late Albert and Mary Winn Okerson. He first built a little home on his father's farm, the present Charley Ledbetter place, but remained there but a few months. They moved to the George Boyd place where they lived for about a year. The next two years they spent on the farm where Mr. and Mrs. Dewey Green now live. They then went to the farm which he still owns and where he lives, about four miles from Cave-in Rock. His son, John, now manages the farm, as for the past eighteen years, Mr. Hufsey has been unable to do such active work.

He and his good wife lived together for forty-eight years, saddened by her failure in health soon after their marriage. For thirty-four years she was almost an invalid and for the past fifteen years of her life she was confined to bed. Five children were born to them, two of whom died in infancy. Those who are still living are Mrs. Mamie Crow, whose home is about four miles north of Cave-in-Rock. Mrs. Eunice Gibbs, who is near the Lambert school and John, who lives on the old home place. There are also eleven grandchildren.

Mr. Hufsey has been an Industrious and thrifty farmer and during his active years took a deep interest in everything pertaining to the success of his farm. While he is now unable to do the hard work, he still takes an interest in it, the care of his chickens being his special task. For one of his age, he is fairly active his hearing is good and he can see to read without glasses.

He is of a quiet and home loving nature but greatly enjoys the companionship of his friends and neighbors. Their visits are a source of much pleasure to him and occasionally he is able to take short trips to see them. The present generation owes much to families such as this to which Mr. Hufsey belongs and we are sure all join in a wish that he may live to enjoy many more years in the country to which his forefathers came so long ago.
(June 27, 1935 HCI)

SEBASTIAN CHEEZIK HUMM

Sebastian Cheezik better known as Bass Humm, who is 90 years old feels sorry for the boys who say they are having a hard time now. Looking out over the hills from his farm home near Stone Church, Bass Humm says that he remembered those hills and valleys being cleared of timber with axes and the ground plowed with old wooden plows drawn by oxen.

Humm said there was real timber in Hardin county when he was a boy, explaining that he saw yellow poplar trees 5 feet through atthe stump, and 100 feet high to the first branch. Trees of that size were sold to saw mills for a $1.00 a tree.

Humm also said that oaks were of tremendous size. He said that he can remember Henry Bright splitting 500 rails out of one oak tree, each rail 10 feet long. The oak Humm said grew on the bank of Mud Creek.

Another incident which was particularly stamped on his memory was the making of two gunwales of a river boat 110 foot long and 28 inches wide at the smallest end, out of one poplar tree. They were made by Patrick Bliss for Louis Lavander. The gunwales were hewn and shaped with a broad axe.

Sebastian Cheezek came to Rosiclare with his mother, when he was about four years old, after his father had died at Saline Mine.

His father's name was Joseph Cheezek and he and Sabastains's mother were born in Bohemia.

Bass said he was born in New York City, and when he about three years of age, his father, a cabinet maker, came to the Saline Mines from New York to follow his trade. An Eastern corporation at that time was developing the country around Saline Mine.

Bass said that his father died about a year after they arrived at Saline Mine, and he and his mother moved to Rosiclare. His mother later married John B. Humm. Sebastian Cheezek and his brother took the step father's name of Humm.

Bass said he worked on his step father's farm until a young man. Then he and his brother August went to Terra Haute, Indiana to learn the shoemakers trade. He said he worked three years as an apprentice, just for his board, without pay, at Terra Haute and St. Mary's. He practiced his trade in Rosiclare, ILL., Leadville, Col., in Missouri, Shelterville, ILL., and elsewhere. Thirty six years ago he bought the farm where he now resides near Rosiclare.

When asked about the price of shoes, Humm said a good pair of sewn shoes sold for $6.00 a pair, work shoes from $1.50 up, and dress shoes $4.50 a pair. A light weight pair of calf skin boots brought him $8.00 a pair.

He explained that he often came from Rosiclare to Elizabethtown, taking measurements for the McFarlans, Twitchells and Ferrells for shoes, then returned to deliver them. Asked if he went to Cave-in-Rock, he said no, that people were afraid to go there years ago. Bass Humm said that he can well remember when most of the Rosiclare property was sold by sheriff John T. Ledbetter for taxes because mines were closed on account of hard times. After this event, Bass Humm, Capt. Twitchell, and Capt. McFarland went to Leadville, Colorado where Humm followed his trade for several years before returning to Hardin County.

Reminiscing, Humm said that he could remember when there was not a single team of horses or mules in the county, everyone then used oxen. We even went to church in a wagon drawn by oxen. He said it was but a few years ago when Harrisburg was a day's drive by team from Hardin County and a day's drive back. He said most of the traffic until a few years ago was by river.

Humm said that he used to ship potatoes from Hardin County to St. Louis by river boat, sometimes making money and sometimes not. He remembers one profitable transaction he bought potatoes at 10 cents a bushel and sold them in St. Louis at 60 cents a bushel, making him a nice profit after paying the freight.

Humm and Lewis Lavander, the first elected sheriff of Hardin County, were neighbors. He said that Lavander used to run a saw mill, and he can remember Lavander sending down men to cut trees on his father-in-law's farm. One tree was so big that it upset the wagon when they loaded it. He said one log was five feet through and twelve feet long and was so heavy that it could not be moved. Finally they burned it.

He said if they had these trees now, they would be worth more than all of Hardin County, but he added, people had to clear the land of trees to make a living.

Speaking of Sheriff Lavander, Humm said that everyone in Elizabethtown was dumbfounded when Lavander brought in Jonas Belt of Cave-in-Rock who had been indicted for killing a man. Jonas Belt was said to be an especially dangerous man and everyone had warned Lavander to take several men with him, well armed, to make Belt's arrest.

But Lavander set out for the Cave on a big gray horse alone and with out a gun. When he arrived at Jonas's house, he saw Jonas sitting on the porch with a shotgun across his knees. Jonas invited him in and they talked awhile and then Lavander told Belt that he would have to take him back to Elizabethtown under arrest. Belt said it was too late to go to Elizabethtown. They might as well have supper there and spend the night. Sheriff Lavander accepted the invitation had supper and slept. The next morning they set out for the county seat. When they arrived in town riding side by side people

were speechless with surprise. Jonas was freed of the charge.
HARDIN COUNTY INDEPENDENT, June 29, 1933.

HENRY W. HURST

Henry W. Hurst is the son of W.C. Hurst of Kansas City Kansas, and graduated from Missouri State School of Mining at Rolla, as a mining engineer in 1920. Mr. Hurst became superintendent of the Hill Side Fluorspar Mines in Rosiclare.

Several years ago Mr. Hurst married Miss Hazel C. McDowell of Durango, Colorado, and they have one small daughter, Miss Leatha.

Mr. Hurst is a thirty-second degree Mason and Shriner and is a member of the Rosiclare Community High School Band, and Past Worthy Patron of the Eastern Star.
HARDIN COUNTY INDEPENDENT, August 22, 1935

LURINDA CATHERINE JACKSON

Lurinda Catherine Barnard was the daughter of Tyra and Elizabeth Jackson and was born August 14, 1850 on a farm now known as the Franklin Jackson farm. Her father came to this place from Tennessee in an early day. Her mother moved here from the state of Ohio in 1823.

The seventh child of this family and the only one now living. She had four brothers, William, John, Andy and Stephen and sisters, Sarah and Liza.

"Aunt Kate" as she is called by everyone, can recall many incidents that happened during the Civil War. She said many escaped slaves passed by her home on their way to freedom, also several officers in search of these men.

Her mother used to sit by the open fire and tell her children of their great-great grandfather, who was President Andrew Jackson, and of his noble deeds.

She remembers well how they raised and stored vegetables and fruits for the winter. Also how they spun and wore dress materials, knitted socks for her brothers and countless other things that are not done these days. Four of her father's brothers went to California in the gold rush in 1849, but none of them returned nor were ever heard from again.

Kate was married to the late John Allan Barnard, a Civil War veteran in 1867. They began their long and blissful married life on a farm now known as the "Bill Conn" farm. Eleven children were born to this union, three dying in infancy. The rest lived to be men and women. Dock Barnard died in 1905 at the age of 26. Mrs. Mallie Holbrook, a daughter, died in Castle Gate, Utah in 1929. Six are still living, Allan of Sparks Hill, John of Wasson, Spence of Elizabethtown, Walter of Cave-in-Rock, Mrs. Alda Barnard of Sparks Hill, and Mrs. Mollie Holbrook of Elizabethtown.

In 1884, she and her family moved to Green Wood county, Kansas, lived there two years and came back to Hardin county where they lived until 1896 when they again left Illinois, moving to Corning, Arkansas. Both of these trips were made in covered wagons and it took a number of days to make the journey. Finally in 1888, they decided to return to Illinois.

Uncle John was the great grandson of Kit Hobbs, who was a great Indian fighter. He killed a notorious Indian chief, who had kidnapped a white woman, and the government presented him with a fine rifle.

For the last eight years of his eight-five, Uncle John was totally blind. Uncle John and Aunt Kate were members of the General Baptist church of Rock Creek.

She lived with her oldest daughter, Mrs. Mollie Holbrook and her oldest grandchild, Miss Ezra Holbrook of Elizabethtown since her husband died in 1939.

She has four children past sixty years of age and her youngest is forty-nine. Aunt Kate has a very sweet disposition and loves company. She has eighteen grandchildren and twelve great grandchildren. All of them visit her quite often which makes her very happy. Her eye sight is very good for an eighty-five year old person.

This article was written by her great granddaughter, Ersa Holbrook.
HARDIN COUNTY INDEPENDENT, Feb 28, 1935

HARDIN COUNTY INDEPENDENT, Feb 28, 1935

I.N. OZEE

Mr. I.N. Ozee, 81 years old, came to Elizabethtown last Saturday morning and spent several hours talking about events of 50 and 60 years ago.

He came into this country with his father's family in 1855, and spent the first year on a farm now owned and occupied by J. A. Oxford Jr., then owned by the writer's father. Ozee's father then bought land less than a mile northeast of Sparks Hill, where they built and moved the next year, and where the father lived until he died some 15 or 20 years afterward.

Mr. Ozee married Miss Fannie Wall who bore him three children, two girls and a boy, Edward, who died some two years ago in Missouri.

Mr. Ozee now lives with his son-in-law, James Mott, near El Dorado, Illinois. He has nieces in Elizabethtown, Mrs. Charles H. Jackson and Mrs. Charley Frailey.

HARDIN COUNTY INDEPENDENT, Aug. 4, 1921

MARY ANN JACKSON JOHNSON

Mary Ann Jackson was born on August 15, 1856, on a farm near Smithland, Kentucky. She was the daughter of the late---- and Lucy Jackson. He mother before her marriage was Lucy Ann Glace. As Mrs. Johnson's family records were accidently destroyed some years ago, she has depended chiefly upon memory for the following facts of her history. According to her memory, her parents were natives of Kentucky, their home being in the vicinity of Smithland.

Her childhood was spent on their farm. She recalls her school days which were spent in a little log school house in which the benches were boards laid over cross pieces extending from the walls. She was taught at home by her father until she was large enough to walk the four miles which lay between their farm and the school.

She also remembers the fields of cotton and tobacco as well as the toil involved in the picking of cotton and the "worming" of the tobacco. A gathering of the neighbors to pick cotton was a social event in those days.

The first real shaw she ever owned made a vivid impression on her mind as she raised sweet potatoes and sold them to obtain the money which to buy it. It was an "Arab shaw with red stripes."

Mrs Johnson never saw coal during her childhood. Her father cut wood for fuel. During the early years "grease lights" were used, and she has dipped many a candle. Their beds were homemade being made of ropes woven on poles.

She never cooked on a stove until after her marriage, but cooked over a fire place or out of doors. The bread was baked in iron pots suspended over the fire.

Wild deer and turkeys were plentiful. The deer came to a place near their home to lick salt.

Though she was a small child at the time, Mrs. Johnson recalls the Civil War. She remembers the soldiers who came to her father's house to obtain food, and how the stock had to be hidden in order to keep them from taking it. Later when she was a young woman of eighteen years, she was wooed by a Union soldier who had survived the war. On November 11, 1874, she was married at the home of her father to Aaron Johnson. Mr. Johnson was a farmer and also a General Baptist preacher. The young couple commenced to keep house on a farm at Green's Ferry, Ky. Later they moved to a farm at Carrsville. Kentucky, and there their children were born.

The father and mother worked hard. Mrs. Johnson not only performed duties of the house wife of today, but as her husband raised flocks of sheep, it became her task to card the wool, spin it, weave it into cloth, and then make linsey-woolsey dresses and jeans as well as knit the socks and stockings which the family needed.

In 1900, one son Aaron crossed the river, and came to the neighborhood of Cave-in-Rock. Mr. Johnson was planning to hold a meeting at Lambtown, so the family moved over to Illinois. Mrs. Johnson well remembers the moving. It took five wagons to bring the household goods. They crossed on a big ferry, It was about midnight when the family reached Lambtown, but they were hungry. The stove was set up and they had supper.

For about a year they stayed at Lambtown. Then they went to Tower Rock where they stayed for two and one half years. In 1904, they came to Cave-in-Rock. Mr. Johnson's health began to fail and the wife shouldered the family burdens.

She cheerfully accepted these burdens and, not only cared for her invalid husband, but worked hard to provide a living for the family. On July 20, 1916, the Rev. Johnson passed away, having been blind for the last three years of his life.

After his death, the widow struggled along doing the best she could to provide a home for her children. However the children soon married and established homes of their own, and Mrs. Johnson was left alone.

Mrs. Johnson was from early in life a member of the General Baptist church. When she came to Cave-in-Rock, she transferred her membership to the Methodist church of that place.She has been a faithful member, attending services, and giving regularly of her means towards its support.

She had one brother and one sister, both of whom died in Missouri, where her father's family moved soon after her marriage.There were also several half brothers and half sisters still living. The brothers are Ceph Jackson whose home is thought to be in Nebraska and Charlie Jackson who lives in Missouri. Another half brother, Newt Jackson passed away at Cairo, Illinois about two months ago.

Mrs Johnson is the mother of thirteen children, six of whom died in early youth. Of these four were sons: Charlie who died at the age of 21, Ewing at the age of 19, George at the age of 12 and one who died in infancy. There were also two daughters, Frances who died at 24, and Laura who lived only 2 years. The living are: Mrs. Ella Blair, Harrisburg; Mrs.2 Eva Prue, Ill.; Mrs. Ida Obermark, West Frankfort;

Mrs. Pearl Eldorado, and Mrs. Joe Frailey, Aaron and Frank Johnson in Cave-In-Rock. There are also nineteen grandchildren and one great-grandchild.
HARDIN COUNTY INDEPENDENT October 8, 1938

JAMES W. KARBER

I hereby make a formal announcement for my candidacy for the office of State Senator from the Forty-Eight Senatorial District, subject to the Democratic Primary on April 9th.

I was born in Elizabethtown and both of my parents were born and reared in Hardin County. My father, Fred Karber, who for the past twenty one years has been the principal of the Ridgeway Community High School, was at the time of my birth county clerk of this County.

I am a graduate of the College of Liberal Arts and Sciences and also the College of Law at University of Illinois. In 1936, I was Nominated and elected to the office of State's Attorney, which office I now hold.

When running for the office of state's attorney, I had two opponents, the people of Gallatin honored me by giving me more votes than both of my opponents together.

My training in governmental problems while at the university together with experience in the State's Attorney's office and in my private practice amply qualify me for the position which I know aspire.

By profession I am a lawyer; However, I own and oversee the management of a good farm to which I give considerable time & attention. I am therefore interested in farming and stock raising.
HARDIN COUNTY INDEPENDENT, Mar 14,1940.

WILLIAM T. LAMAR

William T. Lamar was born June 22, 1851, died December 21, 1923. Mr. Lamar was born and raised on a farm near what is now known as Union School House. His entire life was spent in the Elizabethtown-Rosiclare area.

He was married to Elizabeth Jackson, September 24, 1872. To this union three children were born: Louis, Lillie and Charles. Lillie, the wife of James Robinett, died April 9, 1909. Elizabeth died in 1881.

On May 28, 1884, William Lamar married Laura E. Staley of Chester, Illinois. This union produced four children; Staley, Marcella (died), Otis and Mary.

Mr. Lamar was well known to INDEPENDENT readers, having served as sheriff, assessor, treasurer, county commissioner, and chairman of the county board. HARDIN COUNTY INDEPENDENT, May 22, 1924.

REV. DOCTOR ALLEN LEDBETTER

In his house in Cereal Springs, July 26th, 1926, Reverend Doctor Allen died, the son of Rev. Doctor Ledbetter, pioneer minister. John T. Ledbetter once sheriff, and county official and Mrs. J. A. Oxford who died about 15 years ago and Mary Thornton, now living in Elizabethtown were members of this respected family.

D.A. Ledbetter was born in this county January 12, 1851 and at the time of his death was a few months over 75 years old. He married young. His first wife was Mary, the daughter of Rev. Elihu Oxford and a sister to the writer's mother. She lived but a short time. He next married a lady by the name of Morris who also died in a year or two, but her son Bunk Ledbetter lived to manhood. He then married Sarah J. Gullet, one of the daughters from the respected family of the late Uncle Pomp Gullett of this county. This union survived and became the parentage of a family of strong healthy children.

There names are Della, Ollie, Robert, Adrain, Emma, Ray, and James W. Ledbetter. All of these, I believe, live except for Della.

Patriotism is a well marked trait of the Ledbetter family, and with Rev. D.A. Ledbetter it was very pronounced. In many of his sermons and exhortations he showed warmth and feeling when he touched on the love of his country. When the cry, "Remember the Main" was sounded over the country in 1898, Allen as his friends called him, answered the call, enlisting under

Capt. Richard F. Taylor. He served in this company until the close of the war.

He came back home saying that it was not outside foes that we need to fear, but sin, corruption, and rebellion against God. These threatening evils, he made war on the remainder of his life.

About five years ago, he sold his property in Elizabethtown and moved to Cereal Springs in order that he and Mrs. Ledbetter might be nearer the children and also that he might have a better outlet to his church work. Rev. D. A. Ledbetter lived the remainder of his life in Cereal Springs.

HARDIN COUNTY INDEPENDENT, Aug. 5, 1926.

GEORGE W. LEDBETTER

George W. Ledbetter was the son of James Anderson and Polly Ledbetter. He was born in Hardin County, December 7, 1858. His father is said to have built half of the houses in Elizabethtown. It is said that he would build a house, live in it "swap" it and build another.

The son, George W. Ledbetter, attended West Point Military Academy in the '80's. He returned to Elizabethtown, and with his brothers Henry and James, succeeded his father in managing the flour mill here. He and his brothers also ran the mill at Cave-in-Rock. Later they incorporated as the Ledbetter Milling Co.

It is said that they milled all the wheat in Hardin County back when the county was a one big wheat field. Old residents remember that Hardin County as first one big potato patch and then a wheat field, before the ground was worked out.

At one time, in addition to owning mills in Hardin Co. the brothers owned one in Oklahoma. Twenty years ago, the mill at Cave-in-Rock was sold. Mr. Ledbetter ran the one in Elizabethtown until his retirement a few years ago.

He has been identified with the business interests of Hardin County for the past 50 years. he was a stockholder when the bank was organized in Elizabethtown in 1903, and he has been connected with it since then. He was its president at the time of his death.

He was director of the bank at Cave-in-Rock and formerly been a stock holder in the bank at Rosiclare.

Mr. Ledbetter was a member of the Masonic and Odd Fellows lodges. He has been a member of The Odd Fellows since its organization in Elizabethtown 54 years ago.

Henry, who had been in the milling business with George and James, died several years ago, as did his brother John Quincy Adams Ledbetter, who was a prominent attorney.

George W. Ledbetter, aged 78, life long resident of Hardin County died in the Rosiclare Monday.

Mr. Ledbetter is survived by his widow, Rachel; his son, Mora at Raton, New Mexico; his sons, Charles and Harry, Elizabethtown; his daughters, Mrs. Ora Ramshaw of Los Angles, Mrs. W.B. Pell, Rosiclare; his brother, James, Elizabethtown.
HARDIN COUNTY INDEPENDENT, August 12, 1937

J. Q. A. LEDBETTER

Judge Ledbetter was reared in Hardin County, Illinois. He died in Mcleansboro, Illinois, March 16, 1920.

He has been a prominent figure in law, politics and church work for many years. His first political office was that of County Judge to which office he was elected to in 1873. He served four years in that capacity and then went into private practice. In 1880 Judge Ledbetter was elected States Attorney and served eight years. He was elected to the same office in 1896 and served until 1900. In 1908 he ran for congress from the twenty-fourth congressional district but was defeated.

J.Q.A. Ledbetter was a member of several fraternal orders. He leaves a wife, two sons, and daughter, Grace, a graduate nurse.
HARDIN COUNTY INDEPENDENT, March 11, 1920.

WILLIAM R. LEDBETTER

William R. Ledbetter, 3rd son and 7th child of the late John T. Ledbetter by his first wife, died at Marion, Illinois, November 16, 1909. He was born in this county (Hardin) February 15, 1880.

He moved to Holcomb, Missouri some 10 or 12 years age, taught school, was cashier in a bank, and later engaged in the insurance business.

Two of his brothers, James and Herbert live in Marion and William joined them several years ago. There he worked very successfully in the insurance business, having laid the foundation for a substantial fortune. He also owned a farm in Missouri.

William Ledbetter belonged to a family of 9 children all of whom survive him, and attended his funeral except his oldest sister Mrs. Kate Smith who lives in Arkansas.
INDEPENDENT, Nov. 25, 1909

JAMES LOWERY

James Lowery was an early day editor and publisher of the *Hardin Gazette*, printed in Elizabethtown, Illinois from the early 1870's to the late 1880's. During this time, he reported the events and people that shaped Hardin County. His record of births, deaths, marriages and local news is a major, and often, only source for genealogists researching that area.

James Lowery was born in Hardin County Illinois on 4 September 1841. He is shown in the 1860 census of Hardin County in the family of John and Mary Lowery, along with Matthew and Mary.

On his 20th birthday, James answered the call to arms, and he and other young men of Harding County boarded the Steamer IDLEWILD to join their regiment. He was elected corporal, an honor that he was very proud of. In a letter to the *Independent*, (a successor to the *Gazette*) he wrote: "I was as proud as though it had been Major General." He did not go into detail about his experiences in the Civil War.

James apparently married Elizabeth Ginger? by 1861 ? as his first child was born in 1862. The 1870 census listed his family as follows: James Lowery 29, Elizabeth 29, John 8, Mary 7, Edith 5, Dosha 2. A son, George William, was born in February of 1881. *The Hardin Gazette* carried the comment: .."New boy at the editor's domicile has been christened George William."

James left Elizabethtown in the late 1880's or early 1900's, after(?) he and Elizabeth were divorced, and moved to Abilene, Texas. There, he became editor of *The Taylor County News*. He returned to Hardin County to visit old friends and places of his earlier years, but he lived out his life in Abilene. Apparently there was a group of people from Hardin county living in and around Abilene as James refers to them in one of his letters.

In the years between 1915 and 1920, he wrote a series of letters to *The Hardin County Independent* in which he reminiscences about the early days in Hardin County. These letters were nostalgic, plaintive, philosophical and often bitter in tone. In a letter dated 26 August 1915, he referred to his family. "... The family is scattered over a wide scope of territory.... Quincy lives in Anderson County, Texas. Edith lives in Everett, Washington.... Docia lives on a farm in Jones County, Texas. ... George and his mother live in Everett, Washington... My half sister, Jane Thornton, lives on a farm 13 miles from town (Abilene)... Nettie, another half sister, married D.W. W (unable to read) and lives in town..."

James owned and published *The Hardin Gazette* from 1872? to 1886? His editorial position against the liquor interests created enemies. In a letter to the *Independent*, dated 20 September 1917, he recalled those early days.

" When local options were first voted for Elizabethtown, I was fool enough to enter the war against violation of the law... On account of this the whiskey dealers and all the influence they could control were arrayed against me. I was misrepresented, demeaned, belittled, and insulted..I was frequently in receipt of anonymous letters, some of them making threats and others tantalizing me about my domestic affairs and troubles..."

In his next letter in October, James refers again to the liquor interests.

"In conclusion, I want to say to my enemies, if I still have any back there that I want them to throw their mud into the Ohio River, as they can no longer reach me with it, and pour their vitriol into Hades for they can no longer burn and scar me with it. Then dip themselves into some pool like Solomon and wash away their moral leprosy. ... instead of throwing brickbats, let them cast an occasional bouquet. Let their motto be flowers for the living and charity for the dead. Piles of flowers heaped upon the graves of the dead are meaningless and words of eulogy fall dull upon the ears hushed in death. Send me a flower or send me nothing, and send it while I live."

In July of 1881, *The Hardin Gazette* printing plant was destroyed by fire, along with the editor's collection of Indian relics, mineral collection and library. The fire was the work of an "incendiary," according to James. Apparently someone or some group wanted to silence the *Gazette*. No one was ever charged with the crime.

Undaunted, James borrowed a press and continued to print the paper.

He advertised for Indian relies and people begin to bring in artifacts to the *Gazette* office. After each acquisition, James would thank the donor in the "Local News" section of the paper. His rate of payment was a lead pencil for each arrowhead.

In the 1930,s a friend related an amusing story about Jim's Indian relic collection. A farm boy found an arrowhead and took it to the editor to trade it for a lead pencil. After he obtained his pencil, Jim's pressman called the boy into the backroom to show him a "printers bug." When the boy bent over the press to see the bug, the printer slashed dirty water on him. The printer thought this was a great joke. The boy didn't. He was wearing the only good clothes that he owned and he did not appreciate them being slashed with dirty water. He was a big, raw-boned teenager and he preceded to give the printer a sound thrashing.

In a letter dated 26 August 1925, James

wrote of his loneliness.

"I have a little domicile and that my only company is a black cat which I call Satan... I was sick quite a lot during the summer... and I can not see well enough to read the paper."

He was referring to files of the Hardin Gazette that he used as reference to write his informal letters to the *Independent*.

In his numerous letters, James never mentioned belonging to any particular religious faith, However, he appeared to have had a belief in life after death. In a tribute to a deceased friend, James wrote: " I lie on my bed in the evening and think of the past and then the future and the words come to mind: 'Shall we gather at the river, the beautiful, beautiful river and gather with the Saints at the river Then there seems to come this refrain yes, we shall gather at the river the beautiful, beautiful river gather with the Saints at the river that flows by the throne of God'"

Through out his life, James Lowery had an inquiring intellect. He had a wide range of interests including history, archaeology, mineralogy, natural history, agriculture and climatology. He was a self educated man, and for his day, he was well educated.

Perhaps James's own words describe his life the best. He saw himself as a "... soldier, editor, prospector and recluse..."

James Lowery, Hardin County's pioneer editor, died in Abilene, Texas on 19 September 1925.

JAMES MANHART

James Manhart, life time resident of Hardin County died November 16, 1930. He celebrated his 90th birthday on April 26, 1930. Mr. Manhart at the age of 22 years when the Civil War started, having great sympathy with the Southern cause, walked from Elizabethtown to Cave-in-Rock, crossed the river in skiff, walked to Marion, Kentucky and there enlisted in the Morgan Regiment of cavalry- designated in later years as Morgan Raiders.

He was captured in the Ohio raid, sent to

Chicago, where he laid in prison until exchanged. He returned south about the time the war ended and he then returned home. He has remained here ever since, living in the same property that has never changed hands to this date.

Mr. Manhart has been a member of Empire Lodge, Number 56, I.O.O.F. for over sixty years. He was a member of the Baptist Church and former businessman here in the furniture and undertaking business.

HARDIN COUNTY INDEPENDENT, Oct. 23, 1930.

RICHARD McCONNELL

Richard McConnell was born October 11, 1867, on what is now part of the Dan Frailey farm in Hardin County on the river bank just opposite Weston, Kentucky.

His parents were the late Hugh and Helen Beavers McConnell, both of whom were born in Illinois. He was the fourth of the six children born into this family. His only brother died in infancy. One sister also passed away many years ago. The remaining sisters are Mrs. Mary Yeakey and Mrs. Alma Dowdy, both of Ford's Ferry, Ky., and Mrs. James Ledbetter of Elizabethtown.

When Captain McConnell was a small lad the family moved from the farm where he was born to Kentucky, locating at Ford's Ferry. There he passed his boyhood and early manhood, working on the farm with his father until he was thirty nine years of age.

In 1892 he was married to Miss Lucy Alice Bentley. To their union four children were born. The first, a girl, died at the age of three years. The others are Gladys, who is now at home with her father, and Ellis and Cyrus, who are both river men of ability and who are now employed at St. Louis. The mother died when the last named was but a small child. Several years later, Mr. McConnell married Miss Olive B. Alexander, of Marion, Ky. They have three children: Everett, who like his father, is a man of the river, reliable and fearless, makes his home with his parents; Mrs. Mary Pearson, wife of John Pearson, who with their little daughter,

Patricia Anne, live on a farm near Cave-in Rock; and Richard, Jr. who is now completing a course at Lockyear Business College at Evansville, Ind.

In 1908, Captain McConnell's career as a river man had its beginning in the building of a boat in the barn of his father at Ford's Ferry. The boat, the ESTA, was built by his brother-in-law, R. L. Yeakey.

In the spring of that year the Yeakeys and the McConnells travelled in the ESTA to Beardstown, ILL. There they remained for about a year engaged in fishing. During one period of two months the average catch was 300 pounds of fish every twenty-four hours.

When they returned to Ford's Ferry in 1909, Mr. McConnell had made a trade for the old Lowry farm about one-half mile below Cave-in-Rock. He intended farming there, but the love for the river, and the life upon it, had too strong a pull. He cultivated the farm one summer and then purchased the ESTA, For two years he used her doing job work along the river near Cave-in-Rock. His trade grew as people learned that he was a man who not only understood boats, but could be unfailingly relied upon to do as he promised.

In 1910 another boat was built in the cave here by Mr. Yeakey and was by him named the EGYPTIAN, A two-roomed boat, 38 ft. by 7 1/2 ft. with a glass cabin and a back room for the machinery. It became very popular, as in those days the most convenient and quickest method of reaching Cave-in-Rock, or getting in connection with the rest of the world was by boat.

Travelling salesmen and others patronized Captain McConnell, and soon he began to make regular trips, twice a day, to Rosiclare. During those years he was of great service to the community as he furnished a means of transportation for those who wished to complete their high school course at Rosiclare. Parents of such pupils entrusted them to his care and their confidence was never misplaced.

In 1915, a third boat, the KATHERYNE was built by Mr. Yeakey here in Cave-in-Rock. To accommodate the growing number of passengers and the increased freight, this boat was much larger than the EGYPTIAN. It was 63 ft. by 9 1/2 ft. and had a steel hull.

Twenty years ago, on the first Monday in July, Captain McConnell commenced carrying the mail on this new boat. He made daily regular trips to Shawneetown, then back to Cave-in-Rock and on to Rosiclare. There was a regular time schedule for arrival and departure at the various points along the river, and he established such a record for punctuality that people could almost set their time pieces by the goings and coming of the KATHERYNE.

At this time the family left the farm and moved into town in order that they might be able to give this superior service. In addition to his other work, Captain McConnell has been the agent here for the West Kentucky Coal Company for the past twenty-six years. During all these years he has had an able assistant in his faithful wife, who not only kept the machinery of the home running but also made countless trips on the boat and looked after much of the necessary business.

In 1918 the McConnells suffered a great misfortune in the burning of the KATHERYNE. She was rebuilt, however, on the same hull and again entered the trade. In 1922, the MARY MCCONNELL 65 ft. by 12 ft. and with a hull of steel, was built at Dubuque, Ia. She was equipped with two engines, and in all her years of service a trip was never lost on account of break- down of an engine. After the building of the MARY MCCONNELL, the KATHERYNE was used as an excursion boat, and as a means of transporting men who had jobs at the dam to and from their work.

For sixteen consecutive years Captain McConnell carried the mail through all kinds of weather and in spite of all difficulties. Perhaps the winter of 1917-18 is the one most vividly impressed upon his memory as the river was blocked with ice for several months and deep snows covered the land. Many citizens of Cave-in-Rock will recall how the men went out with teams and shovels and dug through the drifts to Saline Creek. From there the mail and supplies were brought overland from Shawneetown.

In 1924 Captain McConnell, seeing the need for a good ferry at Cave-in-Rock, purchased the landing and commenced to operate the ferry at this place. He soon built a landing of concrete for the convenience of his passengers. He measured the distances for this landing himself and it was so accurately done that when the new pavement was laid connecting it with the end of the street, no changes had to be made. The contractors for the road inquired as to what surveyor had done the work.

Later he leased the ferry right at Elizabethtown also, and a fine ferry boat for that trade was built at Paducah and named for his wife, the OLIVE B. MCCONNELL.

Though the paved roads and automobiles have almost supplanted the use of the river and boats, there is still a great demand for crossing the river. The completion of the road here and its connection with the Kentucky state road will probably greatly increase this demand.

Captain McConnell has seen many years of service, but he has not retired. He is still able to use the pilot's license which he had for so many years. He and his son, Everett, are operating the ferry here, and at any hour of the day or night they faithfully answer the calls of those who wish to cross the river.

The many friends of Captain McConnell are hoping that he may continue to serve the public in that capacity for many years in the future. Katheryne McDonald, HARDIN COUNTY INDEPENDENT, Sept. 27, 1935

JOE MASON

My father, Caswell Mason, was borned in North Carolina about 1817 and moved to Caldwell County, Kentucky when a boy, at which place the writer was borned February 1, 1842. Father moved to Illinois in 1849, to Fayette County in 1853 where he had a brother, Mark Mason. Mark raised quite a large family. Among the sons I remember only Abe and Henry Mason.

Father moved back to Hardin County in 1854, we making the trip both ways in a "prairie schooner." At that time there was only one railroad in the great state of Illinois, the Illinois Central which we crossed at Du Quoin, Illinois.

My wife and I are just back from a visit to Father's old place after an absence of 64 years. We found that uncle Mark and all his children had passed on to the Great divide, but we found quite a number of our second cousins.

In Springfield I attended the G.A.R. Reunion in which 250 to 300 marched out before Governor Lowden who made a fine speech praising the old soldiers for what they did in 1861 to 1865.

I am the 15th child of my parents who had born to them 10 boys and six girls, all of whom save myself and my sister, Mrs. Sarah Oldham have passed on to the Great Beyond. Mrs. Oldham is in her '80's.
HARDIN COUNTY INDEPENDENT, Sept. 27, 1917.

SARAH JANE MASON

Hardin County can this week claim the distinction of being the home of a citizen who is now one hundred years of age. She was born near Princeton, Kentucky, December 11, 1835, being one of a family sixteen children. Her father, the late Caswell Mason, was a preacher of General Baptist denomination.

The family moved to Cave-in-Rock when our subject was thirteen years of age. At the age of seventeen, she married Shepard Frailey, a widower of twenty two years who had one son, John Frailey of Mt. Vernon, Indiana. Mr. Frailey visits relatives there occasionally. Though the couple was married in Kentucky, at the home of a sister, they came back to Hardin County and lived together for thirty seven years in the vicinity of Cave-in-Rock, their home being where Walter Beavers now lives. Mrs. Oldham never left Hardin county after her marriage except during one brief period where she took her children to Carbondale in order that they might have educational advantages.

To their union were born two sons and two daughters. The sons are still living and are

Robert Frailey, of Cave-in-Rock, and Dan Frailey, who lives on his farm five miles east of that village. In addition to the two sons, there are ninety-seven other living descendants including seventeen grandchildren, fifty-one great-grand children, twenty-eight great-great grandchildren, and one great-great-great grandson. Billy Dee Switzer is the youngest one of six living generations. Among the descendants there are five living generations. In 1885, Mr. Frailey died. Mrs. Frailey remained a widow for six years, but in 1891 married Joel Oldham, a veteran of the Civil War. They lived together until his death.

"Aunt" Sarah lives in her own home, though it is necessary for her to have a companion. Until the past year her health has been excellent. She is now confined to her bed the greater part of the time, but she is contented and always gives her friends a warm welcome. Katheryne McDonald, HARDIN COUNTY INDEPENDENT, Dec. 12, 1935.

FRED McCLUSKY

I was born on Jack's Point Farm in Hardin County, April 6, 1881. My parents were John McClusky, a Civil War veteran of Vermont and my mother formerly Lucinda O'Neal of Johnson Co. ILL. At the age of five years, I accompanied my parents who moved to Kentucky and remained there until I was twelve years old, at which time we returned to Hardin County.

At the age of twelve to sixteen years, I worked on a farm for Dave Orr, which is now known as the S. E. Heri farm. At the age of sixteen to twenty one years, I worked on a farm for Jesse Hurford on Big Creek near the old furnace. My wages during the five years I worked for Hurford were fifty cents per day which was considered big money at that time.

At the age of twenty one I went to work for the Rosiclare Mining Company as a "deck hand" at a wage of $1.25 per day. After working at that job for two years, I was promoted through the various jobs until my present job of Mill Superintendent.

I have, however, always maintained an interest in farming, and in addition to my place at Rosiclare, I have a farm in Kentucky under cultivation.

In addition to my mining and farming activities, I have been interested in the welfare of the community in general and have served eight years on the Board of Education of the Rosiclare High School and two terms as member of the City Council of Rosiclare.

Twenty-three years ago I was first elected committeeman of the East Rosiclare Precinct and have served in that capacity and as chairman of Hardin County, ever since. I am at present chairman of the Hardin County Republican Central Committee.

My wife's maiden name was Anna Cruson. She was born and raised in Hardin County and prior to our marriage was a school teacher. We married on the 29 day of March 1903. At the time of my marriage, I rented the farm known as the Charley Dimick place and at the end of three years, bought the place. We still live on the farm, which is located just outside the corporate limits of Rosiclare.

During all of this time, I have worked for the same company and lived at the same location We have three children.

My oldest son, Gordon McClusky, was graduated from Rosiclare High School and later married Miss Della Wamack of Johnson county, a former school teacher of Hardin County. They have one child, Gordena Ann McClusky, 7 years old. Gordon served five years as Post Master of Rosiclare and at present has the mail contract for delivery of mails from Cave-in-Rock, Elizabethtown, Rosiclare and Golconda. My next oldest boy, Rodney McClusky, was also graduated from Rosiclare High School and then attended the Rolla School of Mines at Rolla, Missouri where he was graduated in mining engineering. Rodney was first employed by the Rosiclare Company as chemist and later as mining engineer, which job he still holds.

My youngest child, Irene, was also graduated from Rosiclare High School and later from the

State Normal School for Teachers at Carbondale. After leaving Carbondale, she taught one year at Brookport, and five years ago returned to teach in Rosiclare. She is still a member the grade school teaching staff. She was married to Louden Pruett, a former Elizabethtown boy who studied law at the University of Illinois, and now resides in Rosiclare.
HARDIN COUNTY INDEPENDENT, Oct. 24, 1935

BIGGER MCFARLAND
      Bigger McFarland was born on 20 or 22nd of April 1820 in Elizabethtown Pope Co.[now Hardin Co]Illinois. He was married in early manhood to Miss Pernissa Stuart. Only one child was born to them and it died in infancy. During the wife's fatal illiness,and as death approached she asked her husband to marry a friend of hers. But he never remarried.
      Captain McFarland spent more time in the merchandising and produce business than any other man on the Ohio River. He made thousands of dollars, and the bounties to the poor were constantly falling from his generous hands, and consumed much of his fortune.
      Bigger McFarland died at his home on April 2, 1893 and was buried next to his wife in the village cemetery.
HARDIN COUNTY INDEPENDENT 05 April 1893.

MCFARLAND TAVERN / ROSE HOTEL
      The oldest building in Elizabethtown, and the longest time in service is the Rose Hotel, at present operated by Mrs. U. G.Gullett.
      The room which is the lobby of the present hotel was built in 1817 by James McFarland, who with his family lived there. Other rooms were added from time to time, and people crossing the ferry at that time were lodged there. This was before Illinois became a state.
      The McFarlands were so prominent in the early history of the county that the precinct in which their property was located was named the McFarland Precinct. When Hardin became a county a hundred years ago, the county seat was named

Elizabethtown for Elizabeth, the wife of the first McFarland resident.

When the courthouse and most of its records burned in 1884, the old land book was saved. It shows that there were 200 land grants in the area that became Hardin County in 1839. One of the entries was that of James McFarland, October 19, 1814, whose grant extended from Hosick Creek to Grandpiere Creek, a distance of six miles along the "meandering" Ohio river and one mile in from its course.

The McFarlands donated the land on which the courthouse is built and if it should be moved, the land would revert back to the McFarland estate.

James McFarland was buried in back of the hotel, the marker showing his death in 1837, two years before Hardin became a county. His widow's grave is also there.

The second James McFarland built the eastern addition to the first part of the hotel in 1840, and another addition was built in 1865.

The first James McFarland also owned part of Hurricane Island at one time. But William P. McFarland, executor of the estate of Mathilda McFarland sold 100 acres of the island to Marion I. Steele, January 7, 1907.

R. P. McFarland, son, of the first James McFarland, ran a store in Elizabethtown in the building where Mrs. Josie Fowler now lives.

There is a bell hung on side of the Rose Hotel, the former McFarland Tavern which was bought to this country so long ago that no one remembers exactly when it came from Pittsburgh, Pennsylvania. It has a silvery tone because it has so much silver in it, folks say. It was rung for meals and to signal the ferry boat, before Mrs. Rose took over.

Mrs. Sarah Rose who died last March, had operated and managed the hotel for 55 years before her death. She had rented the hotel from the third James McFarland six years before she purchased it in 1890.

Mrs. Rose parents were Mr. and Mrs. Calvin Baker who came to Hardin County from Georgia in 1840. They lived on the Ben Pruitt farm, then known as the Capt. B. P. McFarland farm where she was born in November 5, 1851.

The future Mrs. Rose was three years old when parents moved to Equality, Illinois, but she moved back to Hardin County when she married Wiley Rose at 17.

After his death in 1869, she operated hotels, having one in Elizabethtown where the phone office is now located, until she rented the McFarland Tavern in 1884. She bought the building six years later and established the Rose Hotel.

Burrell Hall, colored, and her sister, Frankie Woods have worked at the hotel most of their lives. They are the daughters of Helen McDonald who was cook, working at the hotel for Mrs. Rose when Frankie was born 43 years ago. Burrell is 53 years old. she began working at a very young age.

When Frankie was born her mother was living in Elizabethtown, To save the cook trips home, Mrs.Rose had her move her family into a house behind the hotel, where Frankie has lived since she was ten months old. Frankie began waiting tables when she was ten years old.
HARDIN COUNTY INDEPENDENT, June 1939.

DAVID MCMURPHY

David McMurphy. son of John T. McMurphy and Volley Bradley McMurphy, was born 23 November 1838 in Pope County, Illinois. He appears in the 1850 census with sisters, Hannah, Judith, and Elizabeth.

On 24 September 1861, he enlisted in Co. G., Sixth Illinois Calvary, supplying his own mount and "horse equipment." His military records describe him as 5'10" tall, with grey eyes and dark hair. His occupation was given as farmer at the time of his enlistment.

As did many soldiers in the Civil War, David contracted diseases and sustained injuries that impaired his health for the rest of his life. In October of 1861 he contracted measles at Camp Butler Illinois where he was stationed. The measles plus subsequent exposure to weather left him with diseased lungs. He was hospitalized in Camp Butler in 1861 and again at Columbus, Kentucky in 1862. On the 4th of July in Nashville, Tennessee, he was thrown from a mule and injured his back.

Apparently David had recovered enough of his health to reenlist which he did at Germantown, Tennessee in 1864. He was promoted to corporal and then to sergeant before he was mustered out at Selma, Alabama.

His records do not indicate whether or not he fought in any battles. However, his unit the Sixth Illinois, the Seventh Illinois and the Second Iowa Cavalry engaged a Confederate detachment of cavalry and home guards, resulting in 100 enemy dead or wounded and 1600 (estimated) prisoners. The Union losses were three dead and seven wounded.

On 13 March 1870, he married Mary J. Burner, daughter of George and Martha Burner. According to her obituary, she was born near New Madrid, Missouri in a covered wagon. Her parents were en route to the California gold fields. The family settled at Pilot Knob, Missouri where Mary Jane lived until her marriage in 1870. This union produced seven children David's pension records lists the dependent children: Josephine McMurphy, born 20 August 1875, Elizabethtown;----- McMurphy born 22 February 1878; Edward McMurphy, born 16 February 1883; George Washington McMurphy, born 13 May 1885; Maggie Lula McMurphy, born 3 August 1888. The above named children and their birth dates were verified by sworn statements by doctors Gore and Kirkland who attended Mary McMurphy during the birth of these children. Three additional children were born to this marriage: Mary B. McMurphy, born 1874, and Frank Burner McMurphy, born in 1870s, and an infant, deceased.

In 1888, Mary Jane filed for a invalid's pension for David, claiming that he was nearly totally disabled. David lived only a few more years, and died on 5 march 1891. Mary Jane out lived him by nearly forty years, dying on 30 November 1930 and was buried at Paris, Missouri.

SOURCES
1. Military records for David McMurphy, WC 351-611.
2. *Photographic History of The Civil War.* Francis Miller, editor, Vol. 2.

LEVI MCMURPHY

    Levi McMurphy, proprietor of "Valley View Stock Farm," is one of the well-known and respected farmers and stockman of Warrensburg and Post Oak Townships. His splendid stock farm comprises three hundred and sixty acres of land in Warrensburg Township and one hundred twenty five in Post Oak township. The tract of land was entered from the government by John H. Gardner.

    "Valley View Stock Farm," is the home of the registered Hereford, the largest herd in Johnson County. Mr. McMurphy purchased the first registered male in 1894," Ben Imadine," and three years later purchased the first registered cow. At the present time he owns one hundred forty head of high grade registered stock, a large number of which are breeding cows. The imprint of "Ben Imadine's," horns maybe seen in the cement walk in front of the McMurphy residence.

    In 1877, Levi McMurphy and Martha Hicks were united in marriage at Golconda, Illinois, and to them were born eight children, seven of whom are now living: Mary Alice, who died in infancy; Icy, a prominent farmer and stockman of Post Oak Township; Mrs. Pearl McCormick, Warrensburg, Missouri; James, who resides on the home place; J. Henry, a successful farmer of Magnolia, Missouri; William M., Warrensburg, Missouri; Levi Jr., at home; and Ernest, a highly regarded farmer and stockman of Post Oak Township. Mr. and Mrs. McMurphy are numbered among the most valued and substantial citizens of Johnson County.

    Levi McMurphy was born in Hardin County, Illinois, 6 April 1857. He was the son of Lafayette McMurphy and Mornisa Joiner. Levi's siblings were Mollie, John and Matthew McMurphy. Lafayette died and Mornisa married John Hines.

This union produced: Alien, John and George Hines.

Ewing Cockrell, HISTORY OF JOHNSON COUNTY MISSOURI Historical Publishing Company, Topeka, Cleveland 1918.

WEEKLY STANDARD HERALD, Warrensburg, Missouri, July 22, 1927.

JAMES R. MILLER

James R. Miller, the second son of the late John W. and Mary A. Miller, was born in Rutherford County, Tennessee on January 6,1859. At about the time of the Civil War his family moved to Williamson County and later to Hardin County, Illinois. The Miller family located in Rock Creek Precinct, just west of the Rock Creek Store.

James grew up in this area and received a common school education. After receiving his teacher's certificate, he taught for several years at various schools in the county.

About the year 1894, he entered the U. S. mail service, first on the mail packets JOHN S. HOPKINS and JOE FOWLER which carried the mail between Evansville, Indiana and Paducah, Kentucky. Later he transferred to the L & N Railroad which carried the mail between Shawnee town and McLeansboro, Illinois. James was in the mail service for 27 years.

While living in Shawneetown in 1903, he married a young widow by whom he had one child, Mildred. When the child was 9 month old the mother died and James arranged for his brother in Tennessee to rear Mildred.

James R. Miller died at his home in McLeansboro, Illinois September 17, 1922. He is survived by a daughter and a sister, Mrs. Anna Reynolds.

"Roxie," HARDIN COUNTY INDEPENDENT, Oct. 5, 1922.

JOHN H. OXFORD

John H. Oxford, age 50, was born and reared on a farm in north eastern Hardin County Illinois. He received his early training at Yellow Springs School and His normal training was at Southern Illinois Normal University. He then studied at Ewing College and at Oakland City College where he received his Bachelor of Science degree in 1915.

He taught a few terms in the rural schools of Hardin County, but was soon called to the principalship of Cave-in-Rock (1903- 1906) and then to Elizabethtown schools (1907-1910).

He served in the office of county superintendent for Hardin County from 1910 to 1914, after which term he was elected to the Chair of Science in Oakland City College. He served in this position from 1915 until his death.

His family consists of the father, J. A. Oxford; his step mother, Cecil Oxford, now living in Kankakee; Fowler Oxford of California; Mrs. Otto Holbrook of Elizabeth town; Capt. Don Rowan, a step brother of Evansville; Miss Ruth Martin, a niece of Mrs.Oxford.

John Henry Oxford, the son of J.A. Oxford, was killed when his automobile was struck by a train at a grade crossing in Oakland City, Indiana, August 12, 1926.
HARDIN COUNTY INDEPENDENT, Aug. 10, 1926.

SAMUEL C. OXFORD

Samuel C. Oxford was born July 29, 1856 in Hardin County, ILL. on the Oxford homestead. He was one of the second generation of the large Patton and Oxford families.

In the early pioneer days the first generation settled with their parents on Patton Ridge north of Potts Hill. They were Elihu, James, Elias Newton, Morgan and Hannah. These inter-married principally in the Patton family, entered lands from the government office in Shawneetown, developed good farms, built homes and reared large families.

Elihu and James became pioneer ministers, Elihu first county judge of Hardin County, and all of them were classified with what rogues of the time termed "Damnable Law and Church Party," because they stood unflinching for law and order in a lawless wilderness.

Elias wedded Nancy J. Patton. Their sons

were Riley, John Allen, Isaac, Samuel C. and George; their daughters became Elizabeth J. Angleton and Hannah Brownfield. Samuel C. was the last of them to quit the walks of men, and he had lived to see the generation of his brothers, sisters and cousins go, all of except John Oxford, youngest son of Elihu who is living on his farm in Rock Creek Precinct of this county.

In his early life, Sam Oxford married Mary (Mollie) Barnes, who after becoming the mother of Alfred, Millard F. and Walter S. succumbed to a lingering illness, and ultimately to an untimely death.

Only a few years later on returning home from his first college year, the writer remembers quite well what Sam Oxford who was the president of the Central School Board called for me to teach that school and among other things he said, "I have spent about all I have trying to save Mollie's life, and If I meet with a few more such misfortunes, I'll not have anything to give the boys except an education. That is one thing that cannot be taken away from them and I want you to help me push them through."

Later on the writer taught in Yellow Springs District where the father arranged to send the boys a number of terms. He then moved to Elizabethtown for further schooling, and farmed the place the writer now lives, and where he worked as a salesman in some of the stores. Alfred soon married and farmed for himself, but died about thirty years of age. Going out from school, Walter began teaching in his home county. After attending Oakland City College, Millard also taught, but soon gave up the profession for the ministry.

In the mean time the father married Sarah Shipp, who made him an industrious companion and faithful step-mother for his sons. He as a step-father he also raised two girls, Nora and Altie (?) to womanhood.

In his deep interest in learning, Samuel C. Oxford served many years on different boards in his district and townships; and because of his knowledge of values of both personal and real property, he was sought as deputy assessor. In eight years of this work, he wrote the property of every nook and corner of Hardin County; and was asked by friends to make the race for county assessor and treasurer but his aversion to politics kept him from offering for office.

Samuel Oxford died on August 12, 1941. He was active in the International Order of Odd Fellows (I.O.O.F.) and lived the moral principles of that organization.
F.N. Hall, HARDIN COUNTY INDEPENDENT, Aug. 21, 1941.

I.N. OZEE (J.N.?)

Mr. I.N. Ozee, 81 years old, came to Elizabethtown last Saturday morning and spent several hours talking about events of 50 and 60 years ago.

He came into this country with his father's family in 1855, and spent the first year on a farm now owned and occupied by J. A. Oxford Jr., then owned by the writer's father. Ozee's father then bought land less than a mile northeast of Sparks Hill, where they built and moved the next year, and where the father lived until he died some 15 or 20 years afterward.

Mr. Ozee married Miss Fannie Wall who bore him three children, two girls and one boy, Edward, who died some two years ago in Missouri.

Mr. Ozee now lives with his son-in-law, James Mott, near El Dorado, Illinois. He has nieces in Elizabethtown, Mrs. Charles H. Jackson and Mrs. Charley Frailey.
HARDIN COUNTY INDEPENDENT, Aug 4, 1921

BARBARA HUMM REIF

Barbara Humm Reif was born January 5th, 1846 in Malkanner, which was then a little town in the Rhinfaltz, in Germany. Her parents were Fredrick and Anna Barbara Humm, also born in Germany. They were blessed with seven children, one boy and six girls. The boy died at an early age in Germany, and through these many years since then all his sisters save one, have passed on.

In 1857, Mr. and Mrs. Humm and their daughters embarked in a sail ship for America. "Aunt" Barbara Reif, today the only surviving member of this family, tells of the storm that came over the sea, and the great waves rising higher than the ship. Despite the knowledge of the pilot of the ship, he lost his course in the storm, and when the sea became calm once more, the ship was sailing along slowly toward a small rock-bound island.

There was no wind blowing so the pilot decided to land here and wait for the wind to fill the sails once more. The sailing party remained here eight days until Providence favored them with the power needed to move the ship over the sea. Two months and twenty days after setting sail on the Atlantic ocean, they arrived safely on the Eastern Coast of America, the Beautiful.

Among the other passengers on the ship Frederick Humm chose Illinois for his future home after traveling through several states, of which the subject of this sketch spoke briefly today of their stop in Indiana after they had crossed the beautiful Ohio. She spoke of attending church in Evanston, Indiana. Coming to Illinois, they followed the course of the Ohio River, and arrived in Hardin County and settled on a little farm in West Rosiclare precinct, in the same year the family left Germany.

The farm had a small log house surrounded by woods as only a very few acres had been cleared. Little Barbara, then ten years old today recalls to mind how her father set to work at once clearing more ground and with the help of the mother and the girls raising a crop on the farm every year, to feed the family also helping the other families who were less fortunate. This little farm was cleared of most of the timber and the family lived happily there. It is the farm now owned by "Uncle" Baker Finney, north-west of Stone Church. The Humm family later acquired eighty acres of what is now a part of the Anton Volkert farm.

Many years ago Fredrick Humm and wife crossed the sea of death, their daughters also except the one who remains a memorial of days that are gone and as an example to everyone who knows her as she is.

In January 1869 she was married to Nicholas Reif, after which they lived on the farm on which the Humm family had settled, when they came to this country from Germany. To this happy union were born three children, Saloma, now Mrs. George Humm of near Rosiclare; George Reif, now of Equality; Catherine, now Mrs. George Hermann of Eichorn.

After their married life of the first thirty-three years, during which time Mr. and Mrs. Reif, by hard work and thrift and honesty, always living happily by their neighbors, (and Mrs. Reif, today, speaks praises of their neighbors), in 1902 they lost their home by fire and neighbors, friends and relatives helped them.

In 1921 Mr. Reif died. He is survived by his faithful companion, their son, George Reif and their two daughters, Mrs. George Hermann and Mrs. George Humm.

Mrs. Reif lives with her daughter, Mrs. George Humm, near Rosiclare and in view of the Ohio River, which she first crossed seventy-eight years ago.

She has been a faithful member of the Catholic Church since childhood, and her daily life proves the faith within. The people who know her best say what I have just written and more.

She has seven grand-children and eleven great grand-children,, whom she plays with sometimes other times helping them with their lessons. She sews, pieces quilts and though strange, yet true she can thread a needle by lamp-light. When no one else is around to cook a meal, "Aunt" Barbara does not worry, she cooks the meal, and her daughter with whom she lives says her mother can cook as well as she ever could. She has had a number of cases of severe pneumonia, and is not fully recovered from the effects of a bronchial ailment. Yet she is looking well for one of her age, her memory is good, and she has a pleasant smile and a kind

word for everyone.
HARDIN COUNTY INDEPENDENT, MARCH 7, 1935

Barbara Humm Reif

Barbara Humm was born in Germany in 1846 and her parents Mr. and Mrs. Frederick Humm brought their five daughters of whom she was the youngest to this country when she was nine years old.

It took them 88 days to cross the ocean from Germany to America. Eight of those days there was no wind and the boat bobbed about on the waves, she remembers, and then the captain went back and started to America over again. They landed in New Orleans, and from there came up the Mississippi and Ohio rivers by boat to then what was spelled Rose Clare, in Hardin County, near where Mr. and Mrs. Manuel Hermann had located when they came from Germany before the Humms.

Grandma Reif's parents bought from a man named McCarty, the farm near Lonesome Ridge, on the hill above the present road 34, between Stone Church and St. Josephs where Mr. and Mrs. Baker Finney now live. Mrs. Reif attended school in the log school house at Sycamore and Mr. Greathouse was the teacher.

"But I didn't go to school very much," Grandma or Aunt Polly as she is often called, said "I could not speak English and the other boys and girls tried to make me talk for them so I did not go to school to be teased." She remembers spelling bees they used to have then, and there were no paper and pencils. One used a slate and slate pencil.

She was married to Nicholas Reif in the first church at St. Joseph's, a log church building, Jan. 25 1871 by Father Miller from Shawneetown. Her husband's people had landed here the day her parents sailed from Germany

They brought the farm from her parents and lived there till about 30 years ago when the house burned. They rebuilt it, but because of Mr. Reif's failing health, they sold the farm to Baker Finney, and moved to Eichorn, where they lived till Mr. Reif died seventeen years ago.

Grandma remembers that one drove to the stores of Mrs. Miller and Mrs. Lefler to buy clothes and shoes. She said when they landed at Rose Clare, Hardin County was all trees. The stock was allowed to run loose in the woods until farmers got rail fences built, as foxes were killing pigs.

She said that her parents first raised potatoes, as one grows potato in new ground and then grew corn. Alfred Wood brought the potatoes in that vicinity and shipped them to New Orleans.

Friends didn't have parties frequently then as they do now, and the hog killings were in the winter time. Grandma Reif in all her years has never seen a winter as warm as this one in Hardin County. She said the river froze over frequently in her younger days, but she imagines that was because the water was so much lower before the dams were put in.

Grandma remembers deer and wild turkey and quail in Hardin County. She said her crippled sister, Mary, once found two tiny deer in the corner of a rail fence. One became one of their domestic animals. The girls tied a cord around its neck and it was turned loose in the woods with the cattle. It came back each evening with the cattle for a long time until one evening it didn't appear and they never saw their deer again.

Wild and tame turkeys got fed together, then in those days housekeepers made yeast of meal and hop, and baked on Saturdays for the rest of the week. They dried vegetables as they had no cans or glass jars. They had very few stone jars. They made candles in a mold where twelve were made at a time.

" And you had no light after you had them," said Grandma.

Grandma is in excellent spirits, keeps busy crocheting, and piecing quilts, enjoys going to parties at St. Josephs, and plans to attend Hardin County's 100 birthday party. But she thinks they cannot have a cake with that many candles on it... her cake won't hold the required 94 now.

HARDIN COUNTY INDEPENDENT, Jan. 26, 1939

C.D.M. RENFRO

C.D.M. Renfro, 45 years old, was born in Elizabethtown, Illinois. He moved to Carbondale in 1888 when he was a small boy. Dunk as he was familiarly called, visited his native county but a few times after moving away.

Mr. Renfro was a leading young businessman of Carbondale, he and his older brother being sole proprietors of the Carbondale Steam Bakery, of which the deceased has been chief manager for twenty years. He held considerable holdings there in the form of business property and other investments.

He was director of the Carbondale Building and Home Association, a member of the Elks Lodge and a charter member of the Carbondale Rotary Club and a member of the Business Men's Club.

In 1898, young Renfro, then 17 years, old enlisted in Co. C., Illinois Militia and served entire time of the Spanish American conflict.

His mother was a McClellan, who died soon after they moved to Carbondale. He was a son of the first marriage of the late Judge J. H. B. Renfro.

He leaves his wife; one son, Francis; a brother, R. E. "Bob" Renfro; and a half brother, Lacey Renfro of Carbondale. He was a first cousin to Myrtle Rose of Elizabethtown.

HARDIN COUNTY INDEPENDENT, Nov. 5, 1925.

RENFRO, John H.B.

John H.B. Renfro was a native of southern Tennessee, not far from the border line of Alabama. He became a resident of Illinois at an early age, years before the dense cloud of the Civil war shrouded our country in gloom. The the late John H.B. Renfro, of Carbondale, where his life ended on the 26th of October, 1908, grew to manhood in an atmosphere very different in its political character from that in which he was born.

And when the destructive besom of sectional strife swept the land, leaving a trail of blood and ruin in its wake, he joined the forces gathered to save the Union from dismemberment, and fought valiantly for the flag under which his life began.

In his military service he manfully exemplified the valor and resourcefulness of the citizen soldiery of Illinois on one side of the momentous conflict, as he would probably have exemplified the same qualities in the military spirit of his native state on the other if he had remained in the locality of his birth and been reared under the influence of its political teachings.

Mr. Renfro came into being on January 2, 1842, in Lincoln county, Tennessee, and in his boyhood he came to Hardin county, Illinois, where he became established as a farm hand and later took up a tract of wild land which he transformed into a well improved and productive farm.

His parents joined him here. He had obtained what education he was able to secure in the public schools. During his boyhood he had witnessed several public auctions of slaves, which he never thought right, and at the beginning of the war he enlisted in the Federal army, in Company C, Forty-eighth Volunteer Infantry, of which he was third sergeant.

He took part in the capture of Forts Henry and Donelson and the sanguinary battle of Shiloh. In the last named engagement he was wounded in the right lung and disabled for further service for a time, but after recovering his health he rejoined his regiment. He remained with it until August 27, 1864, when he fell from a wagon and broke one of his arms. This accident occurred in the neighborhood of Jonesboro, Georgia, and from there he returned to his Illinois home.

His brother Phenix, who was a boy at home, while hunting got blood on his clothes, and being suspicioned of the ambushing and killing of two northern soldiers was sentenced to be shot. The crime, however, was committed by a neighbor, who came to Phenix Renfro and told him of the circumstances and asked him to get his brother, who was a northern soldier, to save him, but if he could not that he, himself, would come forward in time to save him. Our subject, however, saved his brother.

J.H.B. Renfro was discharged from the service on March 25, 1865, and resumed his residence in Elizabethtown, Hardin county, this state. In the fall of the same year he was elected treasurer of the county, and was reelected in 1867. In 1869 he was elected county clerk, and this office he filled with great acceptability to the people of the county for a continuous period of seventeen years.

Mr. Renfro was first married on May 4, 1870, to Miss Emeretta Leone McClellan. They had two children, their sons Robert E. and C. Duncan Miller Renfro, both of whom are residents of Carbondale.

Their mother died on November 9, 1892, and on April 29, 1894, the father contracted a second marriage, uniting himself with Miss Fannie J. Holden, of Carbondale, he having become a resident of this city in 1888. They became the parents of five children, four of whom are living. They are: Harvey L., Anna Lois, Laura Jeannette and Margaret Josephine. A son, named Samuel B., died a number of years ago.

During his residence in Carbondale the father served two years as township clerk, two years as city attorney and four years as police magistrate and won general approval by the manner in which he discharged the duties of each of these positions. In fraternal life he was a Freemason for a long time, and also belonged to the Grand Army of the Republic. In the latter organization he was a past commander of John W. Lawrence Post, No. 297. Throughout his long service in public life, in the army and in civil offices he never shirked a duty or gave one slight attention. His citizenship was valued wherever he was known, and was worthy of the regard it won.

George Washington Smith, A HISTORY OF SOUTHERN ILLINOIS: Lewis Publishing Co., 1912.

ROBERT EAGLE RENFRO

The rapid progress and development of

Southern Illinois has made the real estate trade active and extensive for many years, given the loan business great opportunities and kept the fire insurance companies in very active and profitable operation. These conditions have also furnished many men with business and employment, and been, as they always are, of great benefit and service to the region in which they have obtained.

One of the most energetic, enterprising and successful men engaged in the triple business specified, in Carbondale is Robert E. Renfro, who has been occupied in these lines of endeavor since 1893, and in the course of his activity in them has been of great service in stimulating the growth and development of all Southern Illinois, throughout which his operations have been conducted in a manner very creditable and profitable to him and satisfactory to all with whom he has had dealings.

Mr. Renfro was born in Elizabethtown, Hardin county, Illinois, on May 25, 1873, and is a son of the late John H. B. and Emeretta Leona (McClellan) Renfro, prominent citizens of that county, the story of whose lives is briefly told in this work. The father, as will be seen by reference in the sketch of him, was treasurer of Hardin county four years and county clerk there seventeen years. He was afterwards a lawyer and pension attorney until his death, in October, 1908.

His son Robert E. began his education in the public schools and complete it at the Southern Illinois Normal university, from which he was graduated in 1893. After his graduation he began his career in business in the department of real estate, loans and fire insurance. He has found the business so congenial, and has made it so profitable, that he has continued his connection with it and steadily enlarged his operations ever since. As has been stated, his dealings now extend all over Southern Illinois, and often involve transactions of considerable magnitude. He is regarded as master of his line of endeavor, and no one questions the excellence or accuracy of his judgment in reference to the value of real estate or the future possibilities of any tract under improvement.

The public affairs of his city have also deeply interested Mr. Renfro, and made him an advocate of the highest moral tone attainable in the government of the city. On a recent occasion he was the candidate of the anti-saloon party for mayor, but the hour was not ripe for the conditions he and that party advocated, and he was defeated at the election. This did not dampen his ardor for good government, however, and he has ever since kept up his demand for it and for every other form of improvement.

The nature of his business makes him energetic and effective in promoting the extension and growth of the city and the development and betterment of every locality in which he operates. But this only quickens and intensifies a disposition that exists in his very character and make-up as a man and citizen. For he is in all things essentially and practically progressive by nature. In fraternal relations he has active membership in two of the benevolent societies so numerous among men, the Order of Elks and the Knights of Pythias. In political matters he is an unwavering Republican in national contests, but has never been desirous of a political office except the local one mentioned above, and this his friends induced him to seek for the good of the city. His religious connection is with the Methodist Episcopal church, in the work of which he is very active and energetic, being a member of the official board of the congregation which has benefit of his serviceable membership.

On Sept. 4, 1895, Mr. Renfro was joined in marriage with Miss Beulah Witt Storm, a daughter of Oliver P. and Emma H. (Haley) Storm, of Jonesboro, Illinois, where her father was a merchant at the time of his death, in 1888, and for many years prior to that. She and her husband have two children, their sons Donald McClelland and Robert Kennon, who are still bright links that bind the whole family into one of the most agreeable family circles in the city

of their home, and help to make the household one of its most attractive and popular social resorts.
George Washington Smith, A HISTORY OF SOUTHERN ILLINOIS, Lewis Publishing Co.,1912.

LAVINA RIGGS

One of the oldest resident in Hardin County is Mrs. Lavina Brown who was 93 on June 15. She makes her home with her only surviving child and her husband, Tom Keeling.

Mrs. Brown was born in Kentucky, the daughter of William and Mary Riggs. Her family moved to the bluff above Cave-in-Rock when she was a young girl.

On January 3, 1867, Lavina Riggs was married to John R. Brown, a Civil War veteran. They lived on Dan Frailey's place at the Bend of the River, starting housekeeping in a building which is not there now. They farmed there, then in Saline county, then back below Cave-in-Rock where Joe Riggs lives now. Fifty years ago, they moved to the present home of Mrs. Brown and the Keelings.

Mrs. Brown had two sisters and two brothers younger than she is who are living. Mrs. Mahalie Thomas lives in Crystal City, Texas, Mrs. Martin Daymon lives at Peters Creek, John R. Riggs is in Arkansas, and Joe Riggs at Evansville, Indiana.
HARDIN COUNTY INDEPENDENT, June 29, 1939.

PLEASANT W. ROSE

One of the prominent physicians of Southern Illinois, whose skill and ability have gained him a wide and enviable reputation, and as a consequence a large and liberal clientele, is Pleasant W. Rose, M.D., of Cypress, Illinois, where he is the proprietor of a drug establishment. Dr. Rose was born on a farm in Grantsburg township, Johnson county, August 25, 1877, and is a son of Pleasant W., Sr., and Mary Elizabeth (Farris) Rose, farming people of this county.

The Rose ancestry can be traced back to Revolutionary times, several of the name having fought as soldiers in the Colonial army. The grandfather of Dr. Rose, also named Pleasant, was born in 1812?, and lost his father in early childhood. His mother took her little family to an unimproved farm in Pope county, Illinois, where the boy grew up to the hard life of the pioneer farmer, and at the age of twenty-two years was married to Mary Ann Ellis, of North Carolina, a member of a poor but honorable pioneer family.

Possessed of untiring energy and a strong determination to succeed, he worked hard throughout his life and eventually was rewarded by becoming the possessor of an excellent farm in Grantsburg township, dying there in in 1873, his widow surviving him a little over a year and dying December 4, 1874. They had five children, as follows: Mary, the widow of D.C. Chapman; J.E.; Sydney A., the wife of J. W. Damron; Maria; and Pleasant W., the father of Dr. Rose.

Pleasant W. Rose was born and reared on the farm on which he now resides in Grantsburg township, and was married there October 29, 1868, to Mary Elizabeth Farris, a native of Tennessee, eight children being born to this union, as follows: Arista A., who married W.C. Graves, formerly a merchant of Vienna, Ill., but now the owner of a valuable ranch in the State of Colorado; Ida, who is deceased; Mary, the wife Dr. H.W. Walker, a well-known physician of Grantsburg; Lillie, the wife of Isaac L. Morgan, deputy state fish warden and real estate and insurance agent at Vienna; William; Dr. Pleasant W.; Sidney; and James W., who is deceased. Pleasant W. Rose, Sr., who now lives on a finely cultivated farm of two hundred and seventeen acres, is enjoying the fruits of his many years of industrious labor.

He is known as a practical, sensible man of affairs, a public spirited citizen and leader of the Republican party in his community, and a man who is devoted to his home and family. He has the entire confidence of the citizens of his community, who recognize in him the type of citizen who has the best interests of his locality at heart.

Dr. Pleasant W. Rose received his early education in the common schools of Grantsburg township, later attended the Vienna High School, and in 1896 entered Barnes Medical College, at St. Louis, Missouri, from which he was graduated April 12, 1899, with the degree of M.D. He began the practice of medicine at Grantsburg, but in 1900 went to Simpson, where he remained for five years, then going to Granite City, where he remained two years.

He came to Cypress in 1907, and here has built up an extensive practice, traveling through the rural sections in a radius bounded by four miles north, three miles west, seven miles south and three miles east of Cypress, finding his high power automobile very convenient in taking him to the home of his patients.

In his profession he has steadily arisen until he now occupies a foremost place in its ranks, and as a business man he has been equally successful. On coming to Cypress he erected a fine corner business block, where he has established a drug business, handling all goods to be found in a establishment of its kind, valued at more than six thousand dollars.

The Doctor belongs to New Columbia Lodge, No. 336, A.F. & A.M., and holds membership in the Johnson County Medical Association, the American Medical Association, Association of Railway Surgeons, and was formerly local surgeon for the Illinois Central Railroad at Simpson.

On May 16, 1901, Dr. Rose was married to Nancy E. (Ellis) Mount, widow of John L. Mount, of Pope county, and a daughter of John and Mary Ellis. She has two sons by her former marriage: J. Leon, who is twenty years old; and William Ellis, who is fifteen years of age.
George Washington Smith, A HISTORY OF SOUTHERN ILLINOIS: Lewis Pulishing Co. 1912

EMMA SCHNEIDER

Emma Schneider was born in the little coal town of Bowlesville, Gallatin County, Illinois on the 28 of March 1862. Both of her parents came from Germany about the year 1852, the former to escape compulsory military service and

the latter to look for opportunities in America.
 Their frugality and willingness to work in the course of a few years enabled them to buy a farm south of Saline River in Enterprise School District.
 Edward Schneider bought a farm nearby and won her as his wife, January 15, 1882. To this union was born one daughter and seven sons. The daughter died at nine years old and one of the sons died in infancy. The surviving sons are as follows: Victor, Ernest, Carl, Oscar, Edward and Henry.
 During World War 1, five of her sons enlisted into the service. Soon after her sons were enrolled in their various military units, her husband received a letter from the State Council of Defense asking that he engage in a campaign of patriotic education in Illinois counties with large German populations. When Edward asked her what he should do, She replied "If you think you can do least bit to help win this war, in God's name go" She went through the cold winter of 1917-18 with only the help of her afflicted older brother.
 Emma Schneider died on June 26, 1920.
HARDIN COUNTY INDEPENDENT, July 15, 1920.

DR. JOHN JACOB SHEARER

John Jacob Shearer was born May 30, 1851 He grew to manhood in Hardin County, Illinois. He married Alice McDowell in the 1870's?. This union produced two children, a son, G.C. Shearer and a daughter, who died in infancy. Dr. Shearer qualified for the practice of medicine and for several years practiced his profession until illness forced him to retire. He worked with his brother in the Circuit Clerk's office while he lived in Elizabethtown.
 The doctor spent most of his life in this county, starting out in his middle age to seek a new fortune. He tried Florida, California and Virginia but returned to Hardin County, buying property in Elizabethtown. He lived there until 1926 when he sold out and moved to Florida to be near his son, G.C. Shearer.
 John Jacob Shearer died November 8, 1926

in St. Petersburg, Florida. He is survived by his wife, son, two brothers, and a half brother. Only one brother, G.W. Shearer, was named in the obituary.
HARDIN COUNTY INDEPENDENT, Dec. 16, 1926

HOWARD SIMPSON

Howard was born February 10, 1876. When Howard reached his manhood and realized that his brother (by a former marriage) and his stepfather, Bill Renfro, had done about all they could do him, he hired out to John T. Simmons to work on his farm. Howard became manager of the farm and stayed with Mr. Simmons for three years.

Leaving the farm, Howard became a barber and worked in Caseyville and Sturgis, Kentucky and Harrisburg, Illinois.

When he was nearing his 23 birthday he married Minnie Brookmier who bore him two children, Oral who died in infancy, and Henry who is married and a school teacher in Harrisburg.

Howard Simpson died Oct. 27, 1939.
HARDIN COUNTY INDEPENDENT, Nov. 28, 1939.

E.M. SMOCK

E.M. Smock the subject of this sketch was the only son of James Smock of this county. He was born October 3rd, 1876 near Rock Creek, Hardin County. His boyhood was spent with his parents on the farm and attending school at Rock Creek.

At about the age of 21 years, E.M. Smock entered the profession of teaching. His 24 years of active service began the first term of school at Pinhook, the second at Douglas, then came four successive terms at Double Box and one at Cave-in-Rock.

There was then a break in his work as a teacher while he served as county clerk. At the close of his term of office, he returned to teaching and taught at Cave-in-Rock, Rosiclare, and Elizabethtown.

Mr. Smock was united in marriage to Miss Annie Shearer, daughter of George Shearer in May of 1906. This home was blessed with sons,

Herbert and Kenneth who with their mother, his sister, and parents survive him.

He was a member of two fraternal orders, the Odd Fellows and the Masons. He became a Odd Fellow in 1895 and a Mason in 913. He was also a member of the Christian Church at Cave-in-Rock.

M.M. Pritchard, HARDIN COUNTY INDEPENDENT, April 6, 1922.

BRITTON STACEY

Britton Stacey, the subject of this sketch, was born near Gainsboro Jackson County, Tennessee. May 1, 1844. He had one known brother, Hiram.

When Britton was about two years old, his parents removed to Kentucky and in 1852 to Illinois, locating on a farm some 10 miles north of Elizabethtown. Here he grew to manhood, working on the farm in the summers and attending the public schools during the winter months, obtaining however but a meager education.

On August. 13, 1862 he enlisted as a private in Co. F, 131st ILL. Infantry and was mustered in on November 13. He was engaged in the military operations on the Yazo River, fought at Haines Bluff, Arkansas Post and the Siege of Vicksburg.

After the fall of Vicksburg, he was taken ill with typhoid fever and sent to the hospital in St Louis where he remained for seven months. He then rejoined his command at Paducah, Ky., and soon afterward (November 14, 1863) the regiment was consolidated with the 29th Infantry and Mr. Stacey was assigned to Co. A of that regiment. For the next eleven months he was at Natchez on guard duty, then New Orleans, Daulphines Island, At the Battle of Spanish Fort and in numerous other minor skirmishes. At the battle of Spanish Fort March 27, 1865, he was severely wounded by the explosion of a shell, his left arm being so badly lacerated that it had to be taken off above the elbow.

On March 22, 1866, He was married to Miss Emma J. Tinsley, the daughter of Jackson and Nancy Tinsley. Emma was born July 13, 1847 in

Allen County Kentucky, coming to Harding County in 1882. No children blessed this union.

After his marriage, he engaged in farming until 1881, when he moved to Elizabethtown where he has since lived.

Mr. Stacey served 12 years as deputy sheriff having previously served eight years as a constable while living on the farm. He was several times elected to a place on the town board and served one term as mayor of Elizabethtown. He was one of the charter members of Alexander Ragan Post. He also belonged to the I.O.O.F. and Knights of Honor. He was serving his second term as County Commissioner at the time of his death on September 7, 1910. Emma Tinsley died on September 6, 1914 in Elizabethtown, Illinois.

THE INDEPENDENT, Sept. 15, 1910 & Oct. 8, 1914

HIRAM MORTON STACEY

Hiram Morton STACEY was born June 29, 1840 in Jasper, Tennessee. He moved to Hardin County Illinois before 1860 as he was listed in the 1860 census in the household of Marback Stacey, age 43 and Elizabeth, age 29 ?.

According to his military records, H i r a m was 5' 10" tall, with blue eyes, dark hair, and a dark complexion. In the census, his occupation was given as a farmer.

On the August 13, 1861, Hiram enlisted as a private in Company A, 29th Illinois Regiment commanded by Captain Charles M. Ferrell of Elizabethtown, Illinois. Hiram saw action at Fort Donelson in February of 1862 and the Battle of Shiloh in the following April, receiving wounds in both engagements. The 29th Illinois distinguished itself at Shiloh, turning back a confederate calvary charge.

In action at Holly Springs, Mississippi, he was captured by Van Dorn's troops and pardoned on December 20 1862. Hiram was discharged at Natchez, Mississippi but re-enlisted the following day (January 1, 1864), and served until he was mustered out at Camp Butler on December 5, 1865 with the rank of Lieutenant.

Hiram Stacey married Serena Adeline Byrman

of Hardin County Illinois in 1862, and she bore him three children: E. J. Stacey, born August 20, 1866; Serena, born October 15, 1869; and Nancy E, born 20 November 20, 1871.

Serena died July 18, 1876, and he married Ida Ella Braughard on September 10 1876, daughter of Jerimiah Braughard, born May 6, 1810 of Covington, Ky., and Lucindy, born April 26 1816., Ida bore him seven children: Cora A, born 29 March 1878; Emma M., born October 3, 1880; Chester A., born July 3, 1882; Barham S., born. February 28, 1884; Lillie M., born April 7, 1886: Shadrick M., born December 1, 1887; and Druscilla, born January 21, 1891.

Hiram was living in Bloomfield, Missouri In June of 1920, according to his pension records. How long he remained in Missouri is not recorded, but he had moved to California in the winter of 1924, probably sometime in January. He died 18 June 1925 in San Jose, California.
Hiram M. Stacey, Pension Record # XC 949-918

JAMES A. TADLOCK

James A. Tadlock was born in Grundy County, Missouri on June 13, 1854. He was the oldest child of the late John B. and Fidelia Tadlock and is the only living member the family, his two sisters having passed away several years ago.

Mr. Tadlock has some memories of his life in Missouri, although the family left there when he was small child. He remembers when deer were so plentiful that a herd came up near the home early one morning and the father shot two before breakfast.

He also recalls the roving band of Indians that infested Grundy county which at that time was very thinly settled. It was his father's habit to put bells on his horses when he turned them out to pasture. At times the Indians stole these bells. On one occasion, he noticed that the bell rang in a peculiar manner. He began to investigate and discovered an Indian in the forks of a nearby tree. He seized his cap and ball rifle, fired and killed the Indian.

In the year 1859, the father brought his

children to Kentucky, coming by boat to Caseyville. From there they went to Crittenden County, where the father worked for a short time at Bell's Mines.

In 1860 they moved to Seller's Landing. At that time he enlisted in the 56th Illinois Regiment and served for three and one half years in the Union Army during the Civil War. During this period the subject of this sketch and his two young sisters were left at the home of their uncle, James Tadlock at Seller's Landing.

Their father lost an eye in the service and was honorably discharged before the close of the war.

When he returned he moved his family a mile down the river to Battery Rock, where he took charge of the ferry between there and Caseyville. The boy James many times helped his father pull the ferry load across the river when it was loaded with Union men. On one occasion fifty Union men were being ferried across the river when a Rebel tow boat came down the river. It was clearly their intentions to run over the ferry boat. One of the Union soldiers fired a shot into the pilot house. The pilot backed the boat just in time to save the soldiers. At another time some gun boats were lying at Battery Rock. He was on one of them when the boat fired its cannon at some Rebel soldiers across the river. As Mr. Tadlock tells the story, "the jar almost knocked my teeth out."

When school was in session at Battery Rock, he attended there and well remembers using an old time Webster's " Blue Backed Spelling book" and "McGuffey Reader." The school was built of logs and the seats were made of split logs supported on pegs and without backs.

In 1873, his father died at 54, leaving the children alone in the world. His son James who was then about nineteen years of age, worked and did the best he could to provide for his two sisters.

In 1877, he was united in marriage to Martha I. Whitaker, who was two years younger than he. The marriage was a happy one, and they lived together in Battery Rock precinct for forty years. To this union sixteen children were born, nine of whom are living: George Tadlock, whose home is near Lamb Town; Clarence, Tadlock, whose home is at Peter's Creek; Richard, Charlie and Freeman Tadlock, of Eldorado; Mrs. Laura Douglas and Mrs. Ollie Crowell, of Cave-in-Rock; Mrs. Ida Burman, of Valler, Illinois; and Mrs. Ettie Littrell, who lives near Lamb Town. There are also forty-two grandchildren and twenty-two great grand- children.

In 1917 death separated the aged couple. Mr. Tadlock then sold his farm and moved to Eldorado where he lived with his youngest daughter until she married. Since that time he has no fixed home, but visits among his children.

While living at Seller's Landing, he fished as well as farmed and learned many things about fishing and about building rigs of all kinds for the catching of fish. He is not content with being unemployed and during the past winter while making his home with his son, George, he knit twenty fish nets and made twenty sets of hoops for them and completed the nets. He also made one dip net.

About fifty years ago, he joined the old Union Christian Church at Lamb and in his own words, has "been living it ever since".

While his hearing is somewhat impaired, his general health is good. He is a small man, wiry and active. He recalls a running and jumping contest for men over fifty held at Shawneetown. He was sixty-five at the time but he beat all the other men. He still enjoys running and jumping with his grandchildren and their friends. He has a store of interesting reminiscences which he relates with such keen enjoyment that is a pleasure to hear him.

For the past month he has been at the home of his daughter, Mrs. Laura Douglas at Cave-in-Rock where he had an attack of influenza. He is now almost recovered and his many friends join in a wish that he may completely recover and live to enjoy many more years of activity.
HARDIN COUNTY INDEPENDENT, May 2, 1935.

R. F. TAYLOR

Captain R.F. Taylor, who is going to be 84 years of age May 5, came to Hardin County in 1873 from Pope county where he was born, to teach school at Battery Rock. He boarded with Jonathan Brown, the wealthiest man in the county, who as a white boy played with the Indians.

Captain Taylor remembers Jonathan Brown telling him that when he was 12 years old, his mother died and he came down the river in a boat with his father to trade with the Indians. They landed near Battery Rock and Jonathan had become engaged in a fist fight with an Indian boy about the same age. The Indians watched the fight, some cheering for the white boy, others for the Indian fighter. Finally Jonathan's father separated them, and made Jonathan return to the boat. He wasn't there long until the Indian boy came to the boat, one side of his face painted and begged that the fight continue for the enjoyment of everyone.

They were there but a short time, when Jonathan's father died, and he was buried by the Indians. Jonathan stayed at the boat and later managed to build a kind of cabin for himself. He was 17 years of age before he saw another white person.

Captain Taylor remembers Brown telling how he was hiking on an Indian trail, near where Sparks Hill in now located, when he encountered another white lad about his age. The other boy said he was Jackie Baldwin who lived on the west side of the present county line near where Bethany church now stands. They were the closest white neighbors for a few years when others settled between Battery Rock and Bethany.

Capt. Taylor remembers that Jonathan Brown died in 1875. His granddaughter was Mrs. Jim Beard and her children, Mrs. John R. Oxford and Mrs. Underwood are residents of the county now. Milt Lewis is a great grandson. Mrs. Jonathan Brown had been a granddaughter of John C. Breckenridge who had been a candidate for president against Abraham Lincoln.

The Hardin County Land Book shows that

Jonathan Brown obtained a deed on Jan. 7, 1836 to land now owned by W.H. Edmundson.

When Capt. Taylor came to this county he was 18 years of age. He was born in Pope county, three miles west of Bethany church. He was the son James P. and Katherine Taylor. He taught at Battery Rock School, Stone Church and then at Elizabethtown.

Then Capt. Taylor went to Bloomington to law school and returned to Hardin County where he began practicing law in 1880. He went back to school in 1882 to complete his work.

Since that time he has been State's Attorney of Hardin County, frequently a member of the Village Board of Elizabethtown, a member of the Elizabethtown School Board, and Master in Chancery of Hardin county.

In 1898, R.F. Taylor was commissioned in the United States Army by Governor Tanner, and took his regiment of volunteers to Cuba in the Spanish American War.

After his return home in Hardin county, Capt. Taylor became a member of the Illinois Legislature.

Capt. Taylor saw them making iron at the Old Furnace, in 1873. He said J.O.D. Lilly from Indiana operated it then and work there continued until 1880, when the Old Furnace closed because iron smelting was done in Birmingham on such a large scale that it didn't pay any longer for Hardin County's mill to operate.

After iron was smelted at the Old Furnace, the bars were brought in cattle-pulled wagons to the river for shipment. Capt. Taylor said the furnace at "Martha" was not running in his time, but there were right smart sized towns at Martha and the Old Furnace when he moved to Hardin county. He said another plant at that time was the Stouglin Lead Mine at Pierre Creek.

Capt. Taylor remembers Lewis Lavander who was first sheriff of Hardin County after it was organized. He said folks were remembering then how Lavander was such a youth that he cried when he thought of the responsibility it would be, when he learned he was elected sheriff of the county. As Taylor remembers they told him the state appointed Mr.Cowsert the first sheriff of the county to serve until the first election.

Capt. Taylor also knew Col. Eschol Sellars the man who built himself a mansion at Sellar's Landing, opposite Caseyville. He was the one that sued Mark Twain for Libel, claiming he was the one Mark Twain alluded to in the "Guilded Age" as Col Eschol. The colonel lost the suit and in later editions the name was changed from Eschol to Colonel Mulberry.

Taylor remembers there was a soldier that fought in the Revolution War, Isaac Hobbs buried on the Job Catt Farm.He said he remembers in 1878 Kit Barnerd published a notice in the county paper asking that neighbors turn out to help clean the grave yard where that soldier of the American Revolution was buried.
HARDIN COUNTY INDEPENDENT, Feb. 16, 1939.

RICHARD FULKERSON TAYLOR

Richard F. Taylor was born in Pope County, Illinois on the home farm on May 5, 1855 and was the third son of James Pinkney Taylor and Catherine (Formault) Taylor. Richard had four brothers, Jonathan, Spencer, Caleb, and William Francis and one sister, Priscilla Indiana. All have passed on to the great beyond except his sister, Mrs. India Flannery, who is a nurse in Cherokee, Iowa.

He received the advantage of the public schools, attended college and became a teacher He acted as superintendent of the grade schools of Elizabethtown and while thus engaged, began the study of law, in 1883 graduating from the law department of Illinois Wesleyan University, His admission to the bar having occurred the previous year. He has since continued in the active general practice of his profession in Southern Illinois and is one of the veteran and honored members of the bar in Hardin County, having served as States Attorney through the period from 1892 to 1996, and then gave his attention to private practice.

In June of 1898, he enlisted for service in the Spanish American War, being commissioned a captain in Company D, Ninth ILL. Volunteer

Infantry. He was in active service in Cuba for months and received his honorable discharge at Augusta, Georgia, after which he resumed the practice of law in Elizabethtown.

In 1914 he was elected representative from the forty-eight District to the state legislature. He is now serving as Master of Chancery. In addition to offices he filled in line of his profession, he has also served on the board of education and as Mayor of Elizabethtown for several terms.

During his term as States Attorney, there were 433 convictions and in one lot there were nine sent to prison. When he left office the county did not owe a dollar.

Captain Taylor is a grandson of Aaron and Mary Lee Taylor, natives of Virginia. Mary was a grand daughter of "Lighthouse Harry" Lee, member of the distinguished Lee Family, which he represented as a gallant soldier and officer of the Revolutionary War. The Captain's father served in the Union Army during Civil War and his religious faith was that of Primitive Baptist.

In 1884, he married to Miss Mollie Ledbetter, a daughter of the late J. Nelson and Rebecca Ledbetter. To this union was born seven children. Rebecca Eunice, a graduate from the Southern Illinois State Normal College at Carbondale, and from the University of Chicago, and for several years had been a successful teacher in the schools of Paducah, Kentucky. Richard Fowler Taylor, also graduated from the University of Carbondale and the Princeton School of Aviation. He was trained in aviation in Texas at Kelly Field and became First Lieutenant in the World War. Following the close of the war, he remained in the service and was advanced to the rank of Major and placed in command of 38th Division in Indianapolis, Indiana. He was killed in a plane crash at Clinton, Indiana on September 9, 1932. Benjamin Herrin Taylor attended school at Deleware, Ohio, and the Missouri Military Academy at Mexico, Missouri. He is now chairman of the Hardin County Democratic Committee and also Investigator for this section for the Sales Tax Department. He resides in Elizabethtown. The other four children, Paul, Mary, Jack and Floyd died while very young.

Captain Taylor lost his wife February 17, 1935 and she was a highly educated lady, accomplished musician and very popular with her acquaintances.
HARDIN COUNTY INDEPENDENT, June 20, 1935.

R.F.TAYLOR

Sixty years ago this month in March 1880, Capt. R.F. Taylor, attorney, aged almost 85, started practicing law in Hardin County in his present office just above the courthouse in Elizabethtown.

Since then he has tried cases before Justice of the Peace Courts, and every other court in Illinois, including the Supreme Court. His first case in 1880 was defending five men charged with murder, accused of shooting from a roadside to kill Brown Ederington, Battery Rock, were cleared.

Since his first case he has defended 200 charged with murder, most of these were in Hardin County, although a few were in Gallatin County. One big case was in Cario, where Capt. Taylor's client, charged with lynching a negro, came clear.

Capt. Taylor said his hardest fight in the county years ago was as one of the defense attorneys representing Logan Belt, when he was charged with the murder of Luke Hambrick. Judge Baker who tried the case, later became Supreme Court Justice in Illinois, One of the attorneys who defended with Capt. Taylor was Mr, Stelle, father of the present Lieutenant Governor of Illinois. It took two weeks for the Belt case to be heard.

Capt. Taylor has not only defended murder cases, when he was State's Attorney of Hardin County, he prosecuted some, He was elected State's Attorney in 1892, and sent nine to the penitentiary at one term of court on murder, assault and rape.

Besides prosecuting or defending in criminal cases, Capt. Taylor took part in civil suits. His largest civil suit involved the ownership of property near the Big Sink which amounted to about $30,000 he said.

When asked about the frequent number of murder cases which seem to have occurred in Hardin County recently, Capt. Taylor said it's nothing like it used to be, that there were always two or three murder trials on the docket in the old days.

Taylor will be 85 years old on May 5. He was born at Grand Pierre, Pope County, the son of James P. and Katherine Furmault He was a graduate of high school in Pope County and taught in that county and in Hardin County for five years to

He first came to Hardin County as principal of the school in Elizabethtown in 1878. From 1879, he taught and attended law school at Illinois Wesleyan at Bloomington intermittently until he obtained his law degree.

In 1880, he started his practice here, and in 1884 he was married to Mollie Ledbetter.

In 1898, he organized Company D, 9th Illinois division here and took his company to Cuba in the Spanish American War.

When he returned, he resumed his practice of law. He was elected to the state legislature in 1914 and served one term there. He has practiced law since then, has been Master of Chancery a number of times, and has that position now.

His office is the one in which he commenced practice 60 years ago, but he has defended and prosecuted cases in three courthouses in Elizabethtown. The courthouse in which he first practiced burned in 1884, the second one burned in 1921, and he continues to represent clients in the one which has stood there since 1926. He represented clients in the Baptist church when court was held there from 1921 to 1926.

Because his Spanish American War veterans' company has an annual meeting in May, Capt. Taylor has invited them to have this year s meeting here with him on his 85th birthday, May

HARDIN COUNTY INDEPENDENT, March 28, 1940

DELILAH ELLEN WALKER TERRELL

Delilah Ellen Walker was born May 2, 1854 in Caldwell County, Kentucky. She was the daughter of James Walker and Mandy Hobbs, a native of Alabama. She was one of a family of seven children. She had two brothers and four sisters. James Walker abandoned the family when Delilah was 12 years of age and the mother was left with a large family to support. She called on the children to help; consequently, Mrs. Terrell's opportunities for receiving an education in school were very meager. She spent her childhood on the farm and took her place in the field, plowing corn, helping with the cultivation of the cotton and tobacco which were important crops in that section.

Another task was the making of maple sugar. She recalls tapping of the trees. Holes were bored and spiles inserted in to conduct the sap to the container in which it dripped. When a sufficient quantity was obtained it was then boiled in large iron kettles over a fire out of doors.

In recalling the customs of those days, she also remembers the parching of coffee. It was purchased green and had to be parched before being used. Mrs. Terrell not only worked in the fields, but assisted with such household duties as young women of those days had to perform, including spinning of cotton and wool into thread and then weaving the cloth and making garments.

On March 1st, 1885, She was married to Joseph E. Terrell, a Civil War veteran. The wedding took place at the home of her mother. Mr. Terrell was a native of Kentucky and his occupation was farming.

In September 1881, the family moved to Cave-in-Rock. Mrs. Terrell remembers many who lived there. Some of the leading stores were the Pelhank store of which the late John Tyer was manager, and the store owned by Mr. Greenleaf. What is now the implement store was owned by

Joseph Mason. Dr. Green and Dr. Hill were the leading physicians. she also recalls Mr. and Mrs. James Ledbetter and sons, Chap and Henry Frayser, Jim Carr and Mitch Pritchard.

After residing for two years in Cave-in-Rock, the family moved out on a farm in what is called the Bend of the River. They remained there for several years, but in 1913 purchased the farm which is still her home.

Mrs. Terrell has four living children. They are Mack Walker (?), Hugh Terrell, and Mrs. Edna Terrell Durham. A daughter, Josephine Terrell died in infancy. Another daughter Mrs. Pink Lewis died in 1921. On August 13, 1929, she was bereaved of her husband who had been an almost helpless invalid for ten years. On November 21, 1934, she lost a son, George Terrell, who was in the service of the army during the World War. She also has twenty-five grandchildren, and seven great grandchildren. Her family are all residents of Hardin County. Her grandson, Clarence Calvert, 18 years of age, lives with her at the old home place, and her daughter-in-law is her almost constant companion.

Mrs. Terrell is a member of the Christian church at Antioch and attends church whenever her health permits. She is industrious and takes great interest in the raising of chickens and geese. She also enjoys the planting and cultivation of cotton, an unusual crop for this country. Last year she raised two 24 pound bags of cotton, picked out the seeds and used it to fill quilts.

Her special hobby is piecing quilts. In her own words she has pieced "enough quilts to fence Hardin County and cover it over." She takes a great interest in finding new and lovely patterns and has one hundred and ten beautiful quilts in her possession. She has made many quilts for others--her handicraft being distributed over various parts of the United States.

For one of her age her health is good. She is happy and cheerful and often comes to town to visit friends.

Delilah Ellen Walker Terrell died on December 8, 1936. Her obituary (HCI Dec.10,

1936) lists children: Mack and Commodore Walker, Hugh Terrell, and Mrs. Edna Terrell.
HARDIN COUNTY INDEPENDENT, Nov. 5, 1938.

REV. JOHN THORNTON

Rev. John Thornton was born in Morgan County, Tennessee, August 11, 1839 and died at his home in Elizabethtown, Illinois June 7, 1911. His family moved to Hardin County when John was two years old.

He was born of poor parentage and grew to manhood as the average poor boy of that early day did without any of the educational and soc- social advantages enjoyed today.

At the age of 20 years, he wooed and won the hand and heart of Miss Mary Ann Ledbetter, and their marriage was consummated on June 2, 1859. To this union were born 10 children, namely: Rebecca, wife of Richard Birch of this place; Doctor E. of Abilene, Texas; Martha, wife of W.D. Aaron of Peters Creek; Sidney, wife of C.W. Patrick of Redland, California; John A., of Cave-in-Rock; Willis C., Deceased; Ida, wife of Clarence Shearer of St. Petersburg, Florida; Phoebe, deceased; Lou, deceased wife of Byrant Mason of Cave-in-Rock; and Henry, of Peters Creek.

John joined the Christian Church and remained a member of that body until 1866, when he united with the General Baptist Church at Rock Creek. He was ordained to the full work of the ministry by the presbytery of the Ohio Association October 11, 1871. He served his church for more that a quarter of a century. He often pastored three churches at a time, Some of them far from his home, often necessitating exposure to inclement weather to reach them.

He was a man of profound reverence, of unfaltering faith in God and implicit trust in His divine promises.
HARDIN COUNTY INDEPENDENT, June 15, 1922.

LAURA TURNER

Laura Erline Ferrell was born August 14, 1879 at Elizabethtown, ILL., the daughter of Joseph Ferrell and Sarah Elizabeth Moore. She was united in marriage to Ira Martin in August 1880, who preceded her in death. To this union three children were born. A son, Julian preceded her in death also.

In 1905, she came to Montana to homestead southeast of Big Sandy. In November 1914, she was married to Charles A. Turner, who preceded her in death. Two daughters were born to this marriage.

For the past several years she has made her home with her daughters, Gladys and Jennie, at Whitefish during the winter months and lived at her home during the summer.

Mrs. Turner was a member of the Big Sandy Methodist Church, the WSCS, and Rebekah Lodge.

Laura Ferrell Turner died in Whitefish, Montana, June 6, 1960. She is survived by three daughters, Fern Martin of Reno, Nevada; Gladys Turner Ferree and Jennie Turner Cowan both of Whitefish; a son, Joe F. Martin of...?

Source: unidentified newspaper clipping, but probably a Whitefish newspaper, dated June 1960.

PAUL TWITCHELL

Paul Twitchell of Paducah, Kentucky, whose ascent of the literary ladder within the past few months has been so extraordinary, is probably the most talked about writer of the younger generation. Just on the other side of the quarter century mark, he is an athletic looking young man who has already achieved success in other fields. But, his novel BROKEN PETALS accepted by a New York publishing house will add a crowning touch to his busy career.

He comes from a long line of English ancestors. His family is one of the oldest in America, widely scattered over the states. His immediate branch of this old pioneer stock settled in Hardin County, Illinois in the year of 1818 and has lived there since, with the exception a few.

Moses Twitchell was one of the first settlers of Hardin County, Illinois, migrating there from Bethel, Maine by the way of Pittsburgh. Moses was a direct descendant of

Benjamin Twitchell who arrived in this country in the year 1630 from England, with a boat load of Puritans, landing at Dorchester Neck, Old Harbor, near Boston, Massachusetts, and took the Freeman's Oath with Reverend Thomas Hooker, a year or so later.

The ancestry of Paul Twitchell can be traced back much further than this to the year of 1085 when Alvered De Inspannic, A Spanish gentleman of adventure, receiving twenty-six districts in which was the district of Turchet from William The Conqueror, for his services in the conquest of England.

In the year of 1461, John Turchet received from Henry V1, the Barony of Audley and was held until 1631, having in the mean time developed the name Turchet to Twitchell.

The long history of the family down to Moses Twitchell is filled with the adventure of a strong family, whose records are found in the annals of many wars such as the War of the Roses, the King Philip Indian War, French and Indian War and the Revolutionary War.

While on this topic, Robert Winch Barrett a member of this family was the first person to be killed in over seas service during the Great War.

And back to Moses Twitchell again who halted his flat boat at McFarland Landing, now known as Elizabethtown, Illinois. There was little thought of the history he was making by carving out a wilderness for civilization. His life was a crowning success; his sons bought more glory on him. Franklin Twitchell, the oldest, was a noted river pilot on the river in his teens when Cave-in-Rock was a famous outlaw hangout for the river pirates. In the spring of 1848 Lafayette, the youngest son, went overland to California, where he dug for gold in the heart of San Francisco. Later, he went to Pike's Peak and returned to organize Company B, 131st(?), Illinois Volunteer Infantry. Brother Franklin was in the 18th Voluntary Cavalry, and, the direct grandsire of Paul Twitchell. The brother's campaign in the Civil War, around Vicksburg, Shiloh, Murfeesboro, against the great Confederate cavalryman Forrest, are legends within the family which outshines those that come down from the early Indian days.

But Paul, the most recent of this old family to gain fame, seems to find things just a wee bit tougher to handle than by shooting Indians and clearing land. He has a bright eye for the future and a quick smile and clears away the task before him with a courage typical of the family name. His recent volume of poetry COINS OF GOLD has pushed him into the limelight.

HARDIN COUNTY INDEPENDENT, Aug. 10, 1939.

MARCELLUS L. TYER

Marcellus Leonidas Tyer, son of the late John and Rufinia Tyer, as born near Cave-in-Rock, Illinois, November 5, 1858 and died July 1, 1923.

His father was one of the early settlers in Hardin County and was a very prominent man in the administrative affairs of the county, having served many years as a member of the Board of County Commissioner.

He was mainly interested, however, in farming, beginning in this vocation in those days when potatoes were the chief agricultural product and New Orleans was the market with the Ohio river flat boat as the link between the market and the farmer.

It was in that school of hard work--that which was attended upon the life of the early farmer when the land had to be cleared and made ready for the plow-- that Marcellus was reared. He being the oldest in the family, was left to share the responsibilities of the farm during those months when the father was on his way to market. Here he learned and had ingrained in him those traits of industry and self-reliance which so characterized his life. He spent a great part of his young manhood in attending and in teaching school. After attending the rural schools, he was further educated in the Normal Schools at Carbondale and at the Illinois Wesleyan University at Bloomington, Illinois. He was very much interested in education and his early thirst for knowledge was never satisfied. On July 26,1885, he married Hannah E. Foster, daughter of the late Horace and Elizabeth Foster. Soon after his marriage, he settled on the farm near where he died and began to devote his attention to farming.

Farming constituted his chief life's work and, with exception of the four years he served as County Judge, he gave his entire time to this business. He was a student of scientific agriculture and used the knowledge thus gained for the solution of his farm problems. He was also an active member of the Farmer's Institute and served several years as president of the County Institute.

Marcellus was a member of the Masonic and Odd Fellows Fraternities. He leaves a widow, eight children, grandchildren, two? brothers, four sisters.
HARDIN COUNTY INDEPENDENT, Aug, 16, 1923.

HENRY VINYARD

Henry Vinyard, son of Philip and Lucinda Vinyard, was born in Hardin County, Illinois, August 27, 1845, and died in Elizabethtown, Illinois, January 10, 1915.

His boyhood was that of the average Hardin County boy of 50 or 60 years ago. At the age of 18 years, he volunteered in the Civil War and enrolled October 9, 1863, in Co. D. 48th. Kentucky Mounted Infantry Volunteers (Captain Hiram J. Belt's Co.) and was discharged December 16, 1964.

On March 3, 1869, he married ----- McFarland, Rev. J.W. Crewdson officiating. To this union 12 children were born: 4 boys and 8 girls. Three girls died in infancy, one at 16, and one boy at 13. Of the boys Philip and William live in Butte City, Montana and Lloyd C. lives in Charlevoix, Michigan. Of the girls, Sidney (now Mrs. W. R. Ledbetter) lives in Hicks, Illinois; Henryetta (now Mrs. J.J. Scheytt) lives in Elizabethtown, Illinois; Clara (now Mrs. Albert Luster) lives in Murphrysboro, Illinois; and Della(now Mrs. Chas. Christensen) lives in Miles City, Montana.

Henry Vinyard was a member of the General Baptist Church for forty years. He was ordained a deacon in the church and afterwards licensed to preach.

His funeral sermon was delivered by Rev. Jerry Rose, a neighbor and life-long friend of the deceased. Henry Vinyard was buried in the Elizabethtown I.O.O.F. Cemetery.
HARDIN COUNTY INDEPENDENT, Jan 1915.

JAMES A. VINYARD

James A. Vinyard was born near Elizabethtown, Hardin County, Illinois, December 8, 1844, died at his home in Springfield, Illinois, October 29, 1917.

James was the son of Rev. John and Eliza Vinyard, pioneers of Hardin County. James grew to manhood on a farm and received his education in the county school near his home. At the age of 22, he was united in marriage with Miss Elizabeth O'Melveny, September 27, 1866, the daughter of George and Harriet O'Melveny, pioneers of Hardin County.

James was for many years a salesman in the dry goods store of C.M. Ferrell and Company, and also with the Emily and William Pleasant Dry Goods Company. He was elected clerk of the Circuit Clerk in 1876 and held that office for two terms.

In July of 1885, James and his family moved to Springfield, Illinois where he was employed as a salesman for the Serberger Brothers Clothing Company until he retired a few years ago.

Surviving are his wife, Elizabeth; daughter, Mrs. Laura? Sprecher; son, John Vinyard; grandson, James H. Sprecher. He also leaves the following sisters and brothers: Mrs. Mary Jennings, East Prairie, Missouri; Mrs. F.M. Fowler, Elizabethtown, Illinois; Mrs. John Hubbard, Karbers Ridge, Illinois; Mrs. D.W. Gustin, Peters Creek, Illinois; W.H. Vinyard, Paducah, Kentucky; Charles Vinyard, Rosiclare, Illinois.
HARDIN COUNTY INDEPENDENT, Nov. 22, 1917.

E. F. WALL Jr.

"If a man puts money in this band, he is entitled to it at all times", stated Mr. E. F. Wall, Jr., cashier of the First State Bank of Elizabethtown, while discussing a recent bank crisis. That statement represents the keystone of Mr. Wall's banking policies as well as it indicates the integrity and straight forwardness of his private and community life.

The dean of Hardin County bankers is a native of this county, son of the late E. F. Wall and Minnie McFarland Wall, was born at Wall's Landing, five miles east of Elizabethtown, which was named for his grandmother, Elizabeth McFarland. His mother died when he was only eight years old, and his stepmother is still living at the old homestead.

Mr. Wall's schooling was received at Cave-in-Rock, Peter's Creek, and Tower Rock, in this vicinity. Later he attended school in Oakland City, returning to Elizabethtown where he taught in Hardin County school for a number of years before entering the banking business.

The story of Mr. Wall's life is the story of the development of banking in Hardin County. For 32 years he has guided the financial welfare of this community, and in all this time he has never missed a director's meeting.

The First State Bank of Elizabethtown, of which he is now cashier, was founded in 1903, only three or four days after the founding of a private bank in Cave-in-Rock. This latter institution, now known at the Hardin County State Bank, was incorporated in 1911. Mr. Wall was also instrumental in the founding of the Rosiclare State Bank, which was opened as a private bank in 1910 and incorporated in 1919.

In the past 32 years, the banking business throughout the country has experienced many depressions and perilous times. Yet, under the leadership of Mr. Wall, the three Hardin County banks have never been in jeopardy at any time. When other and larger and more powerful banks were forced to close their doors, these three banks paid currency. Even in 1933 the doors of the First State Bank were open for several days after the declaration of the nation-wide bank moratorium, and the bank was closed for only three weeks in all, proof enough of the sound policies and principals upon which these banks were operating. When asked how such a record was achieved, Mr. Wall smiled and said, "If a man knows he can't get something, he immediately wants it. If he knows he can get it, it doesn't matter." By showing the depositors that their money was available upon call, an exchange of faith was established and the solidity of the bank assured.

"Our time deposits are higher now than at any time in the history of the bank." was Mr. Wall's encouraging answer to an inquiry about the present financial situation in Hardin County.

Aside from active work as a Mason, and membership in the I.O.O.F., Mr. Wall is also on the board of the M.E. Church, although he is not a member of this organization for he carries his religion in his wife's name.
Ellen Carr, HARDIN COUNTY INDEPENDENT, Sept. 19, 1935.

DR. W. N. WARFORD

Dr. W.N. Warford was born September 5, 1822 in Woodford, County Kentucky and died in Elizabethtown, May 2, 1905 at the advanced age of nearly 83 years.

He was married to Mary J. Shearer, February 8 ?, 1846, who died August 11, 1883 ?. To this union 7 children were born, they are in order of birth: Annie who was the mother of J.W. Henry and Willie White of Elizabethtown and Mrs. Dr. J.R. Gregory, of Cave-in-Rock; Mary C., Martha J., Sarah, William I., John D., and Charles E. (the latter died July 5, 1871). Annie died July 12, 1901.

W. N. Warford was remarried to Martha J. Douglas, February 13, 1887. She died April 1, 1903. After the death of his second wife, he made his home with his son, William P. Warford of Elizabethtown.

Dr. Warford came to Illinois in 1842 ? and engaged in the mercantile business until about the close of the Rebellion when he moved to Indiana. Returning to Hardin County in 1867 or 1868, he settled at Sparks Hill where he remained until 1883, then moving to Elizabethtown where he has since resided.

His success as a merchant was supplemented by an income from the practice of medicine which he began in the antebellum days and ended about a year ago as a member of the Board of Pension Examiners.

Dr. Warford was buried in the Elizabethtown Cemetery next to his first wife.
INDEPENDENT June 15, 1905

WILLIAM P. WARFORD
William P. Warford was born in 1860, the son of William N. Warford.

In 1883, he moved to Elizabethtown when his father bought the general store from C. M. Ferrell. W.P. Warford and John Shell operated it as Shell and Warford, but later Warford bought Shell's interest. He operated the store until 1913, when he sold it to John W. Henry, now circuit clerk.

Mr. Warford has not been active in business in Elizabethtown since then, but owned the property in the block from the corner where the store is located to the ally as well as his own home.

In 1890, Mr. Warford opened the first bank in the county, his private bank in his store which he began managing in 1883. He operated this bank until forty years ago, when it was sold to the present First State Bank of Elizabethtown. Mr. Warford was vice president of the new bank and director for many years.

He married Maggie Price, daughter of Tom Price, on November 26, 1885. She died on March 20, 1934. This marriage produced David, who is vice president of The First State Bank; Mrs. Muriel Duley of Adairville, Kentucky; and Mrs. H.K. Pritchard of Fort Wayne, Indiana.
HARDIN COUNTY INDEPENDENT, July 23, 1943

PHOEBE IRENE WATKINS
Phoebe Irene Watkins was born January 1,

1848, near Herod in Hardin County, but near the Pope county line. Her father was Daniel S. Watkins who was born near Louisville, Kentucky. Her grandfather's home was in a fort which was built as a protection for the white settlers against the raids of the Indians. Two older brothers of her father were killed by Indians when fourteen or fifteen years of age. After this the grandfather brought the remainder of his family down the Ohio River and established a new home in Hardin County, Illinois. Mrs. Oldham's mother, who before her marriage was Susan Watson, was born and raised in Saline county, Illinois.

Mrs. Oldham was the third child in the family, having four brothers and four sisters. Beside herself there is only one other member of the family living. This is her brother, D. W. Watkins, whose home is in Chicago, and who has been superintendent of the Carbolic Acid Gas Company Plant there for the past five years.

When she was only three years of age, her parents moved to Elizabethtown and there her girlhood was spent. In October 1867, at the age of nineteen, she married there Henry Hoewischer, a Civil War Veteran. After their marriage, they lived in Cairo, Illinois for two years. From there they moved to Golconda, where they resided for a time before returning to Elizabethtown.

To this union was born three children. They were Harry, who is foreman of a cotton-mill in Tiptonville, Tennessee; Philip, who is in the government employ at Owensboro, Kentucky and a daughter, who died at the age of five years.

Mr. Hoewischer died in December 1874, leaving the subject with three small children. After his death the little daughter, Maude, died from the effects of burns which she received when the home of the family was burned.

On October 10th, 1878, Mrs. Hoewischer married Thomas Oldham, also a Civil War veteran. They made their home at Elizabethtown but later, moved to a nearby farm. In 1904 they moved to Wayne City, Illinois where they resided until Mr. Oldham's death in 1911. To this union was born one son, C. Fleetwood Oldham. As his home was also in Wayne City, the mother made her home with him and his family. They remained in Wayne City until 1914 when the family returned to their native county and made their home on the farm a short distance east of Cave-in-Rock where they now live.

There are ten grandchildren and fourteen great grandchildren of the Hoewischer family, whose homes are in various places in Illinois, Kentucky, Tennessee and Ohio.

The only grandchild of the Oldham family is Mrs. Ted Frayser who with her husband and their little son, Jimmie, also make their home on the farm with the grandmother, and parents.

In her youth Mrs. Oldham united with the General Baptist Church at Mt. Zion in this county. Later she joined the Methodist Church in Wayne City and remained a member until 1934. When she returned to Hardin county, she then affiliated with the Christian church. Mrs. Oldham as also active in the Rebecca Lodge and held offices in that organization.

Mrs. Oldham possesses an excellent memory. The family records were lost in the fire which destroyed her home some years ago. All the data for this sketch was furnished by her from memory. Her health has been good, and she has not gone to a physician for twenty years except once when a cow stepped on her foot, crushing the bones of the foot and ankle. On account of this accident she has not been so active of late years. Her sight and hearing are impaired, but she is still able to do many things.
HARDIN COUNTY INDEPENDENT, Jan 1935.

CHARLES WILLIAM WESTON
Charles W. Weston was born in Kent County east of London, England, April 11, 1844, and died at Dorrisville, Illinois, November 3, 1925. He came to America with his parents, Henry and Sarah Weston and a younger brother, Thomas. The mother died, survived by a husband and two small sons, Charles and Thomas.

The father enlisted in the Mexican War, leaving his two sons in guardianship and care of a man named Sharp in Hamilton county, Illinois. The father was in General Taylor's division and was killed in battle. Sharp learning of the father's death betrayed his trust by appropriating to himself the means of his wards (which were ample), thus leaving the boys penniless.

Frederick Weston, an uncle of the boys, learning of their situation from a passing traveler, drove to Hamilton County in a buggy and kidnapped Thomas and made arrangement with Charles to follow at night, which he did. He met them in Raleigh, Illinois.

They were followed by Sharp who tried to force them to return, and after some sharp caviling was driven away by the boys'uncle. The boys lived with their uncle several years and were treated kindly and charitably by him and his good wife.

Charles William Weston enlisted in the Civil War at the age 17 years, and was honorably discharged.

At the age of 26 he was married to Miss Margaret Jane Ross who departed this life, July 13, 1902. Seven children blessed this union: Mrs. Lilly Slye, Mrs. Sarah Twitchell, Charles F. Weston, Daisy Leonberger, Mrs. Ella Ashford, and Katherine Weston, also a boy who died at five years.

Charles Weston united with the Bethany Church of General Baptist as a charter member and served as a deacon for 40 years. He loved his church, his Masonic lodge, and was a faithful attendant at both. He loved his country and her flag, and was a regular attendant at patriotic meetings in honor of his country. He also loved music, books, flowers and truth.

Charles William Weston died November 3, 1925 and was buried in the Odd Fellows Cemetery in Elizabethtown, Illinois. This grand old soldier, Christian, and fraternal friend of many, found a last resting place.
HARDIN COUNTY INDEPENDENT, Dec ? 1925.

HARRY WHITEHEAD

Harry Whitehead was born on a plantation in

Old Virginia, Culpepper County, on May 29, 1840, and he will be ninety-five years old on next May of that date. His father, a slave, was Harry Brown, and his mother, also a slave, was Rebecca Whitehead.

He is one of a family of eleven children, all of whom lived to maturity and are as follows: Lou George, Lemon, Phil, Orange and Tildie. The other five were sold as slaves before his memory. After being a slave for twenty years, under a slave master by the name of James Whitehead, he ran away and joined the Union army at Chattanooga, Tenn., serving for two years and ten months.

At this time he was captured and held a prisoner in the Confederate prison for eight months, being captured by Hood's army at Dalton, Georgia, and he was kept busy during this time by being forced to dig pits for men to fight in and also trenches around the cities of Columbia and Macon of that state.

He served in the Union Army under Captain Elliot of Posey County, Indiana. He was given an honorable discharge and mustered out of the service in Nashville, Tenn., in 1865.

After being released from the army he went to Mississippi where he remained for six months with a Mr. Cullins. From there he went to Livingston County, Kentucky and worked for a white man by the name of Pheneas Barnett for about two years.

After leaving Kentucky he came to Elizabethtown in 1868, where in 1869 he was united in marriage to Miss Mella Austin, daughter of Edmund and Nancy Austin. To this union were born eleven children, namely George, Henry, Orange, Edd, James, Jessie, Mrs. Lula Duncan, Mrs. Nannie Bibbs and Miss Gola, the others dying in infancy. Of these only three are now living, James and Lemon of Elizabethtown and Edd of Mt. Vernon.

They were married in Elizabethtown at the old James Kirkham place, known now as the Elisha Robinson farm, by the late James Hawkins, and the marriage license was issued by the late James McFarlan, then the county clerk, and the late Clay Williams was one of the witnesses to the marriage That evening a big wedding supper was served to them by Mr. and Mrs. Austin, a turkey supper it was, and the following county officials were in attendance: Ben Renfro, then circuit clerk, James McFarlan, then county clerk and Wes Ralph, at that time sheriff. This couple lived together for twenty-six years. They began their married life as farmers on the Kirkham farm, later moving in Huffman Alley.

After the death of his first wife, "Uncle" Harry remained single for fifteen years, then he married Mrs. Anna Johnson in 1907. This marriage took place in the A.M.E. colored church at Elizabethtown and was performed by Rev. Bill Barnett. It was a church wedding to which all were invited and welcomed.

"Uncle" Harry and "Aunt" Anna have always lived in the house where they now reside in the north west end of town, just behind the church of which they were both members. "Uncle" Harry lives comfortably, as he is on the civil war pension list, drawing a nice amount each month. In their home they have electric lights and a nice radio and other conveniences, as well as a 1934 automobile which he has driven for him by his nephew, Tannie Whitehead, and they often drive to Harrisburg and other points.

He makes the rounds up town each day to see his friends, considering his age, he is quite a spry old gentleman and liked by all who know him.

His present wife, Anna, was born about 1853, at Benton, Missouri and her maiden name was Ravenscroft. She was about 4 years old when President James Buchanan was elected to office. She remembers the campaign song that goes something like this, "All around the Omnibus, the monkey chased the weasel, that is the way the money goes, Pop goes the weasel." Her slave master, Wright White, was of the Allen Estate and he left Anna with Emma and Mary White, her Mistresses, he going with a party by the name of Dock Mars to the south on a flat boat, thinking his slaves would be freed.

At the time of President Lincoln's term of office in 1861, she went to live with Elsie Barnes, a white lady living on Barnes' Ridge in Missouri, to care for her baby. Barnes' slaves had gone and

Mrs. Barnes had lots of work to do, cording and spinning the all kinds of a farm wife's duties. She remained with her until she was about fourteen years of age. She worked for a short period of time in Metropolis, Illinois and then moved to Crittenden County Kentucky where she kept house for various families.

In December the same year, Anna was married to Dane Johnson in Crittenden County, Kentucky, being married by a Baptist minister by the name of Lark Grisham, in the home of Mrs. Adeline Buckham. They started their married life on the farm of Bob Cofields' and lived there some nine years, then moved to Henry Cook's farm in Kentucky and remained there for about three years. Coming to Elizabethtown, Illinois, in the fall of 1881 and bought the home where she now lives, from the late James McFarlan, paying $125 for the lot alone. This union was blessed with nine children, namely, William, Nora, Willard, Johnnie, Louis, Ellis, Rogers, Bush and Tom. Two of the nine are now living, Roger in Rockwood, Me., and Willard in Anderson, Ind. "Aunt" Anna is a faithful reader of the Bible and stays very close to her home. She is now eighty-two years of age but does not know what month and day she was born.
HARDIN COUNTY INDEPENDENT 24 Jan 1935

HENRY M. WINDERS
    Henry M. Winders was born in the eastern part of Hardin County, Illinois, on April 14, 1848, and died at his home in Elizabethtown, Illinois on March 28, 1915.

In his boyhood the educational advantages of today were unknown, but he qualified himself and won a second grade certificate and began teaching school. Later, he obtained a first grade certificate and soon ranked among the foremost teachers and educators of the county.

At the age 18, he enlisted in Co. D. 48 Kentucky Mounted Infantry Volunteers and served 16 months in the Civil War.

He was first married to Mary J. Coltrin, nee Dunn from whom he was divorced in 1875. On November 12, 1876, he married Mrs. Mary F. Irons, who with her daughters Mrs. Mary Belle

Price and Mrs. Dora Weaver survive him. The second marriage proved more congenial and they lived 9 years in Battery Rock, near Lamb and then moved to Elizabethtown where they lived for nearly 20 years.

Henry Winders studied the law and begin to practice law before the Justice of the Peace and later was admitted to the bar and practiced in all the courts.

Henry served as Deputy Assessor, Deputy Sheriff, and County Clerk. He was also elected as County Surveyor. Last fall he was elected as County Judge. Judge Winder's bearing was that of an intelligent man, not obtrusive but positive in his convictions. He had the courage of his convictions, a man of strong character.
HARDIN COUNTY INDEPENDENT, April 8, 1915.

ALBERT TAYLOR WINN

Mr. Winn was born October 22, 1854, and therefore passed his 80th birthday almost four months ago, at which time a happy family reunion was held. He was the son of the late William Wayland Winn, who was a native of the state of Virginia and the late Nancy Gibbons Winn, who was born near Rising Sun, Indiana.

Soon after his parents were married they left Indiana and came to Hardin county, Illinois, where they established their home on a farm near where Potter's Memorial church now stands about four miles northeast of Cave-in-Rock. There they lived the remainder of their lives on what is now called the "Uncle Billie Winn" place.

Taylor Winn, the subject of this narrative was the second of seven children, he having had three brothers and three sisters. Of all the family, he and one sister, Mrs. Mary Kaegi, of Cave-in-Rock, are the only ones remaining. Probably many of our readers will remember the tragic death of one brother and his wife, Mr. and Mrs. Perry Winn, which occurred October 11, 1926. They were living in Dell, Arkansas, when a cyclone which struck the town that night, completely demolished their home and killed them. They were found lying dead in a neighbor's yard, probably having been struck by falling timbers.

Mr. Winn lived on the farm with his parents until he was about twenty-five years of age, attending school first at what was called Tyer school near the Dewey Green home, later at the Round Top school and finally at the Martin school.

About the time that William and Nancy Winn were married at Rising Sun and left Indiana for Illinois, another young couple, the late Thomas and Sallie Douglas, friends of theirs were also married there. Not long after the Winn's came to Hardin county, the Douglas's also came and located on a farm near the one belonging to the former family. The two couples being from the same place, and undergoing the difficulties of adjusting themselves in a new and untried country, became very closely bound together by the ties of friendship.

Later when the son of Mr. and Mrs. Winn became a young man it was only natural that a courtship should develop between him and the young daughter of Mr. and Mrs. Douglas. This courtship culminated in the marriage of Albert Winn and Sonora "Belle" Douglas on March 26, 1878.

As the father of the bride was then badly crippled from rheumatism, the young couple remained on the farm now known as the "Uncle Tommie Douglas" place for the first few years of their married life.

Later, in 1881, they purchased forty acres of uncleared land at the place where they now live near Cave-in-Rock, and bravely commenced to make a home for themselves and their family. By means of industry and thrift, they succeeded in overcoming the hardships of pioneer life and later added more land to the original forty acres. Mr. Winn, during his early manhood raised much wheat, a crop almost unknown to Hardin county now. He also raised corn, potatoes, cattle and hogs for the market. These things were shipped on the boats which used to ply the river in those days.

Four children came to bless this union,

Mrs. Sadie McDowell, whose home is near Lamb, on route two from Cave-in-Rock, Will Winn, of Weston, Kentucky, Mrs. Nan S. Barger of Cave-in-Rock, and Mrs. Nona Matheney of Shelterville When the children were growing up, the home was a center for the young people of the community for the parents and children were a jolly group and others were welcomed to their family circle.

As the children grew to maturity and married, the family increased, there now being thirteen grand-children, Mrs. Barger having six children, Mrs.McDowell, four, and Will Winn, three. There are also four great grand-children, Willard and Olan Rutherford, sons of Mr. and Mrs. W. E. Rutherford, and Beulah Marguerite and Patty Jo Green, little daughters of Mr. and Mrs, Dewey Green. All are highly respected citizens in the communities in which they live.

Mr. Winn has had one interest from which he has derived much pleasure. He has always had a great love for hunting. In his early days wild deer and turkey were plentiful and he brought in much such game, using a rifle which was made by his grandfather Winn who was a gunsmith. This highly prized rifle is now in the possession of his only son, Will Winn, of Weston, Ky. He won a record for being the best long range rifle shot in Hardin county many years ago when old time shooting matches were held, and kept it until only a few years ago when his eyesight began to fail.

He used to fish a great deal, and enjoyed many hours of fishing at the Frailey lakes, accompanied by his friend, Joe Will Hughes, of Kentucky.

Mr. Winn has always been a man of high ideals, ready to give of his means, and willing to lend his support to all good causes. He has been a man of good habits, a kind hearted neighbor, and a citizen who has stood for law and order.

He and his faithful companion still live at the place which has been their home for fifty-four years, and while they are both physically handicapped in many ways, they are cheerful and

contented and it is a real pleasure to be counted as one among their many friends. The kindly welcome which is always extended at their home enables one to understand why it was a meeting place for their friends in the days that are past.
HARDIN COUNTY INDEPENDENT, 21 Feb 1935

WILLIAM WINTERS

A stranger, for the first time, seeing "Uncle" Billy Winters walking briskly up the street of Cave-in-Rock on a busy Saturday would never think his being within a few months of his four score and ten. But if he lives until the 29th day of this coming October, he will have passed his 90th milestone, for 1845 was the year of his birth.

"Uncle" Billy who is one the few remaining Civil War veterans in Hardin County was born in Ripley County, Indiana. His father who was the late John Winters was also a native of Indiana, but his mother who was the late Margaret Rex Winters was born in Germany. She came to the state of Indiana when she was twelve years of age.

William Winters was one of a family of eight children, he having had four brothers and three sisters. Of the five sons of John and Margaret Winters, John, Dan, George, Owen and William, only William survives. One of his sisters, Carolyn Winters, died at the age of twelve. The others Mrs. Catherine Rucker, whose home was in Kentucky, and Mrs. Mahala Jane Bruner, who was a resident of Hardin County, have passed away more recently.

When the subject of this narrative was a lad of seven years, the family moved to Boone County, Kentucky where they remained for four years. They then crossed the river to Illinois and established a home at Sparks Hill in Hardin County.

When the Civil War commenced, he was a boy of only sixteen, but he went to Elizabethtown and enlisted with the other recruits from this county. He belonged to Co. C. 48th Illinois Regiment Infantry. He was with General Sherman being a member of the 15th Corps from the beginning of the war to its close.

He saw two years and seven months of actual service because on three different times when disabled on account of severe wounds, he was compelled to accept leave of absence and remain under treatment for several months.

When he first enlisted, he was sent to Scottsboro, Alabama. He was first wounded at East Point, Georgia where he received a shot under his right arm. The ball passed through his right lung and lodged under his left shoulder blade where it still lies. At that time he had three month's furlough and came back to Elizabethtown where he was treated by Dr. Wall whom possibly other old citizens may remember. when he was recovered, he returned to his company and was under General Sherman, making the famous "March to the Sea" in 1864. While on this march, he was wounded a second time. On this occasion he was wearing a breast plate which had on it a brass eagle. The ball went through the plate and struck his breast bone.

"Uncle" Billy was also one of the boys who was with General Sherman at the Battle of Kenshaw Mountain in July 1864, which was one of the bloodiest battles of the war. He remembers very distinctly the battle of Ft. McAllister, Georgia, which occurred on December 13, 1864. This battle lasted for five hours and so much blood was shed that it ran in streams over the ground. He received a third injury which was a flesh wound in his left hip.

He was with Sherman at the capture of Richmond, Virginia and witnessed the surrender of General Lee in April 1865.

When the war was over and the great host of Union soldiers marched for two days through Washington, D.C. in a grand parade wearing(?) their torn and blood stained banners, "Uncle" Billy was with them.

From Springfield Illinois where he was "mustered out", in 1865, he returned to his home of his parents at what is known as Sparks Hill. But he soon established a home of his own, for later in that same year he and Miss Susan Delph

Ozee were united in marriage at Harris Creek near Sparks Hill. The young couple first went to Lamb Town where they began their life together on a farm. After a short time, however, they left the farm and went to the river where they made their home on a family boat, a short distance above Cave-in- Rock. Mr. Winters made a living by fishing. At the end of two years, they moved to a farm about six miles from Junction in Gallatin, county.

They remained there for six years and then returned to Hardin county and established themselves on a farm about ten miles north of Cave-in-Rock. At this place they remained and raised their family.

To this union eleven children were born, six of whom are living. The remaining sons are Robert and James Winters of Hardin County, and Ernest of Gallatin County. The daughters are Mrs. Myrtle Patton, of Gallatin County, and Mrs. Della Oxford and Mrs. Annabel Pennell of Hardin County. There are also fifty grand children and sixty eight great grandchildren, many of whom are residing in this county.

"Uncle" Billy makes his home with his oldest daughter and her husband, Joshua Pennell, on their farm near Sparks Hill. He is not strong enough to engage in the heavy work on the farm, however.

He has been a member of the General Baptist church of the neighborhood for many years. He greatly enjoys the company of his friends and they are pleasantly entertained by listening to the great number of stories of the past with which his memory is so richly stored. HARDIN COUNTY INDEPENDENT, May 23, 1935.

William Winters died May 14, 1942, Hardin county's last veteran of the Civil War. (HCI, May 21, 1942)

DR. JAMES A. WOMACK

Dr. James A. Womack, 48 years old, was born and raised on a farm in Hardin County, Illinois. He received his early education in his home school where he received education sufficient to teach. He taught several terms of school, attending college between terms at Enfield in White County, and at Carbondale.

In 1884 he graduated with high honors from the Medical University at Nashville, Tennessee and later took a post graduate course at in the Rush Medical at Chicago.

Since 1884, he has been active in the practice of medicine. He has also been interested in farming and stock raising.

Besides taking a course in medical jurisprudence, Dr. Womack has been a close student of statutory law, having acquired a thorough knowledge of its foundation.

Dr. Womack has been a life-long Democrat and has been an active worker in politics for 30 years. For the past nine years he has been chairman of the Democratic Central Committee of Hardin County. He is now a candidate for State Senator from the 48 District.
INDEPENDENT, July 30, & August 6, 1908.

AARON, Dick 40, Glady 93, Gradie 40, James 40, Martha 17, 288, Rebecca 70, 136, W.D. 17, 136, 40,
ABBOT, Mary 127
ABNER, Wm. 9
ABNEY, Anna 109, 204
ADAMS Allen 35, Anna 112, Belva 42, Ben 49, C.D. 156 Fannie 35, Florence 49, Gladys 108, Hester 42,35, James 40, 42, Jimmie 181, Marie 72
ADKINS, Mary 103
AIMES, Ella 110, 139
AINSWORTH, Josie 110
ALDRIDGE, Minnie 76, Sherman 78
ALEXANDER, Olive 115,245
ALLEN, Mary 99, Anice,120
AMSDEN, Maude 62
ANDERSON, A.F. 69, 64 Everett 88, J.M. 8, Joseph 65, L.B. 2, Melissa 25, Rufus 1 Zodie 84
ANDREW, B.J. 29
ANGELTON, Ida 61, 98 Julie 100, Marsh 8, Millard 14, Nancy 14, Thomas 14
ARBEL, Mary 85
ARMSTRONG, --- 160
ARMSWORTH, Josie 139
ARTUR, Jas. 4
ASBEL, Charles 68, David 133, Viola 134, Asbell, David 133
ASHFORD, Anne 97, Arlie 95, Bertha 95, Carrol 95 Clifford 82, Della 133, Ella 299, 28, Emma 56, Frank 95
ASHFORD, Harry 95, Hazel, 120, John 95, Julie 95 Katie 97, Laura 5, Lon 95, Louis 95, Mary 66, Mollie 97 Nancy 20, Odie 97, Russell 95 Susan 20, Wesly 20, Will 95 William 82
AUD, Nigel 60
AUSTELL, Bertha 125, Enos 125
AUSTIN, Alice 210, Daniel 30, Earl 73, 146,210, Edmond 108, 300, Finney 120, Henry 108, Luther 108, Mabel 124, Mary 206, Mella 108, 120, 300, Nancy 108, 300, Nora 105, Roy 108, Tommie 108
AYERS, Adeline 96, Doe 147, W.N. 96
BADGER, Lula 24
BAIN, Lennie 137, Zora 31
BAKER, 14, 108, 131, 140, 253, Charles 12, Frances 108, 131, 140, Lucy 108, 140, Mary 108, 140, Morgan 108, 140, Nellie 109, Sarah 108, 131, 140
BALDWIN, A.M. 210, Arza 131, C.G. 66, C.S. 96, Chester 9, Dewey, 67, 131, Edith 131, Edward 77, Elizabeth 86, Elmer 131, Elmira 86, George, 95, 131, John 96, Martha 77, Tula 73, Vern 67, Gertrude 131, Hattie, 131, Ida 131, Jackie 280, John, 89

BALDWIN, 96, Sarah 131, Tula 210
BALL, Anna 45, Annie 78,
BALL, Bertus 78, Claude 16, Donald 78, Elsie 78, Myrtle 78, Nora 50, Olive 71, Olive 16, Orvil 78, Raymond 24, Ruea 78, Sarah 78, W.M. 78, 24, Walter 78, William 45
BALLINGER, Edith 66
BANKS, Alice 105, America 84, Arvetta 87, Bertha 128, Clyde 128, Dan 58, Daniel 128, Deb 42, Dorthea 105, Earl 42, 37, Edith 105, Edward 128 Effie 128, Elijah 42, Elizabeth 3, 53, Eller 42, Everett 105, Ezra 128, Georgia 105, Gertrude 42, 105, Gladys 87, 90, Goldie 90, Gussie 90, Hattie 42, Hattie 82, Henry 87 90, Ida 42, Irene 87, 90, J.M. 84, James 105, Jean 105, John 128, Joseph 105, Laura 42, Lloyd 42, Louisa 84, Lucie 105, Mae 105, Margaret 58, Martha 50, Nancy 128, Nellie 105, 128, Nettie 35, Otis 128, 42, Ollie, 42, 197, Opal 105, William 105, 128.
BARGER, Josephine 19, Esther 62, Roena 74, Nonette 104, Nan 110, 305, Earl 104, Bernard 104
BARKER, May 101, Minnie 101, Mose100, Riley 158
BARKMAN H.H. 5
BARLEY, Sam 159

BARNARD, Alda 110, Allan 110, 233, Bill 43, C.W. 26, 43, 141, Daisy 110, 148, Dock 110, 223, Henry 60, J.A. 94, 142, Jerry 31, John 95, 110, 233, kit 282, Lurinda 110, Mallie 110, Mary 151, Mollie 110, 111, Spence 110, Walter 110
BARNES, Charles 113, Dave 138, Emanuel 113, , Henry 18, 42, 138, Jesse 113, Mariah 113 Mary 259, Missouri 18,19, Ollie 113, Ora 113, Wyoma 113
BARNETT, Bill 300, Daisy 1633, Henry 1
BARTON, Elizabeth 123, Nancy 224, Pearl 122
BASCOM, Ben 89, 143, Bessie 114, 138, Daisy 114, 115, 138, Gais 115, 138, Gals 142, Georgiana 67, Grover 114, 115, 138, 144, Henry 112, 114, 138, Josie 138, Nola 114, 115, 144, R.T. 91, Sarah 115, 138, 142, William 114, 115, 138, 142
BASS, Dora 116
BASSETT, Elizabeth 4
BATEMAN, Lonnie 100, Ron 127
BATH, Carolyn 86, Henry 22, 39, 86
BAUR, Arma 129, Jack 129,
BAUR, Oscar 129
BAUGHER, Elizabeth 127 Estelle 53, Fred 127, George

BAUGHER 53, Gilbert 96, Glen 53, Horrell 53, J.H. 53, Jack 96, James 127, Jeff 127, John 127, Lee 53, Lizzie 127, Lucas ? 127, Margaret 127, Martha 127, Mary 95, Minnie 127, Ollie 53, Sam 96, Samuel 127, Thomas 127, Tom 96, William 95, 127
BAYLOU (S) Bernie 53, E.J., 53, Everett 53, J.E. 43 Mintie 53, Ula 43, Willie 53
BAYNE, John 3, 6
BEARD, Augusta? 94, Belle 94, Fannie 51, Henretta 51, 94, James 19, 51, 94, Jim 280, Mamie 19, 46, Mathew 19, Nancy 50, Viola 100, William 50
BEAVERS, Charles 55, Clara 127, Cora 25, 83, James 105, Joe 159, Pete 105, Harriet 35, 111, Helen 106, 245, J.H. 9, Joe 105, John 105, Mattie 105, Ross 111, Walter 105, 111
BEBOUT, Cora 129, Enoch 20, Lora 106
BEDFORD, Ellen 88, J.L. 88 Loren 61, 88, Sarah 130
BELFORE, Jonathan 7
BELL, Anna 104, Charles 91 David 131, Druad 91, Ernest 91, 131 George 91, 131, Hester 40, Issac 91, 131, J.H. 131, James 91, Joe 91, 131, **BELL**, John 131, July 131, Junie 91, 131, Lou 62,
Malissa 190, Maude, 191 131, Orval 91
BELOW, Anna 37
BELT, Albert 90, Allen 96, Bonnie 92, Brownie 90, Burnett 73, C.M. 55, Charles 99, Charlie 90, Chester 90, Clara 117, Clayborn 50, Dallas 90, Dal 55, Dewey 92, Dick 43 Esther 92, Ethel 21, Floyd 92, Frances 99, Gracie 90, Grant 50, H.J. 2, 148, H.L.31, Harriet 114, 208, Helen 90, Hinton 20, Hiram 8, 50, 157, 292, Howard 90, Ida 117, Inez 99, Joel 114, 115, 144, John 31, Jonas 231, Jonathan 4, 55, 114, Josie 114, 115, 138, 144, Laura 34, Lillie 38, 96, Lloyd 92, Logan 8, 34, 284, Lucy 96, M.M. 99, Mabel 31, Maggie 92, Mariah 50, Marion 20, Mary 4, 8, 90, 114, Mila 92, Milas 90, Minerva 17, Minnie 40, 90, 99, Morgan 90, Nancy 109, 147, Noah 96, Non 38, Palmer 96, Porter 96, Robert 73, 90, Rosa 73, Roy 92, Ruby 92, Sarah 114, 144, 115, Theoderic 41, Thomas, 8 20, 117, 73, Viola 96, Virginia 38, 90, W.J. 21, Walter 41, Wendell 90, Willis 117
BELTZ, Ruby 92
BENGALL, Virgie 114
BENNETT, Cora 83, Mag 75
BENTLY, Lucy 115, 245, Samuel 30

BENUM, Richard 11
BERNARD, Allen 74, Austin 16, 130, Daisey 135, Maxie 16 Mollie 125, Spence 233, T.S. 42
BERRY, Katherine 47, L.R. 47
BERTZIN, Laura 42
BERWICK, Nora 97
BETTS, Barbara 73
BIBBS, Nannie 300
BINKLEY, Dr. 160
BINUM, Richard, 218
BIRCH, Al 110, 147, Alex 136, Alice 93, 109, 135, 148, Allie 42, 48, Anna 55, 116, Arthur 42, 55, 116, 136,145 Ben 23, 89, 109, 110, 147, 135, Cora, 109, 148, Daisy 135, 148, Deneen 128, Dewey 110, 135, 148, Dolly 136, Elizabeth 89, 109, 147, Eva 110, 135, 148, George 110, 120, 147, Gladys 120, Harry 55, Harmetta 135, Hyremetty 109, India 78, 113, Jane 89, Jennette 113, John 89, 110, 147, Laura 110, 147, Lula 109, 135? 148, 135, Marion 113, Martha 110, 147, Mattie, 52, , Maude 136, Mollie 71, 89, Ollie 22, Oscar 42, 116, 136, Polly 12, Rebecca 17, 52, 89, 136, 288 , Richard 17, 22, 35, 52, 89 110, 136, 147, 288, Roy 42, 116, 136, Ruby 55, T.A. 41, 145, Thomas 23, 41, Tressie 55, Viola 23, W.H. 69,

BIRCH, W.H. 110, 113, 135, 148, William 109, 113, 135, 147,
BISHOP, Gertie 26, John 51, Martha 74, Ruby 51
BIZZLE, V.A. 137
BLACK, Almedia 125, Emma 60, Isaac 75, James 75, Jonah 75, Leullar 75, Martha 75, Richard 30, Samuel 23, 75, William 75
BLAGG, John 52
BLAIN, George 33
BLAIR, Ella 236, Elva 109, Hepsie 55, Lutitia 41, Sarah 41, Thomas 41
BLAIS, Ella 122
BLAKLEY, Hattie 37, Lizzie 29, Lydia 100, W.T. 29, 37
BLANCHARD, Anna 24, David 24
BLEE, John 143, 218
BLISS, Maria 29
BLOOMER, Charles 18, 75, Lillie 75, Nancy 75
BOATEN, Minnie 96
BOATRIGHT, Allen 116, Anna 116, Charles 116, Fred 116, Hattie 116, John 115, Lenard 116, Louis, 116 Mack 116, Ray 116
BONEFIELD, T.J. 81
BOOTH, Frances 25
BOTTEN, Mabel 94, Milas 94
BOULDEN, Katie 134, Loyd 133
BOWERS, William 56
BOYD, Alonzo 81, Bessie 17

BOYD, Betty 2, Dow 81, 117, Earl 81, Effie 117, Frank 81, George 228, Harold 81, Katherine 157, Lowell 129, Nancy 117, Nell 114, Nellie 132, Nora 81, Otto 11, Pewton 29, Sarah 81
BRADLEY, Volley 254
BRAMBLET, J.M. 21, Nettie 21, Sadie 69
BRANN,---- 4
BRANNON, Earl 87
BRANTLY, Bessie 38, Jimmy 38, Mary 38, Paul 38, Syble 38
BRAUGHARD, Ida 277, Jerimiah 277, Lucy 277
BRAZELL, Charley 89, Rosetta 89
BRECKENRIDGE, John 280
BREEDER, C.A. 113
BREWER, Amanda 131, Ambrose 131, Fred 131, George 131, L.C. 84, Lula 131
BRILES, Pearl 102
BRINKLEY, Alvin 31, Aretha 59, Catherine 31, Lessie 31, Lester 31, Richard 31
BRITTAIN, Amrene 26, Beulah 146, Cora 146, Gladys 146, Grady 146, Harvard 146, Henry 146, Hester 146, Ida 117, Maysella 146, Mildred 146, Otis 146, 151, Pearl 146, Rozella 146, Theodore 146,
BRITTAIN, Thomas, 26, 146, Vada 146, Virginia 146, Wanda 146, Weldon 146,
BROADWAY, Ida 35, Tom 35

BROOKMIER, Fred 42 Minnie 91
BROOKS, Mary 87
BROWN, Beatrice 122, Bill 126, Blanche 105, Elisha 2, Elsie 116, 217, Ethel 96, 121, Fred 121, Geneva 128, George 7, 121, Harry 300, Hazel 122 Imogene 126, John 270, Jonathan 280, Lavina 270, Lottie 31, Margaret 127, Mark 126, Mary 122, Mona 129, Nora 121, Pearl 126, Rachel 103, Rebecca 108, Samuel 4, Seretha 124, Turner 103, Wilfred 121, Winfred 122
BROWNFIELD, Ben, 28, 54, 167, B.F. 164, Clarence 29, 54, Gertie 29, Hannah 14, 28, 38, 167, 259, Ida 29, James 29, 54, 164, Nora 29, Ota 29, Sarah 21, Thomas 38, Ida 164, Marvin 130, Mona 84, Nora 97, Robert 37
BROWNING, Hannah 103, Sherman 59, 103
BRUCE, Oscar 18
BRUMETTE --- 7
BRUMLEY, Asa 23
BRUNER, Jacob 6, J.H. 6, Katherine, 137, Mahala 112, 306
BRUNTLY, Eliza 71
BRYAN, Alice 52, Amanda 53, Charles 52, Cordella 53, Davis 52, Henry 52, J.W. 52
BRYAN, Mary 53, Morgan 52, Nettie 53, Nora 53

BRYAN, S.G. 52, Sylvia 126, Thomas 52
BRYNES, John 146
BUCKHANON, Bursie 71
BURILSON, Anna 42
BURKE, Betty 124, Carroll 124, Ed 124, Marie 110, Ora 124, Raymond 124
BURKHART, Charles 29 Martha 126, Maude 63
BURKLOW, Alice 119, 123, 151, Andrew 123, Andrew 151, Annie 119, 151, Bessie 119, 123, 151 Charlie 123, 149, Cinthia 90, Elizabeth 123, 149, George 123, 151, 129, Jack 119, James 19, 123, 149, Jimmy 129, John 123, John 128, 149, Kate 119, 123, 151, Lela 92, Martha 123, 149, Minerva 128, Otto119, 123, 151, Ray 119, Robert 119, 123, 151, Sam 123, 149, Sarah 119, 123, 150, William 128, 137
BURMAN, Ida 112, 279
BURNER, George 255, Martha 255, Mary 255
BURNS, Sarah 74
BURRIS, Dee 33, Martha 128
BURROUGH, Rose E. 47
BURTON, Edith 111, E.E.14, 202, Lucile 114, 202, Mary 111, Minerva 86
BUTLER, Joe 131, Josie 109, Mary, 109, 172, Pearl 130, Thomas, 109, 172
BYERS, Arkle 136, Eugene 136, Frances 136, J.C. 136, Julian 136, Lizzie 136, Myrtle 136
BYNUM, Elizabeth 79, 117 J.A. 117, Josh 79, Margaret 117, Melvina 80, Myrtle 117, Richard 79, 117, Serena 276, W.T. 79, William 117
BYRAN, Alice 86, Elizabeth 84, Morgan 84, Thomas 84
BYRANT, Carter 38
CAIN, Addie 42
CALBERT, Francis 14, India 118, Lula 99
CALDWELL, Della 118, Ollie 74, Wesley 6
CALHOUN, Letitia A. 18
CALVERT, Clarence 287
CAMERON, 12
CAMBELL, Elvira 30 Mary 30, Mattie 136, Ollie 101, Tom 30, Virginia 30, William 28
CANADY, Anna 34, Howard 34
CAPPS, Joyce 126
CAPON, W.H. 130
CARITHERS, Joseph 102
CARLISLE, Bird 78, James 11, 218, Jane 79, Milas 47
CARMAN, Belle 39, Effie 128, William 39
CARNAHAN, Maggie 116 Carr,
CARR, Alice 57, 01, Cela 46, Hattie 88, James 45, 46, Jim 287, John 137, Leslie 114, Lottie 114, Madeline 14,
CARR, Margaret 14, Moody

CARR, Margaret 14, Moody 14, Noah 14, Pearl 14, Roy 137, Rysdon 46, Sarah 28,46, 64, 163
CARROLL Jennie 108,121, 154
CARTER, Charles 32, Elijah 14, Elizabeth 89, Luia 14
CASAD,---157, Bettie 86, Blanche 30, 107, Charles 6, 30, Eliza 107, Harriet 6, Jane 47, M.F. 47, Mary 77, Orley 30, Otto 30, 107, Raleigh 30, Sebary 77, 127, T.L.A. 30, Thomas 7, 107, Vina 30, 107, Walter 30
CASSICK, Bertha 110
CATELLA, Nellie 91
CATT, Agnes 98, Asa 98 Jobe 987, Joe 282, Mary 98
CAVANDER, J.C. 3, Lula 3
CHAMBERS, James 24, Jane 24, Mary 24
CHAMPION, Elizabeth 38
CHANCELLER, Phinias 126
CHANCY, Allen 128, Theodore 7
CHANEY, Martha 134
CHAPMAN, Mary 271
CHEEK, John 1
CHEEZIK, Joseph 229, Sabastian 229
CHRISTENSEN, Charles 23, 70, 292, Sadie 62, Della 292
CHRISTY, Sarah 89
CLANAHAN, Annie 15, C.l. 2, Louisa 2, Rev. 148
CLANTON, A.J. 142, Andrew 151, Brian 152, Cora 152, Dora 152, Ferrell 152, Martha 152, Mary 151, Mollie 19, Tom 8, 151, 152
CLARDY, Pearl 136
CLARK, Agustus.32, Anice 120, Bobby 120, Cecil 32, 54, 152, Chester 7, Cora 32, 54, 152, Elizabeth 79, 120, Esther 32, 54, 152, Gladys 120, Hazel 120, Helen 120, J.A. 31, 32, 69, 80, John 54, 152, Lawrence 25, Lester 120, Lillian 113, Linda 77, Mabel 32, 190, Mary 32, 152, Myrtle 119, Reba 110, Rose 56, Roy 120, 54, Royal 32, Ruth 32, 54, 80, 152, Sarah 31, 32, 152, Thomas 6, Trice 120, William 23
CLARY, Henry 83, Jerusha 83, Lue 83
CLAXTON, Ethel 132
CLAYTON, J.J., Laura 1
CLEMENT, Clarence 116, Ida 27, 41,65, 103, 116, Ivy 116, John 116, Martha 111
CLEVELAND, Archie 33, Pearl, 49, 61, 81
CLEVENGER, Eliza J. 85
CLIFFORD, Kate 113, 130
CLOSSON, James 131
COCHRAN, ---30, Charlie 98, Helen 120, Joseph 13, 77 Julie 109, 171, Martha 124 Mollie 98, Ollie 84, Reason 98 Ray 13, Rose Ann 84,
COFFEE, A.B. 105, Arthur 105, Mary 102, 105, 134

COFFIELD, Jerry 4, R.L. 8
COGHILL, Joel 4
COCKER, Addie 48
COLBERT,---- 88, Edith 131, Lena 128
COLE, --- 147, Ada 108, 154, B.C.132, 133, Dewey 108, 154 Genevieve 154, 132, 133, James 108, 121, 153, Jennie 108, 121, 154, Jerdie 132, 133 Maravilla 108, Martha 108, 121, 153, Olivia 108, 154, Olivia 108, R.C., 108, 121, 153, 154, R.F. 153, Richard 108, 121, 153
COLEMAN, Hattie 60
COLLINS, Anna 103, B.F. 129, Bessie 17, C. 81, Flossie 137, Frank 129, James 57, John 46, Mary 57, Pearl 129, Rosa 57, Susan 11, Susie. 46, William 57
COLLOM, May 124
COLTRIN, I.A. 114, 127, 209 Coltrin, Mary 24, 302
COMBS, Lula 122
COMPTON, Gertrude 128
CONDITT, Annie 119, 123, 151
CONKLE, Annie 102, 125 Bessie 102, 125, Christopher 102, Eller 84, Fannie 102, Issac 102, John 101, 102, 125 Mildred 127, Sam 102, Sidney 102, Thomas 102, Tom 102
CONKLEY, Frankie 40
CONLEY, Fannie 15
CONN, Bill 233, Claire 136,

COLLINS, Donald 14, Edgar 136, Etta 136, Harold 136, Harriet 136,James 136, Jane 89, Lewis 89, Martha 110, 147, Myril 136, Ollie 28, S.S. 5, 8, Samuel 6, 136, W.F. 14, Walter 136, Wayne 136, William 136
CONNELL, Kate 138
CONRAD, Lucinda 3, Pearl 129
COOK, Bill 24, Ethel 124, Fred 19, Gertie 79, H.B. 19, Harriet 25, Herbert 19, Houston 56, Howard 79, Ida 19, James, 25, 79, John 19 79, Lavena 56, Martha 123, Martha 123, 149, Mary 56, 106, Myrtle 79, Nancy 79 Walter 79, William 25
COON, Martha 147
COOPER, Beula 11, C. 11, Carl 11, Charles 11, Golda 11, Martha 11, Mollie 11, Noah 11, Norah 11, Roy 11, Willard 11
CORLEW, Mary 10
CORNELL, Alonzo 117, Archie 117, Carrie 117, Cleoma 117, David 117, Edward 117, Frank 117, George 117, Laura 117. Minnie 117, Freda 117, Garcie 117, Margie 117, Meredith 117, Millard 117, Nora 117, Vercie 117, Wilburn 117

CORTER, Cain 3
CORTON, Mary 225
CORWIN, Rebecca 160, Theodius 160, Zadock 160
COSBY, Ruth 62
COVET, James 23
COVINGTON, Alfred 62, Beulah 62, Charles 62, 80, Daisy 47, Daisy 105, Esther 62 Hubert 62, John 62, Loyd 62, Mary 62, Pearl 62, Ruth 62
COWGILL, Arthur 78, Mary 76
COWAN, Jennie 289
COWSERT, Aaron 120, Alice 55, 104, Alvin 90, Anna 120, Audra 112, Ben 104, 121, Betty 121, Charles 121, Clyde 112, Cora 109, 135, 148, Burton 54, Ellen 87, Frank 87, Fred 12, Green 120, Harry 88, Jake 54, J.B. 62, John 104, Julius 88, Leona 86, Lila 90, Lonnie 104, Lottie 125, Maria 87, Martha 126, Mary 49, 87, 121, Meredith 117, Nan 90, Nancy 62, 104, Perry 9, Robert 87, Rose 104, Sarah 121, Thomas 121, Ulysses 120, 88, Willie 104, 120, 121, W.H. 12, William 88, W.L. 120,
COX, Allen 118, Anna, 8, 118, Audrie 118, Belle 9, Cecil 118, Clinton 121, D.N. 118, D.N 44, 45, 46, Elizabeth 9, 118, Fred 118, Gilbert 121, 133 Gertrude 131, India 11, James 121, Jane 118, Julie 76,

COX, Mollie 9, Raliegh 118 Solomon 8, 9, 118, Will 94, William 118, 121
CRABB, Charlie 9, Clara 98, Jessie 135, Joseph 85, Oscar 123, Sarah 95, 131, Thomas 131, CRAIG, Jim 7, Martha 50, Nettie 32
CRAIN, Marie 97
CRANE, Gertrude 31
CRANK, Thomas 161
CRAWFORD, R.H. 130
CREAMER, Alley 115, Charlie 115, Howard 126, Johnnie 115, Maggie 115, Minnie 115, Tom 115, 126
CREASON, William E. 34
CREMEENS, John 7
CRIDER, W.T. 18, Helen 129 Don 129, D.F. 129, Ed 129, Earl 129, James 152
CRONKITE, Daisey 97, George 97, Nancy 74
CROUCH, John 48
CROW, Albert 117, Charles 117, Howard 117, Lou 117, Mamie 113, 228, Mary 117, Minnie 100, Russell 117, Thomas 117, Vida 117, Willis 117
CROWELL, Effie 48, John 66, Laura 66, Mary 66, Ollie 112, 279
CRUS, Lilly 101
CRUSE, Gertie 92, Lois 92
CRUSE, Loyd 92, Phene 92, Phoebe 92, William 92
CRUSEN, Mina 89

CRUSON, Anna 115, 251
CUBLEY, Clarence 134, Effie 83, Joseph 134, Miles 134, Sarah 134
CULLISON, Bud 157, Georgiana 67, James 67, Margaret A. 67, Saloma 67 Triphena 90, Tyrphene 67
CULLUM, Bertha 86, Cecil 86, Clyde 86, Clyde 86, Cora 86, E.C. 36, Ethel 36, Everett 86, Ira 86, James 3, John 86, Julus 86, Loren 86, Mary 86, Oma 86, Sarah 86, Theodore 86, Thomas 86, Walter 86, William 86, Julius 86, Ira 86 Minda 86, Nancy 86
CUMMING, Alice 69
CUMMINGER, Daisy 50, Ethel 52, 74, James 63, John 63, Mary 86
CUNNINGHAM, Ann 225 Anna 101, Mary 225, Willis 225
CURE, Hazel 19
CURNS, Minnie 104
CURRY, Clara 54 Elizabeth 116, 215, Etta 79, Helen 129, J.S. 104, John 54, 190, Minnie 19, 54, Owen 160 Rebecca 34, 46, 51, 160 Siegel 19, 104, Willie 54, William 104, Zoa 129
CURTIS, Jane 99, Fowler 123, Madeline 123, Anna 123,
CURTIS, Ethel 123, Katherine 123, Broad 123, Elizabeth 123, Thomas 123

CUTTRELL, Charles 29, Phoebe 29, Zenith 29
DALE, Alice 101, Alma 49, Anna 120, Arza 101, Audrey 47 Bert 101, Cecil 49, Celia 101, Clarence 43, Eva 124, Evelyn 101, George 49, Hancil 101, Hosea 48, 49, James 101, Jane 101, John 101, Julia 43, Lora 101, Luther 49, Manda 46, Mary 127, Ollie 59, 76, 101, Raymond 101, Roy 101 Ruby 101,
DALTON, Charlie 115, Elma 47, H.D. 45, Huber 115, John 115, Marcella 115, Opal 115, Reed 115, Willena 45, Willna 115
DAMERON, Mary 136, Richard 136, Susan 136
DAMRON, J.W. 271, Sydney 271
DAN, Carrie 102
DANIELS Cora 110, Savannah 110, Will 110
DAUGHERTY, Bill 137, James 31, John 31, Lon 31 Pauline 31, Ruby 31, W.E. 31
DAVIS, ---17, Abraham 1, 88, Abram 7, Addie 133, Alma 31, Asa 1, 6, Betsy 155, Brian 41, C.M. 41, Cary 6, Charles 126, Corlin 31, Daisy 20, Dan 156, 160, Dean 112, Dick 24, Don 31, Dora 81.
DAVIS, Edgar 70, 73, 156, 210, Effie 31, 100, Elizabeth 88, Ella 137, Ezra 136.

DAVIS, F.L. 71, Frank 133, George 97, 126, 155, Gladys 31, Golda 73, 210, Hannah 100, Herpie 126, Horace 1, Jeff 99, Jim 70, Joshie 87, Josie 100, 133, Leonard 126, Leslie 87, Letha 79, Lizzie 70, Louise 100, Lucinda 33, Ludwick 99, Lydia 100, Mae 97, Mag 102, Marie 20, Marion 79, Martha 41, 156, Mary 72, 97, 136, 155, Matlida 100, May 22, 24, Minnie 104, 100, 112, Mythel 31, Nancy 99, Noah 126, Nora 70, Olin 72, Ora 124, Otto 126, Pauline 156, Perry 79, Phoebe 27, Ruth 65, Sarah 31, 88, 133, Shirley 156, Sol 3, Stella 131, 201, Susan 97, Sylvia 126, T.A. 70, Tom 100, Tot 156, Van 99, Virgie 79, W.D. 33, 53, 54, 163, W.H. 39, W.L. 70, Walter 19, Wanda 156, Wayne 156, William 84,102,155, Zena 71
DAY, Charles 117, Lena 89,
DAYMON, Anna 112, Della 112, Dola 30, Issac 96, John 96, 112, Lucretia 30, 112, Martin 270, Orin 64, Polly 66, Minnie 30, Wiley 30, 96, 112,
DE INSPANNIC, Alvered 290
DEAL, Anson 15, William 15
DEATTA, Clara 103
DECKER, Addie 134, Asa 24, Asa 98, 111, 112, 137, 139, 161, 162, Bessie 102, 125, C.C. 111, 162, Effie 83,

DECKER, Elizabeth 111, 162, Ellen 134, Eunice 40, Florence 98, 112, 129, 161, Golda 111, 139, 163, Gordon 111, 139, 163, Henry 83, 125, 134, Hettie 35, Jobe 83, John 98, 111,134, 139, 161, Linda 73, Lum 139, Lydia 98, 111, 112, 139, 161, Maria 83, Mary 98, 134, Maurice 24, Melissa 31, 98, 112, 137, 161, Myrtle 111,139, 162, Ota 139, Owen 19, 111, 162, Riley 83, Sarah 83, 134 Savannah 81, 91, Susan 111, 162, 162, Wilma 139
DEDERICK, Ada 108, 154
DELEZYNSKI, A. 1
DELL, Effie 100
DEMERIS, James 8
DENCE, Charles 99
DENEEN, Arthur 55
DENGLER, August 81, Joseph 81
DENT, Elizabeth 52, Fannie 52, James 52
DENTON, A. M. 52, Allen 5, 134, 163, 167, Andrew 163, Arza, 166, 167, Beulah 166, 167, 221, Hannah 5, Ida 29, 164, J.E. 29, 52, 54, James 134 163, 167, 221, Lizzie 21, Loren 166, 167, Mary 5, 28, 163, Matilda 52, Olney 166, Phoebe 164, Rachel 166, 167, Richard 167, Sarah 132, 164, Sudie 164, Virgil 166, William, 21, 28, 52, 134, 163

DERRINGER, Howard 63
DEVAULT, Arthur 31
DEVELLE, Lottie 44
DEVER, Ben 61, Francis 61
Frona 61, Mae 61, Ordway 61
Pearl 61, Rosie 61, Sallie 61
DEVERS, Ben 33, 49, 81,
Edna 49, F.M. 33, George, 33
49, John 33, 49, 81, Mae 49,
81, Marion 49, 156, Ordie 49
81, Pearl 49, 81, Phrona 49,
Rose 49, 81, Sallie 49, Sally
81, Will 49
DEWESEE, Amber ? 86,
Bettie 86, Bob 88, Francis 86,
Leona 86, Leona 88, Minerva
86, Nannie 86, Robert 86
DEWEY, Clyde 14, 15, Emma
14, Frank 14, 15, Jacob 14, 15,
James 15, John 14
DICKMAN, Belle 44
DIMICK, Amada 168,
Amanda 5, 136, Carrie 90,
C.C. 18, 136, 168, Charley
251, Emma 95, 168, Franklin
5, 136,168, George 9, 136, 168
G.F. 18, John 18, Judge 5,
Mable 18, Otis 18, Ralph 18,
Sarah 12, W.E. 124, Walter
114
DINSE, Marie 130
DIXON, Amelia 87, Charlotte
93, David 93, James 93, Lizzie
82, Mary 84, Masie 120
DODD, Emma 135
DOGGETT, Evan 7, Mary 38,
DOMICK, George 28
DONATHAN, Connie 79,
Fredrick 60, 71, 87 Nellie 80
DORSETT, Ile 16
DOSSETT, Bill 21, Eb 156,
Elbert 93, Ethna 21, Fanny 2,
George 93, H. F. 21, Henry 21,
28, 56, 217, I.A. 28, Ida 21, Ila
93, Ile 21, James 93, John 2,
21, Lora 21, Miem 21, Minerva
21, 28, 23, W.J. 28
DOUGHERTY, Catherine 8
DOUGLAS, A.L. 71, 106,
Adiel 156, Burtis 157, Charles
72, Clyde 51, Cora 25, 83,
106, D.A. 106, Daisy 71, Dave
106, Dorothy 139, Emma 106,
Eugene 52, Eula 52, George
55, 56, 106, Gladys 100,
Grover 106, Hansel 51,
Horatio 113, Ida 25, 83, Jeff
106, Jermiah 106, Jesse 113,
Laura 112, 279, Louise 25,
Lula 83, Mabel 106, Marie 52,
Martha 10, Nancy 106, Nora
25, 65, 83, 106, Quentin 52,
S.J. 106, Sally 51,304, Sarah
83, 113, Sonora 110, 304,
Thomas 25, 51, 83, 100,
143, 304, 143, Virgil 107
DOWDING, F.J. 87
DOWDY, Alma 106, 245
DOWNEY, Artimissa 56, 89,
Charles 168, Charles 95,
Clay 83, Commodore 99,
Elizabeth 99, Emma 95, 168
DOWNEY, Florence 44,
Henry 57, 89, 99, 169, Herbert
99, Jennie 57, John 99, Junie
91, 131, Katie 99, Levisa 99,

DOWNEY, Margaret 99, Mollie 89, Nancy 99, Pell 99, William 95, 99, 168
DOYLE, Mary 136
DRAKE, Martha 100
DRIVER, Bertha 169, Ira 169
DRUMM, Anna 32, Carrie 87, Elmer 87, Gladys 87, Harry 87, Jacob 88, Jake 32, Lanie 87, Lydia 87, Martha 26, Mary 87, Myrtle 87, William 32, 87, Willie 87
DUBOIS, Minnie 130
DUKE, Orval 122
DULEY, Muriel 296
DUMONT, John 79,
DUNCAN, Ezra 95, Furdela 102, Hallene 43, Jacob 68, Lula 108, 300, Minnie 101, Nancy 37, Offa 68, 69, Opha 37, Troy 95, William 68
DUNN --156, Dr. 161, Emma 15, Mary 24, 51, T.A. 120, Tot 160
DUNNAWAY, Della 120
DURHAM, Edna 123, 287,
DUSCH, L.D. 80, 105, Louis, 105, L.P. 105, Maurie ? 105,
DUTTON, Albert 129, Andrew 12, Arlen 107, Arlo 129, A.W. 12, Blanche 30, C.H. 105, Charles 12, Clara 24 Chester 107, Ethel 112, Ewell 105, Gordon 30, Hester 105, Hester 107, 137, James 81, Joe 129, Lester 105, 107, Letta 81, Luther 129, Newlin 105, 107, 137, Rhoda 93, Rysdon

DUTTON, Rysdon 46, Stella 129, W.E. 30, Willis 160, Charles 137, Lennie 137, Lester 137, Willie 12
DUVALL, Clyde 69
EADS, Riley 34, Salina 34
EATON, --- 2
ECKMAN, Henry 39
EDERINGTON, Brown 284
EDMOND, Angie 57
EDMONDS, Fred 79, Lou 75, Norah 79, William 79
EDMONDSON, Anzie 101, Bee 85, 156, Bell 171,Connie 85, Emma 109, 172, Ethel 85, Gracen 109, 171, Harve 171, Henry 85, Jane 109, 171, John 109, 171, Julia 109, 171, Mary 85, 109, 172, Newt109, 171, Sarah 171, W.H. 109, 171, Zachariah 171, Zack 109, 172
EDRINGTON, John 3
EDWARDS,---45, A.E. 56, Ab 18, Albert 48, 106, Ben 47, Bessie 113, Claude 73, E.R. 56, Ernest 37, Francis G. 56, George 47, 48, 73, 210, Grace 5, 37. India 29, John 48, Johnie 49, Lace 18, Leniel 210, Louise 37, Mary 110, Mazie 109, Nan 48, Robert 56, Sallie 51, Sarah 173, 178, 188, 193, 223, Tobe 5, W.R. 5, Willa, 48,
EDWARDS, William 29
EICHORN, Anna 32, Christine 92, Doris 28, Elizabeth 92, Jack 32, Jacob 39 92, John 132, 133, 92,

EICHORN, Maggie133, Margaret 92, Martin 132, 133, Mary 32, Sebastian 32, Theresa 132, Willie 92
ELDORADO, Eldorado, Pearl
ELLAS, Sarah 112
ELLEN, Redick 88
ELLIOT, Harriet 10, Hattie 131, Joseph 10, Mary 96, 121, Nancy 10
ELLIS, Alvin 135, Arvil 135, Elva 134, Iva 134, Jane 55, Lula 109, 135, 148, Mary 271, Moses 134, Sophia 134, Sylvia 135
ENGLES, Lucy 99
ENGLISH, Martha 16, Richard 45, James 37, Lissa 37, Issac 37, Nellie 46, Essie 130, C.C. 219
ENOCH, Belle 73, Millard 73, Ruth 73
ENSLEY, Hazel 50, Phoebe 50
ENSLOW, W.M. 73
ESTERVES, Alpha 133
ESTES, Tom 197
EVANS, Jim 116, Mary 116 Richard 98
EVERETT, Emma 82
EVERTSON, May 55
EWARDS, Bessie 69
EWELL, Amerso 21, Arland 106, Frank 106, J. 43, J.E. 21 John 106, Icelez 21, Mary 43, Myrtle 106, Samuel 43, T.A. 43, Thomas 43
FARLEY, Jessie 152, Charley

FARLEY, Charley 152
FARMER, Lilbern 108, Nancy 79, William 79, Wilma 139
FARRIS, Mary 270
FARSEY?, Lizzie 22
FELLOWS, Bessie 35, 84, Fannie 19, 84, Hattie 13, Hettie 19, J.W. 35, 84, Pharis 106, Roy 35, Willie 19
FERGUS, Rose 88
FERRELL, --- 230, A.C. 3, 7. 59, A.J. 28, Albert 3, Alice 131, Anna 103, Andrew 172, 179, Annie 133, Arnold 76, Audrie 118, Augusta 41,133, Belle 15, Ben, 95, Bert 15, 68, 76, 185, Bessie 77, Betty 76, "Booze" 180, C.H. 28, C.M. 3, 94, 293, 296, Carrie 43, Charles 11, 76, 95, 175, 186, Clement 173, 178, 188, 193, 223, Clifford 44, Clifford 68, 185, Cora 87, Dewey 47, Dick 180, Ed 112, 133, 135, Edd 74, Edd 75, Edgar 138, Edward 32, 41, 81, 85, 88, 95, 111, 180, 190, Eliza 175, Elizabeth 3, 48, 68, 70, 104, 125, 175, 184, 186, 187, 189, Ella 53, 189, Emma 54, Emmer 44, Estella 197, Etta 98,129, Eunice 15, 76, Everett 76, Frank 85, 173, Frankie 189, Fred 189, 190, George 45, 46, Geraldine 87, 138, Gertrude 41, Gladys 15, 76, Grace 41, Grover 76, H.A. 53, 54, 62,

FERRELL, H.E. 96, Hallie 111, Harrington 85, Harry 189, 196, Harvey 95, Hattie 196, Hazel 196, Hedley 189, Henry 1, 14, 41, 62, 74, 75, 133, 175, 189, 190, Hettie 75, Homer 15, 76, Horace 138, Isabella 188, J.K.P. 23, J.W. 15, 76, James 1, 76, 87, 94, 95, 125, 138, 173, 178, 186, 189, 190, 197, Jane 52, 178, Joe 22, John 21, 44, 53, 68, 94, 173, 175, 178, 180, 184, 186, 193, Joseph 68, 74, 104, 173, 179, 184, 188, 288, Josephine 186, 187, Josie 36, Julie 76, July 131, Jury 131, Laura 184, 190, 192, Leona 184, Lillie 54, Mabel 32, 196, Malissa 194, Margaret 48, 103, 194, Mariam 184, Martha 28, 173, 175, 186, Mary 17, 189, 194, 197, Milas 72, 74, 75, 189, 190, Minerva 48, 103, Missouri 194, Mollie 99, Nancy 94, 175, 189, 190, 196, Nellie 186, Noland 15, 76, Nora 73, 76, 82, 125, Norman 196, Ollie 28, 42, 173 Omar 36, 94, Ora 45, 46, 116, Orval 28, 173, Otis 196, Perilina 173, 179, 223, Pernett 11, 41, 48, 70, 103,.133 Ralph 15, 76, Randal 15, 76, Rebecca 28, 173, Rella 95, Richard 184, 189, Robert 189, Ruby 62, Sallie 44, 185, 189, 195, Sarah 11, 104, 173, 178,

FERRELL, Sarah 188, 189, 190, 195, 218, 288, Shella 89, Stella 189, 190, Susan 197, Tabitha 178, Thomas 173, 178, 189, 194, 193, Ural 76, Vernon 76, Viola 87, Viola 138, Volentine 195, 192, 197, W.H. 43, William 28, 173, 178, 189, 194, 197, Willie 197
FERROL, Norma 109
FERRY, George 158
FIELDS, Jim 36, Laura 1 Quiller 36
FINCHAM, Junnie 32
FINLEY, Sophronia 117
FINNEY, Baker, 130, 263, Duke 130, Ida 12, Majenta 130
FINNLEY, Lillie 108
FISCHER, Caroline 122
FISHER, Bertha 53
FLANNERY, C.A. 100, Dan 77, 94, Dru 94, India 282, John 94
FLEENER, Clarence 75, Edith 75
FLETCHER, George 85
FLOYD, Alice 91, Grace 39
FLYNN, Charles 42, 61, Charlie 61, 137, Charlotte 42, Clyde 137, Clyde 42, Frank 61 H.T. 61, Isabell 42, J.W. 49. Jackson 42, James 61, Martha 137, W.J. 39, William J. 42, 137,
FOE, John 83, Rella 110,
FORD, Blanch 122, E.J. 53, E.L. 53, Jessie 53, Mintie 53,

FORD, Susie 80, T.J. 122, Willie 53
FOREMAN, Frank 79, Nancy 79, Nema 88
FORMAULT, Catherine 113, 282, Katherine 285
FOSHEE, Emma 47
FOSTER, Alice 27, Anna 72, Asa 63, 108, 130, Clarence 108, Clyde 119, Cora 152, Della 72, Elizabeth 27, 52, 55, 292, Etta 108, Grover 72, H.B. 108, Hannah 55, 292, Henry 108, Horace 27, 30, 42, 52, 55, 63, 75, 90, 108, 292, I.A. 27, 52, 73, 94, Issac 95, Jodie 130, John 52, Joseph 27, Julia 27, 95, Laura 42, 75, Lee 131, Lillie 90, 108, Marion 108, Mary 52, 90, 130, Noah 108, Nora 31, Opal 108, Owen 72, Phoebe 27, Sam 95, Sarah 108, Stella 128, Susa 27, Susan 130, Tena 62, Thomas. 27, 52, 27, 94, Wallace 108 William 27
FOWLER, Bertha 199, Dr. 69, E.M. 198, F.M. 34, 69, F.M. 34. 293, Francis 68, 198, H. 198, Joe 69, 95, Joel 204 John 55, 69, 95, 104, 199 Josie 96, 197, 253, Martha 95, Mary 73, 118, 199, 210, Nancy 199, Newton 68, 198, Panzie 55, Robert 68, 118, 199, 210, Roberta 68, 199, Sarah 95, 199, Thomas 118
FOXX, Minnie 115

FRAILEY, Alex 120, Alta 81, 91, Ann 120, Anna 72, Bill 45, Bob 148, Charles 72, Charley 34,46, 81,105, 234, 260, D.M. 28, 39, Dan 28,116 ,148, 155, 245, 250, Dick 75, Elizabeth 80, Ella 72, Eva 72, Frank 80, 81, 105, Frona 61, Gusta 120, Henry 81, 105, James 137, Joe 122, 144, Joe 237, John 72, 116, 120, Joseph 72, Julia 30, Kenneth 34, Lela 105, Lelia 80, Lizzie 25, 105, 112, Lucretia 112, Maggie 108, Martha 39, Mary 90, 155, Media 72, Nancy 80, 105, Ora 120, Oscar 72, Phil 156, Phrona 49, 81 Ralph 157, Richard 25, 34, 90, 80, 104, Robert 72, 250, 116, Sarah 116, Shephard 116, 249, Tobe 108, William 39
FRAIZER, Fred 109
FRANKLIN, Fannie 84, Jonathan 84,
FRAYER, E.E. 36
FRAYSER, Alex 143, Angie 74, Bob 121, Carl 109, 132, Chap 287, 136, 199, Dola 30, Eddie 56, 132, Elizabeth 93, Ella 132, Ellen 91, 120, 131, 199, Eva 56, Fayette 56, Harley 143, Harry 112, Henry 56, 287, Herbert 74, J.I. 91, James 120, Jim 298, John 74, 91, Kate 100, Lenard 74, 120, Lizzie 79, 102, Masie 120, Millie 78, R.A. 24, R.V. 91, 108, Richard132, Robert 91,

FRAYSER, Robert 74, 105, Roma 78, Rose 56, 132, Ross 61, 74, 78, 88, 121, Rozella 120, Stella 132, Ted 298, Virginius 74, 91, Virginnium 120
FRAZIER, Fred 109
FREDRICK, Joseph 56
FREEMAN, --- 3, Loyd 130
FRICKER, Emma 131, Ethel 131, F.E. 80, Frank 131, Fred 131, Freeman 131, Howard 131, Ida 131, Marshall 131, Mattie 80, Mayme 131, Nellie 87, Stella 131
FRIEND, Ephriam 2, M.B. 2,
FRIEZE, Etta 132
FRISTON, Laura 95
FRITTS, Clarence 77, George 69, John 69, Loren 77, S.L. 69 Sam 2, Samuel 77, William 69
FROHOCK, Henry 87
FUGAT,---144
FULGHAM, Vida 73
FULGHAN, Myrtle 104
FULGHUM, Noah 54
FULLER, Mary 214
GABLE, Jane 92
GAGNON, Minnie 103
GAINES, Addie, 17 124 Earl 42, 124, Jacob 42, Margaret 94, Nemo 124,
GAINES, Neme 42, Ura 42, 124, William 17
GALENA, Mary 85
GALLOWAY, Gladys 77, 127
GANGBARE, Delbert 88
GARLAND, A.T. 105

GARLAND, Arthur 105, Billy 84, 130, Charles 105,144, Dora 93, Doris 103, Earl 54, 56, Earlene. 58, Elizabeth 93, Eva 72, Harriet 22, 35, 93, 111, Henry 22, 93, Hester 39, 83, 84, 130, Joe 105, John 79, 84, 93, 100, 102, 108, 130, Lizzie 22, 79, Mary 22, 79, 108, Minnie 39, 83, 93, 100, Mona 130, Nancy 22, 79, 93, 108, Ralph 130, Ray 105, Rhoda 93, Thomas 56, 79, 93, 102, 108, Wiley 84, 130, William 22, 79, 84, 93, 108
GARRETT, Ada 130
GARVIN, Richard 200
GASKILL, Etheinda 66 Joshua 4
GEE, Emert 52, Everett 52, John 52, Solon 52
GENTRY, Alex 27, Alexander 41, 103, 113, Ben 103, Eliza 125, Elizabeth 41, 65, Eunice 103, 125, Frank 125, Grace 103 Henry 125, Howard 103, Ida 41, 65 103, James 3, 41, 125, John . 27, 41, 65, 103, Lutitia 27, 65, 103, 113, Martha 41, Mary 41, 65, Minnie 103, Ollie 125, Rachel 27, 41, Robert 103, Sarah 41, 65, 103, 113, Thomas 41, Tom 27, 103,
GEORGE, --- 77
GERHARDT, Adelia 62, 73, Alfred 57, Amiel 78, Bessie 82, C.W. 20, 29,

GERHART, Charles 82, 127, Daisy 82, Frank 78, Henry 62, 72, 73, 76, 82, Isabell 27, Jake 78, James 27, Jessie 57, John 82, Joseph 27, Lizzie 82, Luke 78, Mary 20, Melvina 20, Nora 62, 73, 82, Sarah 78, Vina 11
GIBBONS, --- 138, Earl 129, Elijah 129, Elmer 129, J.B. 129, Maggie 129, Minnie 129, Nancy 110, 119, 303, Ora 129, Pleasant 129, Roper 129, Thorne 129
GIBBS, Bennie 112, Eunice 113, 228, Harry 112, 129, Joe 162, Maggie 36, Samuel 112, Sarah 112
GIBSON, Captain 15, Dod 128, Doddridge 128
GIINTERT, Ada H. 25, Clara 25, 70, 72, Frank 22, Frank 25, Howard 22,
GILBERT, Missouri 58
GILLIAM, Mary 87
GILLISPIE, Ruth 92
GINGER, Alice 128, Ann 103 Arch 9, 10, 33, 128, Archibald 85, Bessie 44, Betsy 9, 59, Bettie 69, Bill 91, Braxton 6, Brian 128, C.E. 65, Charles 12 Charles, 60, 75, Clarence 80, Clifford 75, Cradie 26 ,D.V. 69, 74, Dan 91, Daniel 20, 103, E.T. 1, Earl 57, Eli 6, 9, 33, 80, T. 33, Elizabeth 179, 224, Emma 104, Eva 119, Fannie 128, Flora 26, Frank 58, 59, Frankie 31, Fred 26,

GINGER, Grover 26, H.L. 26, Harriet 86, Hattie 12, 60, 128, Henry 26, 44, Hettie 75, India, 74, 91, James 24, 25, 33, 39, 57, 80, 119, Jane 6, 9, 80, Joe 103, John 44, 60, 75, 119, 126, 128, Joseph 26, 128, Junie 26, Katie 33, Laura 75, Lizzie 24, 39, 119, Loyd 57, Lucille 119, Lucinda 44, Maggie 126, Malinda 103, Margaret 56, 117, Martha 1, 88, Mary 11, 10, Maxene 75, Mollie 65, 75, 84, Molly 85, Myriah 83, Nancy 225, Nellie 80, Ollie 75, Orveta 75, Paul 44, Pharris 26, Polly 10, 85, Riley 75, Robert 31, 119, Roxie 91, Sarah 39, Sereda 80, Sylvia 80, T.B. 79, Thomas 57, 80, Walter 119, Warden 119, Willie 12,
GINTERT, Effie 58 Elizabeth 107, Frank 107 Fred 107, John 127
GIPSON, Andy 2
GIRVAN, Georgla 121, Myrtle 121, Raleigh 121, R.L. 121, Vera 121
GIVENS, Rose, 123, R.R.123
GLACE, Lucy 122, 234,
GLADISH, Sam 102
GLASS --- 41
GLENN, Ernest 100, 127,
GLORE, William 93
GOBLE, Aaron 97, Alta 127, Charlie 97, Della 97, Gracie 97, Hattie 97, Laura 97, Minnie 93, Noah 97, Oma 64, Ora 97,

GOBLE, Polly 97, Ross 7, 97, Ruey 97, Sammie 97, Willie 97
GOETZMAN, J.R. 114, 202, Joel 135, John 135, 203, Joseph 203, L.T. 114, 202, Louis 135, 203
GOINS, Amanda 101, 225, Amiel 76, Bobbie 104, Edna 76 Frank 76, 104, George 76, 84, Jake 39, James 76, 78, 84, 104, Joe 78, Joseph 76, Josephine 55, Luke 76, Mary 76, 104, May 104, Minnie 76, Sarah 84
GOLIGHTLY, Rosina 130
GOLSBY, Lucyann 23, Mag 102
GOODRICH, Nellie 71
GOODWIN, John 114, 124, Johnnie 159, Millard 8, Robert 114, 124, Ross 114, 124
GORE, Gertrude 128, J.W. 78
GORWIN, Rebecca 160
GOSSAGE, Wm. 9
GRACE, Ethel 134, I.C. 8 James 5, John 7, 59, Josephine 7, 135, Margaret 76, Maude. 59, Mary 139, 134, Robert 134,
GRAHAM, Alice 12, Ben 13, Elizabeth 99, Joseph 12, 13, Mary 84, Sarah 49, William 84, Willie 84
GRANDPIER,--- 140
GRANDSTAFF, Andrew 102, Madelin 123
GRANT, Ruth 75, Morris 75,
GRAVES, W.C. 271
GREATHOUSE, John T. 5

GREEN, --- 160, Beatrice 96, Beulah 305, Dewey 157, 206, 228 305, Dr. 216, Frank 60, Issac 74, James 74, John 96, Lela 74, Lillie 103, Margaret 206, Maria 96, Martha 74, Patty 305, Sarah 74, W.C. 74, 217, William. 206
GREENLEAF, --- 286, Carol 114, Grace 114, H.A. 114, 216, Joe 114, Mary 114
GREGG, Albert 109, 204, Anna 109, 204, Emma 109, 203, Frank 109, 204, Hugh 109, 203 James 109, 205, John 204,109, Stacey 109, 203, William 109, 205
GREGORY, ---10, ---77, Dora 28, 77, Georgia 127, Gwyn 127, Harriet 107, 127, 208, J.M. 21, J.R. 295, John 107, 114, 127, 159, 208, 209, Mae 63, May 27, Mitty 209, W.C. 107, 219, W.G. 78, Will 27, William 28, 114, 127, 209
GRICE, Effie 128, Sarah 86
GRIFFIN, Gary 58, Harriet 58 Roy 58, Sarah 7, William 58
GRIFFITH, ---21, A.S. 68, 73 118, 210, Alexander 55, Alice 73, 118, Beatrice 93, Catherine 73, 210, Claude 73, 118, 210, Cynthia 121, Doc 21, Edward 93, Edwinna 73, 210, Elizabeth 93, Emma 121, Esther 55, Evelyn 93, Golda 73, 118, 210, Guy 93, James 73, 210, Lenel 118, Lenora 121

GRIFFITH, Linel 210, Louise 93, Marie 93, Mary 68, 73, 210, Maude 54, 55, 73, 118, Millie 93, Ora 93, Paul 73, 118, 210, Sarah 73, 118, Sula 121, Thomas 121, Tony 93, Tula 73, 210,
GRIGGS, Rose 123
GRIMSY, J.W. 7
GRINDSTAFF, Andy 101, Henry 101, Irvin 98, Mira 98, Samuel 18, Samuel 98, Sarah 98, 101
GROSS, Anna 73, Barbara 73, 92, 211, Bessie 35, Blanch 73, Clifton 73, Edith 73, Elsie 12, Eschol 12, 84, Eva 12, Jacob 73, Lydia 98, 112, 161, Olivia 73, Orin 73, Orval 73, Rachel 12, Sorado 12, Sylvia 73, William 73
GROUNDS, George 31, Gertie 92, Julia, 64
GROVES, Dora 152, Malinda 71
GUARD, J.L. 87
GUIDREY, --- 47, Charles 160, Frank 35 160,
GUESS, Jas. 8
GULLETS, W.W. 13
GULLETT, Ben 135, Charles 135, Clara 148, Emma 101, Essie 135, Florence 98, 112, 129, 161, J.G. 69, 108, Jacob 129, James 135, 140, Julia 135, Lucretia 69, Lucretin 129, Margaret 101, 109, 135 Mollie 135, Muriel 91, Noah 135, Pomp 72, 238, Sarah 72, 135, 238, U.G. 135, Waitman 101, 135
GUSTIN, A.A. 69, 143, 149, 212, Ada 119, Alice 96, 119, Amariah 119, Bessie 220 Betty 119, 120, Bill 119, D.W. 34, 293, Dyke 148, Elsie 19, Em 119, "Grandma" 22, Henry 212, Isaiah 1, 119, Lelia 80 Like? 104
H----, Jacob 8, Lizzie H. 8 Monna 8
HALE, Alvin 26, 88, 114, Belle 11, 26, Charlie 114, 124, Clara 54, 104, Etta 114, Freda 93, George 87, Guy 114, James 88, 53, Laura 53, 114, Lolene 114, Martha 53, 88, Ora 26, Robert 88, Thomas 26, 88, 114, Velma 83, 114, Walter 88
HALEY, Emma 269
HALL, Benjamin 76, Beuhla 254, E.N. 29, 54, Elihu 213 Frank 207, Golda 117, Jessie 76, Mary 47, Nicholas 76,
HALL, Ota 29, Wittie 76
HAMBRINK, Byran 134, Clarence 134, Luke 1, Maida 108, 134, Orval 134, Peter 14, P.H. 134
HAMILTON, Henriette 55, Willie 150
HAMMACH, Irving 34, Nora 34
HAMMONDS, Jas. 25, Sarah 25, Sidney 25

HAMP, Andy 33, Augusta 50, Catty 82, Charlotte 3, Elizabeth 93, Hattie 42, Henry 3, 8, 6, 83, Jacob 82, John 82, Louis 33, 56, 82, 93, Mary 93, Nicholas 82, Stella 99, 128
HAMPTON, Ida 46, Tina 3
HANDBRINK, Edna 134
HANDCOCK, J.J. 27, Marie 27
HANNA, Elia? 66, J.E.Y. 129
HANS, Fred 121, Henry 121, Mary 121
HANSEN, Andrew 47
HANUSS, Milley 73
HARDESTY, Frances 114, Frank 74, India 14, 16, Jewell 138, Lennie 138, Mary 138, Nell 94, 111
HARDIN, ---140, Able 136, C.D. 124, Cam 124, Emma 136 Henry 160, India 115, Jesse 124, Julia 70, 120, Mary 116, Milodeen 124, Price, 10, Ray 124, Reed 124, Sarah 124, Yulee 124
HARDRICK.--- 159
HARGETT, H.E. 74
HARPER, Francis 86, Jane 92
HARRISON, Mae 136, Mattie 92, Minnie 117, Myrtle 53
HART, Etta 108, Ezra 16, J.A. 70, Joel 16
HARVEY, Ambrose 4
HASTIE, James 7, 131, Maude 110, Minnie 131, R.M. 139

HATHORN, Ethel 75, Goldie 75, J.W. 75, John 75, Lena 75, Maude 75, Mrs. 4, Myrtle 75, Sarah 54, 52
HAWKER, Hannah 22
HAWKINS, Daisy 82, James 300, Sarah 85, Wilmeta 135
HAWTHORNE, Charley 37, Ethel 37, Goldie 37, Inez 37, John 37, Lena 37, Maude 37, Myrtle 37, Will 37
HAYDEN, Charley 17, Elizabeth 94, 187, Jas 17, Will 17
HAYES, Anna 62, Malinda 80 Tabitha 178, Vada 133
HAZELL, Mary 34
HEALY, Lillie 52
HEMPHILL, --- 1
HENNING, John 215
HENRY, Ellen 136, Ellen 199, Fannie 136, 199, George 131, 136, 199, J.W. 295, James 136 199, John 131,136, 296, Maltilda 52, Mollie 65, Thomas 131, Tom 136, 143, 199
HENSON, Alter 57, Andrew 134, Anna 73, Beula 73, Charlotte 93, Ella 103, Florence 93, Helen 87, Job 93, John 73, 134, Leslie 87 Lula 136, Luna 136, Mae 136, Mary 87, 138, Milley 73, Morgan 73, Murble 73, Norma 57, Otto 87, Pearl 136, Rosa 73, Tom 138, Vernon 73, Walter 89, William 87, 136
HERCHMER, L.T. 213,

HERCHMER, Ted 214
HERI, Bass 15, Elizabeth 15, John 15, Nora 69, Rollie 15, S.E. 250
HERMAN(N), A.F. 15,. 104, 122, Andrew 104, Bill 15, Catherine 111, Christina 73, Christine 104, 122, Emanuel 15, Franklin 77, George 111, 262, John 15, 104, 122, Lizzie 25, Lizzie 122, Manuel 263, Mary 57, 122, Michael 104, 122, Regina 122, Sallie 104, 122
HEROD, Dora 75, 129, Drusilla 75, James 75 T.S. 162
HERRIN, Clara 217, Clarence 217, Elizabeth 116, 215, Elsie 116, 217, Ethel 116, 217, Flora 116, 217, George 116, 215, Harve 217, 219, Harvey 37, Ben 116, 216, Clara 116, James 116, 139, 216, 217, 219, Myrtle 110, O.T. 116, Ressie 216, Tina 29, Walter 116, 217, W.C. 116, Wilford 116, 217, William 116, 215
HERRING, Ben 55
HERRINGTON, Eliza 125
HERRMAN, Andrew 86, Antone 86, Catherine 86, Christina 86, Elizabeth 86 John 86, Mary 77, 86, Michael 86, 121, Regina 86, Sallie 86
HESS, Charlie 56, D.E. 45, David 26, 141, Drura 45, Edward 25, 90, Elizabeth 26

HESS, Elizabeth 80, 141, Issac 45, Jacob 26, Jake 144, Mary 45, Orval 100, Richard 90, Sudie 164
HETHERINGTON, Ann 111, 119, Callie 85, Jane 119, John. 27, 85, Richard 119, Sidney 85, W.T. 27
HICKS, Albert 83, Ann 20, Ben 11, 218, Charles 11, Charlie 218, Elizabeth 135. Fannie 11,218, Frank 83, 129, Henry 11, 218, James 129, Josie 83, Laura 26, Lewis 11, 218, Lora 101, 225, Loy 11, 218, Luther 129, Margaret 218, Marion 11, 218, Martha 256, Mary 218, Milas 11, 218, Miles 26, 79, 83, Milo 11, 218, Mollie 92, Myriah 83 Rebecca 26, Sarah 218, W.J. 51
HIGDEN, Rebecca 3 William 3
HILDPRBECK, ---- 9
HILL, Albert 35, Alice 101, Alice 57, Allan 101, Angie 57, Anzie 101, Bessie 220, Betty 76, Bob 217, C.O. 39, Carolyn 57, 101, Claude 101, Cora 57, 101, Della 97, Dr. 160, Elizabeth 83, 100, 125, Elmer 96, 101, Floyd 123, G.W. 59, 60, 212, 219, George 59, 60, 216, 220, Gladys 13, Goolie 83, Gradie 83, Harve 39, 79, 83, Harvey 12, Hattie 97, Henry 57, Herbert 83

HILL, Hester 39, 83, J.A. 57, J.A. 101, J.W. 143, Jack 83, 100, James 33, 57, 96, 101, Jesse 96, John 12, 60, Kate 59, 78, Kathleen 216, Lora 93, Maggie 101, Martha 33, Mary 40, 100, 110, Minnie 39, 83, 100, Mitty 114, 209, Nora 100, Otto 83, 100, Pearl 83, R.E. 39, 100, Rebecca 220, Roy 83, T.M. 39, Thomas 58, 83, Tom 100, W.H. 39, 159, W.J. 39, Walter 39, 83,100, Washington 220, William 100, 110,

HINDALL, Joseph 85 1, Lucy 79, 85

HINDMAN, Homer 190

HINES, Allen 97, 257, Fanuel ? 133, Fount 11, George 97, 257, John 97, 256, 257, Lula 97, Marion 97, Martha 11, 55, Mary 133, Obe 133, Sophie 98, Walter 97, William 133

HINSON, Joseph 6, Leslie 126, Thomas 6,

HOBBS, Abram 8, Aline 70, Allen 37, 60, 70, 78, Alonzo 56, Amanda 64, Andrew 70, 120, 124, 220, Anna 131, Arch 9, 61, 120, Bessie 17, Burrel 79, Catherine 92, Charles 5, Charlie 128, Dan 65, Dick 6, Dock 61, Elizabeth 27, 118, Elmer 120, 124, 220, Ernest 78, Eula 70, Ezekiel 17, 70, 120, 124, 220, Fannie 70, 120,

HOBBS, Fannie124, 220, Flora 37, Frances 121, 124, 220, George 37, 61, 76, 78, Gertie 79, Grace 37, 78, Hardin 124, Hattie 82, Horace 56, Isaac 5, 16, 66, 69, 131, 282, James 78, 92, Jane 60, Jeff 65, Jefferson 1, 18, 128, Joe 61, John 61, Josh 61, Julie 9, 70, 101, 120, 124, Lela 74, Lois 92, Loy 56, Luther 70, Lydia 65, Malinda 134, Mandy 286, Margaret 92, Marion 9, 65, Marjorie 70, Mary 26, Mattie 87, 133, 87, Minerva 128, Nancy 69, Oral 70, Pearl 123, Phoebe 92, Rebecca 81, 90, Riley 61, Robert 92, Ruth 65, 92, Seba 37, 78, Sherman 128, Sol 120, 124, 220, Solomon 70, Thelma 70, Thomas 18, Tom 92, Vernon 70, Violet 70, Wiley 7, 8, 16, 92, William 10, 64, 65, 92,

HODGE, E.E. 18, Eva 93, Ezra 18, Jessie 19, Jim 19, Leslie 114, Martha J. 60, Thomas 60

HODGES, Emma 114 James 114, Martha 136

HOEWISCHER, Harry 107, 297, Henry 107, 297, Maude 107, 297, Phillip 107, 297 Phoebe 297

HOFFNER, Alice 53, Amanda 82, Delbert 51, Fowler 51, Henry 51, 60, James 51, Raymond 51, Verda 72

HOGG, Ruth 129
HOGON, Henry 86, Jane 86 Opal 86, Ray 86, William 86
HOKE, Emma 121, George 28
HOLBROOK, Betsy 125 Bruce 24, Beulah 111, Cap 88, 101, Cappie 111, Carroll 125, Catherine 125, Daniel 66, Dee 40, 88, 93, Ersa 233, Glady 93, Gradie 40, Harry 88, Henry 24, Joe 66, Joseph 66, Loren 93, Martha 126, Mallie 110, 233, Mattie 88, Mollie 110, 125, 233, Otto 93, 258, Pete 111, 46, P.D. 88, Samuel 24, 125, Susan 111, 162, Thelma 125, W.D. 93,
HOLBROOKS, Alta 23, Bruce 23, Gertrude 82, Henry 23, Minnie 23, Samuel 23, S.R. 116, Susie 139
HOLDEN, Fannie 267
HOLDER, A.F. 52, Charles 52, Ellen 52, Finch 13, Henry 52
HOLDERMAN, - --160 Alva 48, Ester 48, J.A. 48, James 48
HOLLEMAN, Mary 6, Nancy 1, Vina 63
HOLLEY ,--- 39
HOLLINGSWORTH, --- 34, C.M. 34, J.L. 34, Lewis 34
HOLLMAN, --- 33, Della 82, Jessie 82
HOLLOMAN, Annie 133, Bertha 95, Della 133, Ellen 110, Everett 129, George 129, Jesse 133, John 112, Pearl 129, S.A.D. 110, Virgil 129
HOLLOWAY, Hettie 105, John 105, Lee 37,105, Lester 64, 105, Mattie 105, Miley 105, Millard 105, Myrtle 64, Nellie 105, Nora 105, Richard 105, Thomas 105
HOLLY, Columbus 33, Grant 33
HOLT, Frank 108
HOLTON, Beulah 118
HOMBRICK, John 129,
HOOTEN, Lizzy 49, Nancy 50
HOOVAN, Nancy 126
HOOVER, Nancy 20, 100, 108,
HOPKINS, Nellie 134
HORN, Oliver 128
HORNBECK, Charles 90, Earl 87, 90, Henry 90
HOSICK, Adaline 14, Annie 98, Emma 7, Dora 7, E. Smith 98, E.S. 34, Elizabeth 98 Joseph 98, Mary 98, S. 135, S.T. 34, Salina 98, W.S. 95, Martha 7,
HOSKINSON, --- 2, Harriet 22, 93, Lenora 118, Logan 118, Nora 73, Willburn 118
HOSSLER, Adolphus 20, Charles 53, 60, Ida 20, Irene W. 20, Louis 36, 53, 60
HOUSE, --- 31
HOWARD, Anna 222, Beulah 166, 167, Gene 166, Glenn 68, Hannah 78, Harry 57, 222,

HOWARD, Jean 221, Jennie 68, 116, John 57, 68, 222 Lawrence 68, Leon 116, Lillie 221, Loren 57, 221, Lydia 48, 222, Marvin 116, 223, P.E. 167, 221, Pearl 223, P.J. 57, Percy 166, Philip 57, 221 Ray 106, Sarah 221, W.H. 221, W.P. 116, Walter 57, 222, Wesley 223,
HOWE, Jacob P. 17, Sarah 16
HOWSE, Frank 208, Margaret 206
HUBBARD, Ada 224, Alice 224, Alpha 224, Alta 225, Amanda 101, 225, Ann 225, Anna 101, Annie 230, Bertha 224, Bertie 225, Bessie 101, 225, Blanche 230, Charles 29, 96, 104, 193, 223, 224, Chester 101, 223, 225, Clara 225, Cora 224, Dora 109, 205, Edna 230, Edward 96, Effie 225, Elizabeth 224,
HUBBARD, Emma 109, Etta 96, Florence 109, 136, 205, Fred 96, 224, Hattie 29, Henry 96, 224, Hillis 223, 224, Hugh 109, 205, Ivy 96, James 96, 224, 225, Jane 109, 205, 223, Jennie 10, 109, 205, Jesse 225, John 34, 69, 96, 109, 204, 223, 293, Lacey 224, Leonard 224, Lora 101, 225, Margaret 29, Martha 224, Mary 109, 179, 194, 205, Maude 224, Mina 97, Minnie 96, 224

HUBBARD, Missouri, 223, 225, Nancy 225, 230, Obediah 223, 179, Otto 101, Perlina 223, Presley 205, 209, Rhoda 137, Sallie 96, Sarah 224, Thomas 224, William 223, 224, 225
HUBBS, Freeman 114, Loren 112, Rickie 82, Riley 112
HUDSON, Goldey 129
HUFF, Myrtle 55
HUFFMAN, Martha 36
HUFSEY, Ann 100, Dennis 58, Eunice 113, George 79, John 113, Mae 58, Mamie 113, Matilda 113, Nancy 56, 100, Reedie 65, Samuel 113, Anna 228, Charles 100, Charlie 227, Dennic 115, Eunice 228, George 134, 227, John 113, 115, 226, 228, Lennie 134, Loren 134, Malinda 134, Mamie 228, Mary 227, Matilda 227, Maude 134, Nellie 134, Samuel 117, 226, W.F. 227,
HUGHES, E.B. 133, Eliza 113, Elsie? 93, Eva 93, George 32, Ilie 93, J.W. 32, James 32, Joe 305, John 32, Kate 100, Laura 139, Leslie 98, Lora 69, 93, 98, Lycurgus 113, Marshall 49, Mary 67, Mickey 67, 100, Paul 32, Richard 6, 100, Sadie 93, T.A 93, Thomas 93, Wes 1, 29, William 32, 67,
HUMM, Abner 47, Anna 23, 111, 260 Barbara 92, 111

HUMM, C.B. 29, Bass 229, Catherine 39, Charles 47, Elizabeth 23, Fred 77, 111, Frederick 23, 260, Geneva 22, George 132, 262, Harry 47, J.F. 22, James 133, Jennie 57, John 230, Luciene 133, Marzella 22, Mitchell 47, 133, Quentin 133, Thomas 133, Sabastian 229,
HUMPHREY, Denia 40, George 40
HUNTER, Cora 6, Effie 114, Flora 116 217, High 9, J.A. 40, James 7, 46, 126, Jule 46, Mollie 40, Shelton 46
HURFORD, Aaron 64, Alma 72, 101, 72, 102, 102, Anna 72, 135, Annie 102, Arthur 133, 134, Austin 102, Ben 34, 36, 92, 101, 102, 134, Catherine 101, Daniel 134, David 45, 47, 111, Davis 134, Ellen 111, 134,.Eva 134, Gertrude 134, Golda 139, Goldie 111, 163, Hattie 126 Helen 134, Herbert 111, Hiram 101,102, Issac 102, Jemima 111, Jesse 102, 118, 134, 133, 250, Joe 134, Katie 134, Lula 39, Mamie 9, Margaret 92, Martha 134, Mary 102, 105, 134, Nellie 22, Noah 9, 55, 64, 102, 134, Noel 45, Otto 92, Rose 84, Samuel 133, 134, Sarah 102, 124, Suda 45, Sudie 71, Thomas 13, 84, 102, Vernon

HURFORD, Vernon 111, W.N. 64, Viola 134, Wallace 111, W.D. 133, Wiley 102, William 102, 111, 117, 134, 117
HURLEY, Fannie 139, Mary 139, Mose 139
HURST, Hazel 232, Henry 232
HURT, Jane 30 Mary 30, William 30
HUTCHINSON, Betty 124
HYATT, Myrtle 121
ILIFF, Claude 13, Clyde 41
INGRAM, Ben 2, 103, Bert 106, Dick 2, Miranda 103, Nannie 97
INMAN, Jack 80, Opheldia 80
IRBY, Arthur 24, Alice 89, 93 110, 148, Arnold 93, 135, Bill 134, Carlos 89, Earl, 28 89, 134, Ellen 134, Eva 93, 135, Evelyn 93, Fannie 24, Fred 134, Harry 89, James 24, John 134, Howard 127, Katie 134, L.P.14, Lena 89, Margaret 28, Mary 24, Nancy 14, 83, Orval 111, 129, Philip 93, 135, Raum 14, W.P. 59, 129, Walter 134, Wayne 93, William 129, 134, Wilmetta 93, 135,
IRONS, Anna 120, Clint 97, Mary 24, 302, Ruth 97
IRVIN, Addie 15, Carolyn 94
ISHAM, Edd 100, Howard 100, J.E. 58, 70, J.G. 58, 84,

ISHAM, J.M. 70, James 2, 58, Jess 100, Jesse 127, Malissa 26, Margaret 58, Maude 71, 84, Nell 100, Nelle 67, Sarah 84, 127,
JACKS, 150, 156
JACKSON, --- 34, Alonzo 42, Andy 232, Alpha 121, Andrew 94, Andy 110, Anna 135, Annie 9, 102, Bathsheba 66, Beuhla 48, Ceph 236, Charles 9, 46, 65, 234, 260, 234, Daisy 66, Della 112, Dora 124, E.R. 66, Ed 124, Elizabeth 58, 110, 232, 237, Emily 17, Ermine 65, Eulalia 83, Ezra 135, Fred 48, 118, G.W. 15, George 9, 15, 17, 124, Gertrude 41, Harriet 15, John 6, 9, 42, 110, 232, Joseph 9, Julie 95, Katherine 137, Liza 110, 232, Lucy 122, 234, Lula 97, Lurinda 110, 232, Mabel 77, Mae 127, Malinda 76, Marion 34, Martha 42, Mary 27, 122, 234, 122, Mattie 33, Mina 66, Newt 236, Peggy 118, Rachel 93, Rita 18, Roda 75, S.L 32, 76, Sarah 110, 232, Sidney 27, Stephen 110, 232, Susan 17, Thelma 76, Thomas 122, Tom 133, Tyra 110, 232, W.L. 33, Wiley 36. William 9, 19, 34, 42, 65, 94, 110, 118, 227, 232, Yvonne 18
JACOB, Cella 55
JARRELLS, Alma 103, Anna Anna 103, Mary 103, Nancy

JARRELLS, 103, Thomas 43, 103
JARVIS, Jentie 80, Kate 55 Majenta 130, Thomas 80
JEFFORD, James 44, Kelly 44, Raymond 44
JENKINS, ---61, Ada 58, Al 58, 120, Alice 70, Anna 61, Booker 1, C.A.W. 70, Cecil 97, Chalon 70, Charles 110, 139, Clarence 70, Ella 110, 139 Emma 98, 106, 109, Ernest 98, 95 George 97, Henry 61, Herbert 58, 120, Ivy 97, John 70, 110, 139, 157, 227, Josie 110, Loren 98, Margaret 110, Martha 110, Mary 34, 54, 69, 110, Mathew 70, Maude 110, Melvina 98, Mick 1, Myrtle 110, Mollie 139, Nannie 36, Nathaniel 98, 106, Nimrod 110, Nim 143
JENKINS, Opal 97, Phoebe 97, Sarah 82, Sidney 95, Thomas 10, 98, 109, 205, Waldo 36, 61, 97, Weldon 58, Will 157, William 61, 227, 110, Zedick 110
JENKS, Booker 61
JENNINGS, Agnes 30, Albert 16, Annie 82, 133, Dora 225, Helen 91, John 225, Mary 293, Mattie 82, Mollie 125, Nancy 12, Robert 30, Wallace 60
JERRELLS, Charles 64, 135 George 135
JEWELL John 9
JOHN, James 4

JOHNSON, --- 15, A.B. 122, Aaron 122, 235, 237, Anna 108, 301, Arch 122, Bush 302, Buster 127, Carrie 190, Charles 122,127, 236, Dane 302, Ella 122, 236, Ellis 302, Emma 127, Etta 55, Eva 122, 236, Ewing 122, 236, Frances 122, 236, Frank 122, 237, George 122, 236, Gordon 127, Ida 42, 122,236, John 71, 122, Johnnie 302, Laura 122, 236, Louis 122, 302, Lula 122, Marcel 127, Martha 122, Mary 1, 11, 54, 122, 152, 218, 234, Nora 302, Ollie 86, 115, Pearl 122, 237, Robert 127, Roger 302, Roy 75, Tom 302, Willard 302, William 302
JOINER, Anna 73, Annie 122, B.O. 3, Bessie 99, Bessie 128, Clara 29, Clint 119, Daisy 84, Della 50, Elizabeth 29, 55, 86, 97, Emmeretta 84, Essie 50, **JOINER**, Eugen 99, Glen 119, Goldie 37, 75, Helen 119, Hickman 55, 104, Issac 55, Ivy 76, J.T. 91, James 55, 99, John 26, 29, 55, 67, L.E. 39, Laura 67, Lena 128, Lewis 76, Lizzie 122, Lola 38, Loren 50, Loy 50, Lula 91, 99, Maggie 73, Melvina 92, Mildred 99, Mollie 99, Mornisa 256, O.W. 55, Ollie 118, Phil 41, 50, Rachel 80 117, Rhoda 2, Ruth 99, Sam 9, 50, 55, 99, 28, Silas 99, Sol 99, 128

JOINER, Stella 99, 128, Tracy 50, Vernon 76, Virginia 119, Wanda 99, William C. 55, Willie 2
JONES, Alexander 3, Belle 117, Chester 117, David 127, Dena 80, Elizabeth 83, 100, 109, 147, F.M. 87, Francis 36, Gusta 120, Hathryn? 94, Jimmie 77, John 87, Jonathan 87, Joshie 87, Levisa 99, Martha 124, Mary 79, 85 Maude 102, Mercy 87, Neal 117, Nellie 87, Noah 107, Polly 77, Richard 128, Susanna 87, Susie 95, Tom 87, Hugh 15, Mary 62,
JORDON, B.J. 61, J.H. 62 Mary 62
JOYCE, Alvin 38, Arvetta 45, Ella 35, G.W. 38, George 35, Hilbert 45, James 2, John 22, 45, Lilly 22, Martha 2, Oakley 45, Olive 22
JOYNER, Anna 118, Edith 73, Francis 95, James 95, Josie 102, Loren 44, Margaret 13, Melissa 34, Willis 34,
JULIAN, Anice 12
JUSTICE, Mahala 48
KAEGI, Bernard 119, Charles 119, George 95, 119, Henry 119, Herbert 119, 133, 154, Loren 119, Mary 110, 119, 303, Omer 119, Roy 119, Stella 132, Will 119
KAGNER, Sylvia 80
KAISER, Edna 134, Cliff 134

KALLEN, Add 112
KARBER, Ada 93, 124, Adam 7, Amie 44, Bertis 107, Clarence 93, Dorothy 107, Ezra 106, 107, Eula 106, F.C. 10, Frank 93, 106, 124, 237, Freda 93, Frederaca 53, 60, George 49, 87, 106, Henry 8, 106, James 237, John 93, 124, Julie 10, Junie 106, L.A. 93, 124, Laura 138, Lewis 8, Lucy 106, Mary 106, Matilda 8, Paul 107, Will 106
KARNS, Frances 57, John 57
KARRACKER, Arnie 43, 72, Howard 43
KATT, Catty 82
KAYLOR, Mary .62
KEELING, -- I.9, Ada 114, Ed 114, Elizabeth 121, Ellen 114, Emily 6, Eva 114, Frances 120, 121, 124, 220, Fred 114, George 57, J.F. 121, J.J. 9, J.W. 121, James 114, 121, Joe 114, Mary 121, Minnie 134, Nerrissa 9, Pearl 115, Ray 133, T.F. 121, Virgie 83, 114,
KEESES, Anna 71
KELLER, Henry 75, Myrtle 75
KELLY, Maria 87
KEMPER, W.W. 102
KENDELL, Maude 50.
KENDRICK (S), James 33 Mary 33, 53, 54, Ophelia 14,
KENNEDY, Edward 8, Fred 72, Grace 72, Harry 72, Mary 72

KENNEY, Annie 190, Mary 70,
KERCHER, Theresa 132
KERR, A.T. 130, Ada 130, C.C. 160, Clarence 129, E.S. 130, Garrett 130, John 130, Katherine 129, Leslie 130, Mildred 130, Rosina 130, Stanley 130, Susan 130, Tony 129, 130,
KIBBY, H. 131, Mary 131
KIB(B)LER, Daisy 121, E.R. 57 Eddie 121, Edward 89, Effie 51, John 121, Paul 51, Wayne 51, 121
KILGORE, Jeff 43, 53, Laura 43, Willie 43, 53
KIMBALL, G.W. 4, Laura 143
KIMBRO, Anna 135, Callie 135, Cal 135, Earl 135, Elmer 135, Hubert 135, John 135, Mary 135, Nellie 135
KINDLER, Fern 105
KING, Alice 95, Allen 62, 117, Audra 112, Charles 117, Daisy 116, Doras 116, Harold 116, Jewell 112, Joe 98, John 116, 117, Joseph 117, Loren 117, Norma 116, Ruby 62, Triphena 117, Velma 116, Virginia 81, Wallace 112, Walter 81, William 4, 112,
KINNEY, Cephus 104, Frederick 122
KIRKHAM, Charles 60, J.H. 60, James 8, James 300 Lavina 8, Ollie 8

KLINGER, Carrie 98
KNEELING, Addie 17, Arthur 17, Ernest 17, John 17
KNIGHT, Austin 48, David 48, E.A. 48, Ethel 139, Lydia 48, 68
KNUCKY, Elizabeth 4, Richard 4
KOCH, Cecilia 110, John 10, Joseph 110, M.J. 110, Noveda 110, Omer 10, William 110
KORNSTEIN, Ada 119
KOSTER, George 82
KOUPAS, George 102
KRIKIE, Fred 47
LACEY, Noah 127
LACKEY, Archibald 104 Archie 99, Carrie 117, Charlie 133, Dora 143, Frances 99, Frank 133, Julia 80, Mary 104,
LACKEY, Minerva 133, Nancy 99, 104, William 46, 133,
LACY, R.O. 48
LADD, Elizabeth 68,179, 184 188, 189
LADWIG, Hester 24
LAGODZINSKI, Alma 67, Joe 67, Mollie 67
LAGRANDE, C.F. 63
LAINER, Clara 46
LAIRD, Alex 59, Margaret 81 Richard 81
LAMAR, Charles 42, 59, 72, Charlie 238, Edd 72, Elizabeth 6, 237, Laura 238, Lillie 59, 238, Louis 59, 238, Luther 72, Marcella 59, 238, Marie 72,

LAMAR, Mary 59, 238, Otis 59, 238, Roxie 43, Roy 72, Sarah 34, Staley 59, 238, Sula 72, 121, Viola 43, W.T. 6, 34, William 58, 237
LAMB, Arthur 132, Audrey 47, Bertie 47, Charles 47, Charlton 132, George 117, James 79, 117,132, John 117, Lizzie 47, Malisa 117, Mary 117, Melissa 47, Myrtle 79, 132, Randall 132, Sophronia 117, Thomas 16, Thurlow 132, Tommie 132, W.R. 47, 117, William . 16, Willie 117, 125
LAMBERT, Aaron 49, 161, Arthur 49, B.J. 4, Cora 14, David 4, Edna 48, 49, Elizabeth 75, 190, Francis 49, Harve 161, Kate 119, 123, 151, Maggie 70, Minerva 34, Ray 49. 159, Ruthie 92, William 92,
LAMPERT, Ed 134
LANE, Albert 87, Alice 128, Alva 135, 149, Cora 87, 138, Edith 108, Edward 108, Esther 32, 54, 152, G.E. 112, H.G. 108, Hannah 108, Henry 116, 160, Hester 108, Horatio 112, 135, Hugh 87, J.A. 112, Ina 128, Isabell 100, James 42, Jeff 92, Jennie 116, John 92, Joseph 92, Lewis 33, Louis 160, Lou 63, M.S. 87, Mack 92, Mattie 79, 92, Mattix 5, Mina 100, Minnie 99, Mollie 92, Nancy 160, Pete 92

LANE, R.H. 112, Rebecca 160, Riley 92, Robert 34,160, Ruthie 92, Stella 108, W.M. 112, Woodrow 33, W.M. 135 Willie 160, Willis 160
LANIER, Asa 1, 138, Elizabeth 91, Mandy 15, Martha 1, 138, Sam 15 138
LARD, Alice 96, Rhoda 94
LASATER, Connie 31, Gladys 31, James 31, 137, Mary 31, Melissa 98, 112, 137, 161, Robert 137, Sarah 137, T.J. 137, Thomas 31
LATHAM, Sam 92
LATTIMORE, Ross 159
LAVANDER, Addie 126, 136, Alta 136, B.L. 16, 28, 32,
LAVANDER, B.L.40, Ben 32, 39, 62, 79, 82, 123, 147, Bill 62, Cassa 32, Cassie 23, Charles 19, 22, 126, 136, 205, 218, Della 33, 62, Essie 136, Florence 136, George 17, 19, 126, Grace 41, India 136, James 17, 19, 40, 79, Josephine 19, Katie 19, Lewis 17, 19, 126, 136, 231, 281, Louis 22, Mack 10, 126, 136, Mary 3, 39, Thomas 4, 123, Wiley 33, 62, 79, 123, 133
LAWLERS, Louise 93
LAWLESS, Addie 139, John 139, Lulie 139, Robert 139, William 139
LAWRENCE, Abraham 74, Abram 121, Ada 121

LAWRENCE, Addison 121, Agnes 121, Bertha 105, 121, Daniel 74, Elic 121, Izora 103, J.B. 121, J.D. 121, John 88, Sarah 121, Sylvester 121
LAWS F.E. 39, 40, Flora B. 40
LAXTON, Mary 77, Sara 73
LAYOFF Arthur 132, Betty 132, Laura 107, 132
LEDBETTER, Adrain 72, 74, 135, 238, Allen 48, 72, 74, 77, Alvin 76, Anderson 17, Anteline 89, Arthur 117, B.L. 57, B.T. 62, Belle 44, 59, Bertha 98, Bertie 47, Bob 74, Bunk 30, 48, 61, 72, 238, Burlin 130, Carol 117, Charles 63, 75, 117, 128, 227, 240, Charline 117, Clifford 30, D.A. 13, 30, 37, 47, 48, 61, David 14, 105, Della 37, 72, 135, 238, Dick 7, Doctor 238, Dora 63, 80, 129, Dorothy 85, Dossett 40, Dr. 72, E. 17, Edith 89, Elizabeth 3, 61, 75, 100, Emma 74, 78, 135, 238, Emmer 44, Frank 82, Frankie 117, G.W. 46, George 2, 32, 40, 42, 57, 67, 128, 129, 239, 240, Gertrude 42, 53, 67, 105, Grace 40, 240, Grover 82, Harry 128, 240, Henry 3, 85, 95, 105, 128, 129, Herbert 13, 76, 85, 164, 241, 164, Howard 105, Ida 59, 76, Isabell 44, J. 61, J. Nelson 113, J.A. 76, J.N. 24, Jack 76,

LEDBETTER, James 13, 40, 43, 4 4, 59, 63, 72, 73, 75, 105, 117, 128, 129, 159, 238, 240 241, 245, 287, Jim 156, Joe 130, John 1, 13, 40, 57, 59, 61, 76, 85, 94, 95, 105, 117, 128, 159, 230, 238, 240, Joseph 85, Julie 95, June 85, Kate 59, 76, 241, Kenneth 85, Laura 122, Lee 57, Liza 2, M.D.A. 135, Maggie 117, Mahala 1, Margaret 23, 42, 43, 76, 89, Mary 17, 60, 61, 82, 95, 105, 117, 136, 227, 288, May 27, 28, Millard 27, 28, 44, 61, 63, Millington 17, 105, Mollie 24, 85, 113, 283, 285,Mora 128, 240, Nancy 57, 61, Nellie 85, Nelson 283, Ollie 59, 76 72, 135, 238, Ora 67, 128, 240, 105, Otto 114, Pearl 45, Percy 1, Philip 105, Polly 128, 129, 239, Pompey 74, Quince 59, Quincy 76, R.A. 47, Rachel 128, 240, Ray 72, 74, 238, Rebecca 113, 283, Richard 62, 57, Riley 45, 80, Robert 72, 80, 105, 135, Roxie 128, Ruth 61, 81, 85, Sarah 118, 137, Sidney 45, 292, Thomas 18, Viola 43, 117, Virgie 117, Virginia 85, W.P. 23, W.R. 70, 292, W.S. 43, 44, Waitman 135, Walsh 130, Walter 2, William 13, 105, 240, Willie ? 40, Zoa 106, Zoe 106,
LEE, Barsheba 9, Chas 29

LEE, Charles 11, 15, 41, 127, Clifford 114, Cora 41, Daisey 114, Effie 46, 114, Elizabeth 41, 63, Jas 9, John 11, 29, 46, 114, 127, Lula 29 41, 68, 127 Lillian 85, Mariah 127, Malvina 127, Martha 50, Mary 41, Robert 41, Thomas 40, Walter 114
LEIGH, J.J. 70
LEINGEL, Rose 81
LEONARD, Roy 118
LEONBARGER, Charles 132, Clarence 21, Cora 41, Daisy 67, 68, 299, Fred 21, 132, 164, George 21, 132, Gertie 29, John 20, 22, 31, Leon 29, Ollie 21, Rosa 128 Sarah 21, 132, 134, 164, 21
LEONBARGER, Stella 129, Sylvia 73, Wiley 21, 54, 132, 164, William 31
LESTER, Elsie 65
LEWIS, Albert 100, Brown ? 94, Charles 94, 100, Charlotte 94, Cleta 131, Edd 100, Elizabeth 100, Harry 27, Henry 68, 137, Hettie 105, James 27, John 100, Leslie 99, 100, Pink 287, Rachel 137, Rebecca 51, Sadie 100, Ted 87, Thomas 27, 68, 137
LEZYNISKA, L.A. 106
LIEHTENBERGER, Wash.10
LIGHTNER, Ella 36, Ethel 36, Jesse 36, Maggie 36, Mary 36, 53, Noah 15, 36

LILLARD, George 107, 132, Laura 132, Martha 132, Maybell 132, Z.T. 132
LIMBO, Louis 49
LINDSEY, Viola 125
LINER, Allie 25, C. 25, G.W. 25, George 25, Harvey 25, Maggie 25, Melissa 25, Susan 25
LINGAL, Rosie 61
LINGNEL, Rose 49
LIPPERT, Ruth 97
LITTELL, Wilma 66
LITTELS, Milberry 129
LITTLE, Clarence 44, Ebb 83 George 64, Jane 119, Mary 64, Nellie 135, Triphena 117
LITTREL, Charles 66, Ettie 112, 279, Joe 66, Ira 66,
LITTREL, Vernon 66, Willis 66
LIVERS, Angie 55, Effie 24, James 13
LOCKABY, Sarah 199
LOCKE, George 74, Mary 27, 41, 65, W.W. 74
LOCKERSBY ?, Sarah 95
LOCKLAR, Barbara 122 Eddie 122, George 122, John 122,
LOFTON, Willie 121
LOGAN, Carl 90, Charles 90, Enoch 90, Francis 90, James 90, William 90
LOGSDON, Helen 135
LORENE, Orphia 38
LOVE, A.E. 211, Allen 20 26, 60, Clarence 134, Elva 134

LOVE, James 66, 83, Janie 38, John 66, Loren 66, Marion 66, Martha 66, Mary 26, 60, 66, Ollie 66, S.B. 132, Sylvester B. 66, Thurman 134, William C. 66
LOWE, Alfred 40, 41, James 40
LOWERY, Alma, 102, Anna. 49, Bell 22, Clara 12, Dosha 241, Edith 66, 241, Edna 102, Frank 66, George 66, 241, Gordon 60, Henry 102, J.L. 13, 217, J.M. 60, 102, James 136, 241, Jane 71, Jesse 12, 74, Jim 66, John 36, 66, 160, 241, Marie 102, Martha 136, Mary 66, 77, 95, 241, Matthew 241, Miranda 102, Nettie 36, Rinda 99, Walter 66, Warren 102, Wilburn 102,
LUCAS, Mattie 115
LUNDBERG, Anna 29
LUSTER, Albert 70, 292, Clara 292, H.A. 84, J.J. 84, Josie 22, L.G. 84, R.C. 84
LYNCH, Collins 62, James 62
LYNN, Elizabeth 84
LYON (S), Elizabeth 55, Hyremettry 109, 147, James 43, John 2, 109, 147, Nancy 2, 109, Phoebe 13, 197, Rebecca 173, 179, Robert 173
MACRAW, Nancy 5
MADDEN, Anna 88, Buck 88, Charles 10, Clarence 10, Jane 10, John 88, Virginia 88
MADDOX, John 114

MADDOX, Lillie 114, Margaret 114
MAHAN, Alexander 74, Charley 74, Gideon 74, Harvey 74, Issac 75, John 74, Margaret 102, Nancy 74, Thomas 74, William 74
MAHN, Betty 159
MAIR, Robert 108
MALCOME, Sarah 80
MANHART, G.W. 118, James 43, 244, Mary 118, 164, Phoebe 45,
MANN, Addie 125
MANNON, Ross 4
MAPLE, William 71
MARGLIN, Billie 112, Floyd 61, Floyd 61 112, James 31, 83, 94, 112, Katherine 112, Nancy 83, Robert 331, 83, 94, 31, Susie 56
MARLAND, Glenn 135
MARSH, Angleton 69
MARSH, Iva 134
MARSHALL, Anna 139, Charles 139, Clarence 139 Ed 139, John 139, Letha139 Otto 139
MARTIN, Aileen 51, Belle 96, Charles 51, 78, Clara 97, Claude 70, Claudie 71, Daniel 77, Dave 30, 51, 91, Eliza 13, Emma 74, Eugene 107, Fannie 102, Fern 289, Gold 107, Grace 107, Harvey 78, Hettie 107, Imogene 107, Ira 190, 289, Irene 96, Issac 8, James 13, Jane 178, John 1, 8,

MARTIN, Josephine 107, Julian 289, Laura 288, Lucinda 83, Martha 57, 77, Milt 96, Milton 22, Ruth 96, 258, Tristen 65, W.H. 16, W.R. 10, 74
MASON, Abe 248, Anna 29, Bryant 17, 56, 288,Caswell 248, Charles A. 56, E.B. 100, Henry 248, Issac 4, Joe 159, 248, John 21, Joseph 11, 56, 100, Julia 16, 21, Laura 47, Lou 17, 288, Mark 248, Nancy 100, Nora 106, Nora 106, Phoebe 21, Sarah 116, 249, Ulys 132, Walter 40, 56, 100, William 11, 57,
MATBENY, Frank 15 Rolla 15
MATHENY, Job 7, Julie 19, Lucinda 6, Nona 305, Nora 110, Rita ? 58
MATTHEWS, Ethel 134 Floyd H. 52, Harriet 11, Henry 9, Henon 52, John 9
MATHIS, Alice 128
MATSON, Mary 117
MATTINGLEY, Judith . 63 Zachary 63
MAYBERRY, Dora 137
MAYFIELD, Alfred 91, Billie 181, Charles 91, 94, 118, Clyde 118, Frank 60, 118, Frankie 118, Glenn 91, Gussie 91, Helen 91, James 118, John 22, 91, Juantia 118, Ollie 35, Ruby 118
McALLISTER, Katie 99

Mc ALLISTER, Robert 169
McAMIS, Laura 18, Thomas 18, Ross 18, John 18, Laura 115
McBEE, Florence 122 Frankie 65
McCALLISTER, Geo. 3
McCARTY,--- 263
McCAUGHAN, Lula 136
McCLEARY, Etta 102
McCLEAN, Ivy 116
McCLELLEN, ---265, Emeretta 267
McCLOTHLIN, John 102, Margaret 102
McCLURE, V.A. 48
McCLUSKY, Anna 115, Cora 51, 138, Della 115, 251, Denny 112, Esther 112, Fred 51,115, 138, 150, Gordina 251, Gordon 251, Irene 115, 251, Irving 112, James 51, 138, John 51, 112, 138, 150, Kate 51, 138, Loren 112, Lucinda 115, 250, Rodney 115, 251
McGOIN, Arthur 102, Carrie 102, Frank102, Jim 102, Marie 93, 102
McCONNELL, Alma 10, 106 Cyrus 115, 245, Ellis 115, 245, Everett 115. 157 245, Gladys 115, 245, Helen 106, 115, 245 Hugh 115, 245, Lucy 245, Mary 106, 115, 245, Olive 245, Patricia 246, Richard 10, 115, 245, Zoe 106
McCORMICK, Minerva 48, Pearl 256

McCOY, 137
McCUE, Alice 12, Millie 89
McDANIELS,Aaron 123, Arza 60, Nancy 123
McDONALD, Adolphus 66, Asa 129, Della 95, Everett 160, Hobert 53, James 53, Katherine 66, 145, Maude 66, 84, Mayme 75, Ollie 84, Sarah 25, Sidney 25
McDOWELL, Alice 74, 273, Anna 116, Betty 109, 124, Casadine, 123, 126, Charles 85, 123, Clement 109, Deal 27, Dora 65?, 98, 124, 227, Edward 98, 124, Eli 119, 123, 150, Elizabeth 41, Ethel 92, F.M. 123, Gary 109, Geneva 85, George 65, 90, Gertrude 29, Grace 123, Hazel 232, Herbert 85, Ida 65, James 71, Kell 65, 98, 124, Mae 98, Mary 85, Maude 71, May 22, 124, Mora 85, Nannie 65, Nellie 105, Nora 51, 65, Norma 109, Pearl 123, Pry 2, Rachel 119, 123, 150, Robert 123, Rose 123, Sadie 110, 305, Sarah 119, 123, 150, Treva 85, Walter 12, 65, Wayne 65, William 98,
McELROY, Astra 128, Jennie 8
McELVRLY, Gurtie 110
McFADEN, Katie 134
McFALL, Asberry 71, Fleety 71 George 71, James 67, 71, Jessie 6 7, John 71, Josie 64,

McFALL Mollie 71, 89, Ruby 67
McFARLAND, ---230, ---292, Abe 58, B.P. 71, Bigger 9, 252, Druailla 70, Elizabeth 9, 140, 294, James 4, 9, 115, 140, 253, 300, Mathilda 253, Mattie 115, Minnie 294, Pinkney 70, Pinkneyette 23, R.P. 253, Sidney 60, William 70
McGILL, --- 93
McGINNIS, L.H.B. 49, Margaret 49, 87, 87, Mary 87 R.J. 49, Rollin 49, 87,
McGLOTHIN, James 102
McGOIN, Arthur 110, Cora 110,
McGOWN, Ed 11, Julie 11
McKERNAN, Arthur 28, E.C. 27
McKINNEY, May 101
McLEAN, Ora 120
McMILLIAN, Bonnie 92
McMURPHY, Chloe 224, David 254, Edward 255, Emma 234, Ernest 256, Etta 224, Frank 255, George 255, Henry 224, 256, Icy 256, James 224 256, Jennie 224, John 256, Josephine 255, Josie 83, Katherine 224, Lafayette 256 Levi 169, 256, Maggie 224, Maggie 255, Martha, 256, Mary 192, 196, 255, 256, Matt 33, Matthew 256, Mollie 256, Noah 33, 224, Pearl 256, Samual 1, 224, Sarah 224, Silas 224, Tom 224

McMURPHY, Volley 254, William 256
McNEIL, John 34, Dosia 34,
McNUTT, Virginia 103
McTYRE, A.M. 35, Alfred 35, 85, Sarah 85, William 85
McWADE, Agnes 98
MEGILL, Rebecca 83
MEISENHEIMER, R.C. 72
MELLON, Addie 46, Elijah 59, Gus 46, 59, Mary 46, Mary 59
MERRILL, Rachel 103, Robert 103,
MEULLER, Effie 125
MEYERS, Anna 99
MICK, Alex 14, Clifford 40, Freddie 9, Nettie 48, S.L. 61 Shaun? 119, Spencer 9, 14, Walter 40
MILES, ---19, Ada 93, 124, Amie 44, Arthur 19, Arvie 44, Berdie 19, Bird 78, Frank 44, Georgia 121, George 201, Hannah 19, 78, J.A. 78, J.W. 45, 93, Jannie 44, John 19, 65, 79, Lottie 44, Nancy 22, 79, Nora 44, R.N. 44, 48, Robert 44, Will 78, William 19, 45
MILLER, A.A. 78, Alice 101, Anna 27, 257, Annie 78, Bertha 101, Bruce 101, C.W. 33, Charles 16, 33, 97, Charley 97, Daisy 33, 97, Douglas 16, Ed 137, Elizabeth 25, Ernest 85, Francis 23, Frazier 111, Geraldine 11, Glover 101, Gordon 101, Hannah 70

MILLER, Hew 10, Hugh 21, James 51, 257, Jane 13, Jim 5, John 4, 6, 51, 85, 257, Joseph 85, Kate 16, 109, 110, Loren 97, Marshall 85, 10, Mary 51, 257, Mildred 51, 257, Nettie 35, Oliver 101, Oren 33, 35, 97, Oscar 13, Owen 16, Phoebe 137, S.D. 110, S.F.78, Samuel 16, 109, Sarah 10, 73, 210,
MILLIGAN, A.W 106, Abner 50, Bertha 53, Bethel 138, Calvin 7, Cecil 56, Clyde 56, Cora 53, Elizabeth 125, Essie 56, Gertrude 53, Henry 125, Hildred 56, Ila 53, J.N. 18, 53, James 26, 49, 50, John 50, Leslie 125, Lewis 50, Lizzie 127, Mabel 125, Maggie 53, Martha 50, 53, Myrtle 53, Nancy 50, Nora 76, Opal 125, Orval 125, Pearl 125, Ray 125, Rhoda 50, Robert 50, Rosemary 138, T.G. 50, Viola 138, W.H. 50, Wallace 49
MILLIKAN, Amanda 19, J.C. 118, James 73, Ora 20, Robert 73, Sam 20, Thelma 20 Vida 117, Wallace 87, Wm. 7
MINOR, Nancy 31, 94
MITCHELL, Ellen 74, John 6, 74, Katie 57, Mary 16, Minnie 44, Rate 144
MIZZEL Mac 62, Sarah 61
MOBLEY, Emily 139
MODGLIN, Rhoda 50
MONROE, Anna 103

MONTGOMERY, Burtis 102, Charles 102, Edward 102, Elizabeth 102, Etta 102, Helen 102, John 102, Mary 102, Paul 102, Theodore 102, Thomas 102
MOORE, ---16, Anna 55, 71, 113, Bill 64, Buchanan 6, Buck 6,113, Charlie 64, 130 Cicero 5, Cordella 36, Della 22 Dick 130, Dow 61, Edith 105 Elizabeth 18, 184, Ella 158, Eva 93, 135, 137, Frankie 125, George 20, 113, Harrison 37, J.H. 64, Jabeez 5, John 4, Kate 130, Lafayette 66, Maggie 101, Nora 130, Omar 37, Richard 113, Roy? 88, Sarah 37, 130, 288, William 7
MORELAND, Mahallah 18
MORGAN, Alice 17, 65 Amanda 92, Angie 61, Audry 139, Clell 138, Drury 138, Elizabeth 138, George 138, Henry 92, Issac 271, Jane 92, Laura 138, Lillie 271, Melissa 84, Melvina 92, Ray 138, Sarah 17
MORMAN, --- 13,
MORRIS, --238, Anna 27, Charlotte 21, Chas? 21, David 85, Eli 20, Elisha 8, Eva 114, George 36, 85, 120, Herbert 120, James 44, Jordon 50, Malvina 8, Overton 36, 120, Ruby 43, Sallie 43, William 120, William 85
MORRISON, Pearl 123

MORROW, -- 83
MORSE, Phillip 76
MOSELY, James, 1 Wm. 1
MOTT, Ada 75, Agnes 121, Asa 8, Clifford 75, Emma 49, 90, Gertie 75, Gracie 75, James 46, 234, 260, John 8, 75, Marion 5, Mary 126, 179,197, Melinda 5, Millard 75, Myrtle 75, Nancy 75, Nellie 128, Robert 75, Sidney 102, T.M. 205
MOYERS, Catherine 116, Finis 66, Gathal 111, George 116, Glenn 111, Goethal 119, J.B. 66, John 111, Maggie 66, 116, Mary 66, 111, Minnie 111, Molly 66, W.C. 66, 111, Wesley 116, 126, Wm, 66, 116
MOZEE, Dr. 160
MUELLE, Dick 111
MURPHY, John 2, Merta 138
NASH, C. H. 74, Cladys 74, Ecalyn 74, Elton 74, Eva 74, J.W. 74, Lottie 74, Mable 74. Theodore 74, Vernon 74
NAVE, Averett 82, Emma 82, James 82, James 102, Kate 102, Margaret 81,O.E. 82, 102, Ora 82
NEEDHAM, Elizabeth 123, 149, Grace 123
NEEL -- 212
NELSON, Katherine 123
NEWMAN, Bertha 35, Catherine 115, Edward 115, Emma 35, George 35, 115, John 115, Laura 18

NEWTON, Ethel 37, 75, Lizzie 54, Martha 122
NICHOLS, Jennie 55, Myrtle 55?, Samuel 55, Virginia 84
NOLES, Benjamin 50
NOOKS, Maggie 53
NORTHERN, Neal 133
O'HARA, John 69, Laura 69, Lillie 69, Logan 69, Martha 69, Maude 69, Nora 69, Sadie 69, William 69
O'MELVENY, Elizabeth 34, 293,Harriet 34, George 34, 293
O'NEAL James 138, Lucinda 51, 115, 138, 250, Nancy 138, William 8
OBERMARK, Ida 122, 236
ODIUM, Mary 131, William 131
OGDEN, Elizabeth 115
OGLESBY, Katie 58, Grace 86, Virginia 36
OKERSON, --36, Albert 100, 113, 228, Ann 100, Anna113, 228, C.A. 100, Kate 91?, 100, Lottie 100, Mary 100, 113, 228, Nancy 100
OLDHAM, Alex 79, Alex 85, Bessie 117, Beulah 111, Charlie 79, Della 132, Delaney 79, Elisha 79, Fleetwood 107, 298, Frank 111, 114, James 5, 38, 132, Jessie 79, Joel 116, John 69, Joseph 79, Junie 32, Lucy 85, Mae 85, Martha 79, Mary 79, 81, Mattie 105, Nellie 132, Nora 100

OLDHAM, Phoebe 296, Sallie 38, 132, Sarah 80, 116, 120, 148, 249, Susan 107, Theora 100, Thomas 107, 297, Walter 100
OLIVER, Millie 93
OLNEY, Frank 66
OLSHAM, Joel 250, Rose 132
OTWIN, Daisey 114
ORR, David 40, 250, Jack 111
OSMAN, Amanda 92, John 94,
OWEN, Mary 3, Pearl 71, William 3
OWENS, Adiel 124, Asroe 124, Beulah 124, David 59 C.V. 124, Emily 124, Geraldine 124, Maude 91, 131, 59, 131, Orba 124, Pruddie 124, Roscoe 124, Seretha 124, Wanda 124, Victoria, 59
OXFORD, Aaron 14, 16, 59, 74, 91, Adriel 97, Albert 68, Alfred 19, 259, Amy 67, Anna 51, Annie 46, Arch 103, Arlee 81, Armstead 130, Arza 123, 125, Arzie 126, Belle 94, 101, Belva 51, 125, Cecil 72, 258, Charles 78, 125, Charlie 126, Clara 22, 96, Clem 68, Cora 82, 133, Curly 21, Della 112, 308, Dock 37, Dora 51, E.76, Ernest 54, Effie 100, Elias 14, 25, 28, 67, 75, 101, 258, Elihu 20, 21, 33, 35, 51, 67, 72, 238, 258, Elizabeth 17, 132, 259, Elmer 81, Emma 51, 59

OXFORD, Ernest 29, 97, 164, Eschol 100, Eunice 103, 125, Eva 29, 97, Everett 58, Florence 125, 126, Fowler 72, 258, George 14, 29, 54, 61, 101, 259, Grace 14, 59, 74, 91, Grover 40, 70, Hannah 54, 64, 108, 258, 259, Harriet 58, 67, 132, Herbert 125, Herbie 37, Hilda 59, Ida 106, India 14 91, Inez 77, Isaac 14, 59, 68, 74, 91, 106, 259, J.A. 7, 14, 17, 22, 29, 72, 199, 234, 238, 258, J.N. 97, J.R. 6, 35, 51 James 14, 45, 67, 81, 100, 108, 125 126, 258, John 11, 18, 19, 21, 40, 54, 59, 61, 67, 69, 72, 100,103, 159, 165, 257, 259, John 280, Julia 100, 101, Kate 19, Laura 101, Lawrence 68, Lee 18, Lizzie 28, Lucien 51, Mary 51, 61, 64, 72,100, 125, 238, 259, Mattie 72, Maude 125, Mildred 125, Millard 19, 259, Minnie 54, 106, 127, Morgan 67, 78, 82, 258, Nancy 14, 28, 56, 101, 126, 258, Nora 29, 97, Opal 63, 125, Oma 20, 63, 125, Owen 70, 103, Paris 100, 144, Patsy 11, Paul 59, 70, Phoebe 97, Prof. 20, Raymon 100, Rebecca 46, 103, Riley 176, 259, Robbie ?14, Robert 33, 51, 59, Roxie 25, 59, S.C. 14, 19, S.E. 125, Sam 29, Samuel 11, 19, 54, 67, 81, 258, 259, Sarado 76, Sarah 19, 20

OXFORD, Seba 20, Sidney 17, Viola 100, Virgil 61, Walter 19, 259, William 106, Wilmer 14, 58, 67, 132,
OZEE, Anna 51, Anne 104 Eddie 46, Edward 234,260, Fannie131, 234, Florence 90, 131, I.N. 46, 234, 260 J.N. 51, James 85, Joseph 85, Lillian 85, Margaret 10, 85, Mary 51, 85, Rebecca 51 Simon 65, 131, Susan 112, 120, 307, Tim 131, Tom 85 "Tom Thumb" 81, Walter 85 131, Will 131, William 85
PABST, Virgie 111
PACKEY, Annie 102
PAGE, Adli 104, Allen 100 Amanda 64, Clem 137,
PAGE, Flora 78, Flossie 76, 137, Harriet 112, J.J. 165, 33, James 137, John 90, 104, 112, Leula 41, Louisa 33, Lucy 137, Mary 31, 112, Mollie 69, Ralph 137, Rhoda 137, S.M. 100, S.N. 39, Viola 33, W.R. 76, W.S. 137, Walter 104, William 100,
PALFREEMAN, Arabell 225
PALMER, Bertha 130, Calvin 21, 64,Cecil 118 Dora 77, 78, 130, Etta 77, J.R. 63, Jodie 63, 130, Joe 21, John 35, 130, Joseph 50, Josie 64, Lizzie 47, Lucy 31, Mary 35. 63, 77, Missouri 64, Oma 64, Richard 77, Sophia 21, W. H. 130, Wiley 77, Wm.118, Zena 24

PANKEY, Agnes 90, Agnes 111, Arthur 64, 111, C.A. 24, Dal 90, 111, Edith 111, Etta 90, Everett 90, 111, George 111, Howard 61, Iley 90, 111, J.H. 24, James 24, 111, John 24, 61, 111, Lucian 90, 111, Lula 24, Mark 24 Mary 45, 90, 111, Philip 24, Ray 111, Sidney 24, Ward 111, Warden 90,
PARIS, , A.D. 63, A.G. 63, Clara 25, Dr. 54, Elizabeth 41 Ezra 82, J.E. 63, , J.J. 7, James 20, Mack 25, Mary 100, Phil 9 Scott 82, W.J. 2, 4, 63, 82
PARKER, Anna 32, Callie 135 Francis 90, Nora 130,
PARKHAM, Ann 25, Evelyn 53
PARKINSON, Green 34, Harriet 43, Lizzie 87, Mildred 34, William 103
PARROTT, Daniel 39, 133, Joe 90, Josie 39, Kate 90, Lucinda 39, 133, Lula 39, 133, 134, Minnie 90, Nan 90
PARSONS, --- 132
PARTAIN,----61, Anna 98, 139, Bessie 99, Etta 98, 139, George 98, 139, Grover 98, 139, Izora 58, John 138, Mabel 125, Maude 53, Milas 98, Minnie 98, 139, Ollie 98, 139, Ollie 98, Tom 128, Willie 139, Willie 98, Wilson 130
PARTON, James 13
PATE, John 21, 122, W.T.21

PATRICK, C.W.95, 288
George 133,, Lydia 161,
Sidney 17, 136, 288, 111,
PATTERSON, Adela 73, 82,
Doland 83, Harry 106,
Henrietta 116 Ishmael 71, Lena 37, Malinda 71, Margaret 49,
Maude 125, Norman 71,
Robert 107, William 49, 70, 71, 71
PATTON, Adron 38, Alice 13, Alonzo 38, 81, 91, 134, 137, Alta 81, 91, Anna 98, 103, 113, 120, Arza 86, Belvia 125, Billie 137, Bob 127, Cicero 5, 81, 91, Cicero 81, Clarence 78, Clarissa 7, Daniel 19, 81, 120, Earl 81, Ed 125, Edward 81, Effie 81, Elias 7, 28, 163, Elizabeth 132, Ellen 61, Elsie 50, Enos 125, Eschol 132, Ethel 77, 127, Fern 89, Gertie 60, 112, Gracie 38, 101, Grant 13, 64, 163, Granville 78, Hannah 5, 11, 28, 64, 113, Hardin 39, Hester, 146, Hillas 91, 137, 138, Hiller 81, Hiram 39, Horace 137, Imogene 138, James 13, 28, 44, 81,86, 101, 109,127 163, 164, Jannie 44, John 94, 98, 137, Lewis 39, 113, Lizzie 28, Loretta 38, Lucian 94, Lucinda 109, Lucy 96, Lydia 71, Margaret 11,101, 135, 218, Mary 5, 7, 28, 61, 82, 127, 163, Milford 19, Mollie 135, Mora 60, Myrtle 112, 308, Nancy 258

PATTON, Omar 60, Oral 81, 91, Orlie 137,Paul 127, Peggy 127, Polly 85, Rae 135, Rebecca 28, 64,163, Roland 137, Roy 60, 127, S.G 71, Samuel 12, 28, 64, 109, 113, Sarah 28, 81, 113, 163, Savannah 81, 91, Tom 127, Tressia 138, Walter 125.
Warren 81, 120, Will 113, William 9, 52, 81, Willie 86, Willis 120
PEARSON, Bessie 42, Della 42, Effie 117, Essie 42, Eva 64, 123, H.C.2, 4, 42, 64, John 245, Mary 42, 64, 115, 140, 245, Maud 42, Minnie 42, Walter 131, Wiley 42
PEAS, Betty 121
PEEL, Webb 216
PEEPLES, Harriet 2, Henry 2, John 2, Mckee 2, William 2,
PELL, Aaron 143, Betty 119, Billy 169, W.A. 216, W.B.240, W.P. 128, Webb 160
PELLEN, Nancy 197
PENNELL, Anna 92, Annabel 112, 308, Bessie 119, Joahua 104, Lillie 113, Lottie130, Oren 130, Seba 92, William 130
PERNELL, Annie 67, Ed,60, James 67
PERRIN, Ed 25
PERRY, -- 48, Ann 120, Dora ? 65, Edith 91, Elvira 122, Eschol 91,George 135, John 122 Lacey 49, Louisa 49,

PERRY, Mary 135, Ralph 91, Sallie 49, 61, 81, 91, Thomas 91, Tom 33, 122, Velma 91,
PERSINGER, Charlotte 101
PETERSON, Harry 66, J.C. 66 Lena 75, Robert 67
PEYTON, Lora 101
PHILLIPS, Howard 16, Lizzie 136, M. 7, Manassa 6, Susan 6
PIERCE, George 127, Harry 127, Lillie 127, Lucretia 127,
PILAND, Fred 25, Dock 52 George 79, J.B., 86, 167, Jerry 25, Jonah 7, James 106, Joe 106, Joey 167, John 106,
PILAND, John 79, Joseph 106, Kitty 106, Pearl 106. Robert 106,
PILLOW, George 42, Nancy 186
PINNELL, Bessie 123, 151
PITT(S), Alonzo 54, Clarence 54, Yandell 31
PLEASANT(S) Charles 3, E. 3, Emily 293, W. 3, William 293
PLEW, Daniel 8, Serena 42
POGUE, Harriet 100
PORTER, Ethel 123, Fannie 67, 106, Glen 223, James 125, Jennie 68
POSEY?, Mabel 68
POST, Antone 132, Frank 132 Theresa 132
POTTS, Edd 73, Freda 117, John 73

POWE, Sadie 100
PRATHER, Ambie 82, Gilbert 82, Herbert 82, Hulbert 82, James 82, Velma 82
PRENTICE, Geneva 85
PRESLEY, Mae 83
PRICE, Amber 48, Arthur 10, 47, 94, Dora 48, Eddie 48, Eva 122, Fleety 71, Frank 127, Hardin 9, Hillis 137, M.T. 10, Maggie 296, Mary 24, 303, Mintie 53, Morris 47, 64, 94, Robert 140, Rose 140, Thomas 10, 94, Tom 296
PRITCHARD, Andy 39, Carroll 12, H.K. 296, John 39, M.M. 39, Mary 12, Mitch 287
PROCTER, A.G. 23
PRUE, Eva 236
PRUETT, Hattie 67 Ben 44, 138, 253, Clora 40, Henry 138, James 138, Jim 140, John 138, Julius 67 Louden 252, Margaret 109, 171, Mary 138, Sarah 109, 171, Thomas 109, 171, William 67
PYLE, Anna 99, Austin 13, 65, 98, Elmer 99, Eva 119, George 98, Gertrude 36, Jacob 65, Jane 99, John 13, 57, 99, 197, Katie 58, 65, Lucy 99, Mary 99, 98, Maude 99, Nicholas 99, Phoebe 13, 98, Robert 99, Roy 57, Sarah 195, 197, William 99
QUELLEN, Albert 99, Archie 99, Charles 99, Frances 99, John 99, Mary 99, William 99

QUERTERMOUS, John 113
QUORUMFOX, --- 93
RADCLIFFE, Laura 131, Rebecca 25, Susan 25, William 25
RADFORD, Eva 78
RAINER, Sam 12, Hattie 11
RAINS, Bertha 86, Oscar 86
RALPH, Alex 147, Ben 116, Bessie 127, Charlie 46, Cora 133, 12, Cleave 46, Deneen 88 Dora 116, Dorothy 88, Elmer 116, Emma 116, Evelyn 88, Fannie 88, Fred 109, George 109, Gilbert 109, Grant 133, Henrietta 116, James 4, 46, 49, John 71, Mack 12, Nan 4, William 6
RALPH, Josephine 88, Laura 109, 110, 147, Lou 133, Lucie 105, Lydia 65, Mamie 46, Manda 46, Mary 116, Mattie 133, Maude 49, May 109, McClellan 116, Myrtle 46, Nellie 46, 109, Nellie 46, Orval 46, Rosie 133, W.A. 50, 116 W.J. 88, Walter 46, Wes 301, William 71, 116, Willie 46
RAMAGE, Odie 97
RAMSEY, S.G. 33, Charlie 126, Florence 126, Mary 126, Nancy 86, William 126
RAMSHAW, Ora 128, 240
RANDALL, Charles 58, D.D., 58, Daniel G. 58
RANDOLPH, Bessie 42, Lillie 95, Robert 42
RANKIN, Mae 98, 124

RASH, Charles 35, Cora 106, J.E. 106, James 55, L.T. 53, Mary 53, Mattie 33, Maude 134
RATCLIFF, Eliza 53, Emma C. 53, George 53, Joe 44
RAVENSCROFT, Anna 300
RAY, John 149, Martha F. 69 Samuel 69
RAYMER, Sarah 127
READY, Arthur 85
REAK, Bill 64, Drucilla 96, 121, Henry 25, J.D. 62, Judith 64, Mat 15, Matthew 18, 25, 62, Mollie 15, Rebecca 25, 62 Roy 62, Thomas 62, W.E. 62
REDDICK, Claude 61
REED, A.C. 124, Alice 25, 35, 88, 124, Artimissa 57, Elizabeth 5, 6, Emma 136, Ethel 124, Gusta 35, Henry 136, James 124, Lester 21, Lewis 5, Louis 57, Martha 57, Mildred 124, Myrtle 46, 104, 130, R.J. 35, 87, 124, Richard 124, Riley 124, Robert 124, Rufus 12, Russel 12, Russell 25, Ruth 124, Sarah 87, Valier 139 Wesley 12, 87, Willie 35
REIF, ---92, Barbara 23, 260, Catherine 111, 262, Francis 86, 104, George 104, 262, Mitchell 104, Nicholas 111, 262, 263 Nick 29, Saloma 111, 262
REINER, Bertha 98, Carrie 98, Carolyn 94, Dora 98, Elizabeth 118, Elmer 14, 98 Fred 94, Goatlieb 84

REINER, Henry 94, John 70, 94, 98, 124, Katie 14, Margaret 84, 94, Mary 76 98, 124, Louis 98, Phoebe 13 98, Willie 94
REINS, Ida 131
RENFRO, Anna 132, 267, Ben 147, 301, Bill 274, Broadway 132, C.D.M. 67, 265, D.N. 59, Don 269, Duncan 132, 267, Emeretta 268, Francis 265, Frank 38 G.W. 38, George 28 Harve 114, Harvey 267, Howard 35, Ida 25, 35, 83, 132, J.H.B. 67, 265, J.R.B. 59, Jim 58, John 265, 268, Johnny 38, Lacey 67, 265, Laura 27, 267, Margaret 267, Maude 69, Nancy 59, 132, Norton 58, Norton 120, R.F. 265, Phenix 266, Ray 132, Raymond 35, Robert 267, 269, Rosco 132, 35, Sarah 35, Thomas 35, 132 W.H. 124, W.J.B. 35, William 132
REX?, Margaret 112
REYNOLDS, Alex 123, Amerine 123, Anna 38, 51, 257 Asa 38, 211, Ima 38, Janie 38, John 38, 45, Nancy 123, Wilma 38
RHEA, Patty ? 128
RICE, Cecil 122, Denie 122 John 122, Kenneth 122, Oscar 122, William 122
RICH, Nona 39, Nora 100
RICHARDS, Emma 109, 172

RICHARDSON, ---19, Lottie 114
RICHERSON, Ab 129, Albert 79, Clifford 79, Dortha 79, Etta 79, Fannie 79, Glenn 79, Herman 79, Walter 79, William 79
RICHESON, Phene 92, Bettie 96, Drucilla 96, 121, E.R. 96, Elliot 121, 122, Ethel 96, 121, G.S. 121, Mary 96, 121,122, Nora 121, W. H. 96, W.C. 96, W.S. 121, William 96, 122,
RICHELS, Ray 132
RICKETS, Belle 91, Charles 123, Charlie 22, George 4, 17, 22, 91, 123, Hattie 128, John 22, Josie 22, Lavada 106, Mary 22, Nellie 22, Ramon 115, Raymond 123, Walter 123
RICKETTE, John 5
RIDLEY, Jack 106, Myrtle 106
RIGGS, Albert 32, Amanda 72 Cassiday 88, Charlotte 88, Clifford 88, Clifton 88, Dora 130 Edward 88, Electa 88, Ellen 114 Franklin 45, H.B. 64, Hattie 88, Henry 32, 45, 83, J.M. 88, Jeff 9, Jerdie 83, 132, Jewell 32, Joe 133, 143, 270, John 45, 83, 133, 270, Joseph 83, Kenneth 88, Lavina 270, Lenora 45, Mahalie 270, Mary 45, Nema 88, Ralph 88, Rose 88, Sallie 132, 144,

RIGGS, Sarah 83, Twila 88, Vera 190
RIGSBY, Gold 107
RILEY ---160, Ethel 89, Hiram 30, Jane 109, S.A. 63 Susan 63
RITTENHOUSE, Charlotte 101, Hattie 101,144, Henry 101, 149, Lora 101, Permington 101, Rosa 101, William 101
ROBB, Naomi 105
ROBERTS, Etta 136, James 126, Joyce 126, Rebecca 59,
ROBERTSON, Mary 17
ROBINETT,---3, Alice 43 Bluford 3, James 49, 59, 238, Kate 102, Lillie 238
ROBINSON, Appie 89, E.L. 23, Elisha 300, Essie 135, Eva 27, Fred 27, 137, Jake 27, 137, Katherine 114, Mae 49, 61, 81, Mag 135, Mary 27, 57, Rachel 41, Richard 27, 137, Thomas 27,
ROGERS, Almedia 125, Alvin 125, Anna 125, 137, Arvie 44, Charles 125, 76, Ellis 125, Elmer 125, George 125, Ike 125, Isaac 40, 125, 137, Jesse 76, John 125, Lottie 125, Louella 125, Lucy 46, 125, Mary 137, Robert 219 Wittie 76
ROHOOF, Henry 127, Sarah 127, Thomas 127
ROLLINS, Frances 99
ROLLO, William 136

RONDEAU, Mazriah 104
ROSE, ---252, Adaline 96, Addie 48, Albert 96, Arista 271 Bluford 30, Burford? 1, C.A. 78, Cassander 32, 123, Charles 11, 48, 61, Clarence 131, 132 Clement 94, Clifford 114, Cora 86, Cordella 53, Della 66, Dema 91, E.R. 11M, Earl 61, Ed 114, Elbert 48, 96, Elizabeth 96, Ella 97, Elsie 63, Eugene 96, Eula 115, Frances 140, George 23, 40, 48, Harve 61, Hattie 132, Henry 16, 65, Ida 30 46, 271, J.E. 271, J.H. 31, J.M. 18, James 18, 78, Janet 96, Jennie 118, Jerry 94, 111, 293, John 13, 48, 161, Joseph 46, Kate 48, Lawrence 11, Lena 94,111, Lillie 271, Louise 46, Mabel 94, 111, Margaret 68, Maria, 271, Martha 94, 111, Mary 270 271, Media 72, Milton 46, Minerva 28, Minnie 40, Mollie 48, 94, 111, 114, 132, Myrtle 38, 265, Nell 94, 111, Oliver 61, Phoebe 11, Pleasant 3, 12, 23, 132, 176, 270, 271, Ray 132, Raymond 206, Robert 48, Saloma 67, Sarah 1, 14, 140 253, Sidney 271, Walter 40, 61, Wiley 23, 40, 63, 140 Will 40, William 23, 47, 108 131, 271
ROSS, Margaret 299, William 3
ROST, Frank 133, Thresa 133

ROTES, Bosty 23, Harriet 89, John 23, John 121, Sylvester S. 35, Tina 25
ROWAN, Charles 22, Don 22, 258, Frank 22, Mayme 100 Paul 22
ROWLAND, Al 129, Bill 117, Edward 22, Golda 117, James 117, John 117, Maggie 129, Margaret 12, Raymond 117,
RUBENACKER, Mary 86, 122, George 104
RUCKER, Catherine 112, 306
RUDD, Anna 107, Lorenzo 107, Mariah 107, Mary 107
RUMSEY, Alice 95, Bertha 199, Burt 95, D.F. 95, Della 95, Fields 95, George 95, J.W. 95, Lillie 95, Robert 95
RUSH, Adelaid 118, Anna 135
RUSHING, Laura 69
RUSSELL, Alma 103, C.M. 126, Emma 116, Jane 126, Julia 54, Loren 38, Mary 125, Mollie 5, Samuel 5, Thomas H. 38, W.F. 54
RUTHERFORD, Arahable 103, Arch 59, 81, 134, Bet 61, Betty 100, Bryan 132, Clement 109, Elva 109, Eschol 108, Ethel 108, Ewing 109, Gladys 108, Hannah 59, 103, Harriet 132, Harry 108, 132, James 8, 88, 103, 134, Jim 148, Joe 134 Joseph 103, 108, Laura 109, Lucy 125, Lydia 28, 103, 134, Mazie 109, Miranda 81, 103,

RUTHERFORD, Olan 305, Randall 132, Thomas 103, 109, Virgie 109, Virgil 108, W.E. 305, Walter 109, Willard 305
RUTLEDGE, Nancy 12
SADDLER, Hattie132 Samuel 132
SANDERS, Ollie 110, 147
SANTY, Clarence 119, 130, Earl 119, 130, Frank 119, 130, Helen 119, Joe 119, Pearl 119 R.E. 96, Ruery 130, Ruie 119
SAUNDERS, Ollie 41
SAWYER, Matilda 113, 226
SCABOROUGH, James 67, Mary 103
SCHERRER, Regina 122 Thoedore 104
SCHEYTTE, Henryette 292, J.J. 23, 292
SCHNEIDER, Carl 42, 273, Edward 42, 273, Emma 42, Emma 272, Ernest 42, 273, Henry 273, Judge 165, Oscar 42, 273, Victor 42, 273,
SCHNELL, Janice 62
SCHOGGINE, Jesse 128
SCHROLL, Delza 52, Effie 76, 124, Essie 32, 76, 124 Freeman 76, 124, George 1, 7, 76, Gertie 76, Gertrude 124, John 32, 52, 76, 124, Louis 52, Mara 52, Mary 124, Mary 98, Wayne 124, Wayne 76
SCHULTZ, Fred 30
SCHUTT, Clyde 120, Emma 57, Ethel 52, Ezra 120, Jacob 120, John 57, Katie 57,

SCHUTT, Lucy 57, 78, Maggie 57, Mary 77, Minnie 98, 139, Mollie 57, Ricka 81, Virgie 115, Virgil 120, Walter 57, Willie 57, 120
SCHYETT, J.J. 70
SCOTT, A.M. 6, Aaron 123, Bell 109, 171, Charlie 95, 139, E.T. 64, Edgar 64, 123, Elizabeth 123, Euel 123, Eva 95, 107, 136, F.E. 29, 63, Frank 95, 107, 136, Freeman 12, 29, George 12, Gertrude 12, 29, Harrison? 107, 136, Henry 64, 84, 95, 107, 123,
SCOTT, Henry 95 64, Horatio 64, 107, 123, Howard 95, 107, 136, J.M. 64, Kate 64, 123, Laura 95, 107, 136, Laura 95, 107, Lee 95, 107, 136, Matt 123, Maude 64, 123, Robert . 29, 136, Susie 95, 107, Thomas 107, W.L. 29, Walter 12, 29, William 95, 136, Willie 136, Willis 95, 107
SCROGGINS, Dorothy 57, Josephine 41, Louis 57, Saunders 41, Thelma 57
SEAGRAVES, Pearl 113
SEAVERS, Emma 82, Frank 82, Margaret 82
SEGT, --- 15
SEINER, Christena 32, Elizabeth 92, Frank 25, 32, Jack 32, Jacob 25, John 24, 25, 32, Lizzie 25, Margaret 82, 92, Mary 32, Sebastian 32, Tina 25, Wendlin 32, 92

SEINER, Will 25, 121, William 24,
SELLARS, Eschol 282
SEPTER, George 69
SERVER, Daisey 47, 105, Etta 47, James 47, L.D. 47, Lawrence 80, Mary 47, 80 105, Minnie 47
SERVERS, Nancy 74
SHADOWENS, Charlie 90, John 90, Johnie 90, Lee 90, Narlie 90, Oliver 90
SHANKS, Catherine 125
SHAW, Ardes 47, Clarence, 106, 115, E.P. 115, Ed 1, 6, Elma 47, Ephraim 106, Etna 34, George 34, Harry 47, J.W. 10, John 3, 47, Mary 47, Murble 73, Ramona 115, Ward 47, Wayne 47,
SHEARE R, Alice 273, Annie 50, 108, 274, Clarence 17, 288, G.C. 74, G.F. 108, G.G. 273, G.T. 92, G.W. 74,81, 93, 108, 274, George 50, 102, 160, 274, Ida 17, 70, 288, John 74, 273, Lottie 100, Mary 10, 22, 79, 295
SHEARING, -- 135
SHELBY, Anna 89, Anteline 89, Barbara 20, Clara 89, 130, Cora 138, Edith 89, Elizabeth 89, Grant 89, Harriet 89, Jacob 89, James 20, 89, Kate 44, Katherine !30, Margaret 89, Martha 89, Mary 89, Polly 89, Reece 89, 130, Stella 20
SHELDON, Alice 69,

SHELDON, Alsworth 69, Arley 126, Clyde 69, John 69, Katherine 69, Lillie 69, Loren 69, Loy 126, M.L 69, Maggie 64, 126, Mary 64, Oscar 64, Sam 64, Steve 64, Theodore 126 Willie 64
SHELL, A.J. 40, Elizabeth 179, 189, Grace 109, John 296 Lucinda 109, Lucy 99, Moses 8, Solomon 7, 89, Lizzie 224,
SHELTER, Andrew 23, 29, 39, 110 Anna 29, Anthony 62 Anton 4, 23, 29, Barbara 110, Bernard 110, Bonnie 110, Joseph 29, Catherine 92 Cecilia 110, Chtistina 86, Elizabeth 62, Emma 87, Frank 39, Fred 22, Fred 23. George 39, Gordon 36, Grace 39, Henry 39, Joe 39, 115, John 23, 29, Josie 39, Kate 23, 36, Leo 110, M.A. 80, Mary 63, 86, Mitch 39, Nicholas 29, Richard 110, Rosa 23, Rose 62, Sally 29, Salome 23, Sebastine 36, 86, Tina 29, Walter 36
SHELTON, Nora 53, Sarah 130, William 63
SHERETZ, Mary 131, William 131
SHERIDAN, Alice 22, Ann 22 48, Annie 55, Charles 22, Della 22, Edith 75, Elizabeth 75, Eona 75, Eugen 75, Francis 76 G.H. 121, James 75, John 37, Luther 97, May 22, Myrtle

SHELTER, 75, Oasis 75, Owen 75, Rose 75, Rosetta 89, 75, Roy 22, Ruth 75, Samuel, William 22
SHERRES, Regina 86
SHERWOOD, Earl 7
SHEWMAKER, Anna 98, Arzie 52, Asal 49, Carl 107, David 133, Della 132, Dorothy 52, Earl 107, Harriet 133, J.F. 29, James 139, Jess 101, Jesse 225, Mary 7, Milo 52, Nance 133, Nora 139, Norman 52, Sarah 78,
SHIPP, Eliza 12, F.M. 2
SHIPP, J.H. 12, James 44, Mary 52, Pearl 12, Sarah 30, W.E. 12,
SHOCKLEY, James 94, Julia 94, Loy 94, Lee ? 134
SHOEMAKER, Dill 114, Frank 8,
SHOWALTERS, Alfred 63 Lon 137
SHROEDER, Mary 32
SHUFFLEBARGER, Angie 131, Anna 131, Charles 131, Cleo 131, David 131, Gladys 131, Hiram 131, John 131, Laura 131, Minnie 131, Mora 131, Will 131, Willis 131
SHUTT, --- 68, , Clyde 52 Delza 52, Ezra 52, Fred 52, Jacob 52, 58, Katie 58, Lucy 58, Roy 52, Virgil 52, Willie 52
SIEDLER, Catherine 86
SIGNORE, Maggie 25
SIMMONS, ---144, Bessie 82,

SIMMONS, Betsy 155, Fannie 84, George 10, John 22, 7, Lydia 10, Mary 51, May 109, Rosa 123, Virginia 84, Wesley 51
SIMMS, Andrew 116, Cella 55, Elizabeth 2, Frankie 40, Hester 40, Jim 40, 51, 116, Lucinda 40, Mary 40, Rose 55, Thomas 55
SIMONEN, Lunce 30
SIMPSON, Gussie 90, Henry 91, 274, Homer 87, Howard 91, 274, Ida 132, Jennie 62, Jim 159, L.J. 2, Minnie 274, Oral 91, 274
SINANES, Stella 131
SINGHI, F.A. D.76, Vittrice 76
SINGLETON, Nancy 126,
SISCO, Carlos 35, Earl 139. Hazel 139, Jack 139, John 139, Laura 139, Paul 139, Pauline 139, Robert 139, Rosie 133, Walter 139
SISK, Mollie 94
SKELETON, Sarah 113
Stacey 109, 203
SLAGEL, Arthur 58, J.D. 58 Mattie 104, 130
SLOPSKY, Abe 122, Amedee 122, Caroline 122, Edward 122, Morris 122
SLYE, Lillie 68, 299
SMEE, Harve 107, Josephine 107, Maggie 82
SMITH, A.B. 60, Anna 23, 65, 125, 137, Bill 159,

SMITH, Bursie 71, Cecil 90, Champ 3, Charles 71, 72, 118, 137, Charlie 30, 65,138, Claudie 71, Clifford 137, 138, Dewey 113, Earl 68, Ed 128, Edward 68, 71, Elmer 91, Elvis 137, 138, Eona 75, Esther 137, Etta 133, Frank 59, George 65, 113, 137, 138, Geraldine 138, Giles 96, Harley 128, Harry 37, 71, Hatchett 120, Henry 72, Herbert 125, Hester 91, Isaac 72, 137, 138, James 70, 71, Jane 75, John 71, 75, Joyce 137, Kate 241, Leta 137, 138, Lillie 113, Lizzie 75, Loren 118, Louise 41, Lowel 137, Lucinda 96, Mary 68, 71, 72, 137, May 119, Millard 75 Nellie 71, Noel 138, Nola 114 115, 144, Olive 71, Ota 139, Othal 137, Othol 138, Pearl 71, 113, Radford 113, Rebecca 71, Reddick 71, Reed 113, Roscoe 71, Rosie 82, Sarah 103, Sarah 27, 41, 65, 67, 113, Serena 72, Sudie 71, Susan 36, Thomas 41, 72, Walter 137, Will 85, William 21, 44
SMOCK, A.A. 55, Anna 81, Annie 108, 274, Bert 63, Cornellus 70, E.M. 50, 274 Everett 81, Henry 63, Herbert 50, 81, 275 J.M. 64, James 50, 55, 274, John 63, Kenneth 50, 81, 275, Martha 28, 70, 156, Martin. 63, Mary 63, 64, Robert 64, Sarah 70, Thomas

SMOCK, Thomas 4, 55, 64, 98
SNEED, Alfred 103, Alice 103, Annie 98, 103, Billie 103, Clara 103, Carl 128, Della 104, Effie 128, Gertrude 128, Howard 128, Ina 128, Izora 103, James 103, Janie 128, John 103, Leona 86, Lillie 103, Lorene 128, Lucian 103, Silas 128, Stella 128
SNOW, Alfred 139, Allen 75 Harry 75, Henry 75, Lois 139, Vernon 75, 139,
SONNEN, J.T. 50
SOWARD, Charles 89, Clarence 89, Clyde 106, Clyde 89, Fern 89, Mable 89, Mantie 89, Mary 54, Millie 89, Vernon 89, Willis 9
SPECHER, James 293
SPEER, Charles 135, Jesse 135, Mary 135 Virginia 135
SPEES, Bon 65, Robert 65
SPEILER, Frederick 20 Margaret 94
SPIVEY, Candas 86, Dora 84, Francis 86, G.12, Grace 86, Halpa? 86, Howard 73, 99,118, James 12, 23, 46, 73, 84, 111, 118, John 12, 23, 86, Jonas 23, 84, 85, 86, Josephine 86, Leona 86, Lucinda 23, Lucy 12, 24, 84, Lurine 99, Maggie 73, Maude 84, Mercy 87, Milas 40, 86, Mollie 84, Pearl 86, Pink 86, Rosa 73, Rosa 118

SPIVEY, Serena 72, Thomas 86, Wade 12
SPRECHER, James 34 Laura 34, 293
ST JOHN, John 41 Reevie 41, Mattie 57
STACEY, Anna 97, Arveta 99, Barham 277, Betty 121, Brittian 22, 16, 275, Byram, 192, 195, 192, Chester 277, Cora 277, Druscilla 277, E.J. 277, Edd 99, Elizabeth 276, Emma 275, 277, Eva 95, 107, 136, Ezra 99, Georgia 99, Geraldine 32, Gordon 45, Hiram 7, 275, 276, James 47, Jordan 121, Laura 24, 192, 197, Lillie 99, 277, Marback 276, Mary 12, Morton 16, Nancy 16, 275, Nannie 121, Orvil 99, Raleigh 45, 99, Sarah 71, Serena 275, 277, Shadrick 277, Sidney 99, Silas 32, 96, W.B.121,
STALEY, Laura 59 238
STANLEY, Edward 90, Ethel 112, Ewing 90, Florence 90, Gertie 112, Jimmie 112, Minnie 112, Ota 134, Sarah 90, 112
STATHEM, Belle 101
STAYTON, J.B. 112
STEEL, Alexander 118, Charles 118, Della 118, Frederick 118, James 118, Janet 96, Jennie 118, Katie 110 Rodney 118, Sarah 118, Harriet 27, Marion 253,

STEEL, Samuel 4, Stressie 125
STEBER, Ida 103
STEINER, Weintlin 82
STEPHENSON, Charlie 118
STEVENS, Charity 2, Charles 91, Clara 103, Ed 36, John 2, Josie 36, Susa 27, Thomas 5
STEWART, ---- 4, Alice 88, Ida 22
STILL, Arthur 123, Oliver 123 Still, Rosa 123, Rose 123 Virgil 123,
STILLEY, Patsy 80
STOKES, Ellen 61, W.E. 61 William 45
STONE, ---136, Alice 103, 126, Bert 79, Beulah 269, Dan 56, Cassenor 85, Clarence 79, Clifford 100, Connie 85, 87
STONE, Emma 269, Glenn 79 James 79, John 88, 100, Jordon, 77, 79, Lawton 100, Malinda 77, Martha 100, Mayme 100, Milo 79, Mina 100, Oliver 269, Ollie 71, 79, 85, Solomon 8, Susan 79, Thomas 77, 79
STUART, Ida 97, Pernissa 9
STUBBS, Henretta 50, Rosa 4, T.H. 50
STUB(B)Y, Charley 18, Cora 53, Elmer 138, Gotleip 18 Mara 52, Mary 138, Wm. 2
STURGEON, Dorcia 125
STURGILL, Opheldia 80 Rachel 52, W.R. 80
SUITS, Charles 54, 55, 73,

SUITS, Charles 134 210, David 38, Davis 134, Eugene 119, France 38, Harlan 119, Harve 67, 134, Harvey 119, Herschel 119, John 134, Josephine 86, Josie 38, Lavern 119, Maude 73, 210, Milas 134, Mose 134, Moses 59, Nellie 105, Olen 134, Orval 134
SULLIVAN, -- 1, Carrie 47, Charles 47, 106, Ida 38, 59, 76, Minnie 47, 106
SULLIVANT, Bruce 113, Hobart 113, John 113, Mariah 113, Ray 113, Willard 113
SUMMERS, Hattie 103
SUTTON, America ? 127, Arthur 19, Charles 127, John 127, Myrtle 104, Rebecca 28, 64, 163
SWAGGART, Charles 15, Jewell 44, 118, Marie 102, Maude 123, Rosa 73, Vivith 118, Wiley 44, 118
SWEAT, Albert 80, Andrew 84, Daisy 84, Loy 80, Martha 84, Millie 84, Myrtle 47, Zodie 84
SWITZER, Andrew 138 Billy 250, Dee 138, Electiville? 138, James 138, Ralph 138 William 138
SYLVESTER, --- 21
TABER, Frank 118, Freeman 83
TADLOCK, Charlie 106, 112, 279, Clarence 112, 279

TADLOCK, Elvira 122, Ettie 112, Ettie 279, Fidelia 112, 277, Freeman 112, 279, George 112, 279, Ida 112, 279, James 112, 277, John 112, 277, Laura 112, 279, Martha 278, Ollie 112, 279, Richard 112, 279
TANNER, Claude 106, G.W. 106, George 106, Henry 106, John 2, Laura 106, Virgie 106
TATE Ada 114, Ardes 47
TAYLOR, -- 91, Aaron 113, 283, Ben 113, 128, Benjamin 283, Bennie 24, Beulah 63, Caleb 113, Calib 282, Catherine 113, 282, Claude 97, Eunice 24, 113, 128, Floyd 113, 284, H. 81, India 282, J.C. 18, Jack 113, 284, James 281, 282, 285, 113, John 136 Jonathan 113, 282, Judge 1,
TAYLOR, Katherine 281, Lillian 113, Lillie 127, Lucy 45, Mary 62, 113, 283, Paul 113, 284, Priscilla 113, 282, R.F. 58, 94, 127, 136, 280, 284, Rebecca 283, Richard 24, 28, 113, 239, 282, 283, Robert 136, Ruth 97, Spencer 113, 282, 113, Stuart 97, Thomas 136, William 46, 113, 282,
TAYTON, George 107
TEDFORD, Leslie 47, Onita 47, Paul 47, Theodore 47, Willard 47, Mabel 106
TENSLEY, Mary 103
TERR, Betty 63, Curtis ? 63

TERRELL, Commodore ?123 Deliah 123, 286, Edna 123, 287, Edna 123, George 287, Hugh 123, 287, Joseph 39, 123, 286, Josephine 287, Mack 123, Walker ? 123
THACKER, Ben 161
THOM, Mary 66
THOMAS, A.B. 76, 93, Dickie 159, Francis 1, George 1, 7, Horace 31, Kate 48, L.E. 219, Mahalie 270, Marion 36, Mary 7, 31, 125, Matlida 100, Nancy 56, Nettie 53, Vera 121
THOMPSON, Betty 124, Charles 59, Harriet 30, J.C. 76, Jeanette 59, Lula 11, 29, 127, Mary 132, Matthew 1, Rebecca 60, 220, W.L. 68
THOMS, Minnie 131
THORNTON,-- 77, Augustus 71, Bertha 130, Clifford 72, D.F. 99, Doctor 288, E. 71, Electa 30, 99, Erma 99, Henry 17, 61, 71, 99, 136, 288, Mary 98, Ida 70, 288, J.A. 70, J.T. 152, Joe 159, John 17, 30, 35, 98, 136, 160, 288, Lloyd 99, Lou 288, Martha 288, Mary. 61, 70, 136, 238, 288, Nettie 36, Ollie 35, Phoebe 17, 288 Rebecca 35, 70, 136, 288, Rinda 99, Sidney 288, T. 66 Theopolis 30, Willis 17, 30, 99, 288
THORTON, John 13
THRELKELD, 157 Rose 123, Ross 123, Helen 119,

THRELKELD, Louise 25, Lula 83, Paul 124, Ruth 124,
TICHENOR, Frank 52, Granville 122, Blanch 122, Vernon 122
TILLEY, Jean 214
TINKER, Sarah 115, 138, 142
TINSLEY, Alliam 104, Alonzo 130, Archie 104, Charles 130, Clara 26, Cowne 104, E.S. 26, 43, Elijah 152, Emma 16, 22, 275, Horatio 43, Jack 22, Jackson 275, James 43, 104, 130, Marie 26, 130, Martha 99, Mattie 104, 130, Minnie 130, Myrtle 104, 130, Nancy 22, 275, Tinsley, Naomi 104, Robert 48, Theda 104, Theta 130, William 130
TITE, Jessie 129
TOBENSKI, Pearl 86
TOLBERT, Annie 122, Bennie 122, Carroll 59, 129, Cecil 90, Clifford 80, Ernest 59, James 80, John 59, 80, Katie 66, Lacy 80, Laura 122, Marguerette 80, Milas 80, Molly 80, Myrtle 111. 139, Myrtle 162, Rebecca 59, Rich 59, Ruthie 80, Thanor 122, Will 59, 122, G.C. 80
TONNY, Ora 93
TOWERY, J.W. 61
TRAIL, O.C. 130
TRAVIS, Frank 80, Ruth 32, 54, 152

TREECE, Alice 64
TRENT, James 2
TRIMBLE, Mary. 68
TRINT, Esther 92
TROVILLION, Madge 105 Penn 105
TUCKER, Amy 12, Elmer 20, Elsie 72, Emma 20, Esther 112, Henry 20, J.B. 7, 12, 20, 152 John 7, 40, Morgan 116, Roy 20, Susan 20, W.M. 72, Weaver 20, Willie 20
TURCHET, John 290
TURLEY, Eddie 146
TURNER, Alice 61, Anna 49, Bertha 103, Carrie 61, Charles 190, 289, Cora 57, 101, 103, D.A. 5, Ed 64, 103, Edward 26, Ella 103, Etta 103, Fred 131, Gladys 289, Ida 131 Jennie 289, Jno. 9, John 49, 64, 49, Lizzie 49, Laura 288, Loren 103, Loretta 133, Lottie 94, Louise 131, Mary 103, 117, Mayme 26, Ollie 103, Polly 8, Riley 103, Samuel 8, Stella 131, William 49, Willie 49, 131, Wilmer 61
TWITCHELL, -- 230, Alice 126, B.E. 27, Ben 27, Bessie 31, Capt. 27, Charles 126, Charlotte 32, Earl 32, Franklin 126, 290, George 126, J.B. 31, J.W. 27, Jake 126, James 27, Jobe 80, Joe 126, L.F. 27, Lafayette 27, Lafe 126, Lydia 62, Mary 126, Moses 290, Opheldia 80, Paul 289, 290,

TWITCHELL, Robert 27, Sarah 68, 126, 299,
TYER, -- 123, Dolly 136 Etta 77, 132, Hannah 142 292, John 23, 55, 155, 216, 226, 291, Judge 27, 159, M.L. 27, 52, Marcellus 55, 291, R.C. 132, Ressie 216, Rufinia 291, Rufus 55
TYLER, George 13
TYRE, John H. 33
TYREE, Martha 84
ULMSNIDER, --- 202
UNDERWOOD, -- 280, Addie 125, Augusta 94, Bertha 124, Dorcia 125, Effie 125, Fannie 51, J.W. 124, Mary 41, Millard 125, Tressie 125, Viola 125,
USLEAMAN, Clay 85
VAN BIBLER, Andy 97, Anna 97, Francis 97, Elizabeth 55, J.O. 97, Mina 97, Myrtle 97, Sadie J. 97, W.W. 88, 97, Walter 61
VAUGHN, A.W. 139, Alfred 89, Anna 34, 139, Belle 57, Betty 126, Dosia 34, Earl 126, Ella 31, 72, Ellen 20, Fannie 70, 120, 124, 220, Flora 28, Henry 20, Ida 126, India 115, Iva 115, J.W. 126, Janie 128, Jesse 126, Joe 45, 126, Loren 34, 115, Martha 89, Marvin 126, McKinley 115, Melissa 34, Mildred 34, 127, Miles 115, Mindy 120, Mollie 5, Nancy 126, Nora 34

VAUGHN, Oleda 115, Ollie 115, Oscar 115, Pearl 115, Reba 126, Sallie 137, Samual 20, Sarah 83, 90, Sherman 115, Spencer 34, Valier 139, Virgie 127, Warren 28, 139, William 139,
VAUGHT, Minnie 111
VENABLE, Charles 51, Fred 51, Robert 51
VERMILLION, --- 143
VERSON, Norah 79
VICK, Ethel 132, Lee 132, Leonidas 132, Ora 113, Rose 114, 132, Glenn 79
VINSON, Bertha 110, Cleve 119, Ellen 110, Gurtie 110, Hershel 119, Lealie ? 123, Meltin 10, Myrtle 119, Reba 110, Rella 110, T.J. 110 Tom 110
VINYARD, --- 52, A.A. 39, Ada 121, Alex 46, 137, Alice, 96, 119, Alpha 36, Alta 46, Anderson 18, 39, Archie 14, Belle 15, 76, Bessie 56, 113, Bettie 46, Betty 83, Bill 22, C.F. 26, Charles 26, 34, 54, 66, 69, 113, 137, 293, Charley 78, Charlotte 50, Clara 292, Clyde 59, 74, Cordella 36, Daisy 63, Daniel 18, Della 23, Della 292, Dulcie 45, Edd 78, Edward 69, 113, Effie 76, Effie 124, Eli 18, Eliza 34, 29, 70, 96, 293, Elizabeth 293, Ella 137, Ellsworth 126, Elmer 45, 63, 69, Emmer 58, Ernest 63

VINYARD, Ethel 52, Fannie 128, George 41, 54, 83, 87, Gertrude 36, Golden 36, H.T. 44, Hattie 36, Henry 23, 62, 54, 70, 292, Henryette 23, 292, 113, Hosie 69, Howard 69, 113, Ida 45, India 113, Issue 54, J.O. 64, J.T. 36, James 5, 34, 38, 293, Jefferson 14, Jennie 36, Jim 59, Joe 8, John 8, 34, 36, 68, 69, 70, 96, 199, 224, 293, Joseph 45, 59, Josie 68, 96, 199, Lacy 87, Laura 34, 293, Lewis 69, Lillie 16, Lloyd 23, Lora 69, Loren 68, Loyd 70, 218, 292, Lucian 13, 30, 127, Lucinda 23, 292, Lucy 14, Margaret 87, Marjorie 87, Martha 42, 96, 137, 224, Mary 13, 30, 34, 54, 69, 70, 83, 98, 111, 137, 293, Maude 37, 75, Milas 104, Nat 113, Nate 69, Nettie 44, Nevile 128, Ora 114, Oscar 22, Phil 50, Philip 23, 62, 292, Pinkneyette 62, Rachel 69, Roy 93, 124, Ruben 44, S.A. 46, Sarah 87, Sidney 23, 292, Silas 16, Jefferson 88, T.M. 36, Thelma 83, Thomas 36, Trevis 137, Virginia 36, 49, W.H. 34, 38, 69, 96, 293, W.M.M. 30, William 23, 70, 104, 292, Willie 26

VOLKERT, Amelia 87, Anthony 62, Antone 56, 86, 125, Charles 23, 62, Daisy 116, 117, Emma 87, Frank 126

VOLKERT, Frank 87, George 56, 126, Hattie 87, 126, Helen 134, Henry 86, 87, 126, Herman 87, James 56, Jesse 126, Jim 133, John 23, 56, 62, 87, Joseph 62, Leo 56, Lizzie 87, Maggie 33, 126, Margaret 56, Mary 56, Minnie 87, Regius 62, Rita 56, Rose 62, Salome 62, Thomas 87, 126, William 33, 56

VONCREE, --- 11

WADKINS, D.W.107

WAGGONER, A.H. 114, Abner 114, Charles 83, Cora 32, 54, 83, 114, 152, Edna 76, George 83, 114, Jesse 78, 161, Joseph 83, 114, Mae 83, 114, 83, Presley 114, Robert 83, 114, Ruby 83, 114, Thelma 83, 114, Velma 83, 114, William 83, 114

WAKEHAM, 77, 127

WALACE, Levy 26, Riller 26, W.R. 26

WALDEN, Charles 135, J.J. 135, John 135, 220

WALKER, ... 27, Aaron 80, Beulah 124, Cecil 63, Com 63, E.L. 22, H.W. 271, Horace 111, James 286, Jane 54, Lillie 63, M.L. 25, Mack 287, Malinda 80, Marcus 80, Mary 271, Mattie 105, Ollie 107, Patsy 80, Rachel 166, 167, Sarah 25, 80, Steve 22, Walter 166, 167, Will 98

WALL, E.F. 10, E.F. 53, 294,

WALL, Ed 4, Effie 11, Fannie 46, 234, 260, G.A. 53, George 11, Grace 101, 109, Jane 10, Minnie 294
WALLACE, Amanda 53, Ellen 111, Frances 136, James 10, L.H. 30, Levy 141, Melvin 82, Minnie 87, 129, Minnie 87, Pearl 119, Pleas 130, Riller 141 W.R. 141
WALSTON, Susan 107
WALTERS, Dortha 79, Garland 135, Minnie 135, Nancy 199
WALTHER, , Mattie 136
WALTON, Edgar 38, Emma 3, J.S. 4, Ida 29, Jack 30, Maggie 38, Mildred 38, Minerva 129, Tommy 129, W.J. 29, William 1,
WAMACK, Della 115, 252
WARD, Etta 47, Frank 80, 105, Mae 114
WARFIELD, W.P. 94
WARFORD, Annie 10, 295, Carrie 122, Charles 10, D.T. 47, David 20, 53, 296, E.J. 75, Edwinna 73, 210, Flora 53, 54, George 123, J.D. 210, John 10, Maggie 296, Martha 10, 295, Mary 10, 139, 295, Roy 123, Sarah 10, 295, W.N. 10, 295, W.P. 10, 47, 126, 139, William 10, 139, 295, 296,
WARREN, James 7
WASSON, Lucy 140, Pruddie 124
WATERS, Ben 6, Carl 26, Dora 12, 60, Emily 6, Garrell 6, Georgia ? 26, Henry 6, J.G. 6, James 29, 164, Jonathan 6, 12, Martha 12, Robert 6, Willie 18
WATKINS, Alta 127, Bessie 127, D.W. 287, Daniel 107, 297, Elizabeth 36, 127, Essie 127, Gilbert 125, Grace 97, 125, Harry 127, James 127, John 125, Linda 125, Phoebe 107, 296, Susan 107, 297, William 125, 127
WATSON, Allene 89, Alvin, 128, Bessie 44, 77, Bonnie 65 Bruce 77, 127, Dellar 89, Deneen 128, Donna 128, Douglas 128, Ethel 77, 127 Florence 77, 127, Gertrude 77 127, Gladys 77, 127, Harry 77 127, Herbert 65, James 77, 92, 127, Mabel 77, Mae 127, Marion 77, Overton 128, Sebary 30, 77, 127, Susan 297, Theta 130, Thomas 77, 127, Toy 123
WATTERS, James N. 54
WEAST, Mae 43
WEATHERBY, Geo. 4
WEATHERINGTON, Alice 91, Elva 91, Harry 91, Mable 91, Muriel 91, Stella 91, Herbert 91, Lula 91, 99, Harrison 91,
WEAVER, Addie 139, B.P. 64, Dora 24, 303, Saline 179
WEBER, Effie 100 Minda 86,

WENTON, Josie 100
WESTON, Charles, 41, 67, 68, 298, 299, Daisy 67, 68, 299, Elizabeth 29, Ella 68, 95, 299, Frederick 68, 299, Henry 68, 298, Katherine 68, 299, Lillie 68, 299, Margaret 299, Sarah 68, 298, 299, Thomas 68, 298
WHAL, Fred, 74
WHEELER,Elizabeth 43, Fred 74, George 18, 43
WHELLER, A.K. 93
WILLIAMS, Bell 11, Granville 11, Jeff 11, Joe 11, Hattie 11, Mary 11, T.L. 11
WHIPPLE, Doris 138
WHITAKER, Martha 112, 278
WHITE, Albert 10, Anna 10, Emma 301, Eva 110, 135, 148, Gradie 83, Henry 10, James 10, J.W. 10, Kate 13, 76, Loren 83, Marshall 10, Mary 301, Pearl 62, Renfro 10, Willie 10, 295,
WHITEAKER, Alice 128, Astra 128, Elizabeth 128, Geneva 128, Gertrude 128, Hall 128, Mark 128, Martha 128, William 128
WHITEHEAD, Anna 301, Edd 108, 300, George 108, Gola 300, Harry 108, 120, 300, Harry 108, 300, James 108, 300, Jessie 108, 300, Lemon 108, 300, Lou 108, 300, Lula 108, 300, Mella 300, Nannie

WHITEHEAD, Nannie 300, Orange 64, 108, 300, Philip 300, Rebecca 108, 300 Tilde 108, 300
WHITESIDE(S), A.B. 75, Elizabeth 96, India 17,Malinda 76, Mary 49, 60, Sam 49, 60, Sidney 60, Thomas 76
WHITTAKER, Ambrose 5
WILCOX, Mattie E. 58
WILKERSON, John 28, Jordon 134, Lydia 103, 134, Rose 75, Sylvia 134
WILLIAM, Broadway 35, Gwendoline 57, Marion 76, Vernon 57
WILLIAMS, Alonzo 51, Annie 133, Belle 114, Bertha 105, Bertha 121, Blanche 105 Clara 51, Claude 77, D.W. 77 97, Dan 74, Dean 105, Dora 137, Earl 77, Edgar 54, Elijah 74, Elizabeth 70, Ella 36, Elsworth 54, Emma 74, Emory 105, Ethel 74, Euls 54, Eva 77, Fern 105, George 6, 19, 70, Harriet 15, 114, Heloise 74, J.C. 105, James 54, Jeff 54, 88, 54, Joe 105, John 70, Louise 74, Lulie 139, Majorie 105, Margaret 75, Marion19, 26, Mary 96, Milas 19, Mollie 41, Myrtle 117, Naomi 105, Nora 77, 97, Opheldia 80, Otis 77, Pete 70, Pete 70, Phoebe 137, R.H. 105, Rachel 80, Richard 79, Robert 9, Roena 74, Roland 133, Sallie 68, 185,

WILLIAMS, Sue 105, Sylvia 135, T.L. 5, 11, 114, Theodore 54, Thomas 15, 105, 137, Travis 74, Vera 105, Virgil 54, W.P 14, 80, William 96, 134
WILLINGHAM, Elizabeth 42, Gertrude 17, Hallie 111, R.H 17, 32, 42, Virginia 46
WILLIS, Elizabeth 29, James 29, R.V. 68, 199
WILSON, Marvilla 108, 154, Martha 121, Rosie 56. Thelma 125, Zelpha 124
WINDERS, Belva 119, F.M. 64, Henry 24, 302, J.W. 119, Mae 119, Marie 119, Mary 64, 302, Nora 119, Roxie 119, Susie 119, Sylvester 37
WINGATE, Bessie 114, 138, E. 90, E.C. 7, Edward 90, Em 157, Emma 49, 90, Hanson 144, James 49, 90, 144
WINGATE, Louisa 49, Mary 157, Rosa 49, Rose 90, Sidney 90, Tyrphene 67
WINN, Abaslom 6, Albert 10, 119, 303, Andrew 118, Charles 55, 119, Charlie 49, Cora 49, Ellen 118, Etta 49 55, Harriet 133, Hepsie 49, 55, Irene 119, James 29, 49, 55, 118, Jesse 49, Jim 133, Lee 29, Mary 110, 119, 303, Minnie 49, 133, Nan 110, 305, Nancy 110, 119, 303, Nona 305, Nora 25, 83, 110, Perry 110, 111, 303, Sadie 110, 305, Samuel 48, 55, Thelma 49, 119

WINN, W.H. 55, Will 305, William 49, 110, 119, 303, Willie 118
WINTERS, Alice 119, 120, 123 151, Anna 120, Annabel 112, 308, Anne 104, Bessie 81, Bill 104, Billy 120, Carolyn 112, 306, Catherine 112, Charlie 120, Dan 112, 306, Daniel 11, 29, l 74, David 120 Davis 120, Dell 120, Della 112 120, 308, Doris 138, Ernest 112, Finney 120, George 10, 112, 120, 306, Gertie 76, Gertrude 124, James 104 112, 308, Jane 29, John 74, 112, 120, 306, Mahala 112 306, Margaret 112, 120, 138 306, Martha 175, Mary 138, Millie 120, Myrtle 104, 112, 308, Nancy 32, Norma 138, Opal 86, 120, Owen 112, 306 Phoebe 120, Robert 104, 112, Robert 308, Samuel 41, 52, 88, Susan 130, 307, W.H. 81, William 112, 120, 127, 130, 306
WOLRAB, Clara 70, Elizabeth 69, John 69, Maggie 70, Mary 70, Mattie 69, 103
WOMACK, Celia 50, Cynthia 76, Dr. 54, George 15, J.A. 76, 87, J.H. 76, J.T 76, James 308, Joseph 26, Joshua 1, Marion 26, Martha 55, Nancy 50, Sarah E. 15, Vina 30, 197, W.L. 15, 76, W.W. 76

WOMACK, Walter 15, William 26, 43,
WONTING, James 16 Sam 16
WOOD, Alfred 139, Katie 139, Leonard 41, Sarah 139
WOODRUFF, Lucy 137
WOODS, Emma 22, 97, Frankie 254, Roscoe 94
WOODY, Margaret 48
WOOTEN, A..H. 80, Elmer 80, Laura 42,
WORFORD, W.T. 87
WORRELL, Inez 32
WRIGHT, Dink 45, Fred 137, Hicks 137, Jackie 45, Mary 137, Ruby 110, Sallie 137, William 137
WRINKLES, Oscar 5
WRISTEN, C.W.36, D.W. 36
WUTHERMAN, Fred 135
WYATT, Ellen 87
XANDER, Maria 115
YANDELL, Clara 135
YARBER, Betsy 133, Etta 133, Ettie 37, James 37, John 37, 133, Loretta 133, Robert 133, Vada 133, Wiley 37
YATES, Bill 91, Josie 109, 172, Mrytle 37, 75,
YEAKEY, Cathy 5, James 4, Mary 106 245, R.L 40,
YORK, Britton 20, Jeppi 3
YOUNG, E.V. 117, Ernest 133, Eunice 137, Gertrude 134, Lewis 137, Lydia 111, 139, 162, Phoebe 137, Vaughn 137
YOUNGER, Hulda 62
ZIEBELL, 184
ZIGLER, Adam 19, 57, 58 78, , Andy 58, Elizabeth 58, Emma 20, 58, Frank 57, 77, Franklin 58, Fred 58, George 58, Jacob 58, John 20, 58, Katie 58, Lucy 58, 78, Mary 57, 58, Minnie 20, 58, Philip 58, Walter 20, 58, William 19, 58,
ZILK, Frank 101
ZIMMER, Barbara 110, Bill 33, Peter 82, 89, Sophia 56 Thomas 56

www.ingramcontent.com/pod-product-compliance
Lightning Source LLC
Chambersburg PA
CBHW071951220426
43662CB00009B/1087